CW00429629

Hope and Shared Values

DR. HASSAN B. AKBERALI

Hope and Shared Values

A Reality Check

First published as Paperback and E-book on Amazon

ISBN: 9798651326785

All photographs from author's private collection taken by him, friends or relatives

Dedication

Dedicated to the women in my life for their inspiration - my late mother, late mother-in-law, wife and two daughters - and my late father, with whom I did not spend a close childhood, but glad I made him feel proud of me.

CONTENTS

A Salute to the By-Gone Generation

My main purpose is to pay tribute and gratitude by reflecting on the hardships and achievements endured by a special group of people in search of a better life. This is not a historical account seen through the eyes of the migrants, their associates or an expert on the subject, but a personal reflection of a collection of thoughts based on events heard over the years from third parties about their ancestors. I have put together snippets of shared history, courage, hard work and feats of survival, which I believe is a fair narrative of what happened, to give an overall perspective of the circumstances and difficulties faced by the intrepid settlers. In many ways it ties in well with that of my great-grandfather and grandfather, how they may have reached and ended up in East Africa. I dedicate the following narration in the loving memory of all who followed similar journeys, before and after my ancestors, so that their endeavours and sacrifices are not forgotten.

Generally speaking, most migration to East Africa started from the 18th century onwards, because of the challenging times in Gujarat. People were not well-off as such, and worsened further because of the famine. They also had large families and many mouths to feed. Parents arranged engagements and marriages for their children, as young as twelve, when they reached puberty. Extended family and people from the same village shared strong bonds and values. It played an important part for moral support during the journey, and the first point of contact on arrival, in search of a new life in foreign lands. Some migrants were as young as ten years of age. In most cases, if not all, money for the journey was borrowed from village lenders on family guarantees, or a verbal contract based on trust, to work on arrival at their destination for the sponsor for two to three years, who would also provide food and accommodation, usually a floor in a shop or a warehouse.

During their perilous journeys, the intrepid travellers faced hardships, like getting lost during bad weather, ship captains sailing in the wrong direction, and a drifting ship getting marooned in a remote place for months, and waiting to hitch a lift from passing ships. At the same time, desolate voyagers surviving on meagre rice rations, or hunting animals for food, and spending whole days boiling seawater for a pale of drinking water. Despite hardships, the marooned remained optimistic, did not worry as long as they remained healthy, because they were at least alive, had fresh air and food. In the midst of all this, mothers even gave birth, and a new life raised hope. There were also occurrences of looting, sailors wanting to kill male passengers to confiscate womenfolk and goods, and at times, just prayers and luck saw them through, whilst a few unlucky ones perished.

On reaching their destination, a network of contacts got established over time, as a deep sense of comradeship and brotherhood existed amongst all the settlers, whether Christians, Hindus, Muslims, Sikhs and others, especially at times of thefts, fires, sickness or any hardships, because settlers went to the aid of the victims with acts of philanthropy from successful settlers, wealthy or not, but willing to give a helping hand for others to rebuild their lives and businesses. It served as an informal network of communication amongst themselves and to send news back home - like a 'bush telegraph', which kept people abreast of business opportunities and job offers, similar to the modern concept of 'network marketing'. On taking a job, the new employer would settle the outstanding debt (bond money) with the previous one. Business opportunities grew as successful traders opened more shops along the route, to cater for the needs of construction workers, as the railway lines progressed inland under the German and British rule. Not only new sales, management and other jobs were created by the shop owners - Dukawallas in Swahili - but they also required a network to transport their goods resulting in more business opportunities. I heard stories of an entrepreneur who started a transport business with donkeys, ferrying goods inland from the seaport of Mombasa, equivalent to a goods train that eventually went all the way to Nairobi, rift-valley settlements and Uganda, with ongoing sickness, facing casualties for both of people and donkeys, and also got robbed by the locals. But some locals were also very helpful and acted as guides, just like Mzee Hassani, who helped my great-grandfather and became a part of the family. Other intrepid settlers started catering businesses serving the needs of the railway workers.

Some succeeded, others failed, yet they never gave up, as they had no choice but to survive, rebuild and start again, and how people's luck can also change. An example of this is when a shop owner would throw away some rotten potatoes imported from France in a plot opposite his shop. One day he went to clear the overgrown grass, and found potatoes underneath. He gave some to the local people to grow in their villages, and bought their produce to sell in his shop, opened more branches and started an export business. Such opportunity benefitted not only him but also others, and was good for the economic well-being of the nation. The family in question is known as Batetawalla. Their original surname is Morbiwalla, just like my great-grandfather, as they also originated from Morbi, and therefore distant relatives of mine. Confused! Let me link it to the surname conundrum that I mention later. Another word for potato is Batata in Portuguese. The name has been adapted in Gujarati and other Indian dialects as Bateta, and as he had a business selling potatoes; he was also known as Batetawalla.

Whilst some of the migrants became wealthy and educated, others despite trying did not succeed. What it does show without doubt, we human beings share the same values, and are ready to face life's challenges and tragedies, and if given a degree of chance, we can all achieve something in life. This is a testament to the tenacity and Africa's abundant opportunities that for more than one-hundred-and-fifty years the migrants of Western Gujarat managed a peaceful and mostly prosperous existence in East Africa, without firing a single shot or bloodshed. I feel privileged to share those qualities of a fortunate history of shared values, multiculturalism and social cohesion of racial co-existence, well before such concepts became acceptable in the West.

Map of Journey

The Great Trek by Sea and Land from Morbi to Mombo via Muscat and Lamu

Prologue

L ittle did I know, it would become my '*eureka*' moment, that a posting by my wife on 1st October 2019 on a family WhatsApp group would start a chain of thoughts and lead me once again to actually put pen to paper on a book project, which I have agonised about for a decade, collecting ideas, but failing to come up with an actual format or incentive on how to go about it. My wife forwarded the following meme attributed to Bill Gates, when someone asked the richest man in the world 'Is there anyone richer than you in the world?'

To which, Bill Gates replied,[1]

"Yes, there's a person who is richer than me."

He then narrated a story...

"It was when I wasn't rich or famous. I was at the New York airport and I saw a newspaper vendor.

"I wanted to buy one newspaper and I realized I didn't have change. So, I left the idea of buying and returned it to the vendor. I told him of not having the change.

"The vendor said 'I'm giving you this for free,' on this insistence I took the newspaper"

"Coincidentally, after two to three months, I landed on the same airport and again I was short of change to buy a newspaper. The vendor offered me the newspaper again. I refused and said I can't take it as I don't have change today too.

"He said, 'you can take it, I'm sharing this from my profit. I won't be at a loss.' I took the newspaper.

[1] Lessons Taught By Life https://youtu.be/kMOMx0rLnOo

"After 19 years, I became famous and known by people. Suddenly I remembered that vendor. I began searching for him. After one and a half month, I found him.

"I asked him, 'do you know me?' He said, 'Yes, you're Bill Gates'.

"I asked him again, 'Do you remember once you gave me free newspapers?'

The vendor said, 'Yes I remember, I gave you twice.'

"I said, 'I want to repay that help you offered me that time. Whatever you want in life, tell me, I shall fulfil it'.

"He said, 'Sir, don't you think by doing so, you won't be able to match my help?'

"I asked, 'Why?' 'He said 'I helped you when I was a poor newspaper vendor but you are trying to help me now when you have become the richest man in the world, how can your help match mine?

"That day, I realized the newspaper vendor was richer than I was. Because he didn't wait to become rich to help someone"

"People need to understand that the truly rich are those who possess a rich heart rather than lots of money. Kindness makes you the most beautiful person in the world, no matter what you look like."

To cap it all, a month or so earlier, I was forwarded a Facebook post written by an old family friend from my hometown in Tanga, about life and memories from the 1950s in Tanzania (Tanganyika), which had a mention of my family roots. I was further encouraged by the many biographies and memoirs I have read in my lifetime, which I borrowed from the local library. I am an early riser anyway, and when I have a sub-conscious idea brewing, I tend to get up even earlier rearing to go, like I did on 2nd October 2019, the next day after my wife forwarded a WhatsApp message with fresh exciting thoughts on how to start on the project that had harassed me for many years.

The omen looked even more relevant for me to convey the views of the man in the street' because of the following coincidences linked to eminent leaders. The 2nd October happened to be the birthday of the great and much acclaimed Mahatma Gandhi as I have read about the efforts of this great man, and watched the much-celebrated film *'Gandhi'*, as well as having read a few critical works questioning some of Gandhi's actions, raising doubts relating to his motives. Such is the reality of life that in a 'free progressive world' we are told everyone is entitled to their opinions and views, however conflicting or divisive they may be. On the same day, it was also the day Boris Johnson gave his first maiden speech as Prime Minister to the Tory party faithful at their annual conference in Manchester, a place I have very fond memories of. As expected, he gave an eloquent speech rousing the Tory party faithful and elevating their hopes even higher with promises of 'one nation conservatism' with investment in schools, hospitals and twenty thousand more police officers, once Brexit gets done, come what may by 31st October 2019.

A week earlier, Jeremy Corbyn as leader of the opposition party roused his Labour party faithful at their annual conference in Brighton, saying that Labour is ready to govern the people of Britain, and will address all the hardships, injustices, austerity and the wrongs inflicted by the last nine years of Tory government.

The LibDems, not to be outdone by the other two political parties during their party conference in Bournemouth, gave their speeches with more promises, blaming the other two main parties and pledging to put everything right, whilst conveniently forgetting their broken pledges, when in the 2010 coalition they helped the Tories to enact severe austerity disproportionately on the poor and the disadvantaged, and the famous tuition fees U-turn, as well as supporting hostile immigration policies.

The irony being, despite all these pledges by politicians, as well as past record investment in education, NHS, welfare, police and much more, raises the question why stakeholders (ordinary public) still find it difficult to get GP appointments, quality education, justice and so on, implying that those responsible are not doing their job properly; whereas in real-life, if the ordinary people did not do their job properly or managed home budgets, would dearly pay for the consequences. It seems that it is easy for the 'establishment' to get away with serious scandals and other abuses of power.

I first became interested in politics in 1992 as an owner of a retail newsagent, when I wrote to the PM, John Major, as the small family run retail business sector was going through a difficult period, due to certain government policies. The sector was subjected to unfair trading practices, because of the newspaper wholesale distribution monopoly, as well as increases in Uniform Business Rates, rent and other overheads. As if this was not enough, the government relaxed planning permission regulations to appease big retailers, which resulted in a surge in out-of-town shopping centres with ample parking space, reduced rates and rent that favoured supermarkets. Apart from the difficulties faced by the small retailer, it had other detrimental effects, resulting in empty shop premises in town centres and high streets. All this was allowed in the midst of the much proclaimed 1980s phrase (mantra) 'free market forces'. Unfortunately, the small family businesses face the same problems as in the 1990s. It is disheartening that after twenty-eight years of pledges, similar to those for the NHS, education, welfare, jobs and so forth, we face the same issues, except they are named differently!

My approach is to highlight certain events and salient aspects of reality perceived by a lay person. Like the many born in the 20th century, I strongly believe in hope, fairness and trust. I am sure those born in the 21st century would expect governments and stake providers should not ignore stakeholder's aspirations, but place them foremost above anything else. There are many reasons for undertaking this mission, a daunting task in itself. I feel that our democratic rights should not be taken for granted, and regain the initiative to protect the much-valued liberal freedom that others have fought for, by giving their lives for our well-being. Nothing, absolutely nothing would have changed for the better in our country or the world, if ordinary people had not challenged the wrongs over the centuries, and taken a stand on small and big issues to make life better for themselves and others. I admire hugely eminent as well as ordinary people who stand for social justice, which they deeply believe in. But we do not know the names of the vast majority of ordinary people, whose good deeds we can honour, like those of our family ancestors, so that they do not get swallowed and forgotten in history. In everyday life and in politics you need your head, as well your heart. One is no good without the other. Solutions are found in thinking through a problem with a clear conscious, not solely in an emotional way, however angry we feel, or disapprove of others views.

I have been keen to write my account since 2010, because of national and world events, such as MPs expense scandals, migration crisis, and wars, in addition to personal experiences of unfairness at work, involving a public body and the refusal of a UK visitor visa for my mother and sister after two very close family bereavements. My project has had many false starts, and seemed like an overwhelming task, especially with my lack of professional writing experience. But now I have no excuse, other than to make a concerted effort to get on with it. I do not like regrets, and in most cases I have been fortunate enough to fulfil ambitions in my own small way, which is why I am writing this memoir. I sincerely hope there is something for everyone in this story; inspiration, motivation, advice or simply just a little background of the reality for our politicians to understand that there is more to life than just empty words of hope and pledges. This is part of my story, the tale of a man whose life was shaped by his experiences of writing to politicians.

1

Early Beginnings

t is a history of survival and enterprise of one family that began with an individual taking on the challenges of life headlong with feats of endurance, sacrifices, failures and courage, in search of a better future for himself and his family. It is also a history of shared human values in search of hope and fairness, when faced with adversity.

About two hundred years ago (1718 A.D.), a famine gripped Saurashtra in the peninsular region of the state of Gujarat, India on the Arabian Sea coast. The entire region laid waste as the agriculture shrivelled, and water supplies dried up. During the famines and economic hardships of the late 18th and early 19th century, individuals and families were left with two options to avoid hardships. They were forced to look for new ways of making a living. Some relocated to other parts of India, but those with adventurous traits looked at wider horizons for a better life, with the option of sailing to East Africa, because at the same time, Gujarat was opening up to a wider world. In the early 19th century, the South Indian ports in Gujarat were also linked to Arab ports, like Aden and Muscat, and the trading centres of Mogadishu, Zanzibar, Malindi and Lamu, along the north-eastern coast of Africa. It is said that Vasco da-Gama made use of a sailor, Ahmed ibn Majid, from Gujarat to navigate from Zanzibar to India, an indication of the importance of South Asian and Arab traders already operating in the Indian Ocean region, well before the arrival of European explorers. The map of the Indian Ocean shows there was a long history involving the exchange of people, trades, ideas and crafts between West India, Middle East and East

Africa. The perilous journeys were made in triangle-sailed dhows, to harness the seasonal monsoon winds.

Later in the late 19th century, around 1895 A.D., there was also a steady emigration of workers, encouraged by the British, who were looking for a cheap skilled labour force to work along the indigenous African tribes to build the railway line from the East African port of Mombasa to Nairobi, Kenya. Before this, camel had long been used to bring coastal trade goods such as silk, spices, ivory, porcelain, slaves and incense to inland empires. Both routes played important roles in the lives of impoverished Indians. It steadily established a body of determined young enterprising men on the Dark Continent. Albeit, the British migratory route was safer, with fewer risks, sacrifices and hardships, guaranteeing employment, which played a crucial role of transporting many Indians who were escaping famine, rather than those solo adventurers or small groups who travelled with Omani Arabs. The history of human migration in search of a better life in East Africa is a feat of exceptional endeavour. Africans, Arabs, Europeans and Indian families, just as in others parts of the world, had to navigate through rapidly shifting political and economic situations, as well as survive the challenging inhospitable prevailing forces in alien surroundings.

My great-grandfather, Hassanali, was from Morbi, another coastal town in Gujarat, which had well-established trading links with the Middle East. He had heard from the Arab sailors of the possibility of sandalwood growing inland in East Africa, which was already well known in India and the Far East. He must have literally thought he had struck gold and worth exploring. The sandalwood is a small tropical tree, which lives as a root parasite on around three hundred tree species, absorbing water and nutrients, without major detriment to its hosts, usually grows sprawling upright or intertwined with the host, and living up to a hundred years. One tree can host only one sandalwood, so it is scarce, and it takes a trained eye to locate one, by rummaging laboriously through the thick forest, adding to the price value. Certain cultures place great significance on its fragrant and medicinal qualities. The wood is burnt in Hindu religious rite (rich Hindus also use it for cremation), burnt on the perpetual fire in Parsi temples, and is used in joss sticks by Chinese Buddhists. The oil is used by Muslims to bathe their body before burial, and in the West, it is used in scented soaps, powders and perfumes. The golden coloured oil is extracted from the red heartwood and roots, which has higher oil content, and commands high prices. While the rest of the tree, with low oil content is used for fine woodcarving purposes, such as rosaries and sculptures, instead of oil extraction.

It was sometime in the middle of the 19th century when my great-grandfather, Hassanali Morbiwalla, left India, well-before the British migratory route of railway workers became popular. He hitched a ride with Omani Arab sailors for Muscat, and the onward journey was regularly trodden by the Arabs, landing on the East African coast in search of the sandalwood tree. Life was difficult on these small ships of 80 to 350 tons, 40 to 60 feet long with wooden hulls and lateen sails. The passengers slept on deck and clustered in groups supporting each other, sharing one dream of a better life. They had no privacy, cooked their own food, and lacked any competent medical service. The ships bobbed and rolled off the monsoon seas, even in calm weather, and seasickness was very common, no one escaped the storms during the voyage. On the whole, a frightening experience.

My great-grandfather's movements after landing in Lamu or Malindi off the Kenyan coast, remains a total mystery. But, without doubt, the family history clearly shows sandalwood was discovered in neighbouring Tanzania by my ancestors, whether it was him (Hassanali) or his son, Akberali (my grandfather), remains another riddle. I do not know how old my great-grandfather was when he landed, whether he was married at the time, and if not, when and where he got married. Also, I do not know when and where my grandfather was born, how many siblings he had, or where he got married either. One thing I know for sure is that my father, uncles and aunts were born in Nairobi; my father Badrudin Akberali Hassanali (seventh of ten siblings) was born around 1928; however, I do not know why they were born in Nairobi. How I wish there was at least one surviving family elder whom I could now ask, or had paid more attention to what they were saying when they were alive. A lesson most of us realise later in life is not to take anything for granted when it is too late. Of course, like anyone else I would very much like to know everything about my family history, and would probably have approached life differently. But now it is in the past and no point in regretting not finding out all this information before, so I just look to the future. This is why I have mostly relied on the recollection of various bits and pieces of material, and personal experience of events while growing up in Tanga. The following small account of early family history is based on my logical deductions from the recollection of dates, facts, places and events.

I often recall hearing that it was sometime in the 1890s that my great-grandfather, Hassanali Morbiwalla, arrived in Mombo, Tanzania. What led him to Mombo? How he got there? Was he alone or was my grandfather with him, is anybody's guess? I think the reason could be found by looking at the local geography, and the fact that Mombo bears evidence of the beginnings of a thriving business empire in the early 20th century, in my family's history. Mombo, a sleepy little village with a few African inhabitants and dwellings is nestled at the foot of the beautiful Usambara Mountains, and is remembered by most as the start of the long winding hill road to Lushoto in the Usambaras and beyond. It is situated about 90 miles Northwest of Tanga, which was described by explorer Richard Burton in 1857 as a 'patch of thatched pent roofed huts, built upon a bank overlooking the Indian ocean', with an estimated population of 4000-5000, which included fifteen Baluchis and twenty Indian merchants.[2] The Germans took control of the coastal strip of the mainland by buying it from the Sultan of Zanzibar in 1891, by way of 'gunboat diplomacy', calling their colony Tanganyika (now Tanzania). In the same year Tanga was designated a township, boosting its status, followed by large scale investments by private German commercial interests. The inland areas of Usambara Mountains were opened up, as reliable roads and bridges were constructed which are still used today, and a short stretch of railway line built near Shume with a plan to extend the railway line from Shume to Lushoto and even further; although this did not happen, and still remains as it was in 1893.

Tanga became an important seaport; whereas, Lushoto, formerly known as Wilhelmstal, became administrative centres during the German occupation of Tanzania for the coastal and Usambara regions. A pier with a railway line to the interior was developed. In 1893 the Germans started construction work on the Usambara railway line, with the line reaching Korogwe in 1902, Mombo in 1904 and Moshi in 1911. The railway line was built to develop trade with the fertile northern plantation regions growing sisal, coffee, tea, rice and a range of food products. Sisal was introduced by the Germans in the late 19th century.[3] It was in 1893 when a visionary German Agronomist, Dr Richard Hindorf, introduced the sisal plant *Agave sisalana*, to start the industry in Tanzania. In its heyday, Tanga was the world's largest sisal producing region. Lushoto, situated 4,590 feet above sea level was connected to the Tanga Railways at Mombo, by a road built through the Usambara mountain range with hazardous hairpin bends, which had to be negotiated with extreme care. In WWI, Tanga was also at the centre of a major battle fought between the British and the Germans.[4]

Sisal was the main commercial cash crop in the past, and still grows in Tanzania today, but with a less commercial value in Tanzania today. Traditionally, sisal has been the leading material for making ropes and twine. It was widely used in marine, agricultural and general industrial fields because of its strength, durability and stretchable properties, as well as its resistance to deterioration in salt water. The sisal filled a vital role in rope production for the German naval fleet, and the manufacturing of sacks to export agriculture products from the colony. With the outbreak of WWI there was a dramatic increase in the demand for sisal, which could not be met by the fledgling sisal plantations that were just established by the German East Africa Company in Tanganyika, to sustain the production of sisal fibre. However, the wild form of sisal-*Sansevieria ehrenbergii*

[2]Tanzania Safari Guide; Tanga, The Indian Ocean Coast
https://www.tanzaniaodyssey.com/blog/cadogan-guide-to-tanzania-the-indian-ocean-coast-tanga/
[3] Moffett, J.P. (Editor) Tanganyika: A Review of its Resources and their Development, 1955. About Sisal
https://ntz.info/gen/b00459.html
[4] Anderson, Ross: The Battle of Tanga 1914, Stroud 2002: Tempus.
https://encyclopedia.1914-1918-online.net/bibliography/AN3G75H7

(poor man's sisal), a close relative of *Sansevieria trifasciata* (mother-in-law's tongue), grew in proliferation in the northern Tanzania region. It was known to the Akberali Hassanali family from their wide travels in that neck of the wood in search of sandalwood, allowing them to take advantage to meet the growing demands for sisal, using their recently acquired old truck.

As I have previously mentioned, it is unknown what led great-grandfather, Hassanali, to Mombo and how he got there. Although we can make an educated guess, by examining the local geography of Mombo to provide some answers based on logical deductions. I know the railway reached Mombo in 1904; however, it is believed that my great-grandfather arrived there in the 1890s independently. Mombo is ideally situated at the base of the Usambaras at the crossroads on the way to Moshi and Lushoto from Tanga, and sandalwood is well suited to grow in mountainous localities. It is likely that my great-grandfather, who was on a mission to find sandalwood, may have heard about the Usambaras during his travels while in Kenya, as they are located southwest of that region. I had often heard from various family members and local people during my childhood visits to Mombo that the Kenyan border was within walking distance from some of the places like Shume, and other remote villages from Lushoto. Similarly, the Shimba Hills in Kenya, located some 20 miles southwest of the seaport of Mombasa, lies roughly in the same direction of the Usambaras. It seems likely that the Shimba Hills could have been one of the first prospective sites scoured by my great-grandfather after landing in Lamu or Malindi, situated about 70 miles north of Mombasa. It is equally possible that during his travels searching for the elusive sandalwood that he may have gained local knowledge of the area from the local African tribes,[5] leading him to enter Tanzania from Kenya, either via the mountainous Usambara route to Lushoto and Mombo, or via the coastal route to Tanga, as the Kenyan border is less than 40 miles from here, then proceeding to Mombo by road.

There is evidence of close friendships built during the travels by my great-grandfather and grandfather with people of the local Wasamba Usambara tribe, and many others from varied backgrounds. At this stage, I would especially like to mention Mzee Hassani, who became a very close family friend, and whose sons were given important posts in the business, as foreman of the timber sawmills, and especially his eldest son, Abdi Hassani, who was to play an important role later as chairman of the Cooperative Workers Union at the Mbwi sawmill. Mzee Hassani and his son, when in Mombo, would share meals with the Akberali Hassanali family. Mzee is a Swahili word of great respect, used to address an elder. In fact, Mzee Hassani's home village, Shume, played an important role in the quest for sandalwood.

---

[5]Digo - Peoples Group https://www.peoplegroups.org/explore/groupdetails.aspx?peid=14924

I have fond memories of the Usambaras, with streams running with cold water, lush surrounding greenery, and the friendly local Wasamba people greeting passing cars by waving and smiling, displaying beautiful white teeth. I have climbed a few of those peaks in school holidays during visits to Mombo on my own, or when I went camping with friends in the Usambaras. I also have memories of visiting the remnants of a pilot plant, which was in close vicinity to Shume, which was a humble basic furnace built out of stone to generate steam, a simple method used in India for the distillation of sandalwood oil, as well as my uncles and father mentioning that great-grandfather and grandfather experimented with the steam process in the kitchen, and built the prototype based on this. This shows the ingenuity of human beings to find solutions, despite not attending school or having any formal education, and speaks volumes for the shrewdness and pioneering skills of my ancestors, including others in distant lands over a century ago. I feel that my genes, for the interest in scientific research, must have come from my great-grandfather, and I owe him a lot for the privilege of this.

Once again, I do not know if it was my great-grandfather or his son, my grandfather, who discovered sandalwood in the Usambaras, and established the family distillery and timber sawmill business in Mombo. Neither do I know my great-grandfather's age of death, nor his burial place. However, I do know for certain that my grandfather passed away in 1952. It was soon after my grandmother, Rukaiyabai Akberali Hassanali, who died sometime after my birth in 1951. Both my grandparents are buried in Tanga, and I last paid my respects in 2012 when I last visited Tanga after the passing of my mother, Batulbai Badrudin Akberali. I can say with certainty that it was my grandfather Akberali who established a family business in 1905, aptly named Akberali Hassanali & Sons; its main base was in Mombo. I know this because if it was my great-grandfather, Hassanali, then the business would have been named after him. Also, an advertisement aptly named after my grandfather confirms that he established the business, because it appeared in the 1962 edition of the primary school magazine that I attended. I can also clearly recollect seeing company letterheads giving the names of the partners of the business, the six sons of Akberali, and listing the main business as saw millers and distillers of sandalwood. It seems from family chitchat the two activities only became the main business after WWI; although the company was established in 1905. Life was pretty hard and uncertain in those times, in all aspects, which was due to adverse living conditions and food shortages. Before the war, the family dabbled in various business activities to make a living, but when the war broke out, not only did it cause more hardship, it also provided business opportunities and strength, just like the famine in Gujarat (India), which seems that these sorts of adversities often bring.

The business really began after the defeat of Germany.[3] Soon after the war ended, the family embarked on their business venture, the cherished dream of establishing the sandalwood distillery and sawmill at Mombo. By now, they had already discovered a subspecies of the true Mysore sandalwood growing in the Usambaras. Their team of local people and Mzee Hassani extracted and produced sandalwood oil using steam at the makeshift distillery in Shume. Later, they also found sandalwood growing in the plains of the Pare mountain range, home of the highest free-standing mountain in the world, Mount Kilimanjaro. Shortly after the war, grandfather, Akberali, got the idea to improve the yield of this valuable oil from the chips of the red heartwood and roots, which has a higher content of oil than the offcuts of sandalwood that he exported for use in cremations and wood carvings. He also ordered a somewhat ancient type of basic machinery from the perfume capital of India, the great city of Kannauj, and installed a distillery plant at Mombo, which was later modernised using a second hand boiler from a railway steam engine to generate high-pressure steam. All these efforts increased his extraction rate of the oil by 2½%, which helped him to face the stiff competition from India, and the fluctuating competition from Sudan, China, Burma, and Singapore. Mombo became known as a place for exporting oil, not petrol or engine oil, but for the unique and lovely fragrance of sandalwood oil, valued in 1960 at about £20 a gallon, £470 in today's money. Mombo also got recognised as the only place on the African continent with an industry that competed with India, in the production of sandalwood products. The Akberali Hassanali family, as pioneers of sandalwood were also known as the Sukhadwalla family, and it is an opportune moment to clear the conundrum associated with the family surname.

*****

Amongst some Indian sects from Gujarat, it is common to have surnames associated with places of origin, town or country where they were born, the same as with old English names that were linked to trade. The Gujarati word Sukhad means sandalwood and Walla describes a person's place of origin or trade. The literal translation of Sukhadwalla, means a businessman of sandalwood. My great-grandfather was named as Hassanali Morbiwalla, as he came from Morbi in Gujarat. In olden days, it was also prevalent amongst Muslims of Indian origin to have two surnames, because in the Muslim faith the children are named, as the son or daughter of their father. However, as if it was not confusing enough, let us confuse it further. For some reason in our family, the surname is Akberali after my grandfather, instead of Badrudin after my father, which is my middle name. The reason could be that in those days most mothers gave birth at home; therefore, it was not uncommon for birth details, like names, dates or place of birth to get recorded differently, and entered incorrectly, and birth registration formalities for official documents were not of the utmost urgency. It also involved travelling long distances, and often delegated to those familiar in official matters, such as a family member, neighbour or friend. It could just be that when I was born, I know father was in Mombo, and details just got noted wrongly by the person officiating on his behalf, or it could have been family policy to use the surname Akberali for all grandchildren, I am not sure. But I have noticed some surname variations amongst cousins. I have continued to use the surname Akberali for my wife, Femida (Femi) as her married name and for my daughters, Naamah and Ummehani, as their maiden names, not Hassan as a surname, but as a middle name. By the way, Femi's maiden name was Dungarwalla, as her ancestors came from a village called Dungar in Gujarat.

When I was five, I remember my mother saying that she was told by a teacher living in our neighbourhood to send me to school at the start of the academic year. I went with a neighbour and got enrolled as a Sukhadwalla, because I suppose that is how the whole family was known. It would have made no difference, even if my parents had taken me, because the teacher would have filled the admission form anyway, due to my parents being unable to read and write, and even if they were aware of the discrepancy in my name, they would not have dreamt of questioning the teacher. The Sukhadwalla surname got carried right through when I came to Manchester. I first noticed the discrepancy when I applied for a passport in 1973 to travel to the UK at the age of twenty-two. I decided to get it sorted, and changed my surname to Akberali to be consistent with the passport and birth certificate. On my BSc degree certificate from Dar es Salaam, it still bears the Sukhadwalla surname. In fact, my PhD supervisor still mentions about my name change, and I do not believe that names define one's destiny or future. Call it a coincidence or insignificant, but I would like to think my family and I have benefited with the Akberali surname alphabetically, such as it is listed first on the ballot paper or ahead in queues when lined up alphabetically, but then who knows, we may have lost out by not being further down the list as a Sukhadwalla, and as far as we are concerned, it is now a *fait accompli*.

*****

Later the Akberali Hassanali family went onto to discover a distant cousin of *Brachylaena hutchinsii*, growing in thickets over the dry parts of Tanga Province, their local name is Muhuhu, highly prized in East Africa and Europe for parquet flooring, which has been used to make many floors of famous places in Britain, and other parts of the world, where it has been used for school floors, museums, ballrooms and factories. Private homes that have to stand up to rough treatment have floors laid with Muhuhu timber supplied from Mombo. The family also extracted oil from the Muhuhu sawdust produced as a by-product, and built more sawmills at Tanga, Korogwe, Mbwi and Kwamsisi, not only saw milling

Muhuhu, but also other well-known East African hardwoods. In addition to that, they also established an engineering/mechanical workshop business in Tanga.

Enduring family friendships developed as life progressed in the relative calm in between wars, with many pleasant memories. In particular, I would single out the story of a beautiful friendship nurtured in the Usambaras with the Kamal Khan family, well before I was born, because of the important part the sons of the Khan family played in my life. It was 1937 when events were changing in Europe. The Spanish Civil War had begun; Chamberlain succeeded Baldwin as the British Prime Minister, while Hitler's troops marched into Austria. In India, the British introduced provincial independence, and the Congress Party, led by Jawaharlal Nehru, professed his stance against Fascism, Nazism and Japanese militarism, in sympathy for those oppressed. India was ready to join Britain to fight the oppressors, based on a firm guarantee of future independence; otherwise, it would mean aiding British Imperialism. At the same time the demand for a Muslim League Party, led by Mohammed Jinnah for a Muslim homeland, was becoming louder. Tanganyika was a distant place from the turmoil in the world order. The only daily connection to the outside world was the soundwaves transmitted from London and Delhi, heard on a Philips or Murphy receiver. The evening news from London started with the chimes of Big Ben at 6 pm, and was a must for many Indians making a living in remote places, who strained their ears to catch the latest news from the outside world.

Kamal Khan was referred to as Khan Saheb by everyone, because Saheb is a form of address or title placed after a man's name or designation, as a mark of respect. Khansaheb returning from home, which is now known as Pakistan after 1947 partition, was asked to go to Lushoto to take over the charge of the police station in the British colony. He was recently married man with a young wife. When he arrived in Tanga, he proceeded on the German built Tanga to Moshi railway line, disembarking at Mombo, and travelled to his Lushoto destination by road. The friendship started with my uncles, Ebrahim and Taibali, the two eldest sons of my grandfather. As the eldest of the six, the brothers would drive family trucks to Shume to collect sandalwood. Sometimes it would be late in the evening and dark by the time they finished loading the timber onto the truck, before continuing on their hazardous journey home, even in daylight it was dangerous, because of its winding narrow roads, steep drops and hairpin bends. Quite often the brothers would sleep in the truck, but with the arrival of Khansaheb, they found it difficult to refuse his generous hospitality, and would stay the night at his place, and leave the next morning after breakfast for more sandalwood foraging, or to return to Mombo. In due course, the Khansaheb family were blessed by the birth of four sons.

Over the years, the Akberali Hassanali family established more business interests, employing perhaps a thousand or even more people, and Mombo prospered under the collective efforts of Akberali Hassanali & Sons. The company was managed by one particular brother, who had attended school and had a good command of English. He lived in Tanga with his family, while the other five brothers ran the day-to-day business interests in Mombo until the 1970s, away from their wives and families, who had to live in Tanga for their children's education. A family home got well established in Mombo, and the sawmill and distillery business expanded, which were situated along the slow-flowing tributary of the Pangani River. The family also operated the Usambara Petrol Station and an Inn at the crossroads to the Usambaras, Tanga and Moshi, not far away from the railway station. Every weary passing traveller who stopped there to fill their tanks with petrol, were graciously offered cold passion fruit juice free of charge. It became another family trademark, because it was very tasty and thirst-quenching. In return, the hot traveller would bless the family, as the cold drink flowed down their throat. When I recall talk of such times, it brings back happy memories for me, and has made me emotional while writing this account, because of how total strangers appreciated simple acts of good deeds of kindness, such as quenching their thirst or hunger. Those in need of help, in case of mechanical breakdowns, were assisted with repairs in the well-equipped sawmill garage, enabling them to continue with their arduous journeys on murram roads and tracks built with stones and gravel embedded in soft laterite soils, while those arriving late, were offered a place to sleep and food at any time during the night. It was an open-door policy for those in need in the Akberali Hassanali family.

2

Forgotten History

I find it a fascinating adventure how my great-grandfather and grandfather, with his wife and six sons laid the foundation of an enterprising business, well over a hundred years ago. It must have been a struggle for survival that required endurance, trust, sacrifice, family unity and historical sentiments. I also think with sadness of those unlucky migrants who crossed the *kalapani* (black waters) in a dhow from India to Africa in the middle of the 19th century, and onwards, without success. Our family owe so much to those who had the courage to travel across an unknown ocean to a mysterious destination, referred to by others as the dark and forbidden continent, without any navigational experience, just hope and dreams. These were astonishing feats in themselves. Indians had already made their presence in East Africa, well before the Europeans, without firing a single shot, national army, gun boats, war, carnage or bloodshed. They had endured a lot to carve out an existence, not just for themselves, but also helped in the development of many nations, then and even now in their new adopted countries. I would like to think there are many lessons that can be learnt of shared values and feats that can be built upon for the good of humanity as a whole. In reality, the history of East Africa is an exceptional past of pioneering adventure of African, Indian, Arab and European people. Equally disheartening in the case of my family business and many others, with exception of a few businesses from that period, only survived one or two generations. The main reasons were due to the rapidly shifting political and economic environments in Kenya, Tanzania and Uganda.

South Asians in East Africa are written out of history books from the colonial era, and their true contributions and sacrifices are often overlooked. They also do not feature in the subsequent textbooks written on Tanzania, Kenya and Uganda history after these countries became independent. In fact, if mentioned at all, they are seen as people who were expelled for exploiting Africans, and played no important part in the national histories. Besides, Asians are not part of the Indian national history, because they had migrated before independence. If they do get a mention, they are not part of the European colonial history, except for being 'middlemen' who could be employed for the colonial projects to build railways or other tasks. What history books do not give is an accurate account of Asians, like my great-grandfather and many others, who all played significant roles in nation building, long before the Europeans. Even the Europeans in those days did not know, or perhaps for superiority reasons, did not want to acknowledge that the early contacts between Indians and East Africans went back two thousand years. The very first undisputed written evidence of these early contacts is in the Periplus of the Erythraean Sea, written by a Greek merchant in the 1st century A.D. In fact, when Vasco da-Gama arrived in Mozambique, Mombasa and Lindi in 1497, he was surprised at the number of Arabs and Indians he encountered. In fact, history books do not even mention that Indians were already in East Africa before the British explorer Richard Burton[2] in 1857, the German colonial ambitions - by way of 'gunboat diplomacy', and in the form of the German East African Company[3] - or the arrival of the British in the First World War.[4] As victors, the British had also engineered a collapse of the German currency by circulating forged notes, leading to the widespread trade disruptions, affecting Asians very badly, but they still survived the calamity. Even such sacrifices, hardships and resilience, did not get mentioned, just taken for granted and ignored, as it is today in the West.

In those days to the Germans and British, the Indian was just a 'colonial subject', and unlike European settlers, was not entitled to the protection of the colonial civil law. The traders were subject to the same harsh treatment that was given to the defenceless Africans, and forced to compete with the colonial companies and settlers, without any support or recognition. What the history books also forget to divulge is that Asians faced anti-Indian legislation in housing, business, education and other restrictions in public life. This led to the founding of the Indian Association in Mombasa, as early as 1900, giving a voice to institutionalise and collect the grievances from Asians about government legislation and high taxes - compared to what the British and Europeans paid. The association became instrumental in defending the political and economic interests of Asians in East Africa. It was a never-ending cycle. Often the colonial powers would argue that they had to look after the welfare of the Africans, but Asians always demonstrated that Indians were not against any legislation in favour of Arabs and Africans, but against legislation discriminating them, playing one group against another. Such discrepancies existed for tax reductions on fresh butter, cigarettes, milk and ghee, where ordinary Asians, Arabs and Africans would not benefit at all, as they could not afford them in the first place, or the quantities purchased by Europeans, as the they were able to buy large amounts, but basic items, such as rice and kangas worn by African ladies, had duties on them.

In the mid to late 19th century most new South Asian migrants in East Africa depended on the goodwill of other migrants, because they had left their friends and relatives in India. Also, family and community members back in India would repay the money they had borrowed for the voyage, so they often arrived penniless after spending their savings, or were even looted en route to East Africa. This made it impossible to acquire credit to buy food, or even a small mattress to sleep on, when they arrived at their destination. Many did not speak English, Arabic or Swahili, but despite such obstacles, survive they did, and what they achieved they built through sheer spirit of individual enterprise and stubbornness, without an army or the backing of a powerful military nation, which needs to be applauded and acknowledged. The Asians continued to grow, supporting and helping each other in their common goal to succeed in whatever capacity they could. A migrant would work for his sponsor for many years to establish credentials, and eventually earn the trust of the sponsor, allowing them to receive goods on credit, with which to establish his own business. Once established, he would return to his town or village in India to secure a bride, and after some years the pattern would be repeated with another relative.

Building any business is one thing. Surviving the business challenges is another. Especially those most difficult ones not under your control, such as political factors, ideological issues and cultural obstacles, which no one can forecast, and overnight could destroy years of hard work spent building-up a business. The post-colonial East African era resulted in the nationalisation of Asian businesses and assets built over one-hundred-and-fifty years. Before independence, the worldwide influences of different political economic ideologies played an important role in building a new nation state. One question posed was whether Tanzania, formerly Tanganyika before the union with Zanzibar following an army coup in 1964, should follow a more socialist, or a capitalist pattern. Tanzania chose an African Socialist Democracy, named *Ujamaa*; Whilst, Kenya chose an African capitalist ideology, I am not quite sure what that meant; whereas Uganda, under General Idi Amin, chose an anti-Asian business policy. To cap it all, the loyalty of Asians, as Indians from the sub-continent were now referred to, was always questioned by the opportunist African political leaders for their own policy failures to gain popularity, which led to physical attacks, looting, misguided nationalisations of Asian properties in all three countries, followed by expulsions of Asians in Uganda after 1971. It also became difficult for British Asians in Kenya to get visas to do business, as they were now considered foreign nationals, so they left for Britain. All such events wiped out generational life savings, leaving families facing unpredictable consequences. As the migration gathered pace in the 1970s, the British popular press went on its periodic overdrive of scaremongering, stating that Asians will bring with them criminality, diseases and welfare dependency.

Sadly, all these events led to immeasurable psychosocial impact, uncertainty and personal insecurity, which would affect and hurt any human being, especially if you spent so much of your life running your own business, building it from scratch with sacrifices, and sharing success by investing and supporting local communities through philanthropic acts, even helping and supporting the African political independence cause. Such acts of nationalisation and recriminations cuts the umbilical cord between you and your place of birth, your roots and identity. This is precisely what happened, despite our best intentions and wishes that led people like myself and many others, who were third and fourth generations born in East Africa, to seek new futures elsewhere. It is such events that makes one seek a better education and opportunities on foreign shores, leading humans to contribute to the economy and well-being of their adopted country, just like their forefathers did some one-hundred-and-fifty years ago, when they set off on their perilous migrations.

The migrants to East Africa like my ancestors and others were successful, because they helped each other. During the first weeks or even months after arriving, migrants stayed with relatives and friends, or if they had none, in community houses. These houses were informally organised, often on the premises of an Asian trader, who had already become established in East Africa. Many migrant families did not forget what it had been like to be poor themselves. In fact, there were many cases whereby some Asians had lost everything, but with the help of others, they became very successful businessman, and engaged in philanthropy (charity). Religion, cultural and family heritage are important sources for personal development, and performing charitable acts for the less fortunate meant a lot for those pioneering souls. Something we can all learn from, because humanity as a whole, need each other, not only when in need, but also in times of plenty. Hence, further reflecting the basic shared human values in various forms, but with the same overall objectives, to provide a better future for their children, so they can lead a prosperous life than the previous generation. The irony is that such values are compartmentalised in the West. For example, Britain has the conservative (Tory), socialist (Labour) and liberalism (LibDem) values. However, what those pioneers in East Africa believed in most was humanity, and most importantly not to forget what it felt like to be on the receiving end of hardships and inhumanity. If we look closely, such values have been practiced universally to varying extents since the beginning of humanity in one form or another. What the past migration from the Western shores of the sub-continent to the East African shores achieved were acts of liberalism, conservatism, socialism, reformism, and traditionalism. What is more noticeable is that people practicing these shared values was normal, and passed down through generations, which raises an important question, how did they learn to practice liberal, socialist and conservative ideologies, usually associated with Europe? They had not attended schools or universities, nor visited the West, so how did they learn to practice such ideologies? What it does highlight is that humans share similar survival instincts and beliefs, work hard to provide a better future for their children, provided they are given opportunity to do so, in a safe, not a conflict-ridden environment. These shared values are universally accepted, because if people are free, then this allows them to control their own destiny and well-being, with the role of the government to make it possible, by alleviating obstacles so individuals are able to realise their dreams and aspirations.

Various Indian business communities often built and funded their own places for religious worship, schools, hospitals, sports and other amenities. Most Asian migrants and Africans depended on the goodwill of rich migrant families. The Muslim religion played an undeniable crucial role in the Akberali Hassanali family, since charity and good deeds is one of the five pillars of Islam. Everyone has the need for others, and caring for children, spouses and immediate relatives is a basic instinct of human beings. The first step in 'charity and philanthropy' is to go beyond the boundaries of immediate family and loved ones. This means surpassing the extended family, or one's self-defined community. The second requirement is acceptance of a certain degree of self-sacrifice, not to expect anything in return for the charitable contributions and voluntary work one has given; not even respect or social prestige. The final step is to allow all communities, race or nationalities to have access to the charity. This amounts to humanism in its purest form.

On the surface, it may appear Indian families play no important role in political developments and socio-economic changes, because it is not well documented; however, on closer examination of academic research written on various aspects of African history and newspaper accounts shows that this is not quite true. Indian families, like my family and others, have played important roles towards the economic development of East Africa. Not only that, but also a political role in the independence movement and post-independence progress, welfare of the workers, in addition to the philanthropic well-being of the local community. In short, the Akberali Hassanali family have played important roles in loosening racial and religious boundaries. My ancestors in East Africa served the colonial officials, as well as the Tanzanian independence movement, and in the end, from the small seaport of Morbi in Gujarat in India they ultimately became 'world citizens', well before the term was even invented. The pioneers arriving to the shores of East Africa arrived with an enterprising attitude, hard work and sacrifices with minds of a prototypical businessman to pursue wealth to improve life, not only for themselves, but also for others. This I feel, highlights the similar adventure spirit in me, to seek further education and a better life, when I flew in comfort to the UK in 1973 to face new challenges in a foreign land, which in no way can be compared to the hardships that my ancestors faced, but challenges of a different sort. It has also allowed me to always respect people as human beings, in my fledgling ambition to serve public duty, which I hope also gets instilled in my children and grandchildren.

My paternal grandparents Akberali Hassanali   Early photograph of father and mother.
and Rukaiyabai Akberali Hassanali.

My maternal grandparents Ebrahimjee Mamujee and Fatambai Ebrahimjee Mamujee (circa 1970
s).

Like most families, we did not have a camera when I was young. I bought my first camera in 1978, an Olympus OM10 when employed at Manchester University, which I still have. Early photographs are taken by extended family members and friends.

Camphor log loaded on Albion FT 101 for transportation to Mombo with uncle Taibali.

Triumphant arrival of Mvule Log in Mombo on Albion FT from the Usambaras with uncle Taibali (front left), cousin Mustafa (right), Mzee Hassani (in white cap).

Mombo Health Clinic built for Mombo residents and surrounding areas

Mombo Primary School built by the family.

Mombo Mosque built by the family.

At the mosque inauguration from eldest (r to l) uncles Ebrahim, Taibali, Noordin, Fazal, father and Taher

Sandalwood distillery and staff hut at Mombo with Usambaras in background.

Usambara Petrol Station, prime location, at the cross roads to the Usambaras, Moshi and Arusha from Tanga and Dar es Salaam.

Usambara Inn next to the petrol station.

Uncles Taibali and Noordin with Tanzanian Agriculture Minister Bill Bryson in Mombo.

Donation ceremony of Mbwi Sawmill to the workers co-operative attended by President Julius K. Nyerere (seated in white cap) and from his right, Abdi Hassani (seated), uncles Fazal (standing) and Taibali (seated).

Getting ready for ploughing land with uncle Taibali on far right and Mzee Hassani standing next to him.

A lot of hoeing saved and a happy group of Women Association members.

3

Upbringing, Education and Gratitude

I was born in 1951 in Tanga sixty-nine years ago. I recall my mother, Batulbai Badrudin Akberali, mention that at birth, my grandmother was saying a son has arrived for Badru, short for Badrudin, which was my father's name, and she was very happy. I also remember well my mother often saying that I was born in the early hours, just before the call for morning prayers, and my grandmother took me on her lap whilst she was on the prayer mat.

Events were bringing a change in Europe, Africa and all corners of the world following the end of WWII. Historians regard the 20th century as the most cataclysmic in the history of mankind, because for the first time the entire population of the world was affected directly or indirectly by two world wars, one after another, changing the face of civilisation. The West would never be the same again, but neither would the Third World. Soon after the colonial empire dissolved, the world was engaged in the storm of rage, confusion and uprisings. For Europe, practically centuries of supremacy and complacency were shattered. Suddenly alone, the Third World found it equally hard to manage and embrace alien ideologies of democracy and Western concepts. The World could no longer be regarded as one single idea, one right colonial standard, as well as many other differences.

Like most towns, Tanga also has a fascinating history. It was a famous place for the sisal plant that went around the world, because of its maritime use, and where Germany and Britain fought – 'The Battle of Tanga' in WWI.[2,3,4] Tanga was then the second largest town in Tanzania, with a population of 70,000, a multi-ethnic multilingual community comprising of Africans, Arabs, Indians and Europeans. The Africans, formed the majority, and belonged to the *Digo* Tribe,[5] followed by Arabs from the Middle East, mostly of Omani origin. Indians, the third largest, comprised of various sects from the Indian sub-continent. The last group were the Europeans, mostly made up of the British and others, such as Greeks, Germans, Italians, Portuguese, and Americans.

The prevailing colonial political and socio-economic environment meant that the Africans, Arabs, Indians and Europeans led segregated lives, living in distinct areas with separate schools, sport centres, and other amenities. Prior to 1951, there were two primary schools. The Germans built the Tanga School in 1895, not necessarily driven by an ideology to educate the local tribes, but it was more to satisfy their needs of colonial power, so they could communicate with the local people (Africans) to exploit the natural resources of the land. Tanga with its safe harbour and proximity to the Usambara Mountains was recognised as a potential agrarian land for planting cash crops, such coffee, tea sisal etc. The Tanga school was run by Catholic Missionaries for Christians of African and Indian origin. A second school was built in the 1940s by the philanthropic Karimjee Jivanjee family, with the main intake of Indians from all sects, few Arab and African children. In the 1950s, two more primary schools were built for children from specific religious sects, one by the Ismaili community, and another by the philanthropic Taibali Sachak family, which I attended from 1956 to 1963. If I recollect, the annual intake was about thirty to forty children attending each school. These two schools allowed the non- religious school to increase its in-take for African and Arab pupils, and the same Karimjee Jivanjee family went on to build the very first secondary school in Tanga for non-Europeans, with an annual mixed intake of about two hundred from all communities and race.

While growing up in Tanga, it was natural to form close friendships with people from African, Asian and Arab origins. We mingled freely to study, talk, play and attend parties as equals, with no inclination we belonged to a different race, creed or class. I was not aware of derogatory racist names, which I came to know and hear later after coming to the UK. The only contact I had with the Europeans was at school. Our headmaster, Mr Hornsby was British, and a strict disciplinarian, not impartial to using the cane. I was at the receiving end on a few occasions. Not for academic reasons, but for dress code and misbehaving outside school hours, when riding a bicycle on the right-hand side of the road instead of the left, because that side was for pedestrians and horse riders, so they could see oncoming traffic. A lesson I never forgot! However, one never publicised such incidents. I would not have dreamt of telling my mother. Even if I had complained, she would have said that I must have deserved it for misbehaving, and would tell the teacher to punish me if I misbehaved at home, a no-win situation, so best to keep such matters private. Mr Cook taught geography, and there was a temporary teacher, Ms Gardner, for 6 months who taught English before 'O' level exams in 1967. The rest, about less than fifteen, were Indians, with one African teacher for Swahili. They were all great teachers, and I can still name many of them. Apart from teachers, the only contact with other British people was during cricket matches when asked to play against or in their team, when short of fixtures or players. While growing up, the atmosphere amongst Tanga residents was one of broad-mindedness. Not one of harbouring prejudices, based on issues related to national or international politics, because historically this is what divides human beings. No one questioned differences based on race, creed and class, but made the most of the prevailing conditions by giving opportunities to one another. We were always taught to respect our elders, teachers, property and each other in the society we lived in. Discipline and respect came naturally. I can say it has done no harm, and has served me well.

After independence in 1961, the top priority for the government, under President Julius Nyerere, was to provide free primary education up to year seven for all citizens, irrespective of race, class and creed. He was an eminent graduate of the Edinburgh University, a teacher himself, and referred to by Tanzanians as Mwalimu (teacher in Swahili). The newly independent Tanzania had few schools and teachers, with insufficient resources to educate everyone, but Julius Nyerere built a platform for all Tanzanians to receive primary education; increasing the intake of African pupils. Schools were situated in bigger towns and villages with very limited places. My mother did not attend school, but she was very farsighted, and mixed with every community and faith, regardless of their background. She came from a large, not well to do family, and was one of ten children; despite this, her parents made sure they had love, food and shelter being their most pressing priorities. I have very fond memories of my maternal grandparents, Ebrahimjee Mamujee and Fatambai Ebrahimjee Mamujee, who passed away in the late 1970s. My mother got married at the age of thirteen, and played a pivotal role in the formation of my ethics, education and character. At a very early age, my mother instilled in me that education is the wealth of an individual and the nation. So, I owe it to my parents for their foresightedness, as well as my teachers and friends for their help in my life's endeavours.

Education is the great engine for personal and social development. It is through education that a homeless girl or the daughter of a labourer can become teachers, a boy of a farm worker or dustman can become a doctor, the son of parents like mine, who never went to school, can attend university, or even consider a political career in a great nation like the UK to serve public duty. Education is what we make out of what we have learnt at home and within the schools we attended that separates one person from another. It is extremely important that children are not limited by lesser facilities, because of their social background and upbringing, so that their progress is not inhibited by what they read, think, or dream to achieve. Quality education for all children, irrespective of social status, is an investment in their future, as well as the nation's, not a waste of money, or time. A marked disparity should not be allowed to exist in the funding between state and public school, otherwise great variation(s) in educational achievements, and social mobility is bound to exist.

It is true that education on its own will not bring success, what is also needed is hard work and determination, and a lot of successful business people did not attend school. What quality education does is allows an ordinary person to open their mind to apply common sense - the knack for seeing things as they are, and doing things as they ought to be done, so they are able to make informed decisions, and not fall victim to extreme forms of religious and populist political indoctrination that preaches division and hatred. I believe to be 'educated' does not mean being 'literate', and having a university degree, and that an 'illiterate' person is not a wise person. We often see people without a university degree, with just basic quality education, or who have not even attended school, can also be 'educated', because of possessing a higher 'degree' of common sense. Good education should not only prepare a child for a better future and social mobility, but open up their mind to apply common sense and logic, not in one's specialised field, but an ability to understand humanity in all aspects of life. I hasten to add that there are examples of eminent leaders, who have had impeccable education, but this may not have given them the correct values, so they became extremely capable of inflicting atrocities and pain on others.

In that respect, we need to embrace an education curriculum with wider benefits, especially in the early formative years of a child's education at home and school. In fact, while doing research for this book, I came across a lot of correspondence and press articles written in my lifetime, which reflect consistency in the real-life concerns that I have raised over the years, as it will become apparent later. I also came across a detailed letter I had written to headmistress, Mrs Daphne Caless in 1995, of Pyrford Primary School, which our daughters attended. It was basically to thank her and the staff for teaching our two children, and preparing them for their future. Amongst other points, which had transpired during our various meetings, I concluded, 'health and education is an individual's and the nation's wealth, and a good standard should be made available to all'. This became one of my slogans in the 2017 and later elections, highlighting my belief in the importance of quality education for everybody, young and old, and I believe that it is never too late to learn anything in life.

My mother was a spiritual person and a devout Muslim. Like most Muslims, she was religious, but not at all fanatical. She used to read the *Koran* every morning until she died, and later in her life offered services to recite the whole

Koran on behalf of others unable to do so, because of time and other constraints. I brought the copy she used back with me from Mombasa, which is now used by my daughter, a proud possession of hers, and I am sure it will protect her children. My mother lived her life praying for my well-being, so that I succeeded in education. She taught moral values rather than religion, and those values and her prayers have guided and helped me in my life. When I look back, it has protected me very well throughout my life. She was also very particular to mark my birthday according to the Islamic calendar, 8th *Jamadil Ula*, instead of 15th February, as she would be more aware of the Islamic calendar dates to help her honour yearly religious events, instead of the Gregorian calendar. When I left home in 1970, wherever I was, mother wrote nearer the time to my Islamic birthday to remind me on which Gregorian date it fell on. After marriage, she would then remind my wife to make sure my birthday got celebrated on 8th *Jamadil Ula*. Even then, it often got forgotten, but not now, because that was the day when mother passed away, so no one forgets, including my daughters and sisters. My mother also taught us that to be good Muslims you had to respect people, regardless of faith, class or race. I have always put integrity, trust and accountability at the top of my agenda, which I strongly believe to the extent that it instinctively became my main topic in 2017 and other campaigns, when I stood for elections to serve for public duty.

My mother always welcomed everyone to our house, so we had an open house policy, whether they were Muslims or non-Muslims, as multiculturalism (social cohesion) was instilled in me at a very early age, as reflected from my friends' circle. For that I give full-credit to my mother. I dwell on these matters very often.

*****

Mother willingly and selflessly always put her family first. Her life was not driven by material things or personal gain, but simply in doing the best for others. It did not matter what walk of life they were from, she always treated everyone equally and with respect, as fellow humans. She never forgot her family roots, what it meant to make ends meet on a meagre income. She knew what hunger felt like, and what it was like to go without things. Mother believed that it does not cost anything to be friendly with those in need, such as the elderly. She had an inner strength, which allowed her to go that extra mile to help others. When I went to Dar es Salaam University in 1970, I only saw my mother during the holidays, but she was always in my thoughts while I was away, and I knew for sure that I was in hers, because she always prayed for my well-being from the day I was born. She loved me very much, and I know she was very proud of the person that I have become. It is the learned behaviour and the core values she infused in me that ultimately defines the person I am today, someone who respects people, keeps promises and honours commitment. After I settled in the UK, my visits were even less frequent, in thirty-nine years I made a total of nine visits, but we wrote to each other frequently, especially nearer the time of my 'Islamic birthday'. Later on, I often spoke to her on the phone after I got married. Despite being physically apart, when she passed away on 30th March 2012, 8th *Jamadil Ula* 1433H; her memory still remains fresh in my thoughts. I believe and feel her prayers are still helping my family and me.

*****

My father also came from a family of ten; he was the fifth of the six brothers. Although we led a comfortable life, we were not that well-off, despite having a huge business empire, which was strictly managed and controlled by one particular uncle. Father just abided by what he was told to do, or was expected to do; he had no jealousy, just the greatest respect for his brothers and others. In the eyes of others, the whole Sukhadwalla family was wealthy. But in reality, this was far from the truth, because all important and financial decisions were made by one uncle, so if my mother needed something costly for the home, she would often ask his wife to put in a good word, even if father wanted to borrow the family car when he visited Tanga. The immediate extended family comprised of forty. I recall sayings from my paternal grandfather to his six sons, telling them about the importance of living as a united family, because it is "difficult to break a united bundle of six sticks than one stick." I must say, when I was growing up that I noted my grandfather's wish was well adhered to in every sense by the whole family, especially father. That is the incredible part, which I suppose is partly down to the culture, we respected not only our family elders and one another highly, but everyone. I cannot stress enough the unity that held us together as a family, through thick and thin; we never had any disharmony and never thought to think differently. We were all there to help one another, although none of us was financially rich, but we had rich hearts, and nobody was allowed to go hungry, even strangers.

*****

I did not spend much time during my childhood or later years with father. I often remember thoughts of family and people who knew him, mentioning he was a simple, honest, humble and quiet individual, who placed trust in others, expecting them to behave appropriately. I received an urgent call from mother when father was taken to hospital, and admitted into the intensive care unit. It was Saturday 12th March 2006. Femi and Naamah who are adept with computer skills said I should not waste time, but fly there immediately. I am glad I heeded their advice, and flew out the same night. I spent the last few days of my father's life by his bedside. Although we did not communicate in my childhood, I could see the joy in his eyes when he saw I was there when it mattered most. I last saw him on Wednesday the 16th when I left his bedside at 10pm, and my Kenyan cousin was also with me. She saw me feed him, spontaneously caress his head and kiss his forehead before leaving. On the way out she said it was a lovely gesture, as she knew of my childhood relationship with father. We received a phone call at about 2am from the hospital, requesting us to return. We had a feeling what it was about, and found that my father had passed away. Those last four days made up for all the years of lack of contact between a father and son.

*****

I was brought up by my mother in Tanga while father lived in Mombo. We saw my father about three or four times a year, so we had a distant father/son relationship, up until the day he passed away peacefully. I never missed him when it came to making important decisions, as my path was laid out automatically, because of my academic results. All I had to do was graft and pass exams with the encouragement and support of mother. I worked hard, not only academically, but also in extracurricular activities. When I needed to make any decision, education related, mother would ask me to seek my uncle's opinion. To be honest, he was not that bothered in such matters, as I was not expected to do well in school. It was mother who ran the home on her own and catered for all our needs, and it was her dream that I did well in my studies. Mother was a strong believer in the value and importance of education, because she believed it frees people from poverty, since an educated person could not be oppressed, as he or she can think for themselves. She would ask her friend's sons, who were older than me, doing well academically to coach and encourage me, which they often did. I always took full advantage of this, as they were good role-models for me. I recall well that my mother was keen that I always mingled in good company. To do that I had to be of similar calibre, not only academically, but also at sports and socially, so as not to get treated as a general dogsbody, but also not forgetting my humble roots to respect people, irrespective of their background.

I have always considered being very fortunate, as I have mingled with friends and peer groups from academically successful families. My genes for hard work may have come from my father, but from mother came wisdom: she used to say, "You will learn even more from friends who are good at school." I was never afraid to learn or work hard, even today, I am ready to learn from anyone, and I am not ashamed to admit if I do not know something. I will take the trouble to find out, or learn by asking. Here I would also like to mention Khansaheb, who had four sons. He got transferred to the Tanga Police Station and lived not far us. The four brothers were older than me, brilliant both academically and in sport, especially hockey, later they all qualified as doctors and practiced in Germany, Tanzania, the USA and UK. The eldest, Khalid Kamal Khan, had a medical practice in Dar es Salaam when I was at the university, and acted as my guardian. Hamid, Arshad, and the youngest, Majid, coached me when I needed help in maths and science. They all had a soft spot for my mother. Khansaheb looked smart in his police officer's uniform; he was fond of me and wanted me to do well in school, to succeed in life, as he was aware of my father's education and family handicaps. I made friends easily in Tanzania and later in the UK, especially in Manchester and Woking. My friends circle was made up of a very cosmopolitan group. All these factors played a crucial role in my early and later life, which has helped me to progress.

When I was growing up, secondary places in government state schools were limited, as would be expected in a newly independent nation, with a fledgling economy and few infrastructure facilities with a long list of priorities, such as poverty, health and jobs. Instead of shunning responsibility, the government addressed the situation by introducing an education policy, where each primary school pupil had to sit for the National Territorial Exams to secure a place in secondary school. At that time, there was only one secondary school in Tanga for the whole region, offering about two hundred places for those with good exam grades, who attended the many primary schools. Competition was intense. It meant that many pupils, even with reasonable results, failed to secure secondary places, and those from rich families were sent to the only fee-paying private school in Tanga or abroad. Those from disadvantaged families had to work hard to pass exams to succeed in life, and education was one way of achieving that. We received top-class quality primary and secondary education, far better than the private school, from dedicated teachers with the best teaching facilities, studying Cambridge 'O' level and London University 'A' level syllabuses. We sat the same Cambridge examinations required of students in Britain. Exam papers were marked abroad by the respective boards. In order to gain 'A' level places, which again were limited (about thirty), only those students who got a first grade in their 'O' level exams were offered places, followed by a few with second, and even less with third grades. From 1965 onwards, after I completed my 'A' levels, there were less than a thousand university places at the newly opened Dar es Salaam University or scholarships for studying abroad, which were granted based on 'A' exam results. To qualify for the limited government scholarships to attend university, whether in Tanzania or abroad, students had to sign a contract to attend National Service prior to attending university, which led many Indian students from well-to-do families not to sign a binding contract, and after 'O' levels they left to pursue an education abroad, mostly in the UK.

I was delighted when I passed my Cambridge 'O' level examinations in 1967 with a first-grade. I was excited to let mother know, so called out to her from outside the house before going in. She was in the kitchen cooking lunch, and came out running to hug me. She had a knife in her hand. Our next-door neighbour came out to intervene, thinking I was being attacked. Mother's first concern was that I should go at once to inform my uncle. I did not stop for lunch, and left. I waited for him to arrive from the office. When I heard his car, I rushed to give him the good news and he said, "Fine, so you have passed. What are you going to do?" I reminded him that I had come for advice a few months ago, asking him whether I should stay at home after 'O' levels or go abroad for 'A' levels. Staying in Tanga meant pursuing education through government grants and signing-up for National Service, with no option for me to decide my future education career. I informed him that his reply was that we are Tanzanians and have nowhere to go, only to change his views so easily four years later when it came to the future education and ambitions of his two sons. But to tell the truth, he did not think I was capable of doing well in 'O' levels, as I was the first in the whole family to achieve that feat. Later, I was given an opportunity to go abroad after 'O' levels by a non-family member. I was also gifted a parker ink pen in recognition of my achievement by Tilak Raj, a brilliant engineer in charge of our family engineering workshop, just like my father, he felt really proud of me. I have still got the pen, kept as a treasured past memory.

In 1968, in my first year of doing my 'A' levels, I was elected as treasurer to serve in the Interact Club, which was affiliated to the Rotary Club of Tanga, and got invited to attend their monthly lunch meetings to give a report of our activities. The Chairman, Shaukat Karimjee, was a direct descendent of the philanthropic family who had built the first primary and secondary school in Tanga. He was also a medical doctor, who was well known for his charitable deeds towards the poor. On finding out that I belonged to the Sukhadwalla family, he was curious who my father was, as he knew my uncle well. He was pleasantly surprised when I told him it was Badrudin, and he replied "I didn't know he had a son, but he must be proud of your achievement." He took me aside to offer me a scholarship in the UK for further studies, and told me that I should discuss this offer with my parents. I mentioned the conversation to my mother, and she said that I should discuss it with my uncle, who told me to flatly refuse the offer. It was because he was worried about people asking why the wealthy Sukhadwalla family could not afford to send their first successful son abroad. My uncle was more concerned about his reputation, because he was well known in Tanga. By the way, I am not sure when my father came to know about my 'O' level results, perhaps when he visited us next, or my mother may have asked my aunty to convey the news when my uncle next phoned Mombo to discuss business with other uncles. But one thing is for sure, the pleasure I had of making both my mother and father proud of my modest academic achievements that I could see etched on their faces for the remaining years of their life, which was apparent when people used to ask father for the secret behind his son's achievements, because he never attended school.

*****

In 1970 when I was in National Service for the first six months, my uncle and aunty made a special trip, traveling about three hundred miles to see first-hand what it was like. Upon their return to Tanga, my aunty mentioned to a very good friend of hers that after seeing my plight and living conditions in the camp, there was no way she would let that happen to her two sons. Little did she know that although mother did not move in the same 'posh' circle, her friend's husband was a lawyer with a strong reputation for philanthropy, including a member of the Rotary Club, and in a small town like Tanga, everyone knew each other. Therefore, the friend would have had heard of my 'O' level results, a big achievement in those days, and the desire of my mother to educate me. My aunt's friend mentioned to my mother on hearing the hypocrisy and attitude of my aunty towards her sons' education, and not concerned about my future. It turned out my uncle's elder son, within months was taken out of school in Tanga and sent to Mombasa in Kenya to pursue his 'O' levels there, which he just managed to pass, and came to the UK in 1973 to gain 'A' levels followed by a business course. Not sure what he ended up doing, but he had an easy time, being bought a furnished house and a car to pave the way for his younger brother to follow, and his parents visited them regularly. In a way, like any other motherly instincts, my aunty was just looking after her sons' well-being and interests, just the same way my mother wanted me to succeed, and do better than my father. It was my uncle, as patriarch of the family, who had other ideas, acting with self-serving interests for the betterment of his sons' future. I bear no grudges. I had invited my only surviving aunty and her sons to the wedding of my daughter, Ummehani, in 2013. Even now, I have highlighted, not from an acrimonious point of view, but just to give an honest account of reality, as any memoir should give; that not everything is perfect, but to make the most of a situation.

When I met my cousin in the UK, I raised the issue of unfairness and a distinct lack of opportunities in the field of education for those in the family, without an influential voice, such as my father, whose son, despite a proven track record of passing prestigious exams, had to rely on scholarships and attend National Service. I suppose it must not have gone down well. So, in 1975 when I went to Tanga, my cousin who had preceded me must have told his father my views. I could sense tension amongst influential uncles and cousins, which I could not figure out. It came to the upsurge on the last Sunday, before my departure to the UK, when mother answered the phone from my aunty, to say that my father and I were summoned for an urgent meeting at their place. We were completely unaware of the reasons. I asked my aunty what it was all about, and she shrugged her shoulders pointing to the lounge where my uncle was already seated with three other uncles. I was asked to sit on the floor next to him, and he ordered me to relate the conversation I had with his son. I obliged dutifully, and he asked my father for his views. As usual, father kept quiet. I said it had nothing to do with my father, and it was unfair to place him in the firing line. My second eldest uncle stepped in to arbitrate, cooling down the situation and asked me to apologise, which I did as a mark of respect, and being told not to hold such conversations in the future with his son, and I never did. However, my parents felt the consequences of my actions for six years after that meeting, which became progressively worse after I dedicated my PhD thesis to them, where I put 'to my parents who made it possible'. It was only until my uncle, who managed the family business passed away in 1981, when the tension eased.

I am pleased that both my daughters have had good results, attaining MSc first-class degrees in pharmacy from UK universities. Their university education was paid for by earning money from summer and week-end jobs, our support, as well as winning bursaries and scholarships without ending-up with student debt. I can vividly recall during a visit to Mombasa in 2005 when my Kenyan cousin and I were reminiscing past childhood memories. She mentioned about the 1975 incident, because a week prior to that her father, mother and elder brother came to Tanga for a visit while I was also there. She said the visit was pre-planned, as my uncle had asked them to come over to sound them out about me. Thirty years later, I found out from her that the rest of the family members sympathised and agreed with what I was saying, and did not take my side for self-serving interests, because of the fear of facing similar repercussions handed out to me, and it is true that people keep quiet when they 'know which side their bread is buttered'. I have been pretty close to my Kenyan cousin, because I spent quite a few childhood school holidays in Mombasa, as it was my mother's birthplace. I also visited my maternal grandparents and uncles, who always welcomed me, and were very proud of my academic achievements. My Kenyan cousin went onto say that she knows me well, and maybe some of my views might have been shaped sub-consciously, by being treated as the 'black sheep of the family'. I suppose she could be right. My uncle's attitude may have stirred and influenced my thoughts, in terms of what it means to believe in hope and fairness for others. It could also be because of my mother's influence, who never forgot the needs of the poor because of her own upbringing, even after marrying into a relatively well-off family.

In a way, I can proudly say the enterprising person in me, with a get up and go attitude to face new and different challenges, like coming to the UK to seek a better future, are similar to that of my ancestors in the 19th century. It also suffices to say that the National Service experience has made me a better person. In 1967 I went hitch-hiking around Kenya, Uganda and Tanzania, covering about three thousand miles in a month with two close classmate friends, Nizar Shivji and Pradeep Amin. What an experience! Something that was unheard of in those days. Especially by sixteen-year-olds, because of infrequent traffic flow and remoteness, hitching lifts on trucks, nights spent by the roadside in remote areas. We stayed with relatives and Gurudwaras (Sikh temples). In fact, when we visited my aunty in Nairobi, she told my mother off for allowing me to go at such a young age on such an adventure, but this is what mother was like, she always wanted me to make the most of opportunities. If I had not gone, I would not have had a chance to visit much of East Africa at a fraction of the cost, and free entry to the National Parks, because we were students. I spent a few school holidays with many friends camping in the Usambaras. I made the most of the opportunities I had, but whether I would have achieved more if I had been sent abroad, I will never find out, but such is life!

4

Manchester

ollowing graduation from Dar es Salaam University in 1973 with a BSc (Hons) Diploma in Education, I taught at the Old Moshi Secondary School. At the University, I was with my good school buddy, Nizar Shivji, and also developed a very good lifetime friendship with Moosa Jiwaji and his family. During my BSc course, my lecturer Dr Mike Pearson motivated me to consider a PhD degree in marine biology abroad. On his advice, I wrote to Professor Edwin (Ted) Trueman at Manchester University, it was the only university I wrote to for a place, because of my research interests, and I had heard of Manchester, in relation to a local lichen species (a type of green algae) growing there, which had turned black during the industrial revolution, because of smog pollution. I was also interested in going to Manchester because I had heard of the tragic loss of lives of the Manchester United Football Team in the Munich air crash. It must have also been fate, because the UK became my future home and destiny, in search of a better future, just like my great-grandfather who had heard about sandalwood from Omani Arabs, so he landed in East Africa.

I arrived at Heathrow Airport on 9th September 1973 on an East African Airways VC10. It was my first experience travelling on a plane, let alone setting foot on foreign land. I landed wearing a double-breasted suit and a tie, which I had worn for the first time, and had to be aided by a friend to tie the knot of my tie, something I have still not mastered, and rely on my family to do this. I was not overwhelmed by the strangeness of the place, because deep down I believed if I was respectful and polite, others would reciprocate. I had never been surrounded by so many Caucasian people before, but that did not intimidate or bother me in any way. I remember with great fondness the first experiences of the British people, and at the airport they lived up to my expectations, as they were helpful, friendly and courteous. After asking for directions, I took a coach to Victoria Station, and then a train to Manchester. Looking out of the coach and train, I could not believe I was in the country from whose education system I had benefited from during the colonial and post-independence era. I arrived at Manchester Piccadilly Station with my green suitcase, it was raining, and Manchester lived up to its reputation of being a rainy city.

It was Sunday, and thinking there was no point heading to the university, since it would be closed, I asked for directions to a nearest cheap B&B. I was directed to one in Ardwick, where I stayed the night, and had my first meal, ending up at the Star of India restaurant on Oxford Street. The menu was quite confusing. I never knew so many different types of curries existed, to me a curry was a curry. You always learn new things! The next day I met Ted, and after finishing registration formalities, I was told to find a place to live, and was directed to the university accommodation centre. I was given a list of addresses by Mr Taylor, so I could find a bedsit, a name I recall as he was the wicketkeeper in the same university staff cricket team that I joined later. I was not familiar with finding my own accommodation, because at Dar es Salaam University, accommodation was automatically provided. I realised it was a different system at Manchester, and there were no places left in the Student Halls of Residence, as I had not booked. Without thinking, I hopped on a bus, after asking around for directions. When I reached the destination, I found no one was at home, and proceeded to the next address on the list with similar results. It was getting dark, so I returned to explain to Mr Taylor my situation, and he put me up for the night in the student guest room. He suggested it would be better if I phoned before setting off on my 'Gulliver' travels in a new land. I made quite a few phone calls, but was told there were no vacancies, informing them that I would ask Mr Taylor to update his records, which I did. He just smiled, as if to say there were other reasons, which I found out later. I tried a few more numbers, but it was getting late again, but then I was told by Mrs Lawton that she had a vacancy, I was so relieved and accepted the bedsit on 16 Rippingham Road in Withington, without looking. It was much colder and damp inside than outside, with no central heating except for an electric fire on a meter - 5p lasted about 30 minutes or even less, a luxury I could not afford. I went to bed wearing a few layers of clothing. Hot water was at the discretion of my Irish landlady, and very rarely switched on. It did not matter, as I used the bedsit for sleeping only, because I worked late in the research laboratory, and later I found out that there was a shower unit in the basement floor of the department building, which I used, as well as facilities in the Student Union and sports centre.

Arriving in Manchester was a defining moment in my life. It was not easy, but a tough existence for the first couple of years. I received some financial assistance from the British Council towards university fees, as well as from my family. I worked hard and spent most of the time in the laboratory, and walked wherever I could. I made friends easily, something which was instilled in me at an early age. As time progressed, I became quite popular, not only in the Zoology Department, but also with the other staff, as we shared the building, and later I collaborated in research with some of them. Ted recognised my academic potential, and had a soft spot for me. I also benefited by being given more hours to assist undergraduates in practical classes, which improved my financial position. I made some endearing friendships. Everybody needs friends who you can share your happiness with, and help you when it is needed most. I have been fortunate to make many friends in my life. Even though, I have not been in regular contact with many, because just like me, people have moved on, I still carry fond memories of many friendships and events that helped shape my life. Friendships, which one never forgets are those that blossom in foreign lands, just like my ancestors, when they landed with their few possessions in East Africa. I value all the friendships I have made since, as they have all made a difference to my life. I pay tribute to all my friends.

One of the very first close friendships I developed was with David Evans, a research officer who specialised in electronics, who I came to know, because the research I was involved in comprised of electronic techniques to monitor animal behaviour. It was not long before David invited me to his place for meals, we became more than just good friends, we were like brothers, and I call him 'Bro' to this day. To my children, he is Uncle David, and his wife, Aunty Liz. We managed to convince a few people who could not believe, for obvious reasons that we were brothers. We concocted a yarn that we shared a common father, who was a Muslim, and was allowed four wives. Later, George Kamel, a PhD student from Egypt, also became our brother. We all had hairy chests; David had Welsh ancestry and carried a good tan, and like George, had a lighter complexion. Whereas, I used to get away by telling people that I had got my mother's darker genes. It would be impossible to list all my friends, so I will only mention a few where appropriate. I also became good friends with Dr Keith Marriott, my PhD supervisor, and his wife Glen, who were a part of my Kenyan episode in 1982, which I will mention a little later.

In 1977, I moved to a better bedsit on 17 Birchfield Avenue in Longsight, with a separate kitchen, better washroom facilities and a gas fire, a luxury compared to the previous one. Another good friend, Pat Yalden, a technician married to Dr Derek Yalden, willingly helped me to move my belongings, which had by now grown a bit more than just the one green suitcase. The following day, during a coffee break, Pat told other colleagues how I managed to survive for four years without any consequences to my health, and she was pleased to report my new abode was much better. I must take a moment to mention my good friends Lesley and Jack Kelly. Lesley would often ask if I needed any shopping done, something I am still not keen to do, so I did not go without food. I was awarded my PhD in December that year, and I invited my landlord and landlady, Mr and Mrs Connors as my guests at the graduation ceremony, instead of my parents. Both were chuffed by the cordial welcome they were given at the reception that Ted held in my honour in his office. They were touched by my gesture; an experience they said they would not have had, as their children did not go to university. I was glad I made them happy, which I know is how my parents would have felt.

The research went well, and I wrote my first research paper prior to submitting my PhD thesis. It appeared in the prestigious Nature Magazine, which specialises in publishing novel research, which is equivalent to the Bible of the scientific world. On the strength of my research findings, Ted applied for a Natural Environmental Research Council for a grant worth £33,000, to employ me as his post-doctoral research fellow for four years. I conducted research on the behavioural, physiological and biochemical responses of marine organisms to environmental stress, and published papers in reputable scientific journals, with a major research review in Advances in Marine Biology, and established a working model on the toxicological effects of copper from the organism up to the cellular level. It was the second time that both my parents did not attend my graduation. I dedicated my PhD thesis to them for making it possible, and knew they must have felt very proud, because during my first visit to Tanga in 1978, since graduation, as well as later ones, I witnessed first-hand how my parents must have felt, because I was warmly welcomed by everyone I met, family friends, neighbours and community elders. I was invited by Mr Chaudry, one of my only surviving teachers from the past who lived in Tanga and was a neighbour of my parents, to address meetings at the Tanga Rotary and Round Table Clubs. I could see he felt so proud. I was even more humbled when eminent people of Tanga were keen to mingle with me, which would have been impossible before. They said they felt proud of my father, known as a Mr Thumbprint, as he could not read or write. I heard about their friendly banter with my father, saying that your son cannot only read, write and speak in public, but had also published research papers in reputable scientific journals. It was then I realised that copies of research papers I posted home that father would ask people what they meant, as he did not have a clue; nevertheless, he felt very proud. Both mother and father did not even know what PhD meant, except for the word doctor, so when people asked them what it meant, my parents would tell them that 'I am a doctor of the sea', showing their foresightedness to understand the importance of education. That is why I believe in quality education, because it raises hope and fairness, not only to get a better job, but change attitudes towards others, and not become victims of hatred, dividing our society.

I started my employment as a post-doctoral research fellow in January 1978, after I was granted a work permit by the Home Office. My research went from strength to strength, I wrote more research papers, mostly as a sole author, and quite a few in joint authorships. I also visited research institutes, assisted in PhD supervision and lectured undergraduates, in addition to attending various national and international research conferences with Ted or on my own, and carried out research with colleagues from other departments, especially with the late Dr Mike Earnshaw, with whom I developed a close friendship. In the same year, I was appointed as a tutor to look after student welfare at Owens Park, a University Halls of Residence. I was provided a one bedroom flat: a lounge, bathroom, kitchen, 24-hour central heating, hot water and meals in the student cafeteria. The accommodation was a luxury compared to the previous two. I was consistently making new friends, such as Bob and Liz Frost, Hywel and Christine Thomas and many more. Something Ted, Mike and Keith noticed I did with ease, from people of all walks of life, whether from the same vocation or not, and a quality of mine they made sure to mention when writing references for job applications.

*****

In January 1982, I was appointed at Kenyatta University, Nairobi, Kenya on a two-year lectureship contract to teach marine biology. This also gave my two sisters the opportunity to move to Kenya for a better future, as I was given a house on campus. The plan was that later our parents would leave Tanga and join us, as they were getting old. In July 1982, David (Bro), Liz, Keith and Glen came for a four-week Kenyan holiday. They stayed on the campus visiting various national parks, and after a week we took an overnight train to Mombasa to spend a fortnight on the coast in a rented villa. On the return journey to Nairobi on 1st August, we were told at the last station, a junction 5 miles from Nairobi that the train was going no further, and we should all embark and make our own way back to Nairobi, as there was a military coup. We found out that the university campus was the main target, because of student revolt. Our first concern was for my sisters, as we had left them behind, but did not know how to get in touch. I remembered their friends phone number, and managed to get through. It so happened they were visiting them over the weekend. I asked them to stay put, not to go to the campus until they heard from us. We were stuck and left to our own devices to make our own way to safety from the middle of nowhere. Lady luck was on our side, as the last train to leave Nairobi for Mombasa stopped at the same junction. We heard from others on the train that we should not proceed to Nairobi, as the situation there was very bad. Bro phoned the British High Commission in Nairobi who offered no help or advice, so we decided it would be best to return to Mombasa, but told there was no place on the train. I asked Bro to wave his British passport as it would carry more weight than my Tanzanian passport in this type of situation. It worked! We managed to board the train, and helped two Germans in the process. I haggled for a compartment for us, and again luck was on our side. On the same train there was a fellow British stationed at the Mombasa Mission to Seaman, which helped us to get through army barriers, because when we arrived in Mombasa there was now a strong military presence with a barrier looking for rebels from Nairobi, restricting entry into Mombasa. The British person who we got to know, approached the barrier waving his passport; saying in a stern manner, "Diplomatic Mission," omitting Seaman, and we all got waved through. We went to his place, and then returned to the seaside villa we had vacated. It so happened that it was not let out, and we were able to stay until the situation improved in Nairobi. We returned to Nairobi after a couple of days, collected my sisters on our way to campus, and were able to get back in time for my friends to return home to the UK, as the airport re-opened the next day, but they were concerned about my safety and that of my sisters. We still joke about this situation to this day, saying that they would never get a holiday like the one I had planned, a real adventure with a military coup thrown in for free.

*****

Obviously, Bro and Keith had experienced first-hand the precarious situation in Nairobi, and on return to the UK they managed to get a few hours a week (part-time) lecturing at Manchester Polytechnic. Bob Frost offered me my previous tutorship post at Owens Park, which took care of my accommodation on my return to the UK. Mike Earnshaw wrote a letter inviting me to Manchester to complete some outstanding research. I was granted leave of absence from Kenyatta University, and left in September 1982. I decided not to return back to the university, because it remained closed for an indefinite period. I resigned due to the uncertainty of the coup, and asked my sisters to move to Mombasa. At Manchester University, I was offered an Honorary Fellowship, which allowed me the use of facilities for research. It was a productive research period. I wrote a number of research papers at that time, increasing my scientific credentials in my field. I also started applying for permanent research and lecturing positions at Manchester University and elsewhere. I got short listed often when I applied for suitable posts, because I had a good CV, with some thirty-five publications, as well as lecturing and academic experience gained in just five years since completing my PhD. Unfortunately, I was always unsuccessful. I often found after the interviews that the main reason was that I was either over qualified or underqualified for the position. In one instance, I was shortlisted for two separate positions at the same research institute within a period of six months, but still unsuccessful because of the previous reasons. At times, I would be asked about my Tanzanian education, if it was of similar or as good a standard as that in the UK, despite knowing from my CV that my qualifications were British affiliated. I would politely reply, saying that I was granted admission to Manchester University based on Tanzanian qualifications. I now have a PhD granted by a British University, and all my publications were published in reputable British journals. I persevered applying for jobs without getting anywhere. I then applied for a full-time post advertised in the Physiology Department at Manchester Polytechnic, where I was lecturing part-time, since returning from Kenya. I was shorted listed again, and although I was unsuccessful, I continued to share the teaching with the successful candidate, Dr Gary Warburton, who confided in me that he could not understand why I did not get the job. He also mentioned this to Bro, as they played rugby for the same club. Gary and I also collaborated on a research project, which I proposed. Such incidents in my academic career made Bro, Mike, Keith and others feel bad. They started to mention that I should look around and see how many lecturers are of ethnic origin. I realised it would be difficult to break into the system, even if I had the same, or an exceptional talent than a non-ethnic candidate applying for the same position.

In August 1984, I visited my parents, who were now staying in Mombasa with my sisters. It was good to visit my maternal uncles, aunties and cousins. I also met Femi, when I went to buy a post-card from the stationery shop, which was owned by her family. We had a friendly conversation, so I went back a couple of times and asked her out. We got along well, so I proposed, and then we got engaged towards the end of August, and planned to get married in December. On my return to Manchester, I mentioned my plans to friends, and obviously they were pleased. I was offered a tutor's flat for married couples at Owens Park, and invited my friends to the wedding. Unfortunately, many of them could not attend because of prior commitments, but Ted and Doreen Trueman said they would come. It was a fitting gesture by him because of his role, not only as my guru (teacher), but he was a fatherly figure to me during my time at Manchester. They had a good time in Kenya, meeting both our parents. I saw the joy on the faces of my parents meeting a real professor, and sharing meals at their home. In early 1990s, Femi and I visited Doreen with my daughters after Ted's death, and she confided that Ted felt he should have done more to get me a permanent post at the university. I said it was in the past, and I would always be grateful to him. On return to Manchester, I now had a companion, so we decided to plan our future. Femi had qualified as a medical secretary in the UK, at Kings College in the late 1970s. She was business minded, and suggested opening a retail shop, and I thought why not, as I was getting frustrated with my academic career. We had some savings, and with the support of a helpful bank manager, Jack Chapman, we decided to move down South to make a clean break, and found a suitable business in Woking with the help from her brother, giving us both a new chapter in our lives.

5

Of Business and First Political Dialogue

In April 1985, Femi and I packed our bags, and left our Manchester home to start a new life. We travelled to Woking in a hired van with all our belongings, and our good friends, Mike and Kasey Earnshaw, helped us by driving the van.

In the first week of taking over the retail shop in June that year, we had a break-in, followed by a second robbery six months later. On both occasions we lost valuable stock, without receiving a penny from the insurance company, despite having paid our insurance premiums in advance, and we were assured by our broker that we were fully insured both times. In the first instance, the broker failed to instruct us not to exchange prior to the insurance risk assessment survey, if informed, we would have definitely delayed exchange of contracts by a week or so. On the second occasion, it was because the broker had failed to disclose the first break-in to the new insurers. Insurance in my opinion is a con, if not short changed by the insurers, then by the broker, which is what happened in our situation for not doing their professional duty. There is only one winner, not the insured, but the insurer. We decided to cut our losses and not pursue the matter further legally for professional negligence, as he was a good friend of my brother-in-law. However, my advice would be to double-check any advice given by any professional, broker or not, friend or not! We did not take a defeatist attitude, but tried to remain positive and just got on with our life, trying our best. So, that is how we took these two setbacks, as well as future ones.

As mentioned, honesty, respect and moral values are in my genes, which may have come from my mother, but the genes to trust people may have come from my father, as I remember he was no different to me in placing trust in others. I would never deceive or hurt people, because I expect others to behave the same way. I do not short change anyone, whether in business, employment or otherwise, and always do an honest day's work (paid or not). I will give a candid opinion, so not to mislead, making sure that others do not have to pay or suffer because of my mistakes, or misjudgement. So much so, if I have given somebody my word to help, I will do my utmost to honour it, come what may! I am also particular, and believe it is only courteous to reply when someone takes the trouble to write to me, especially when written in their own time and expense. I equally believe professionals, for example lawyers, accountants and brokers should be held accountable for their actions, particularly when they advise one thing to attract business from a client, and then change their tune later. It should also be no different for politicians when they make pledges to get elected, only to default what they have said. I suppose such beliefs may have been the underlying reasons for my interest in politics, and views on accountability towards others in society.

Femi and I slowly developed our retail business, worked hard, added new product lines, and remained open seven days a week. We increased our customer base with a friendly professional approach. Overnight, we had a lot to learn, relying on each other to develop our fledging retail business. Femi was good, as she had business experience. Whereas for me, the switch from academic to business life required an ability to learn a whole new career quickly in commerce, such as customer care, because 'the customer is always right,' VAT returns, business management, accounts, banking, paying wages, health and safety, food hygiene, stock control, and dealing with suppliers. I had done a basic book-keeping course, as an option in school, which served us well. In 1986, our first daughter Naamah was born, and then Ummehani (Hani) in 1990. I must say, they were very considerate and remain so. They were both born on a Saturday night, so that their father could be present at their births, and I must admit, they have made us proud. On both occasions, my father-in-law, Fazleabbas Dungarwalla, and mother-in-law, Mafuzabai, had flown over from Mombasa, being an immense help, both at home and in the shop. They were great in-laws, and over the years they visited us many times. We have plenty of fond memories of them. After the births, Femi did not shun responsibility, she would come to the shop after 9.00am with Naamah, leave about 3.00pm while I opened at 5.00am, closing at 6.00pm, except on Sundays when we closed at 1.00pm. Femi would take Naamah to the cash and carry, pushing her and the goods around on the trolley. When Hani was born, Naamah had started school, so Femi would drop her off and then come to the shop with Hani. It was tough, but we persevered, and at least I had the opportunity to spend more time with both children in their early years, as they literally grew up in the shop, something I did not do with my father.

*****

My wife and two daughters merit a mention. Femi has been a pillar of support in my married life, with her constant encouragement and hard work. She also comes from a big extended family of uncles, aunties and cousins, as well as a wealthy business background with her father at the helm, but her feet firmly on the ground. She has been an important part of our struggles and happiness, in spite of all the difficulties, being a full-time partner in running the business, and most of all, did not flinch from her motherly role to raise our two daughters. She has remained an indispensable part of my life for help and comfort, even when we faced great frustrations. Femi endured all obstacles with exemplary fortitude, and never wavered from any of her duties. Of course, like in any marriage, we have had our fair share of differences, which we accepted, agreed to differ and got on with life. Femi's support not only helped me to honour my own life's responsibilities towards my parents, but she allowed me time to pursue political issues too. Such qualities have served to reinforce my respect, love and growing affection. What is important is that Femi has a very caring attitude towards people. She also never failed in her duties as a daughter towards my in-laws in their old age, especially when my mother-in-law suffered ill-health, and her father needed help to organise their lives before she passed away. In May 2001, I am glad I made Femi leave immediately for Kenya when her widowed father was admitted into hospital. Naamah also went as he was very fond off her. They spent the last ten days of his life by his bedside, and did the same for me in 2006 when my father was taken-ill. I feel that her good deeds and their prayers are still benefiting us today. Femi's caring nature and willingness to help has attracted appreciation of the public in her various jobs, and more so now in the community pharmacy and health care system. She manages me, the house, the extended family and work responsibility with great ease, except she prefers my cuisine to hers, because she knows mine is better. I also speak on behalf of my two daughters, sons-in-law and grandson, our love for her will never diminish.

I have been further blessed with two lovely daughters, sons-in-law, Husein Katabjiwala and Mustali Sarkar married to Naamah and Ummehani respectively, who are like sons to me, and are stable in their thinking and a great support, and a grandson, Taher Sarkar. Both daughters are qualified pharmacists and happily married. As mentioned, I have been lucky. They never gave me the usual teenage grief and sleepless nights, and seem to be aware of their family responsibilities and respect for others. I am glad that the next generation are close to one another, and happy that they all get along.

*****

We survived the 1990s recession, including the 1992 'black Wednesday' and faced other obstacles, such as paying more than double the rent, restrictive trade practices, and Uniform Business Rates. All small family retail businesses were also facing unfair competition from the out-of-town shopping centres, encouraged by the government's relaxed planning regulations, and other incentives, which was also having a detrimental effect. For example, there were now many empty shops on the high streets, causing the town centres to become derelict.

In 1992, for the first time in my life I felt the need to raise the real-life difficulties faced by the small family run businesses, specifically the independent retail sector (corner shops). Therefore, I decided it would be best to write to the Prime Minister, John Major, since I believed it would be his duty to listen to the concerns of the ordinary person. I also got the impression, when seeing him on TV that he was a man of integrity and conviction.

Ever since my first letter twenty-eight years ago, as an 'ordinary man in the street', I have written a few hundred letters in total to five PMs, a number of cross-party politicians eminent people and the press. To publish all those letters would require a volume of its own. For the ease of convenience and to maintain a coherent flow, I have given a summary from various letters that I have written since 1992. The original letters cited in the book can be read in its full entirety in the appendix. I have chosen a collection of letters to give a wider account of the real-life concerns and issues that I have raised over years.

My first letter was to John Major on 20th January 1992, which I also forwarded to Neil Kinnock, Paddy Ashdown, Norman Lamont and my local MP, Cranley Onslow, stating that my main concern related to the fate of small businesses, not party politics. Ever since, I have held the same consistent views to serve everyone by writing to cross-party politicians, which covered the following nine points.

> 'I would like to highlight the role of small businesses in a stable economy, which create more jobs than big businesses. The complex multitier VAT system and red tape was an administrative burden affecting small businesses' profits, in addition to being prone to abuse, and needs to be simplified. Rent reviews should be realistic, not based on hypothetical inflated demands. The Uniform Business Rates were an unfair compliance cost, and the small business sector has to work harder to survive, by not being a limited company. Small businesses also get penalised when limited companies declare bankruptcy, with directors only starting new firms later after offsetting their debt. I feel we need better control of inflation, by tackling the root causes, instead of entirely

relying on interest rates, as well as address restrictive trade practices and planning regulation, which favours multi-nationals, at the expense of the small business sector'.

I must say that I had a prompt reply from the Downing Street Communication Office, who thanked me, this was followed by detailed replies from Mr A V M Gallagher in the Treasury, Department of Trade and Industry and HM Customs and Excise, which is now a part of HM Revenue and Customs, as well a courtesy thank you reply from Neil Kinnock and Cranley Onslow. I felt humbled on receiving the replies, irrespective of whether it made a difference or not, is another thing. The courtesy of replying reinforced my belief and trust in British justice, administration and accountability. Something I had learnt to expect from the British when growing up in Tanzania. It also allowed an ordinary person to exercise their democratic right through elected politicians and lawmakers.

Sadly, this is a trait not that prevalent with present politicians. I will share my experience, highlighting similar public disenchantment of the many, not just in the UK, but worldwide with politicians and democracy. It is an irony how real-life concerns have not changed that much in the last twenty-eight years. How history repeats itself? The same old problems popping up, despite past pledges made by politicians to address them, with the same pledges repeated once again by the present ones, only disguised differently.

To give one such example, the government pledged urgent action to address retailers' and unions' concerns to help struggling high streets based on the new data showing the fastest increase of empty shops in nearly a decade, such as pubs and restaurants.[6] Incidentally, it was one of the points I raised in my letter to the PM, and regularly with other politicians in the 1990s. Regrettably like today, the voices of the public are ignored. What the politicians need to realise is that events do not happen overnight, and they need to listen to the people. We need pro-active solutions, not reactive knee-jerk policies that cost the tax payer more in the long run, causing undue hardships. Unfortunately, the small retail business sector continues to face the same age-old problems, like the Uniform Business Rates, high rent, restrictive trade practices, compliance costs and bureaucracy (red tape). What the people are promised today by the government is a repeat of the 1990s government mantra of 'revitalisation of town centres' dressed as 'regeneration of high streets' in 2019!

---

[6] The Guardian: 'English towns and cities get share of £95m regeneration fund' 14 September 2019 https://www.theguardian.com/society/2019/sep/14/english-towns-and-cities-get-share-of-95m-regeneration-fund

I then wrote to Cranley Onslow on 28th October 1994 (letter 2) on the subject of the UK National Lottery, and the unfair selection procedure adopted by the operator Camelot, which basically amounted to a restrictive trade practice. I had written before the actual launch date, in November 1994, as I drew a comparison with similar situations of unfair practices that had existed in the newspaper trade, which the Monopolies and Mergers Commission partly addressed after costing the tax payer over £10m.

> 'I am writing on behalf of other retailers affected in Woking and elsewhere. I am raising concerns of the selection criteria of the National Lottery, which could open up the proliferation of unfair trading practices. I am not saying that we do not approve of the government's decision to launch a National Lottery, far from it. But I am alarmed at the unpublished selection criteria of the lottery outlets adopted by Camelot. Basically, Camelot has been granted a government monopoly to market a product, allowing them to manipulate the market structure to suit its own interests, which we believe is wrong. I am requesting that those responsible should look into the selection criteria, and Camelot should broaden the selection process'.

Sir Cranley was always ready to help and follow-up the matter, and took interest in the outcome, which was later to become the subject of the Parliamentary Select Committee inquiry into the National Lottery in 1996, and I was invited to give evidence at the hearing, which I will mention later, but by that time I had already surrendered the shop lease.

Around the same time in 1993, I discovered some sinister practices by chance in the accounting and processing methods of the newspaper monopoly wholesalers. It started when I had some spare time to check the twenty-page weekly computer printout invoice from the wholesaler. Like most retailers, I did not check the weekly invoice meticulously, just settled the invoice without fail in a week, so as not to face the threat of supplies getting stopped, because the newsagent was at the total mercy (even now) of the designated wholesaler. Besides, retailers do not usually have the time every week to check each itemised invoice entry, they just took/take the wholesaler's word, as we had no choice to go elsewhere for supplies, or to lodge formal complaints. Initially I started with some basic random checks of items returned for credit against my copy, and soon found irregularities. For example, I had returned five copies of a certain periodical, but was credited for less or none, and at times told I had returned a wrong title from the one they had requested. At first, I gave them the benefit of the doubt, but continued meticulously with a focus on credit returns. I soon realised the errors were not isolated incidents, but very common. It roused my suspicion that either I was going senile, at the young age of forty-two, or I had forgotten how to count to ten! What is more, I do not like blaming or pointing fingers at others without making sure it is not me who is at fault. So, after completing the weekly returns bundle, I would ask Femi to check my paperwork. At times, I would even ask customers to double check it for me. Not surprisingly it made no difference; it was always my fault, according to the wholesalers. Once my suspicion was aroused, I kept a much closer check on all invoice entries, by setting up a system for cross-checking.

With time my monitoring technique improved. I discovered more errors, some serious ones, always working in favour of the wholesaler, such as overcharging, VAT oddities and inaccurate entries. I suppose my scientific research discipline was useful to find solutions to a problem, but more importantly, it was a question of my integrity, as well as expecting others to fulfil their obligations of honouring the trust placed in them by others. I set up a diligent approach to monitor flaws in meticulous detail of the accounting and administration procedures of the monopoly wholesaler, and worked out the weekly loss to a retailer's profits. It took some time to understand what was actually happening. I persevered and gathered evidence, at the same time attending to the daily demands of running a small family business. Once I had plenty of evidence, I raised the issue with the Woking branch manager, and got nowhere. After more failed attempts, I wrote to the area manager with a similar fate, making me even more determined not to give up, as I knew what was happening, and the consequences it was having on newsagents' profits. Small retailers face immense competition, not only from the big retail chains, but also government policies. So, I wrote to the company's chief executive officer, explaining the situation. I heard instantly from the managing director of the wholesale operations and the South East regional director, seeking a meeting. It is amazing how people's attitudes change when in the wrong and challenged with factual evidence, to the extent that Femi was given staff to help in my absence by the senior management of the company, when I was invited to attend meetings locally, and in various other parts of the country, to discuss their accounting mistakes I had unearthed.

In 1994, I had more meetings as they soon realised, I was telling the truth, and not making it up. Their whole attitude towards me changed. I was flown to their main head-office to meet very important people in the organisation, followed by more meetings and visits with various departmental heads. It was because I had made them realise that I had not only found a way to monitor their complex weekly invoice, but found solutions in resolving the problem, and calculated the weekly percentage loss of profits to the retailer, which generally went unnoticed. Over the year, it was a colossal amount working in the favour of the wholesaler, because of the monopoly and captive customer market they enjoyed. I was offered a ten-day legally binding contract to work as a consultant, where I was getting paid £300 per day, plus help for Femi while I collaborated with their technical experts, disclosing all my findings. This then gave them the final say to decide whether to implement my findings to rectify the situation or not, and I would have no further say in the matter, as I had to sign a non-disclosure statement. It was a lot of money then, and even now, with a good possibility of a career opportunity, if I played my cards right! I was not happy, not because I wanted more money, but because I wanted the situation to get rectified to benefit other corner shops, as I did not want it to get brushed under the carpet. Therefore, I sought the advice of legal experts, and was encouraged that the best way to bring out my evidence into the public domain was to go to court to expose the errors, compelling the wholesalers to rectify their accounting irregularities. Once the court action was filed, the wholesalers soon offered an out of court settlement, which I was advised to accept by my lawyer, who then told me I had no other option, because if I did not accept it, and the judge found the offer was reasonable, I would be liable for all legal costs, theirs and mine.

I was not pleased at all, because I had acted on my lawyer's advice in the first place to go to court, if I wanted to bring out the evidence to the attention of the other retailers. Now I was told otherwise! Surely one would think they would have known of the likelihood of an out of court settlement. If I had been made aware of this in the first place, I would not have hired the services of a lawyer, and saved a packet on legal fees, because I was more than capable of recovering my own credit, having got so far with the wholesaler when they had already accepted my evidence. The only reason I went to court was to benefit others. Funny how legal experts change their tune, despite giving advice to go to court in the first place, only to end up advising later to accept an offer. I would once again be in similar quandary later on in my life. This just reinforced my belief that law is a mugs game, with costly legal fees, with the high odds stacked against the victim. Highlighting that this is a violation of one's basic civil rights, such as tenancy, employment, consumer, and a simple dispute then becomes a mind-boggling exercise for an ordinary person, when it comes to seeking justice, allowing those individuals or companies, including the government (at the tax payer's expense), with financial and legal clout to exploit all known legal loop holes and delaying tactics to frustrate those seeking justice by acting within the law, and getting away with their actions scot-free. The victims on the other hand, who do not have financial clout, find it difficult to get any proper justice that they deserve.

Reached Kampala with Pradeep Amin, half way, another about 1,500 miles (4800Km) to get home.

Feasting with comrades on army food (1969).

Photo break during secret army manoeuvres behind enemy lines

After twelve weeks basic training, ready to engage and frighten the enemy

Fashion pose. My shorts were trousers last worn by Warwick Davis of Star Wars fame.

With brother George and Mr Connors.

Jubilee year PhD graduation with supervisor Dr Keith Marriot (20 December 1977).

PhD reception held in my honour by Professor Ted Trueman flanked by Mr and Mrs Connors.

Ted Trueman (far left) at Clifford's retirement with his wife (centre) and other staff (1981).

With the famous Marine Biologist Sir Maurice Yonge and wife at International Symposium in Perpignan, France.

Brother David when we went camping outside Tyndrum, Scotland (1982).

Abandoned souls waiting by the rail side planning the great escape. Keith with arms folded with Glen and Liz on either side, myself in blue jeans and other escapees (1st August 1982).

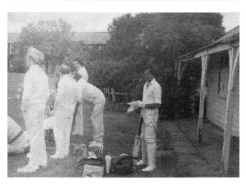

Dreaming of a big innings to attract England selectors at Urmston Cricket ground (1983).

Proud moment for mother (seated) next to Ted and father (seated) next to Doreen meeting a real Professor in their home and sharing a meal with him. Femi is seated next to father (December 1984).

6

SIR and Voluntary Campaigns

In 1994, my brother-in-law who was aware of my daily battles and struggles with the monopoly newspaper told me to listen to the Dawn Traders programme on Spectrum Radio, broadcasted at 5am, and I soon realised that I shared similar business problems with other listeners. This show highlighted how the newsagents were disillusioned with their trade bodies, who were meant to serve and represent their interests. I was pleasantly surprised they were not only discussing the concerns I had raised in my first letter to the PM, but also issues relating to the monopoly wholesalers; such as late delivery, shortages, profit margins and general lack of customer care; although, they were not at all aware of the actual invoicing errors. I thought I had found solace, namely 'a problem shared is a problem halved'. I soon realised it was not that simple, because most of the views aired on the radio remained unresolved for a long time. Contrary to my expectations, it worked out the other way; whereby instead of getting help from other retailers, I ended up taking up their cause, and became involved in the discussion on the relevant issues. I got invited as a regular contributor and also appeared on other rival shows, like Sunrise Radio, and I also read similar reports in various trade press. I expressed my views on wide ranging issues affecting the small family run retailers, and it did not take long to find out from the many interactions on the radio shows and trade journals that there existed a lot of resentment within the sector, and a lack of confidence, in terms of representation by the main trade organisations. I have never been an affiliated member of any political party to-date; it was also true that I never belonged to any trade organisation. In fact, I did not even know of their existence until I started listening to Spectrum Radio, and reading the trade journals of the disenchantment that existed between the members and their trade bodies.

It was not long before I formed the Society for Independent Retailers (SIR) with the support of other business owners, to tackle issues pertaining to small family run retailers. SIR was a voluntary organisation, based mostly on my initiative. As time progressed, it became clear to me that those who joined SIR were fully paid members of the other two long well-established trade organisations, who were meant to look after their interests, but I remained undeterred to help others. To me, it was a form of civic duty, and borne the brunt of all the work that had to be done, in order to achieve justice for all. I also started writing letters to cross-party politicians, and encouraged others to lobby their constituent MP, by sending the same letter I had written. SIR generated a lot of interest amongst cross-party politicians, especially from Tory MPs, as a party in government. I got invited to attend meetings with ministers in the Department of Trade and Industry, Department of Environment, and the then Department of National Heritage to discuss issues affecting the owners of small family retail shops. SIR led successful campaigns, and I was invited to act as a consultee to the DTI and Department of Environment Committees on issues relating to the EU directive on unit pricing and revitalisation of town centres respectively. In the 1990s, the definition of small businesses used by the government was too broad, as it was based on the number of people employed, namely small (0-200), medium (200-1200) and large (1200-over) businesses. It meant family run businesses with no employees, except family or part-time staff were grouped wrongly, and affected them more disproportionately in terms of government policies and compliance costs. It resulted in the family retail businesses being overlooked, when it came to targeting specific government policies towards the sector. SIR led the campaign to draw the attention to ministers of the problems relating to the government's definition of small businesses, and its effects on the sector. Over time, the definition got refined to nano, micro and small to medium enterprises, which made some improvements, but still failed to address the issues relating to a lack of a level playing field faced by small retailers, namely restrictive trade practice, monopoly wholesalers, and the threat of out of town shopping centres.

In November 1994, the National Lottery was launched with Camelot appointed as the successful operator by the government. Camelot embarked to select lottery outlets based on the Cadbury database, which was part of the Camelot franchise. What this meant was that those retailers who did not have accounts with Cadbury got discriminated against, amounting as a restrictive unfair trading practice. It was a hot debate on the radio, as well as in the trade press, which I had already raised with my own MP. SIR lobbied cross-party politicians, which led to a parliamentary inquiry held by the National Heritage Select Committee in 1996. SIR, together with other trade bodies got invited to present evidence at the hearing. The findings led the Select Committee to make recommendations that Camelot should not only make their selection process more transparent, but also give reasons to those unsuccessful applicants to help them improve their selection chances.

In 1996, SIR collaborated with the Asian Business Association of London Chamber of Commerce to conduct a research survey into the 'Prospects of the Independent Retail Sector'. It was published in September 1996, and highlighted hardships faced by the small retailers. The report of the findings was launched at a press conference, and it got wide coverage on TV and in local and national newspapers, such as the Financial Times, The Guardian, The Sunday Times, Daily Express and Mail on Sunday. I also became a regular feature, receiving wide coverage in the trade journals, like the Convenience Store, Retail Newsagent, Retail News and the Asian Trader. I received letters from traders asking for help, and encouraged me to keep up the good work. SIR got invited to join campaigns with fee-paying trade bodies, like the Association of Convenience Stores, except the National Federation of Retail Newsagents. It was mainly because the National Federation of Retail Newsagents considered SIR a threat to their membership base, as they supported restrictive trade practices, enjoyed by them and the monopoly wholesalers. The irony was that their members were not aware of the accounting anomalies, and how their profits were affected by the same wholesalers, because of their monopoly status and lack of competition; whereas, SIR was more concerned about fairness, and a level playing field for all family run retail businesses. In short, four years after first writing to the PM in January 1992, SIR raised the profile of the family run business sector, as reflected in the following examples of national and trade press headlines, such as 'SIR lobbying hard', 'Second sitting at the commons for SIR', 'Retailers urge MMC probe', 'Sainsbury's joins lottery debate' and the 'Coming out of the shadows'.

At the best of times I conducted SIR affairs whilst managing my own business, using personal funds and resources to attend meetings at the House of Commons, Whitehall and elsewhere. I corresponded with politicians and various eminent people, as well as often writing articles for the press, and at the same time serving customers. It just goes to show the drive, multi-tasking ability, resilience and sacrifices owners of small businesses have to make to survive, often taken for granted by politicians and customers alike. I often attended SIR matters, leaving Femi to run our business, at times I would return late from London, but without fail opening on time at 5.00am, come rain or shine, even during the famous 1987 hurricane. It would be misleading to suggest politics was high on my agenda when I was a boy, or at the University of Dar es Salaam and Manchester. However, what I have always believed, since settling in the UK, is to make sure to exercise my democratic right, which I have also instilled in my children and others, and not to take this for granted.

7

The In-between Years, 9/11 and 7/7

N ot everyone fulfils or even finds their dreams come true; however big or small, what is true from the moment one is born is that we all have dreams and live in hope, inspired not only by the family, people we meet, books we read and images we see. More importantly, what we are promised and told by political, religious and community leaders this is what we can at least expect in a fair society, a level playing field, as long as one is prepared to work hard and not take things for granted, as a God given right.

On 15th December 1995, it was our eleventh wedding anniversary. Femi and I decided to surrender the shop lease, as it was getting more difficult to make ends meet, due to increasing overheads, such as the 133% increase in rent demanded by the landlord, on top of the rise in Uniform Business Rates, and compliance costs. All our energies were now focused on developing our life once again from the beginning. It felt the same when Femi and I left Manchester in 1985. Like any other parent, we now had to think about the future of our daughters. I continued with voluntary efforts to serve SIR, attending meetings with individuals and politicians, giving radio interviews and writing articles in trade journals. Although it was proving difficult to continue on a voluntary basis, as I had to rely on personal efforts and funds. Therefore, I stopped active campaigning on behalf of SIR in 1998. I was forty-seven at this time. I am a firm believer in voluntary work, and continued to serve the needs of the wider community, by drawing on my experience gained in real-life. I assisted others by successfully defending immigration tribunal appeals against the Home Office. I have also helped individuals at the time of bereavement, because it is important in Islam not to delay the burial of the deceased, as well as keeping my hand in garden landscaping and maintenance of community amenities.

Looking back to the time we surrendered our lease in December 1995, I often think how we managed to survive, because it was like taking another leap into the dark. I have always adopted a positive attitude, because it is how you react to a situation that is important, as there are always lots of people in the world worse off than you. Such as, people who do not know where their next meal will come from, do not have a roof over their heads, or through no fault of their own, see their loved ones die in front of them in times of conflict. This would be my definition of real sorrow and loss. So that is how we looked at life, not in a defeatist but positive way, rebuilding our lives, by making changes and sacrifices. We surrendered our lease to focus on our Akberali Pickle range that we had started in our kitchen at home, and it looked promising from the market research we had undertaken when we tested the product range on our customer base in the shop. This was the first Christmas festive period since 1984 that we could enjoy together, as we did not have to open our shop. But like many people, we had bills to pay and a young family to think about. In the new-year Femi got a job at Shoe-City in Woking, and I focused on developing our pickle manufacturing business from the kitchen, making small batches at a time, due to the restricted space. It was cumbersome, because before and after each batch, the kitchen had to be re-organised. On the other hand, with an increase in demand, we needed more workspace and an efficient way to increase production.

In December 1998 the newspaper wholesaler whom we had filed proceedings against in 1994 made an out of court settlement, which our solicitor advised us to accept, or face legal costs. So, we decided to invest the settlement sum in the best possible way. We came to the conclusion that the right way to proceed would be to minimise overheads, such as rent, Uniform Business Rates, and lessons learnt from the past. We got a purpose-built conservatory extension attached to our home; this was because if we were unsuccessful in our new venture, it would be a capital investment. I was fortunate that with my scientific background I used ingenious methods to develop the manufacturing process with a minimal capital sum. Also, because of my university contacts, I acquired second-hand laboratory equipment for free, such as water baths, in addition to sourcing stainless steel tables and other equipment from catering auctions, and where necessary, improvised to overcome handicaps. Back then, a stainless-steel mixer would cost about £10,000, apart from being impractical, due to limited space, it was also well beyond our budget. I needed to think outside the box to solve the problem. I then had my eureka moment, by purchasing a cement mixer from Wickes, costing about £90, and got the barrel coated with a food-safe plastic for

£150. We also enhanced our manufacturing process and output by using other creative methods, without compromising on quality. We improved the filtration process by using a domestic vacuum costing less than £100, and a Black and Decker hot-air blower to seal bottles. All this resulted in us manufacturing a range of authentic products comprising of pickles and sauces, based on hundred-year-old family recipes, under the brand of Akberali's. The products we manufactured were free of artificial ingredients, colour, preservatives, oil and modified starch. Our customer base was mainly located in London and the South-East, which comprised of Nuffield Hospitals, delicatessens, golf courses, Bluebird store, grocery shops and sandwich bars. We also generated interest from an importer in France and Germany.

*****

I felt the need to speak up for 'the silent majority' of law-abiding ordinary people, not only ethnic, but also non-ethnic, because often very few seem keen to raise their heads above the parapet. In most cases, ordinary people like me, do not have time to engage with politicians, because of daily work and family pressures, or feel it has nothing to do with them. At times, the public also just put up with the situation, even if it affects their daily lives, such as social harmony, public services and so forth. It seems that people tend to place trust and look up to the government with a firm belief that politicians know better, as it is their duty to resolve matters in national interest. Many feel that even if they try to speak up, nobody will listen, something I must agree with, which is what I have found over a period of twenty years of bitter experiences faced when I have tried to do so. However, despite time constraints I still remained undeterred in my efforts to speak out where appropriate, in a helpful way, without personal motives or approaching any politician for a favour.

This is also because I believed, in comparison to other countries, we in Britain have successfully fostered a wider cultural diversity, in terms of harmony and mutual respect, and we need to take further advantages of these gains to overcome racial prejudices and handicaps, faced by the ethnic communities, and understand how it is undermining social harmony, which is then exploited by religious and political leaders to fuel hatred and anger because of certain government policies that are alienating communities, and has done more harm than good for ethnic people. At the same time this has generated resentment within the indigenous population, with consequential negative effects. Equally the onus is on the ethnic people to put their own house in order, by not taking the goodwill of the indigenous British people for granted, and should stop listening to the backward thinking of 'radical Imams' (local preachers) and foreign governments with unscrupulous agendas who sermon hatred and division, based on religious beliefs.

I therefore wrote for the first-time to Tony Blair on 29th February 2000, because I had felt encouraged by my early baptism, when I had written to his predecessor John Major on 24th January 1992 (letter 1). Unfortunately, I do not have a copy of that particular letter of 29th February 2000 to Tony Blair. Except that my effort did not merit a worthy response, other than a sentence from the Direct Communications Unit; 'I am writing on behalf of the PM to acknowledge your recent letter'. It was signed with a pre-printed signature of Zulma Fernandes dated 3rd March 2000, and nothing else. I took comfort that at least I got acknowledged, which I found later was very rare in many subsequent future dealings with politicians. However, I was not going to be discouraged, and immediately wrote again to Tony Blair with reference to the implementation of government policies for the ethnic people.

Letter 3 - 4th April 2000 to Tony Blair

> 'I am writing to give you a perspective based on real-life experiences of a proud British citizen from an ethnic Muslim background. The UK reflects a land of immigrant activity, which can be attributed to the British people, together with what is prominent about ethnic people, in terms of respecting the law, hard work, enterprise and family values. Despite well-meant government initiatives, ethnic people are seen as second-class citizens, because of institutional prejudices, which filters through into the neighbourhood, workplace and schools, with a stereotype impression that ethnic people have a peculiar lifestyle, relying on welfare benefits, in spite of making significant contributions to the economy and in other fields. Such behaviour affects career, commercial and social prospects of ethnic people. It is crucial to bring cultures together, as an important part of mainstream politics and British way of life, based on mutual respect, instead of compartmentalising people. So, I am raising the question, why many initiatives in existence for years have failed to make an impact for ethnic people and their businesses'.

I then cited examples of politicians being out of touch with reality, showing that it resulted in a significant waste of financial resources and money, which could be spent more wisely to improve public services.

I received a reply (letter 4) from the Direct Communication Unit, saying that I would hear from the Department of Education and Employment and Department of Trade and Industry; however, I heard nothing. I gave up, as I was not getting anywhere after I approached Stephen Pound MP, who replied with a short polite note saying, 'I very much hope that the government is able to make use of your considerable talent and expertise'. What is worth noting, is that what I had raised, over nearly twenty-eight years ago is still being addressed today with politicians and their team of special advisors, who are searching for answers and wasting resources without making progress.

It is worth mentioning that I had written the letter well before the tragic 9/11 event, highlighting some of the concerns, which only became the focus of the government after the sad loss of lives, and subsequent suffering. Not only that, but the 9/11 has led to further conflicts and crises we are still witnessing. I am in no way claiming I had the solution to all our problems, but one thing is for sure, the concerns I raised would have alleviated some of the suffering and hardship. On top of that, I had already raised the question of radicalisation and Islamophobia before it got firmly established. If those concerns were listened to, then some of the underlying issues could have been addressed earlier, with better results and use of financial resources.

*****

In October 2001, I took full-time job as a garden caretaker with the Commonwealth War Graves Commission, and also a three-night part-time job at Tesco to supplement our income, to meet the needs of a growing family. We continued to manufacture pickles at weekends to supply our established customer base. In 2006, Akberali pickles joined forces with CPS Limited with plans to expand further, which did not materialise, and I soon realised the company had other priorities. Due to this, after dismantling all my equipment and facilities at home made it difficult for me to restart this business all over again. Femi left Shoe City to join Lloyds Bank in 1998 as a cashier. In 2002, she took a job at Rowlands Pharmacy, and qualified as a pharmacy technician, and joined Boots in 2011, where she is still working today. It shows that one should never give up, or take anything for granted, and rise to life's new challenges wherever necessary, and change course.

*****

It was Tuesday 9/11. I was in our purpose-built conservatory manufacturing pickles when I received a phone call from Femi, and she asked if I had seen the news on TV. I said, "No," and switched on the TV. I saw the shocking horrible images unfolding right in front of me. Like many, I just felt numb, forgot about pickle manufacturing, and even now feel lost for words, describing those events after so many years later. My fears were brought home when my eleven-year-old daughter, Ummehani, came home from school on Thursday 13th September 2001. I was equally concerned of the severe consequences Muslims will have to suffer, not in the UK, but world-wide, because of the vile actions carried by the few in the name of Islam. I have always felt that as individuals we all have an important role to play, and should speak out when things go horrible wrong. We should not just expect prominent leaders to speak out on our behalf. At the end of the day it is the people who suffer, and know what it means to be at the receiving end of government policy failures. I feel it is important to speak out and let the politicians know that the public may have some pragmatic solutions, something I was trying to highlight before 9/11, but was ignored. I will always stand-up at a time of crisis, especially for the ordinary 'man in the street' who have to face the consequences, because of the actions of bigots, dictators or even democratically elected leaders. It is not that I consider myself a prominent figure, an official spokesman or an authority, but feel I have a public duty to draw attention to the policymakers about the reality of situations, and what it means to get tarnished by the actions of others. As an ethnic person, I am more mindful that we need to play a positive role in our host country to alleviate tension, and diffuse the situation. You may call it stubbornness, infectious optimism and plain courage or even stupidity, but to me, it is better to try my level best contributing in a pragmatic manner, as there is always room for a wide range of opinions for the good of society and humanity as a whole.

Statements promoting segregation and killings are only harming Islam, as if the ethnic Muslim community did not face enough hatred and resentment from the damage inflicted upon them by a few outspoken Muslim clerics, like Abu Hamza, and out of the blue along comes 9/11. Not everyone follows their faith to the last degree, and this does not make them any less worthy than others. If we think about it, even the self-proclaimed custodians of Islam or political leaders belonging to Islam or any other religion, do not practice their faith to the letter, because no faith teaches that killing defenceless civilian people for self-serving egos is permissible. We should all respect those whom we meet, just as it is our duty to respect the country in which we live in, and its traditions. It is hardly a difficult task, and it is a formula for success in all walks of life, as well as one's personal life. No one is asking anyone to agree with every word someone utters, or indeed to agree with every custom of any land. We are all obliged to allow people to hold their own views and follow their own traditions, and most importantly, respect the law of the land. We all have to abide to rules. A family unit cannot function without some sort of rules, even animals in the animal kingdom follow a set of rules; otherwise, how can we call ourselves 'civilised' if we cannot follow simple rules of life?

I knew what happened on 9/11 had nothing to do with my faith of Islam, or what I was taught by my Muslim parents. It is not what we or other Muslim parents have taught our children. This is not what we, or the vast majority of fellow Muslims practice. In Islam, the love for fellow humans is an important part of the faith. Islam is not just about prayers and fasting, but striving for betterment in this world, and the world hereafter. Islam also teaches that if an individual correctly provides for the upbringing of his family, such as their learning and good manners that individual will take them all to paradise, be they young or old, including his employees or neighbours. A person who is sinful will impart to his family bad manners, and will take them all on the road to hell. I did not know what to do, so I thought the best thing one does during difficult times is to seek comfort from elders, and eminent individuals in the society, with experience in such matters. I suppose it is also the start of writing to cross-party politicians on such atrocities and other crises, some examples of which I will mention later where appropriate. I wrote the same letter below the next day on 14th September 2001 after what my daughter was told in the history lesson to the following dignitaries: HM The Queen, HRH Prince of Wales, Tony Blair PM, the US Ambassador - William Farish, Leader of the Opposition - Ian Duncan-Smith, Stephen Pound MP, and past Tory party leader - William Hague and John Major.

'I feel the need to come to terms and seek solace in the wake of the outrageous and audacious atrocities on 11th September in New York and Washington, which we have all witnessed and deeply shocked.

I, like the majority of peace-loving people, condemn these acts of barbarism. I feel deeply saddened and numb, and it affects all those who cherish and believe in democracy.

Such vile and cowardly acts of barbarism conducted by the self-proclaimed fundamentalists and bastions of Islam are contrary to the faith. My Islamic upbringing has taught me to practice 'that the love for your land of domicile is an important part of the faith, and that religion is not just prayers and fasting, but striving for betterment in this world and the world hereafter'. Therefore, it is not Islam that is the enemy of mankind, but the perpetrators living amongst our midst, and unfortunately, they come in all shapes and disguise to further their cause and egos.

I suppose ethnic communities will have to endure some backlash from certain sectors of our society, but hope that common sense will prevail amongst the majority, and with sensible media coverage, it will ease our anxieties. We must not let undesirable elements from any sector undermine the good race relations of our multi-cultural United Kingdom.

A poignant reminder was brought home on Thursday, 13th September, when my eleven-year-old daughter came home from school. She mentioned 'whether it was true what they were taught in the history lesson that the events in New York and Washington were because of Islam'. My wife and I had already experienced such snide remarks since the sad event, but it would be difficult for innocent young minds to comprehend such atrocities.

Finally, I trust you will convey our heartfelt condolences to the President and citizens of America that we deeply share their grief in this hideous slaughter of human lives, which has had a direct or indirect effect on us all.

We pray to God (Allah) to grant you strength to rid us of evil terrorist networks for the betterment of our society, so that good human values will continue to prevail from the sad sacrifice of the innocent lives we have lost.

Yours most respectfully'

It was comforting to receive replies on their behalf, as well as personal replies from the Ambassador - William Farish, William Hague and Stephen Pound, Mathew Taylor of the Foreign and Commonwealth Office and the Counter Terrorism Policy Department. Below are direct quotes of a few lines from some of the replies received.

'Her Majesty's thoughts and prayers are of course with all those who are suffering as a result of the disasters on 11th September, and she appreciated your thoughtfulness in letting her know of your comments'.

'His Royal Highness believes strongly that the world in which we live, can only become a safer and more united place, if we all make the effort to tolerate, accept and understand cultures, beliefs and faiths different from our own. The recent terrible events have only served to emphasise one of eternal and painful lessons of human history – that hatred breeds hatred, and violence breeds violence'.

'On behalf of the Embassy community and my fellow Americans, I want to thank you and your organization for your kind message of comfort and support following the September 11th terrorist attacks on the United States. During this tragic time, we have been moved by the outpouring of sympathy from all corners of the United Kingdom. Acting in unison, we will bring peace and security to the world. Thank you for your kind words'.

'But the current crisis is not only a challenge for the international community; it is also a reminder of the need to improve political stability throughout the world. We must also intensify our efforts to resolve conflicts, defuse tensions and work for peace in the Middle East, Africa, the Balkans and elsewhere. We must tackle terrorism itself and, with equal resolve, the circumstances which fuel it' (Mathew Taylor).

'Like you, I absolutely condemn the terrorist attacks in the United States. I also very much agree with you that the actions of terrorists are utterly incompatible with Islam, and that we must not let reactions to these events undermine good race relations' (William Hague).

'Thank you very much for your letter of 14th September, the sentiments of which I entirely agree with' (Stephen Pound).

I felt comforted, assured and hopeful that humanity would come together in its hour of grief, and leave a better legacy for future generations. However, I hasten to add that I was under no illusion, denial or delusion of reality that there is a simple answer or a silver bullet to solve the inherent problems undermining social cohesion, through a simple top-down, quick-fix state intervention. Although, state action is absolutely necessary, it is insufficient on its own, or if carried out in isolation, by only listening to vocal communities and individuals shouting the loudest. Strangely enough, my letter of 29th February 2000 and subsequent letter 3 on 4th April 2000 were both ignored by Tony Blair PM, written well-before 9/11, covering a number of concerns and issues, which later became a subject of many investigations and policies, costing millions of pounds (if not billions), loss of lives and suffering. I am not saying 9/11 would not have happened, but a different realistic approach based on listening to ordinary people, would have helped alleviate some of the future events and crises.

Unhappily, 9/11 was followed by the equally evil atrocious act by some home-grown extremists on 7th July 2005. I again recall it well; it was a Thursday. I had a morning appointment for a minor surgery under local anaesthetic at Ashford Hospital in Surrey. The TV was on and there was a newsflash at about 10.00am. We all watched in great horror and shock as the news was unfolding. It just makes the body and mind go into a state of shock, which is difficult to explain exactly, except I know that inherent goodwill exists amongst the British people (indigenous and ethnic origin), and humanity worldwide, except for a few extremists. It therefore makes me try even harder to stop the actions of a few religious and political leaders, who try to divide and rule, by preaching and encouraging hatred, and what could be a more important cause than when it pains you to witness unnecessary suffering and loss of lives, when you know you can help alleviate some of those miseries? If anything, it makes me even more determined not to give up.

Once again, I wrote to Tony Blair PM on 6th September 2005 (letter 5), highlighting the main points I had made in my previous failed attempts, so I will only mention some brief extracts from the letter. I know I was expecting too much from our politicians, but I was not to know that then, it is only now, after a few hundred attempts that I have become wiser not to expect anything, not even an acknowledgement, but I am an optimistic person, and do not believe in giving up hope or trying.

In the letter I mentioned that I had written previously and hoped on his return from China, India and the UN summit that my letter on this occasion will be brought to his attention by his advisers. I highlighted issues raised since 1990s related to small family businesses and ethnic communities, with cross-party politicians. I said:

> 'We will overcome natural difficulties and always rise above man-made obstacles, but need a closer scrutiny when formulating specific policies, projects and measures, by placing subtle emphasis and incorporating initiatives for ethnic people within the mainstream to overcome prejudices, with less use of patronising initiatives and red-tape bureaucracy, as opposed to knee-jerking policies. Since the sad and tragic event of 7th July, I feel that I really want to make a positive contribution to improve social cohesion in our multicultural UK. Also, the government should not confine debate(s) with leaders of Muslim communities who shout the loudest, but also include input from the vast silent majority of ordinary Muslims, whose involvement and views continue to remain unheard. I propose that the government should pursue long-term proactive policies and projects, in areas such as religious and civic studies, as part of the curriculum in religious schools (Madrassas), and schools to boost public relations. It would help ethnic people to become an integral part of the mainstream, and not get alienated. This would act as deterrent to unscrupulous individuals or organisations, with their own motives or political agenda. Later or concurrently, a similar practical approach can be successfully adopted for other communities, so that they do not feel left out, and thus achieve a true multicultural society, at peace with one another in the UK'.

I received a prompt reply (letter 6), a one-line postcard from the Direct Communication Unit with a printed signature on 15th September, soon after I had posted the above letter first class on Friday the 9th. Assuming my letter had reached the appropriate place without delay on Monday the 12th, it took only six days for them to reply, especially when the PM was away from 13th - 14th September in New York for the UN summit meeting. It was astonishing how quickly the short curt reply was sent, considering that the Civil Service usually do not respond so quickly to an ordinary person, at the best of times. It was an unfortunate reply, which did not deter me, as I passionately believed that during difficult times, we need to combine our efforts to prevent future disasters. I forwarded my letter 5 - 6th September 2005 to Stephen Pound to see if he could assist in my endeavours, which he did, and he explained the outcome of his kind efforts in his letter dated 18th September 2005 with the following response:

'Dear Hassan

Further to your letter, and following our meeting, I have spoken to the Parliamentary Private Secretary to the Prime Minister, and expressed the disappointment that you and I both felt at receiving a standard response to your recent letter.

Apparently, the Prime Minster has received 3,000 letters from groups and individuals, wishing to offer their advice and assistance in these difficult times. It would be simply impossible for Mr Blair to respond to these individually, and I hope that you will accept that his lack of courtesy in not doing so in your case should not be seen in any way as indicating a lack of respect for your views, or the experience that you bring to the subject.

With best wishes'

Unfortunately, what the Private Parliamentary Secretary did not recall, or was aware of, was that I had written well before the tragic 9/11 and 7/7 events on 29th February 2000, covering some of the underlying concerns relating to ethnic communities and radicalisation, long before Tony Blair got inundated by three thousand letters from groups and individuals, who all woke up after these monstrous attacks, and not before.

Perhaps, thinking of the common good is the right way to end what I regard as a special moment of hope, to steer humanity away from any form of extremism, by inflicting unnecessary hardship and suffering on each other, as I have always said, no lasting harm will come to Britain, because of all the faiths which are allowed to practice freely - some enjoying more rights in this country than in their own country of origin. All the prayers said on this blessed land will protect us from the permanent harmful effects of such atrocious made by man-made acts. That is why I remain undeterred, and I will continue to persevere with more effort, despite being consistently ignored.

8

Misplaced Hope in Politicians

Never did I ever contemplate when I penned my very first letter on 20th January 1992 to a PM twenty-eight years ago that I would embark to write my own memoir to highlight personal experiences. Equally, little did I know that the sentiments in some ways would reflect those felt by the many. What a coincidence? I did not even realise when I wrote my first letter that the trust in the political class would be at its lowest ebb following Brexit, scandals and government policy failures. I am fortunate to have the habit of keeping a record of most of the written work in my own simple orthodox manner, so I can give an accurate account of the challenges faced by an ordinary person who tried to engage with politicians, and exercise my democratic right. I hope the real-life experiences will serve to explain why the public feel disenchanted with politics.

When I decide to do something, I like to start immediately. So, I threw myself into this new ambitious project. I have relived my experiences by reading the letters written over the years, and now I am recalling what I wrote to politicians over that time, so I am able to give a detailed and accurate chronological account based on the evidence of my efforts when dealing with those in power. The archive speaks for itself. My prime motive of this memoir is to provide a record of the efforts and events from the perspective of the ordinary 'man in the street'. A record, specifically, for the attention of the 'defenders of society', highlighting the consequences of their actions, which otherwise would be lost to posterity. I have approached the whole colossal task, not in an accusing way, but in a positive manner. I hope my experiences will be taken in good spirit in the national interest by politicians, in their quest to serve public duty. Even if my efforts make no difference, I will have no regrets. In my own minuscule way, I hope the record of the events will inspire others, by showing them that we all have a positive role to play to improve the world in which we live in.

For my own satisfaction, I feel those past efforts have not gone to waste. The hours spent writing numerous letters over the years has served a good purpose to provide an accurate and honest account of my tireless dealings with the political class. What is so satisfying is the consistency in my convictions, integrity and work ethics over the years. In my numerous correspondences I raised many issues affecting ordinary people, which subsequently led to some serious consequences. I have already mentioned that I had raised some important real-life concerns well before 9/11 and 7/7, including a lack of a level playing field for small retail businesses. Quite a number of those issues and concerns the government is still trying to grapple with. My main concerns are with how some events could have been addressed earlier at a fraction of the cost to the tax payer, causing less public suffering. This is why I feel it is necessary to shed light into how the same unresolved past issues still haunts us today. I had no direct motive, in terms of monetary gain or power, whilst remaining politically unbiased, but just wanted to show politicians that they should take time to listen to the public, as they may have something worthwhile to offer. The aim of writing this memoir is to share my perception of what is happening in this country; and explain how I have become an inseparable part of the political system. Not as a politician, but as an ordinary member of the public, revealing real-life issues to the law-makers who are formulating government policies. At the same time, I want to give a deeper insight into how detached the 'establishment' has become from the people. For example, when it suits, politicians are quick to proclaim with eye-catching slogans and empty words that they are elected to exercise the democratic will of the people, by listening to them, and they 'entered politics to make life better for others.' In reality, such slogans are far from the truth.

I strongly believe that much of government legislation, policies and initiatives are extremely important for social cohesion, but we cannot just legislate our way out of trouble, by ignoring the underlying issues and root causes by passing more laws. We have got to stop spending too much time talking, and start doing something about the problems before they get out of hand. We need to address peoples' hopes and multiculturalism in a positive manner. We can only achieve such goals with pro-active policies, not knee-jerking reactive measures that alienate people further away from the mainstream, which causes resentment between communities. It is with this optimistic approach that I have continued in my quest to raise real-life concerns of ordinary people to the to the attention of cross-party politicians. My main focus has been for the good of the people and nation. Where appropriate, I have raised concerns relating to political failures affecting everyone, but equally, not hesitating to speak out when I have felt ethnic people are in the wrong.

Over the years, I have written to so many Tory, Liberal and Labour politicians, even foreign ones. The main aim was to always be supportive to whichever political party happens to be in government, or even in opposition, which I have done, as I felt that it was my democratic duty to engage in national interest, without joining any particular party. I have already given a detailed description of my attempts in the previous chapter when I wrote to Tony Blair, which received a casual polite rebuff, basically telling me 'don't bother us, we will call you'. The following is a chronological account, giving brief summaries of the contents written subsequently to umpteen politicians. As before, I have given a salient summary and a commentary from selected letters to highlight wide-ranging issues raised over the years. I would like it to go on record that except for a handful of cases; I have not had a reply, not even an acknowledgement. In this and other chapters, I will cover the period from 5th September 2005 until 11th September 2019.

In 2005, the Conservative Party, like any party after a major election defeat was still going through the process of blame, reorganisation and self-discovery. In the process, the party went through a few leadership contests in the aftermath of the landslide victory in 1997 by New Labour. I always believe in giving credit where it is due. This is what I did when I heard that Kenneth Clarke had decided to contest the Tory party leadership. Letter 7 below was written to Kenneth Clarke on 5th September 2005. In my letter I stated he had political conviction to be a worthy leader both in opposition and government, and lead from the front.

> 'I have recently felt that political leaders led through appeasement politics with knee-jerking reactive measures, instead of pro-active policies, when in government or opposition, and I am outlining the areas that need closer scrutiny when formulating specific policies to enhance social harmony. I have interacted on a regular basis with cross-party politicians and Tory MPs when in government, and had the pleasure of meeting you in 1995'.

I did not hear from him.

I also wrote to give credit to David Cameron when he won the Conservative Party leadership contest.

Letter 8 - 31st December 2005 to David Cameron

'I would like to congratulate you on your election victory, and wish you well, and that under your leadership the Tory Party will be a voice for change and optimism, and adopt a constructive approach to hold the government to account. I am outlining real life concerns facing ordinary people that I had also raised in the past with Tony Blair'.

I was so encouraged to hear from his office (letter 9), thanking me for writing, suggesting that the best thing would be to copy my letter to Sayeeda Warsi, who was the chair of the party, and ask her to get in touch with me directly. It would be the only time I would hear from his office. Regrettably, not even as a matter of courtesy an acknowledgement from the Direct Communication Office when he became the PM in May 2010 in the coalition government. I wrote to him again on a few occasions, and the novelty of hearing from his office soon wore off. I acutely suffered by believing politicians would reply, only to find out that once they got elected or became PM, they would not even bother!

I was fortunate to meet MP, Stephen Pound at a function held at the Foreign and Commonwealth Office to commemorate the long-standing bond between Britain and India. As I had interacted with him in the past, I mentioned about the letters I had written to the Secretary of States, Jack Straw and Hazel Blears, regarding social cohesion and integration of ethnic communities into the mainstream. He asked me to write a short note to highlight the points I had covered in my letters to them.

Letter 10 - 20th June 2007 to Stephen Pound

'I am enclosing the letters I had written to Jack Straw and Hazel Blears with reference to the government policy initiatives within the context of ethnic communities, multicultural Britain and the consultative process post 9/11 and 7/7. I am also highlighting the findings of the most recent surveys relating to a lack of ethnic integration due to red tape bureaucracy and awareness of government initiatives, which reinforced some of the underlying causes preventing social harmony that I had consistently raised over the years with John Major, Tony Blair and other politicians'.

I heard nothing further on the matter.

On 27th June 2007, I had written to Gordon Brown to congratulate him when he became PM after he had given his inaugural speech on the steps of Downing Street, but heard nothing back. So once again I wrote to him on 16th May 2008 (letter 11), despite not hearing from his office in June 2007. In my letter I highlighted that,

'I have written to you, as well as your predecessor Tony Blair, Jack Straw, Hazel Blears and others where I suggested various practical initiatives and objectives to achieve social cohesion and integration of ethnic people into mainstream politics, and the British way of life'.

In my letter I also gave reasons why past government initiatives had failed to achieve integration, because when formulating policies relating to ethnic communities, too much emphasis was placed on politics of appeasement, spin, 'sofa style' leadership and reliance on certain individuals claiming to be the 'defenders of ethnic communities. I went on to say that it is about time that the experiences of the ordinary people leading everyday life were taken on board.

As I did not hear from his office, I wrote again hoping on this occasion the views of an ordinary person would get heard, and to improve my chances I also copied my letter of 10th June 2009 (letter 12) to Gordon Brown to Stephen Pound.

'I am raising concerns relating to social cohesion and the rise in right-wing extremism and fascist's parties seen under the disguise of democracy during the European elections, because of the public's apathy and resentment towards politicians. As a parent, I dread to think the legacy we will leave behind for our future generation bearing in mind that in the last century significant British, Commonwealth and Allied lives were lost during the two World Wars to prevent the spread of fascism'.

I suggested policy initiatives to enhance participation of ethnic people into mainstream British politics.

I was lucky to receive a reply (letter 13), and felt it was because I had copied Stephen Pound. But it just regurgitated a similar reply I had received four years ago from another PM, except this time it said 'Mr Brown receives thousands of letters each week, and regrets that he is unable to reply personally to them all'. It went onto say that 'your letter has been forwarded to the Department for Communities and Local Government, so that they may reply to you directly/', which they never did.

Incidentally, it was the second time I was told about the PM receiving thousands of letters, which I was also informed about in December 2005. That time by Tony Blair's Parliament Private Secretary and it would not be the last time I would be reminded by somebody else how busy the PMs are. Such attitude gives the impression that they feel that ordinary people are stupid to think that PMs have nothing to do except wait every morning with their letter opener for the postman to arrive. Of course not! I completely recognise that PMs and politicians are extremely busy people, with immense responsibility, and as they often remind us that they are totally committed to serving public duty in national interest, and unlike an ordinary person, I would not expect them sitting doing nothing or have any spare time to waste. That is why they are provided an army of well-paid advisors and aides, paid by the tax payer to rely upon. They also have a chain of command, comprising of top legal experts and other professionals at their disposal to assist. Not only to open letters, but after reading, advise PMs on important matters, if something merits further consideration. The constituent MPs also enjoy generous allowances and perks, paid by the tax-payer, to help them serve public duty. I wonder what would have happened if I had enclosed a donation cheque for a large sum in aid of the Labour Party. I ask myself if the chain of command or the Parliament Private Secretary would have then felt obliged to bring my letters to the attention of Tony Blair and Gordon Brown, despite receiving thousands of letters each week!

Sayeeda Warsi appeared on 22nd October 2009, on BBC Question Time, as a guest on the panel with Jack Straw and Nigel Griffin of the British National Party. So, I sent letter 14 on 23rd October 2009 to Sayeeda Warsi because I was impressed with how she presented herself on the programme.

> 'You rose above petty politics on BBC Question Time, and like you, I strongly agreed with the BBC's decision to invite Mr Griffin, as it would be wrong to stifle debate, especially in a thriving democracy like ours, which we should not take for granted, nor forget that people of this great country and its colonies fought two World Wars with immense sacrifices and loss of lives, to protect freedom and basic human rights. It is debatable whether it was the right format, because of unfair hostility shown towards Mr Griffin before and during the debate, which prevented discussions relating to actual policy issues. The main political parties also have a responsibility to listen to the concerns of those who turn to the BNP or other extremist groups to prevent them from joining such groups. Now is an opportune time for the political parties to relinquish appeasement politics and address the actual issues based on pragmatic policies, to leave a better future legacy for our children'.

I did not hear from her.

In 2009, I was having problems with my employer, Commonwealth War Graves Commission, and was sacked after subjected to the flawed internal disciplinary process. I sought advice from the CAB. They suggested to seek justice through the Employment Tribunal, informing me that I could either contest myself, or hire a solicitor to act on my behalf. I told them that this was beyond my budget, so the CAB advised me that it would be best to contact my local MP for help to qualify for legal aid.

I wrote to my constituent MP, Sir Humphrey Malins. This was the first time I had written to him, because the last time I had written to my constituent MP it was to his predecessor, Sir Cranley Onslow on 28th October 1994 (letter 2). I must say, both were exemplary in the truest meaning of democracy, putting constituents first, before self-serving party interests. It was such experiences of standards in public duty that I expected most politicians would be of similar ethical standards. But this was not the case, and even more so after the general election on 6th May 2010, despite pledges by various PMs in their inaugural speeches given on the steps of 10 Downing Street.

In my letter 15 on 2nd October 2009, I briefed Humphrey Malins about discrimination at my place of work and why I had lodged an Employment Tribunal Appeal for unfair dismissal against my employer, based on the advice given by the CAB, and managed everything without any professional help.

> 'The trial has been scheduled for Monday 9th November 2009, but the Commonwealth War Graves Commission's legal team tried to get the claim dismissed without fruition, and the judge has advised me to seek a solicitor's help because the hearing can be a daunting experience for a layman, in terms of preparing statements, witnesses, cross examination and other procedures. I have also sought help from the Surrey Law Centre, bar-Pro Bono, Legal Aid and philanthropic individuals, without success as I am not on welfare benefits'.

Sir Humphrey Malins visited me at home, and I showed him the intimidating letter from the Commonwealth War Graves Commission with whom I was having employment problems. In the letter dated 9th October 2009, their Legal Director issued threats based on past Tribunal judgements, he wrote that:

> 'We believe your unfair dismissal claim is doomed to failure, and in all these circumstances your schedule of loss is wholly unrealistic. I wish to emphasise that the cost to the Commission of defending the discrimination claim will be in excess of £50,000. We want to make you aware that the Commonwealth War Graves Commission intends to recoup from you at the end of the trial the costs it has incurred already, and those which will be incurred. In view of these further costs and the significant disruption that will be caused to some 12 members of the Commission's staff for periods upwards of 2 weeks, I have instructions to offer you £15,000 in full and final settlement of all your claims. Your wife was present at the last hearing and we urge you to show her this letter'.

Basically, the Commonwealth War Graves Commission were acting as judge and jury, scaring me to withdraw my claim saying I have no chance of winning. Just before the hearing on Monday, I had a phone call on Sunday from their barrister, reminding me about the out-of-court settlement. He also said I should discuss this with Femi, whom he had met when she accompanied me during the preliminary hearings. Obviously, they were playing on her sentiments. It so happened, JP Jenny Wilkinson, our daughter's school housemistress, and a very good family friend had come for dinner. She said barristers do not come cheap, but are worth the money they are paid. They are in the business to win for their clients at all costs, whether right or wrong, and that I should consider the offer carefully, even if I am right, because of my lack of legal expertise. I knew apart from the in-house team of legal experts, the Commonwealth War Graves Commission had hired one of the top barristers in the field, and he did not come cheap from what I had heard through the grapevine from ex-colleagues. Besides, I could see Femi, Naamah and Ummehani getting extremely worried. Reluctantly, I decided to accept the offer, knowing full well that all the evidence I had gathered on discrimination and wastage of public funds, would not get to see the light of day. The settlement offer was least surprising, since it would be against the interest of my ex-employer, which would have given them bad publicity, due to the five-day hearing being scheduled the day after Remembrance Sunday. Just like the monopoly newspaper wholesaler, it would not have looked well for their reputation, if the evidence came out into the open, especially in the case of the Commonwealth War Graves Commission, a well-known public organisation engaged in noble causes, looking after the heroes who gave lives to save humanity from evil practices. What still puzzles me to this day is if they were in the right, why make an offer? After all, the Commonwealth War Graves Commission was going to recover their costs from me anyway. Also, if they lose, the tax payer would foot the bill. Despite the settlement on this occasion, unlike the newspaper wholesaler, I felt the workings of a public body funded by the tax payer should not get brushed under the carpet, and it was important the public learnt about discrimination and wastage of tax payer's money that was happening in public institutions. I even wrote on 12th November 2009 to HRH The Duke of Kent in his capacity as President of the Commonwealth War Graves Commission to draw his attention to the workings of the organisation which after a promising initial response from his Private Secretary got me nowhere despite subsequent attempts on my part. In some ways my effort was a pioneer to the 'Race Audit' which Theresa May would later announce to look into the 'burning injustices' happening in Britain as her top priority after she became PM in 2016, and if any of its findings have been implemented remains doubtful.

I therefore wrote to Sir Humphrey Malins on 9th November 2009 (letter 16).

'I am requesting your esteemed guidance and support to bring to the attention of minister responsible for a public body like the Commonwealth War Graves Commission, to highlight the underlying issues relating to discrimination and the flawed internal disciplinary process'.

I gave the reasons why I had lodged an Employment Tribunal Appeal, and reluctantly accepted an out of court settlement, because of legal stress and intimidation. I admitted there are Trade Unions, but emphasised that a Parliamentary Select Committee inquiry will serve well to address the underlying workings of a public body, so that such practices are not allowed to continue, and should be prevented from happening again to others.

Sir Humphrey Malins made representations on my behalf for a Parliamentary Select Committee inquiry. He wrote to Robin James, Clerk of the Defence Committee, and said he would get in touch when he hears from the clerk. After a few exchanges with the clerk whilst waiting for the outcome, Sir Humfrey Malins wrote to me on 23rd February 2010 (letter 17). He told me to be aware that he is retiring on Election Day, and that parliament is likely to be dissolved in a few weeks' time. Although he was sure that his successor 'the excellent Conservative candidate, Jonathan Lord, would be very happy to take on my case, but that he would need written authority from me to pass on my file to his successor, if that is what I would like him to do when the time comes'. As requested, I gave Sir Humfrey Malins written authority on 24th February 2010 (letter 18) to pass on my file to his replacement candidate, Jonathan Lord.

Soon after the general election on 6th May 2010, I wrote to the newly elected Woking MP, Jonathan Lord as I was instructed by his predecessor, Sir Humphrey Malins, whom I had given authority to pass over my file to Jonathan Lord to make representation on my behalf for a Parliamentary Select Committee inquiry to highlight the workings of a public organisation, and the difficulties faced by the ordinary people.

So, I wrote to Jonathan Lord on 8th May 2010 (letter 19). It was the very first I had written to him. I first congratulated him on his election victory, and as my MP I also took the opportunity to introduce myself.

'I am following the instruction and advice given to me by your predecessor and as your constituent, I look forward to your support in light of the pledges made during the general election to vote for change in the 'Big Society' of 'New Politics' accountability and transparency of government, in order to make the democratic process more accessible for the ordinary people'.

I heard from Jonathan Lord (letter 20), thanking me for my good wishes, and he stated that he will try to write back about the other issues that I had brought to his attention when he had some time. After a few unhelpful exchanges, I soon realised my MP was ignoring me, and not interested to make constructive representations on my behalf, as reflected in his reply (letter 21). I had also requested appointments on a few occasions to meet in person instead of writing, which he has never obliged to do to this day. He point-blankly said that "if I felt so strongly about local or national political issues, then I am always at liberty to stand for election myself, or to get involved in appropriate charities or pressure groups."

This was the second time that I had failed to seek justice. On both occasions my main reason was to highlight the reality faced by the ordinary 'man in the street'. For me, above anything else it was more to do with underlining the actual difficulties and stress faced by the public, when it came to exercising their rights within the rule of law and policies, determined by the lawmakers and the government, when dealing with public or private organisations. I believed that the best way to achieve justice was to go to court and bring it out into the open. However, both times I had to settle for an out-of-court settlement, so as not become a victim of the justice system myself, if the court found the settlements were reasonable. Something which the legal teams of both defendants knew well, based on their experience in such matters. Although I got an out-of-court settlement, I paid the ultimate price to seek justice, because I got sacked, and the truth remained covered. Whereas, the wastage of tax-payer's money by a public organisation and the workings of a monopoly wholesaler's practices went unpunished, and are allowed to continue. I would eventually feel vindicated when an MP in 2014 who later rose to high levels of public office found the behaviour of monopoly newspapers totally unacceptable, and decided to fight on behalf of the newsagents. At the same drawing caution not to raise my hopes, so that I did not get disappointed, while waiting to find out if leopards do change their spots!

What this does show is that for the ordinary public, the whole business of getting justice is easier said than done. The public end up as victims, whether they win or lose in the courts; but those with financial clout, it is a win-win situation. They can afford to take out a writ to prosecute anyone, and defend themselves well with the best legal teams money can buy, whether they are guilty or not, by using the justice system to cover-up the truth, because they know how to exploit the loop holes and delaying tactics in a legal system that is meant to provide justice. Or as a last resort to avoid bad publicity, they can make an out-of-court settlement, which is then written-off against tax returns as expenses, not costing them, but the public purse.

Politicians should listen to public concerns and not ignore them, or take too long to respond to their repeated pleas of help. Even if politicians do listen, it is only after a major public outcry, suffering or loss of lives. I am not making it up, because the proof is in the pudding, and sadly nothing has changed. How often have we heard during election campaigns and victory speeches of the social injustices that exist in our country? Just to give one such example, Teressa May in her inaugural speech on 13th July 2016 on the Downing Street's steps spoke of the, "seven burning injustices," and ordered a 'Race Disparity Audit' to tackle it. However, nothing was achieved by the time she was forced out of office by her own Tory MPs in June 2019, except another failed initiative, wasting tax payer's money. Not to be outdone, her successor, Boris Johnson in his victory speech made a similar pledge, re-packaged as, "one nation Conservative" to reach out towards all sections of the electorate. Such admissions by politicians clearly acknowledge that the ordinary public face discrimination and injustices in their daily life, reinforcing the situation faced by myself and many others.

One thing for sure, I was not going to allow anything to put me off, especially by the rebuke from my MP. I continued to write or copy him into letters when I thought appropriate, to raise various real-life relevant issues. It was a constant struggle to write, as I was either getting patronising replies or forgotten altogether, and so I would write again, but still got nowhere. In a sense I felt that I had to stand-up for myself, and the public; no matter how large or small an issue may be, persevering with the satisfaction that at least I was trying. Despite frustrations, I was not going to get disheartened or deterred by the inflexible attitude by those in power; otherwise, I would have given up a long time ago. I was often told by friends that I must be mad to persevere, as it is not going to make any difference. I continued to bedevil the politicians, because of the gravity of the situation faced in real-life as an ordinary person. The main reason I wanted to make cross-party MPs aware of the wider implication of their laws and policies on people, was because I do not like regrets in life for not trying. At least in some way it has served a rightful purpose. It has enabled me to give a written record of my experiences, based on years of personal efforts. I can now narrate how those in power ignore the public. Not everyone has the time to write to politicians, but most have the ability to make some kind of contribution. When a constituent tries to practice their democratic right to get heard, seek help or even offer constructive advice, those in power deflect public duty and show contempt.

I felt that I was denied access to my democratic right by my MP, so I explored other avenues, however hopeless or farfetched they may have seemed. My first port of call was with the Speaker of the House of Commons. In my naive way, I thought he would have some regulatory role to monitor the conduct of MPs, to ensure they fulfilled their public duty honourably.

Letter 22 - 6th December 2010 to John Bercow

> 'I am highlighting the handicaps faced by disadvantaged people with no legal finances, lobbying or media clout to gain access to the democratic process, as I have been told by my MP to stand for election or join a protest group(s). I am enclosing copies of letters that I have written to give a deeper insight of the situation'.

I was surprised, but pleased to hear (letter 23) from his secretary, explaining that he has no responsibility for the actions of members outside the Chamber of the House of Commons, and the way in which they choose to deal with their correspondence is entirely a matter for themselves. Like everything in life, the benefit of hindsight is a great thing. It was foolish of me to expect help from any politician, even the PM, let alone the speaker. I should have realised long ago not to place trust in any politician, because no one would break rank and rock the boat. The only reason I wrote to the speaker in the first place was in an act of desperation, as I wanted the truth to prevail. I wanted to bring government and the lawmakers recognise their lack of accountability and wastage of financial resources by a public body. Sadly, it was not to be, but I believed that it was only a matter of time for the truth to eventually prevail, albeit after a major scandal and a costly public inquiry, to learn important lessons after the culprits have long retired on good pensions.

Undeterred, I continued and once again wrote (24) to David Cameron, this time in his role as the PM of the coalition government following the general election on 6th May 2010, just as I had written to his three predecessors. I thought it would be a new era in politics, because after a long time, Britain had a coalition government, and also during the general election campaign he pledged to lead an inclusive government.

> 'I have written to you previously when you were the Leader of the Opposition and I hope on this occasion my letter will be brought to your attention. Over the years I have also written to your three predecessors and raised real-life concerns, focusing on social cohesion and the role of ethnic communities, which in a way compliments your vision of the "Big Society." As a nation, we have great opportunity to stimulate and benefit from the historic ties with the Commonwealth, as partners of choice. I would like to reiterated that when formulating government policies, too much reliance is placed on a few individuals and organisations claiming

to be gatekeepers of ethnic communities, and it seems those who shout the loudest get listened to, not those at the grass roots level who lead ordinary lives. This does not mean that eminent people should be ignored, but at times they can be misinformed, because on reaching their respective positions they get out of touch with reality. I am suggesting that we need to adopt pro-active ways to listen to the views of ordinary people, instead of appeasement politics, spin and 'sofa style' leadership of the past'.

Unfortunately, I never got a reply or an acknowledgement. My many requests were also ignored by Jonathan Lord to make representation on my behalf. I was surprised by the change in attitude of David Cameron's office. They had the courtesy to reply when he was a Leader of the Opposition, but now as PM did not even have the courtesy to acknowledge my correspondence, let alone reply. As a leader, it does not set a good example for any MP, let alone one belonging to his own political party!

I decided to change tack and wrote to Nick Clegg, because during the general election campaign in May 2010 he came across as a political leader more willing to listen and engage with the ordinary people, unlike the leaders of the established parties, who took the electorate for granted. Now as a Deputy PM, I thought he was in a better position to practice what he preached, and deliver the 'New Politics' he had pledged with greater accountability and access to the democratic process for the ordinary people.

Letter 25 - 18th December 2010 to Nick Clegg

'I am writing to you to highlight the real life concerns and handicaps faced by the disadvantaged, in terms of social mobility and discrimination at work, and the advice given to me by my own MP to stand for elections or join protest groups if I felt strongly about local or national issues. I have decided not to heed my MP's advice, because to wait five years for the next election will be too late to address real life issues. Also, I lack financial resources or private donors to fund my political activities, and I believe in a peaceful democracy of electing an MP to represent concerns of ordinary people, irrespective of party political and individual interests'.

I also enclosed copies of letters to David Cameron and my MP. Again, I did not hear from him. So much for 'New Politics', it is more like old politics! I remained steadfast, as I never give up easily for a good cause. In my follow-up exchange of 13th January 2011 (letter 26) to Nick Clegg, and I said,

'It was with deep regret I had not heard from your office, not even an acknowledgement following my letter of 18th December 2010. During the 2010 general election campaign, it felt really good that at long last the nation will deservedly get clean conviction-based politics, a break from the self-serving politics of the past. Sadly, this was not to be. It is no different from seeing the disharmony during the Prime Minister's Questions when the government apportions blame onto everyone else but themselves. Especially, when politicians are often heard saying they entered politics to 'make lives better for others'. This is not so, because the ordinary people face the brunt of the consequences of severity, and made to suffer for the greed and mistakes of the bankers, politicians and government advisers. The voters are tired of the politics of appeasement, and a bog of broken political promises of the recent past. The present coalition government is no different'.

On this occasion, I was fortunate to receive a reply from his office. I was told that my letter has been forwarded to the Department for Works and Pensions, so that they could reply to me directly, as the issues raised are more appropriate for them. I received a long-winded bureaucratic reply, without answering the actual issues with an unidentifiable signature.

Michael Gove was another politician who impressed me, when he appeared on BBC Question Time, because of his views.

Letter 27 - 14th January 2011 to Michael Gove

'It was refreshing to listen to politics of conviction, instead of appeasement politics and broken promises, under the cover of 'New Politics', and good to hear your views, together with that of Charles Kennedy, especially on the question relating to 'English baccalaureate' tables. Like many others, I believe quality education and good health are the two most important requirements to equip future generations, to give them a good start in life. This will help address social mobility and social cohesion. It requires a strong commitment from politicians, and sound practical policies to tackle the underlying root causes facing people in all aspects of everyday life today. I compliment you on that. Unlike recent examples in parliamentary democracy, you showed dedication to better the education standards for all, irrespective of background. We need politicians and experts like you, with conviction to render civic duty, and to eradicate obstacles and hardships faced by disadvantaged people. The public expect politicians to voice honest opinions, not just empty words and rule by knee-jerking reactions to the 24-hour media. It was wrong to stereotype an entire community with comments that Jack Straw made on 8th January, and I agree with you. It is important to listen to ordinary people from 'within ethnic communities'. I just wanted to highlight my experience when I have tried so hard to engage positively over the years on a range of real-life issues, only to be ignored, not just by Jack Straw, but many others'.

My optimism after watching Michael Gove was short lived. He also joined the long list of politicians, as I did not hear from him, not even as a matter of courtesy, an acknowledgement. However, I had met Simon Hughes in 2009 at a function to mark Ahimsa (International Day of Non-Violence) on 2nd October, the birthday of Mahatma Gandhi. I decided to write to him, as he was now a minister in the coalition government. In my letter I stated he was a voice of reason championing everyday issues faced by his constituents (letter 28 below: 17th January 2011).

'I hope you will bring real life experiences of disadvantaged people to the attention of the government, since their voices in stark contrast to the rich, very rarely gets heard. Parliamentary rules prevent the ordinary 'man in the street' to exercise his democratic right, when denied this by their own MP. If the coalition government believes in delivering its agenda of 'New Politics' based on fairness, transparency and accountability, it is vital to listen to the views of the ordinary public, and the difficulties they face in their daily lives'.

I did not hear from Simon Hughes. So, once again I wrote to Nick Clegg, because I believe in 'fortune favours the brave', and just like the students who felt let down over student fees that was introduced by him, I was not going to give up easily on his pledge to deliver 'New Politics' as coalition partners in government. On this occasion I wrote with reference to the programme on BBC 2 'Posh and Posher', to draw his attention to similar relevant points I had raised with him, Jonathan Lord, Simon Hughes, David Cameron and Michael Gove, which letters I enclosed.

Letter 29 - 5th February 2011

'Over the years, I have tried in vain to highlight the handicaps raised in the programme of the lack of social mobility and social harmony. It is because outside the Westminster bubble the public without financial, legal, lobbying, media or social clout face great difficulty to access their democratic process of getting heard, despite the much-promised age of 'New Politics'. It is also very disheartening, especially in the wake of the answers given by David Cameron at the Prime Minister's Questions on 15th December 2010 on the terrorist attack in Sweden, he said "we need to ask the right questions about Islamist terrorism." This is an irony when

I have taken the trouble to ask the right questions, and also provide solutions, and I have faced nothing but consistent contempt and arrogance, not only from him, but also his two predecessors, as well as my own MP. Besides, when asked on 2nd February 2011 by a Labour MP about the plight of a sick child, David Cameron replied that an MP should do his utmost to help constituents in all matters. This is a bit rich and condescending for him to say. When in my own experience, all members of the government have shown clear contempt, and not even bothered to reply to an ordinary member of the public. It is far below any standards one can expect from those paid by the tax-payer to serve public duty. Politicians are not setting good examples for mere mortals to follow'.

I also drew his attention to the report by Sir George Young where he said "the pollical system is deterring people from less affluent backgrounds from becoming MPs". I did not hear at all from Nick Clegg or his team.

By the way, earlier on 27th January 2011 (letter 30), I had written to the BBC presenter himself, none other than the famous no-nonsense interviewer politicians dread, Andrew Neil, commending him on the programme.

'Thank you for your provocative programme, which exposed unfairness in our political system based on politicians drawn from an even smaller social pool and networking contacts, who run the country'.

I then related my personal experience with the political class, and complemented the main thrust of the programme. I went onto to say that he should raise the dilemma faced by ordinary people with politicians, when they next appear on his show to score political points.

I also did not hear from him, not a dickie bird! I would say that it was not a great advert for the programme. Around this time the big political debate in parliament and on TV, such as Andrew Neil's the 'Politics Show' and 'BBC Question Time' were deeply focused on terrorism, radicalisation and Islamophobia, with a lot of focus on Islam, hatred and racist attacks directed towards Muslims, because of the terrorist attack in Sweden, and also comments made by David Cameron at the 'Prime Minister's Questions' on 15th December 2010, as mentioned above. I decided to take the plunge once again and wrote to Jonathan Lord, despite his and David Cameron's indifferent attitude, increasingly becoming clear to me that they were never interested to listen or accommodate real-life concerns I was trying to raise.

Letter 31 - 16th February 2011

'It is insulting of David Cameron to criticise British Muslims for not playing their part to address radicalisation, with his 'sound bites' during his televised 'Prime Minister's Questions' and speeches. When David Cameron, and especially you should know how many times I have tried in vain to do just that. I even requested you, as my MP to make representation on my behalf, which got me nowhere. So, such remarks do not help. Just like his predecessors, Mr Cameron has echoed reservations and concerns on 5th February 2011 in Germany, but offered no solutions. Whereas, I had written to him on 30th July 2010 and copied that letter to you, when I said we cannot afford complacency after 9/11 and 7/7 events, and we need to address it head on, as it threatens true harmony in our society and British way of life. I had also listed specific cost-effective pragmatic solutions'.

Another initiative of mine got ignored, falling on deaf ears as I did not hear from him, regardless of the pledges of 'New Politics', accountability and the rest! Whilst watching 'Prime Minister's Questions' on 16th February 2011 I heard Bernard Jenkins, Chair of Public Administration Committee, inform the PM of the launch of a public inquiry into the 'Big Society', the flagship policy of David Cameron. I took the opportunity to write to him, requesting him to invite the ordinary public to give evidence to the committee, which will serve well to highlight their real-life experiences. In my letter 32 of 16th February 2011 to Bernard Jenkins I wrote that,

'The government's views on the 'Big Society' to alleviate demand on public services were positive values for the well-being of a healthy society. However difficult to put into practice, because when people try to engage, they just get ignored, not only by David Cameron, but many politicians, and even other members of the coalition government'.

I also enclosed the above copy (letter 31) to Jonathan Lord, as an example. I also did not hear from him, but I remained resolute and undeterred. I widened my efforts further by approaching chairpersons of other parliamentary committees, hoping to inspire them to listen to the 'man in the street'. I met Keith Vaz on a few occasions, and wrote to him in his capacity as the Chair of Home Office Select Committee for his esteemed support.

Letter 33 - 26th February 2011

'I approach your good self not with the intention that ethnic people should be treated differently from the mainstream, but far from it. Also, I appreciate MPs can only make representations on behalf of their constituents. However, I am writing because of the interrelated nature of the issues which fall within the remit of your committee, namely multiculturalism, radicalisation and obstacles ethnic British citizens face to obtain family visitor visas, especially at the time of bereavement'.

In my letter I also stated that if he would bring it to the attention of Ed Miliband, who was the Leader of Opposition, so he is aware of the real-life issues faced by the ordinary people, as I am doubtful that he would get to see my letter, if I wrote to him directly, as it is evident by the contempt shown to the average person on the street by politicians of all political parties. I thought this was the next best approach to take. I heard nothing further from him.

Overwhelmingly I felt let down during my numerous attempts to exercise my democratic right. Many would have just given up, if this was the way politicians, paid by the tax payer elected to serve public duty. It is a worrying sign, when especially the trust in politicians is at its lowest. What fate lay ahead for others in democracy for the future generations? Anyway, despite the rebuke from my MP, I persevered and wrote yet again to Jonathan Lord (letter 34: 9th July 2011). Informing him,

> 'I am once again making reference to the pledge David Cameron had made to end the cosy relationships during his watch; whereby political parties have flouted over the decades with detrimental consequences on individual rights, by instilling better scrutiny and accountability amongst politicians, media and the police. I would like to remind you of the promise of 'New Politics' made by him to deliver fairness, freedom and responsibility to restore public trust in democracy. I hope, as my MP you will support the many requests, I have made to make representation for a parliamentary inquiry into the workings of a public body to unveil malpractices, collusion and wastage of public funds, by the top-heavy management'.

I failed miserably to generate any interest from him, as he did not even bother to reply, despite the pledge made by David Cameron to deliver 'New Politics'. Anyway, despite my reservations mentioned above, I wrote to Ed Miliband on 15th August 2011 (35) with reference to the riots in London, and elsewhere in England. I said it was refreshing to hear that he was calling for an inquiry that gave communities a chance to describe what their lives are like, and what may have caused the eruption of violence. I said we need to get to the bottom of the reasons behind these riots, by listening to real-life concerns of ordinary public without social clout, instead of relying on the age-old practices

> 'Society would be served better if politicians would listen and respond directly to the ordinary people, instead of relying too much on the so called 'experts'.

I then gave examples of double standards and improper behaviour amongst politicians and the real-life issues faced by the public outside the Westminster bubble, and continued to say how in many cases the 'experts' despite making mistakes and warning about their past reputation, still get a second chance. A perk that is not available to the public without contacts, and it is this sort of attitude and a lack of trust that has resulted in the reputation of politics being at an all-time low. I highlighted my years of experience and a lack of empathy when I tried to engage with cross-party politicians to raise real-life concerns of ordinary people.

I also did not hear from him, which serves to highlight that politicians from all parties are only interested to interact with the ordinary public at the time of elections, when touting for votes!

It would be an understatement to say I was getting frustrated or angry at times, by the lack of even a short thank you note for taking the trouble to write, let alone a proper reply. Nevertheless, I persevered. I was not going to be put off or feel let down by speaking honestly, plainly and frankly, no matter what people thought or said about me. I always believed that in the end, the truth would triumph. So once again I wrote with a positive approach to Jonathan Lord, as I felt the effects of government policies on the ordinary people mattered. In my letter 36 of 15th June 2012, I said

> 'I welcome in principle the proposed new immigration rules, which the Home Secretary was considering to introduce, but register my strong concern on the subject of dependent's entry into the UK, and I hoped the government will not enforce a blanket ban on all dependents with stringent financial burden, but make provisions for dependents of bona fide British citizens, on the grounds of extended family responsibility. I know that you are aware that I am an ardent supporter of fair, but tough immigration rules to control unscrupulous immigration, not unfair rules at the expense of others to bring net migration down by setting arbitrary targets that penalises British citizens, who have embraced and made the UK their home'.

I requested that he makes representation to register the above concerns. I did not hear from him. Yet another effort bites the dust! Over the years I often raised concerns over illegal immigration, so I felt the need to raise it with Jonathan Lord following the BBC Panorama programme on illegal immigration. In my letter 37 of 22nd January 2013, I thanked him for one of his rare replies to my many efforts ignored by him. But I said,

> 'I disagreed with the statistics you have listed to justify the government's stringent policies are working to stop the increase in immigration. In reality, there is an ever-increasing number of over stayers not reflected in the statistics, who have violated original visa terms, and granted leave to remain in the UK. In a way a government amnesty to tackle the backlog. The statistics are misleading and meaningless. We can all see the failures of successive governments to tackle illegal immigration, which is the main reason behind the subsequent backlog of bogus asylum applications of over 450,000 announced by the United Kingdom Border Agency. It could actually be higher, as statistics can be tailored to avoid controversy. I would like to remind you of my past efforts on the subject reported by Panorama relating to 'ghost' (bogus) immigrants, with genuine asylum seekers forced underground. It can be tackled if approached with determination and with pragmatic cost-effective solutions, before it is too late. The coalition politicians must listen to the concerns of ordinary people, and not call them a "bigot", like Gordon Brown did to Gillian Duffy during the 2010 elections, when she raised her concerns about immigration. Politicians should listen a bit more to the ordinary people, and not just rely on 'experts' and expensive public inquiries to learn lessons'.

Well as usual I did not hear from Johnathon Lord, but continued to remain optimistic, in spite of past failed efforts, even when I tried to enlist his help on numerous occasions, which were also ignored.

I decided to write to the PM in the wake of the senseless murder of drummer, Lee Rigby, because I strongly felt how a series of major issues, just like 9/11, 7/7 and others, has the effect of heightening tensions within communities. I copied Jonathan Lord to keep him abreast, hoping he would assist me in my efforts (letter 38 – 25th June 2013 to David Cameron).

> 'I would first like to apologise for taking up your valuable time, and I am only writing in support of the 'New Task Force'. We must bring perpetrators to face justice in courts, something their so called 'spiritual leaders' deny others, as they do not blow themselves up in order to go to paradise. I suggest the need for long term pro-active solutions, and not short-term knee-jerking remedies. I would like to list various initiatives under these broad headings: transparency, less reliance on leaders or individuals who shout the loudest, charities, awareness, representation at the grassroots level to enhance civic duty, social

cohesion, abolish the outdated term 'ethnic people', and illegal immigration. Despite some well-meaning government policies and initiatives, ethnic people continue to feel like second-class citizens, and are treated as such. I have been trying to raise real life concerns and issues relating to ethnic communities since 2000 prior to 9/11 and 7/7'.

It goes without saying I did not hear from David Cameron and my MP, not even an acknowledgement from the Direct Communication Office. Just like past initiatives, the 'New Task Force' also seems to be gathering dust somewhere!

One of the main reasons I persevered is that I believed in a varied Britain, and ethnic leaders must fulfil their duty to make sure they respect the law and culture of the land, no matter how baffling it may seem. After all, Britain is not asking them to change their religion, and they should not expect everyone else to agree with theirs. If the religious leaders believe they have a divine right, they should than practice their faith with greater transparency, not behind closed doors or scared of public scrutiny. There is room for all religions in this world! No individual faith has the outright authority to claim they have got it right, whilst the others are all wrong. This has also been the fault of successive governments, who as an easy option have mollycoddled ethnic religious leaders, as well as the rich, to act as advisors or gatekeepers to tackle radicalisation, but the government have been taken for a ride by them. In fact, the self-appointed ethnic advisor's main interest is self-serving to feather their own nests, expecting to be bestowed with honours and eminent positions. Instead the government should listen to the real-life experiences of ordinary people who are able to see the world, not just through the ivory tower and eyes of the so-called 'experts', but through the network of close and evolving personal relationships at community and individual level.

Whilst watching the Prime Minister's Questions on 17th July 2013, I heard frustrations and anger raised by a Labour MP, and witnessed the arrogance of David Cameron played out openly, he did not even bother to reply when the MP, David Wayne, wrote to him on behalf of his constituent. I wrote to the MP in question to share my experience (letter 39 of 18th July 2013).

'I am not one of your constituents, but share similar real-life experience that was raised at the Prime Minister's Questions. Bearing in mind, if an MP is treated with contempt by David Cameron, what hope does a mere mortal like myself, or anyone have with no financial and influential clout expect from cross-party politicians and government advisers. It was not only David Cameron, but many others have ignored my efforts including my own MP, who told me to stand for elections'.

I was pleased to hear (letter 40) from David Wayne, he told me he would "keep on trying." It was completely reprehensible and insulting on the part of the government to even contemplate certain policies in the first place, such as the bedroom tax. When they do carry out certain costly ill-thought polices, it just shows how out of touch they are from the ordinary 'man in the street'. Their actions not only cause unnecessary suffering and loss of lives, but also results in the waste of tax-payer's money and resources, which could be spent more wisely, improving public services. I did not hesitate to write to Jonathan Lord yet again on 26th July 2013 (letter 41), when the Home Office decided to insult immigrants with their 'Go Home' billboard van campaign. This not only showed a hostile Home Office attitude towards immigrants in general, but also put lives of bona fide ethnic people in danger. The campaign was a cheap political stunt by the government pretending that they are doing something about illegal immigration.

> 'I was not at all happy by the recent government gimmick. It was nasty and unpleasant politics of divide and rule, at the expense of bona fide British Citizens like myself, my children, and many others. This will only serve to cause more racial tension, hatred and abuse for law abiding ethnic people and their families at their work place, schools, neighbourhoods and other public places. I am reminding you of my numerous efforts, all falling on deaf ears. If the government was really serious about tackling illegal immigration, radicalisation and social injustices, and promote social harmony, then politicians should sometimes listen to the 'man in the street'.

I once again did not hesitate to remind him how many times my efforts got ignored not only by him, but also by David Cameron.

Disappointingly to say Jonathan Lord did not reply. The foregoing accounts do not only disclose how I have persevered, regardless of the contempt I faced from the 'establishment'. More prominently, my loyalty without the support from any politician, let alone my MP was not going to stand up and speak out when things are wrong. As suggested by Jonathan Lord that if I felt that strongly about local or national political issues, then I am always able to stand for elections myself, or get involved in appropriate charities or pressure groups, was not exactly the answer that one would expect to get from your MP. I thought by engaging in a positive, responsible and respectful manner with those elected to serve public duty would have been more acceptable. I do not consider myself a career politician or an activist, I am only remaining true to myself, with a firm belief that nothing, absolutely nothing, would have changed for the better in our country or communities, if people had not over the centuries taken a positive stand, or contributed on issues small and large, for the benefit of all. This is what I have tried to do since 1992. Unluckily, my disappointments do not end here, as I was not prepared to give-up easily, especially if it is for a worthy cause, and not at a cost to the tax payer.

9

More Disenchantment

I heard Priti Patel, the upcoming and ambitious rising star in the Tory party, on the Asian Sunrise Radio. She showed that she was very concerned about the 'newspaper wholesale distribution', and was very outspoken about her disapproval of them, informing the listeners on the radio show that she was going to lead a campaign against the wholesaler's control over restrictive trading practices. Hearing her was music to my ears; at long last we have a politician who is convicted to stand-up for the ordinary person and not her own self-serving interests. I told Femi what I had heard, and she confirmed that we now have a politician with the burning desire to address real-life issues, and hopefully the truth about newspaper wholesalers will come out into the open.

Hence, I wrote immediately to Priti Patel on 27th March 2014 (letter 42).

> 'It is refreshing to hear that an MP is willing to raise concerns, pertaining to the everyday lives of ordinary voiceless people, and making it known that an independent inquiry is long overdue. It will shine a light into the wholesaler's conduct and abuse of the monopoly, which undermines the basic commercial viability of the newsagent'.

I also mentioned that I had a significant amount of evidence showing how the 'newspaper wholesale monopoly' actually affects newsagent's profits, which will help immensely in her campaign. I was overwhelmed when I received a prompt, personally signed reply (letter 43) from her. A rare feat for me to hear from politicians, let alone acknowledged letters, when I have written to them in my own time and at a personal cost so many times. Priti Patel thanked me very much for writing to her regarding the debate that she had initiated in parliament on the news supply trade. She went onto to say,

> 'I am grateful for your interest in this matter and would be very interested to review the evidence you have gathered in relation to the wholesalers. During the course of the debate, the minister who responded suggested that the new Competition and Markets Authority could re-investigate this issue and any evidence I have, may assist them to make this decision'.

For me, it was an historic event. A politician willing to serve people! Priti Patel was one of the only three non-constituent MPs I have ever heard from, other than Stephen Pound and David Wayne. I replied immediately, so as not to keep a VIP waiting in their deliberations, due to the heavy demands on their valuable time to make important decisions. I could not contain my joy. It felt Christmas had come early!

Without further ado I replied to Priti Patel on 24th April 2014 (letter 44). In my reply I reminded her of the substantial sensitive evidence meticulously compiled over a period of years relating to accounting errors, and if she would advise how to send it to her. Regrettably, my hope in the political class was short lived. After all, most career politicians these days are motivated by self-serving interests, above anything else. I heard nothing further. I waited three months and wrote a follow-up letter on 16th July 2014 (letter 45). I was forthright, and stated that:

> 'I am not writing to you in a whim, but acted on the advice of your office to write to you, and I have spent time doing so. I hope you will not use the excuse of receiving thousands of letters, now that you have become a minister'.

> I explained how I had given her the benefit of the doubt, and believed she really shared concerns of ordinary people, to uphold standards in public duty. I also mentioned that no wonder the chairman of the Committee on Standards in Public Life has warned the PM to make sure politicians are aware of their duties to be honest, open, accountable and selfless, or face lack of public trust and disenchantment with Westminster village politics and star struck politicians. I contacted her office, and got nowhere. I wrote again on 4th September 2014 (letter 48). I was straightforward, and stated that,

> I suppose as you have not bothered to even acknowledge my letter, that you will understand why I feel aggrieved, especially when at your request I took the trouble in my own time to offer evidence on the

newspaper wholesaler, and why the public do not trust politicians. I was wrong to think that you are a dedicated politician actually concerned with the views and well-being of plebes, and now with your ministerial appointment, it is more likely you will more occupied addressing interests of lobby groups with financial clout, and the newspaper wholesale monopoly will reign supreme at the newsagents' expense'.

As expected, the trail went cold despite two reminders, as a final attempt I even phoned her office and got nowhere. I found out the reason for the indifferent attitude adopted by her. In the case of Priti Patel, from being a backbencher MP in March 2014, she became the Right Honourable on 15th July 2014, as Exchequer Secretary to the Treasury, followed by a promotion on 11th May 2015 as a Minister of State for Employment. Later, she rose further to higher levels in public office as Secretary of State for International Development on 14th July 2016, but 'forced to resign' on 8th November 2017 in an undignified manner, for misconduct in public office, only to make a comeback within two years to an even higher role as the Home Secretary on 24th July 2019, because past conduct or performance does not affect politicians or hinder their promotion prospects, unlike the ordinary public in everyday jobs. She was handsomely rewarded by Boris Johnson when he became Prime Minister for her loyalty during the Brexit campaign led by him. My experience highlights that as a backbencher MP, Priti Patel was prepared to take up any cause to get into the limelight and seen to be doing something prominent. However once promoted, her priorities changed for her self-serving interests and she sang from the same hymn book as all the other politicians. The dates of her promotion coincide when she lost interest in the plight of newsagent and newspaper wholesale monopoly, so this was no longer her top priority. So, a mere mortal such as I, has no chance of ever hearing from the Right Honourable Priti Patel ever again. After all she was a politician, and her self-serving interests came first, and just like leopards, they do not change their spots.

I suppose experiences like this, and many others may have played a crucial part in my political awakening, later to stand for elections to serve public duty and restore trust in democracy. What is so disheartening is that nothing has changed, in spite of concerns raised in the past by other politicians, and recently by Priti Patel, a senior government politician making pledges to address the monopoly enjoyed by newspaper wholesalers. The House of Commons Hansard of 19th March 2014 has an official record of the parliamentary speech given by her, where she says that "the wholesalers' controls of the newspaper supply chain, and their vice-like grip on independent newsagents can only be described as a near monopoly." She went on to say "I make it my business to visit many independent shops, particularly newsagents, and I always ask about the number of newspapers they are selling. I remember when I was a child, the bundles of our Sunday newspapers being enormous. We were dealing with hundreds and hundreds of newspapers on a weekend alone," but she went on to say "that really the landscape has changed completely," she was conveying this was due to the drop in sales. Her eloquent speech now just seems like an echo of words, they mean nothing, just empty promises, because her priorities have changed to self-serving interests and ego. Is it any wonder trust in politicians is at its lowest ebb?

Yet again, I was not going to be discouraged and continued to persevere, when I felt it was appropriate to exercise my democratic right. It was in light of the announcement that Eric Pickles, the Secretary of State for Local Government and Communities had written to Muslim leaders, asking them to do more work to root out extremists. David Cameron followed with his statement that everybody needs to help tackle the problem of radicalisation. I wrote to Jonathan Lord on 20th January 2015 (letter 49).

> 'I would like to remind you that it was an insult to law abiding Muslims, like myself and many others, when you and David Cameron should know it is not true that Muslims have not offered to help, when I have personally tried many times to offer help to find solutions. What can Muslims do when Mr Cameron, his office or a constituent MP has no appetite or time to listen to the voice of ordinary people, or as matter of common courtesy even acknowledge their letters'?

I once again attached letters written over the years, and requested Jonathan Lord to bring them to the attention of David Cameron and Eric Pickles. Like before, I heard nothing more from him.

Theresa May would be the fifth PM that I wrote to on 14th July 2016 (letter 50). After congratulating her I wrote:

> 'Your speech was moving and very eloquent. It was full of political convictions and vision to build a union, not just between the four nations of the UK, but all of our citizens - every one of us - whoever we are, and wherever we are from. It is important for ethnic communities to become an integral part of the mainstream, and that your vision gives hope based on fairness for the good of all the people, irrespective of creed, class and race. Despite well-meant initiatives from successive governments, sectors of ethnic people feel treated as second class citizens. However, it is equally important for ethnic communities to realise that it works both ways, and by becoming an integral part of the UK they will not get easily swayed or fall victim to the tiny minority with an unscrupulous agenda, who promote and preach racial, political or religious hatred. I

pray to God to give you strength to govern people, to lead a prosperous life in peace in the UK, Commonwealth and worldwide'.

I also copied my letter to Jonathan Lord to keep him in the loop. I received a reply (letter 51) from an unnamed Correspondence Officer, thanking me for my letter to the PM. It also said that my letter has been forwarded to the Department for Communities and Local Government, as they have the responsibility for the matters raised. Then I received a standard band aid bureaucratic reply from the Department for Communities and Local Government, informing me of government initiatives that have invested millions in community projects. I heard nothing further on the subject.

Just after a month I wrote again to Theresa May again on 28th August 2016 (letter 52).

> 'I would first like to apologise for taking the liberty to encroach on your valuable time, but felt it was necessary to write with reference to the launch of the 'Race Audit of Public Services' on 27th August 2016. I hope on this occasion, unlike your predecessors that valuable contributions from ordinary people from all backgrounds will be heard and allowed to engage. In the past, it has become fashionable to address concerns, with complex expensive policy initiatives to absolve responsibilities, instead of a simple and less expensive transparent pragmatic approach. In the process, millions of pounds have been squandered and failed to achieve the desired objectives to enhance social mobility and integration. We need practical initiatives to tackle radicalisation, Islamophobia and other discrimination, by engaging people at a grass roots level, which would help to prevent individuals getting swayed easily by bigots or groups, acting as gatekeepers with their own unscrupulous agenda(s)'.

I gave a salient summary to underline interrelated areas that needed to be considered within the context of the 'Race Audit', and again, copied my letter to Jonathan Lord. As before, I got a reply (letter 53) from an unnamed Correspondence Officer, thanking me for my letter. It also said my letter had been forwarded to the Cabinet Office, because they have the responsibility for the raised matters. I heard nothing further from the Cabinet Office or Jonathan Lord. I persevered despite more failures. I was not going to give up, especially now with the launch of the 'Race Audit' on 27th August 2016. Maybe, I felt 'third time lucky', but I will go further, it could have been my continued optimism that one day I would be heard, and my efforts will come to fruition. Whatever it maybe, I was extremely exuberant and full of hope by the launch of the 'Race Audit'. I felt at long last the political leaders were beginning to show greater commitment, conviction and empathy, with a realistic approach to address the underlying root causes undermining social harmony and social mobility. Something Theresa May's predecessors tried to achieve, but failed to accomplish to find solutions to the same age-old problems. Regardless of the main gist of promises by Theresa May's predecessors victory speeches, they were no different from hers, except for the choice of words. Unfortunately, I found out later that even her pledges failed to see the light of day, before she got evicted from Downing Street. This would not be for the last time either, because the public would hear similar pledges repeated once again using different word choices with greater bluster with the same underlying trend uttered during the 'second coming' of Boris Johnson on 13th December 2019. We can only hope we have better luck this time with him.

Once again, I decided to write to Theresa May on 14th October 2016 (letter 54). In the letter I asked,

> 'Why are we addressing the same issues over and over again pledged over the last two decades ago by your predecessors that it now requires a 'Race Audit'? This shows past initiatives have failed. If anything, we need to ask why, despite years of government policy initiatives, projects and grants, we are still faced with the same old problems, such as Islamophobia, discrimination, radicalisation, hate crimes and other burning injustices? Is it because past policy initiatives, instead of fixing root causes with a pragmatic approach, have often been a 'catch-up' exercise, or have they been just rhetoric? Like many ordinary British people, ethnic and non-ethnic alike, whether Muslim or non-Muslim, I am equally concerned with what is said, not said, done or not done in the name of religion and democracy. We cannot afford to discard lightly the public's disenchantment with the 'establishment' seen during the EU referendum, as well a surge in UKIP right wing political extremism and turmoil in the Labour party. I am pleading with you to give me one opportunity to elaborate in just one area, which requires harmonising of laws to look at viability, implementation and credibility of my proposals. For example, how to tackle forced marriages and women's rights without compromising UK culture or faith traditions, before considering other areas. Tackling forced marriages will help address women's rights, to protect vulnerable women, and encourage their involvement at the grass roots level. The government has nothing to lose, but a lot to gain at no extra cost'.

I also mentioned about my previous two attempts of helping with such issues, and hoped that the letter would not once again fall on deaf ears with a standard generic response with an advice to visit a government website for more details. I concluded that on this occasion, I was optimistic, and that with the esteemed support of Jonathan Lord, who I had copied into the email, I would not be disappointed and shunned by her advisors. Again, I heard nothing further.

I decided to write to Jonathan Lord on 14th October 2016 (letter 55). In my letter, I requested if he would make representation on my behalf, and enclosed a copy of my letter written to Theresa May. I received a reply (letter 56) from him saying he has passed my letter to the PM's office, but that I should not expect a miracle, as I am not going to hear from her since she has a busy schedule. Instead a staff member will consider my letter very carefully; making sure it is passed onto the most relevant person. That said, I heard nothing further, not even an unsigned post card from the Direct Communication Office in Downing Street. I wonder how quickly I would have heard if I had enclosed a cheque with a large sum in my letter to the PM, as a donation to the Tory party. The reader will note the dilemma I have faced over the years when I have written to PMs. All efforts ignored, except on rare occasions for a one-line reply when I have sought MPs support, ignored or informed not to expect a response from the PM, because of their busy schedule.

All I can say, I cannot be accused of not trying my best. It is because I long for the day when fellow human beings can live in social harmony, while being able to celebrate their differences, including their religions. We have all got to find a way to live together in harmony. I felt the events leading to the 2016 EU referendum, and the fallout afterwards needed to be discussed in an open manner, in the interest of the country as a whole. Like the majority, I had also voted to leave in the 2016 referendum. My decision was more to do with my allegiance to the Commonwealth, and not the 'Little England' vision of the European Research Group made up entirely of Tory EU rebels. Once again, I made another concerted effort and wrote to Jonathan Lord on 13th November 2016 (letter 57), as I knew he was a leave supporter too. Not only because of that, but as his constituent, to listen to my less costly pragmatic ideas within the context to enhance social harmony and mobility, and copied my letter to Theresa May.

'We need real democracy, hope, justice and fairness to reflect the expectations of the people in the 21st century, not the same old politics of divide and rule, money talks, contempt, apathy and fear. I am aware that the PM has a busy diary, but I was optimistic that with your esteemed intervention I stood a better chance to get heard by Theresa May's team of experts. As your constituent, I had hoped to be given a degree of opportunity, as it takes a lot of time and effort for an ordinary person to express thoughts on paper with no support. This shows genuine conviction and not an obsession to write for the sake of it. Most of all, it feels painful when ignored or given patronising replies. Like many ordinary folks without media, lobbying or financial clout, it is disheartening when genuine efforts to engage in the democratic process gets discarded lightly by the establishment. We have witnessed social disharmony, allowing 'radicalised individuals' to capitalise and claim democratic victory, with undertones of religious and racial hatred. I hope I get an opportunity to make a positive contribution to enhance social harmony and mobility, and I appreciate your advice given in the letter of 30th November 2010 'to stand for election or get involved...' But, I would rather do so through the existing democratic process. Also, I do not have the financial backing for election expenses, nor am I a career politician; although I passionately believe in the importance of thinking in terms of 'US' and not 'THEM'; whereby communities are at ease living in harmony, with mutual respect, not alienation, mistrust, or get swayed by the tiny minority with unscrupulous tactics, preaching religious, racial and political hatred based on prejudice'.

On one of the rare occasions I heard from Jonathan Lord on 23rd November 2016 (letter 58). He referred to a reply from the minister, no name mentioned; he had read and claimed was sympathetic and straightforward. As I had not received the minister's reply, I requested him to send me a copy. He categorically refused, stating:

'I will not waste my staff's time digging out old letters from you'.

I wonder why he objected so strongly to send me a copy, after all, it would not have been that long ago, so could not have got lost, or filed in the wrong place. He continued,

'Please note that I and my very small team would be very grateful if you would only contact me very, very occasionally from now on, and preferably only if a NEW issue arises that you feel compelled to raise. This will then enable me to serve all my other 73,000 constituents and their families properly; I am sure you understand'.

But he then added,

'P.S. To my previous email, if you do have practical policy solutions to prevent radicalisation and promote social harmony, of course I would be very happy to receive this information. I would read such a letter or email very carefully indeed, and send it to the most relevant minister for their proper consideration and response'.

As before, I got a reply (letter 59) from an unnamed Correspondence Officer, thanking me for sending a copy of the letter I had written on 13th November to the PM, Theresa May.

I replied immediately in response to yet another ultimatum given by Jonathan Lord not to bother him. However, on this occasion he did not tell me to stand for elections or join a protest group.

Letter 60 - 24th November 2016 to Jonathan Lord, I thanked him and said,

> 'I have noted the tone of the contents, and assure you as my constituent MP that I will not even contact you 'very, very occasionally from now on', so you can serve the other 72,999 constituents and their families properly. I apologise for wasting your time, never mind my own time, and my selfless efforts at no cost to the tax payer. If governments of all political parties were serious about social harmony and mobility, then why during the PM's speech outside 10 Downing Street from the late Baroness Thatcher to Mrs May on 14 July 2014 after the election victory is reference made in one way or other to address the same old issues related to social harmony, mobility and racial hatred....If progress had already been made, why would they all make it a top priority'?

I thought Jonathan Lord's attitude towards me was inappropriate, bearing in mind he chose to be a career politician and serve public duty, for which he was handsomely paid for by the tax payer, as well as enjoying other perks. I was merely stating the facts that politicians of all parties, whether in government or opposition are cynical, not only during election time, but also afterwards, because of the disharmony and accusations witnessed by the public in the House of Commons. One would expect agreement, if divisions between various classes did not exist, and Mrs May, like previous PMs, would not have to make it a top priority in her inaugural speech on the steps of Downing Street.

After nearly a year, I decided to reach out once again as Jonathan Lord's 1 of 73,000 constituents, and wrote to him despite his blunt message to only contact him 'very, very occasionally'. In the twelve months break when I last contacted him, we had a snap election on 8th June 2017, which I contested, as I felt it was the only option left for me to gain access to democracy, and as expected I lost. The reason for writing was because of the Channel 4 programme 'The Truth about Muslim Marriage' shown on 21st November 2017. Although, I was not expecting a reply, or even for him to make any representation on my behalf, I just wanted to keep him informed.

Letter 65 - 22nd November 2017 to Jonathan Lord to alleviate suffering,

'I am writing as it may affect some of your remaining 72,999 Woking constituents, and alleviate suffering for them. I draw your attention to my letters to Theresa May, where I had covered the actual concerns raised in the Channel 4 programme, where I offered solutions. If the lawmakers are serious, it is still not too late to tackle women's rights, not only in the context of forced marriages, but generally speaking. We must ask the right questions, as to why some sectors of society still remain affected, Muslims and non-Muslims alike. Also, we need real life pro-active measures with less costly solutions, by listening to the public, not complex expensive solutions to simple issues. The suffering faced by women has nothing to do with Islam, but more to do with the self-appointed custodians of Islam, who have their own agendas, and our politicians have no qualms selling arms to them, allowing these hypocrites to flourish and rule unhindered. We can announce many expensive 'Race Audits' public inquiries and other initiatives to learn lessons after the damage has been done, but in reality, we are just wasting valuable public money feathering lawyer's pockets, who exploit loopholes, without serving main objectives'.

I was pleased to receive a response (letter 66) from Jonathan Lord. However, I would like to point out that since contesting the general election on 8th June 2017, and subsequent local elections, his attitude towards me, when I have written to him has been courteous and appreciative, worthy of mentioning. He replied with a slightly longer reply, not short and curt as before, but I hasten to add, I did not write that often since that fateful reply of 23rd November 2016 (letter 58), and the jury is still out on whether he has actually made practical representation on my behalf. From his reply, he had made no serious representation on the specific issue of forced marriages, but instead made a general one-word statement.

I therefore replied to him on 7th February 2018 (letter 67), thanking him for enclosing the generic reply from the Home Office Minister, Victoria Atkins, saying,

'I am sorry to say that the reply did not address the actual problems related to forced marriages, other than list costly long-winded initiatives. In reality the initiatives are not working, because if they did, then women would not be suffering. What I am proposing is not new legislation, but simple solutions with right balances and checks to make effective use of existing laws, and less costly initiatives to empower women. We are celebrating one hundred years when women were given the right to vote, and let us hope we do not have to wait another one hundred years to tackle pertinent issues affecting their everyday life'.

I heard nothing further! All along I have never been under any illusion or deluded to think that I would succeed in changing anything. I only wrote when I felt it was necessary to express real-life concerns, and if possible, help alleviate hardships, even in the tiniest possible way. I believed that the elected politicians considered it was their responsibility to serve public duty in the best interests of the people, and only they could make a real difference to people's lives.

It was due to another scandal that led me to write to Jonathan Lord again. This time in the wake of the Windrush scandal and hostile Home Office environment, which I had raised with him many times before, based on first-hand experience with my dealings with them (Home Office).

It was now over a year when I last wrote to Jonathan Lord, but this time I thought it was important to highlight my concerns in letter 68 on 26th April 2018 to him.

'I would like to mention that the PM and Home Secretary are in denial when they claim the Windrush scandal has nothing to do with those immigrants who are in the UK legally. This is not true, because at the end of the day, all immigrants face the same consequences, because it is the word 'immigrant' not 'illegal immigrant' that sticks in the public's minds. I want to remind you about the 2013 campaign 'Go Home' vans with billboard signs by the Home Office, under the then Home Secretary, none other than Theresa May herself, now the PM. It is the ethnic British immigrants and our UK born children who have to face hostility, unlike the non-ethnic immigrants from Australia, New Zealand, or Canada. At the same time, we have to be conscious that ethnic immigrants will get blamed or singled out for shortages in public services, or civil unrest. Also, no amount of compensation paid to the victims for the suffering caused by failed government policies will bring back lost lives and the opportunities they may have missed in their life. Above all, the money for this is coming out of tax payer's pockets, not the politician's, and cuts to public services without any detriment to politicians for their mistakes. I hope my efforts will not get ignored, although I am not expecting a reply or anything good to happen, but please do not ignore the concerns which I have raised consistently over the years'.

I received a prompt reply dated 27th April 2018 (letter 69). Jonathan Lord was very apologetic about the anxiety and confusion, and was sympathetic. He thought that the officials had handled this matter, particularly in relation to its treatment of these entirely blameless and hardworking citizens, in an utterly shameful manner. He listed the steps the government has taken, which I thought was futile. As usual, it was after the damage had been inflicted, as politicians were not listening to the people's pleas when needed. He agreed with me and the PM that there was no place whatsoever for discrimination of any kind, whether on the basis of colour, creed, sexuality or gender, against citizens with a bona fide right to be and remain in the UK. I responded without delay.

Letter 70 - 27th April 2018 to Jonathan Lord, and I was frank in my response,

> 'Your reply offers no assurances to a constituent with a 'legal' immigrant background, especially when we can see how those bona fide 'Windrush generation' suffered, even after half a century of making the UK their home. Perhaps you feel sorry, as you had voted for some of the most draconian immigration laws to be passed, when Theresa May was the Home Secretary, without realising the harm it would inflict on legal immigrants like myself, and many of your other constituents. It is a symptomatic lack of understanding and empathy of what 'legal' immigrants actually have to endure in real life, because of the hostile environment created by the government. Moreover, blaming officials is like passing the buck, and an easy 'get of jail card'. This is not a game of monopoly. It is not officials, but the government who decide policies, and blaming them is not the answer, but an excuse to wriggle out of responsibility. The specific examples I have given are not unique to me or uncommon'.

What I was trying to highlight to him was that it was not real-life difficulties faced by 'illegal' but 'legal' immigrants like myself, and the children born in the UK with the correct paperwork, and it makes no difference even when a formal complaint is raised, because that just gets ignored and falls on deaf ears, with a bureaucratic response. The 'Windrush' fiasco, like every other major crisis does not happen overnight, but from small beginnings, when pleas of help are ignored, ending up in disaster and suffering. There is no reason for him to feel sorry about the Windrush saga, but it would be reassuring if politicians offered to look into the issues when raised, so they do not get brushed under the carpet, and ignored.

Yet again, I was pleased to receive a prompt reply from Jonathan Lord on 2nd May 2018 (letter 71). He thanked me for my comments, which he said he would certainly keep in mind over the coming weeks and months. Saying:

> 'There is obviously work to be done around immigration at the Home Office, but I am delighted by the promotion of Sajid Javid to Home Secretary. You will be aware Sajid has been very critical of the Home Office over the Windrush issue, and brings to his new role his own experiences of emigration to the UK from Pakistan, as a child in the 1960s and 1970s. I believe that his promotion is a sign that the

government is aware of the need to tackle this problem urgently and sensitively. I am also confident that he is the right man for this job, and I look forward to supporting him in his efforts to make sure that the Home Office works as fairly and effectively as possible, for both the Windrush generation and for everyone else. With regards to the lives of everyone who is in the UK legally, either as a full UK citizen, or a highly-valued immigrant, I would point out that we have very strong anti-discrimination laws here, which say that everyone should be treated with the same level of respect, in line with the fact that we are all equal before the law. The rise of Sajid Javid from the son of a bus driver, to one of the great offices of state, is a wonderful metaphor, I think, for the social mobility that we should all wish to see. Thank you very much once again for taking the time to bring your thoughts to my attention. I presume we may see each other at the count on Friday'.

Letter 72 - 5th May 2018 to Jonathan Lord, thanking and confirming that I was indeed on time at the count on Friday, but that we may have missed each other, as I had to leave early, since I had prior engagements before his timely appearance.

'I am so glad that after all these years you have realised my intentions to reach out to cross-party politicians, which is based on genuine convictions to make a small, but positive contribution as a British citizen, with an immigrant background from the Commonwealth. It is not the fault of civil servants, because they serve and politicians decide, as late Baroness Thatcher revered by the Tories had said. Without the political will and empathy of real-life experiences, Sajid Javid or Mrs May will not be able to tackle the problem, even if Sajid Javid happens to be the son of a bus driver. By the government changing words from 'hostile' to 'compliant' is just meaningless, because the term 'illegal' immigrant is a red herring, diverting attention from failures in government policies. Immigrants are used as cheap fodder to win votes, by pandering to the right-wing press and political groups'.

I went onto focus on a number of points for his consideration that I had revealed before, such as radicalisation, social harmony, forced marriages and discrimination. I suppose I did not hear from him because he had decided to conclude the matter.

It was not long before I had cause to write to him yet again, due to certain concerns I had raised over the years, which were now openly transparent in the form of Islamophobia in the Tory Party. I reminded him I had raised similar concerns since 2000, faced by British citizens of ethnic origin in their everyday life, and the specific allegations made against the Tory party were not new, but long overdue.

Letter 73 - 31st May 2018 to Jonathan Lord

> 'The Tory party's response citing the recent promotion of Salim Javid as the first Muslim Home Secretary does not mean that Islamophobia does not exist within the party. Let us not get carried away by Salim Javid's promotion as an end to all our problems, whilst ignoring many other injustices. It is worth bearing in mind that Sajid Javid on many occasions has maintained he is a Muslim in name only, and until recently did not openly speak of his Pakistani heritage. Maybe he thought it might hinder his political and other careers, but now seems fine to capitalise on this by publicising it at every opportunity, to make the most of his ethnic heritage. I hope politicians will refrain from using ethnic British citizens as cheap fodder when it suits to attract votes, as it has detrimental effects in their everyday life. I would also like to remind you of the dog whistle politics adopted by the ex-PM David Cameron at the Prime Minister's Questions in his support of Tory Mayoral candidate, Mr Zac Goldsmith, by attacking Mr Sadiq Khan'.

I concluded that the country cannot progress by alienating sections of the population and Islamophobia, a form of discrimination, just like antisemitism in the Labour Party that must also be rooted out, and that the Tory Party should not remain in denial by claiming a few changes here and there as being a victory. Once again, I was pleased to receive a prompt reply dated 1st June 2018 (letter 74) from Jonathan Lord. He thanked me again for my thoughts in this and previous emails of 5th May (letter 72), which he had read carefully and noted the contents. However, I was not at all surprised by his reply when he conveyed that,

> 'I do not accept all what you say in this latest email, and I think that the cynical and unacceptable way you speak about Sajid Javid (and his assumed motivations), perhaps betrays a wider animus you might have against the Tory Party. Locally, I am delighted that a quarter of Conservative Borough Councillors in Woking are of Muslim or Black and Minority Background (BME), and this is also true of a quarter of our Tory Woking County Councillors. This is, I believe, a much larger figure than the actual percentage of Muslim and BME voters locally. The Tories also have more Muslim and BME councillors locally, than all the other local parties put together, and in my first year as an MP in 2010, Woking had the first ever Muslim mayor of Woking, who was also a Tory, and gave this wonderful 'first' a high billing in my maiden election victory speech'.

As expected, Jonathan Lord in his reply was extremely defensive, and strongly disagreed that Islamophobia exists in the Tory Party. All I can say is that instead of tinkering with a general inquiry into prejudices within the Tory Party, the party would have nothing to worry by holding an independent inquiry into Islamophobia, which is also what the ex-Chair Baroness Sayeeda Warsi has been calling for. In fact, I would say the same about antisemitism within the Labour Party. Politicians ought to stop kicking the can down the road, keeping their heads buried in the sand, hoping that by ignoring the problem it will go away. It will not! If anything, it will only get worse. Just like ignoring a final payment notice, does not mean that the debt will go away. He was also wrong to say in his reply (letter 74) that I have a 'wider animus against the Tory Party'. Because if he remembers, I have always been open and honest, and where appropriate given credit where credit was due. I have also been equally critical of Labour and LibDem politicians, including ethnic people and Muslim clerics. What Jonathan Lord conveniently forgets is that the Tory Party has been in government for the last ten years. They cannot keep blaming others for their policy failures and take credit for everything else, and ignore real-life concerns of ordinary people. Just like when they promised an end to austerity, but then we see a rise in homelessness, foodbanks and poverty. Especially when politicians constantly remind us that 'we are all in this together', and when the public try do to engage, are told everything is prefect, and they (the public) have got it all wrong.

I did not reply back, as I saw there was no point in doing so at this point. It is this sort of attitude of denial, which is at the root cause to the underlying issues facing social harmony, discrimination, radicalisation and social mobility, irrespective of creed or race. Whenever those who get called out for racism, politicians or public alike will try to wriggle out of the controversy, claiming "I am not a racist," since they know many BME people. Unfortunately, what they do not seem to realise is that knowing a BME is one thing, whilst living the life as one is another, which are two different issues. The matter of forced marriages surfaced again, when on 2nd January 2019 Sky News featured the findings of an investigation by the Times newspaper into the Foreign and Commonwealth Office, making forced marriage victims pay for their rescue. It revived my previous interest on the subject, despite failed past efforts when I tried to offer solutions to tackle the scourge of forced marriages, which Jonathan Lord and Theresa May ignored, except for a patronising reply from Victoria Atkins, raving about various government initiatives, the contents not even worth mentioning. Only to suffice again, and I would argue that if they are so good, why do women still suffer from it? I was not going to be deterred and immediately wrote to the Foreign Secretary, Jeremy Hunt. Of course, I was not expecting any response from him. It would be foolish of me to expect a reply when I was not even his constituent, not that it would have mattered, based on my experience with my own MP.

Letter 75 to Jeremy Hunt on the same day 2nd January 2019, after apologising for taking the liberty of writing directly to him as a non-constituent, I said:

> 'It was important to write to you because of the misery faced by the defenceless victims. The suffering that is taking place at this moment in time could have been alleviated, if my efforts had not been ignored and discarded lightly by Jonathan Lord and Theresa May. It would be my pleasure to forward the three letters subject to confirmation by your office to do so. These self-explanatory letters will give you a deeper insight that solutions do exist to tackle the misery faced by the victims of forced marriages'.

As expected, Jeremy Hunt's office did not reply, and I wrote to him again after waiting a month.

Letter 76 - 4th February 2019 to Jeremy Hunt, where I initially apologised and appreciated that he had a busy schedule, and did not expect him to reply personally, because unlike the ordinary public, politicians have staff at their disposal paid by the tax payer to help serve civic duty.

> 'In the current climate of the Brexit debate, the political class need to reflect more on their actions. May I remind you of what Kenneth Clarke, 'Father of the House', eloquently said during the Brexit debate on 29th January 2019, that "the political class need to be aware the public are looking at politicians with contempt, and if we are trying to restore confidence in our political system, and if current shambles continues, I hate to think where such behaviour will take us next in British democracy." I am not chasing unicorns, but believe real-life issues affecting ordinary people can be tackled. It just needs a realistic approach with the right checks and balance in government to alleviate the scourge of forced marriages and other atrocities. The victims should be left under no circumstances to face the future at the mercy of others to fend for themselves. I hope this time my efforts will not go to waste, and your office staff will not ignore my efforts blaming that the Foreign and Commonwealth Office receives thousands of letters and it would be impossible to reply to all'.

Regrettably, I did not even receive an acknowledgment as a matter of courtesy, not even a thank you postcard for taking the trouble of writing to him, with a rubberstamp signature. I remained undeterred and sent another reminder.

Letter 77- 4th April 2019 to Jeremy Hunt, this time I sent the letter to his constituency address to increase the chance of my letter being brought to his attention. I begged him, as a respected senior member of the government to listen to the real-life concerns and 'burning injustices' referred to by Theresa May on the steps of Downing Street that ordinary people were facing. I did not hear from his office, with another effort of mine ignored by the political class. The 'establishment' reigns supreme, despite pledges. So, I gave up!

After years of plotting, political chicanery, switching sides, fanning flames attacking minority groups and name calling, at long last Boris Johnson's dream as a five-year-old to become "king of the world" came true, when he achieved his ambition by getting elected as leader of the Tory Party on 23rd July 2019, and replaced Theresa May as PM after playing his part to undermine her during the Brexit debate, despite also making policy blunders as the Foreign Secretary.

I wrote a detailed five-page open letter dated 9th August 2019. In my letter 80, I was forthright and relayed,

> 'I hope with great respect that what I have to say to you, you will take in good spirit the views of a law-abiding ethnic British citizen of Muslim origin, whose loyalty like many Muslims, is foremost to the UK and social harmony. Now that you have got elected by Tory Party members, how will you look into the eyes of the minority groups of ethnic people you have attacked with dishonest fiction and name calling during your career in politics and journalism? Also, how will you now look into the eyes of over two million British Muslims without prejudice, or how can British Muslims trust you as their PM, when you have attacked them with remarks inciting hatred towards them? The innocent people you like to attack cannot reply back, because the very 'free press' will not give them time of the day or an opportunity to pen an answer to your vile and puerile claims, despite living in the same liberal democracy. As a journalist, one would expect you should not run scared, but first check your facts by engaging in debates with other scholars to allay your fears instead of spouting drivel by hiding behind press articles or speech lecterns'.

I went on to question the content of his essay titled 'And Then Came the Muslims', where he wrote 'there must be something about Islam that indeed helps to explain why there was no rise of the bourgeoisie, no liberal capitalism and therefore no spread of democracy in the Muslim world'. I counteracted his claims with a long list of facts. I finished by saying that we all have a lot to offer, Muslims and non-Muslims alike, especially during these challenging times ahead after Brexit, and we can do this without adopting the pound-shop populist divisive politics of Donald Trump, by fanning the flames of Islamophobia to propel grubby electoral ambitions.

As expected, I did not hear from his office. I wrote again on 12th August 2019 (letter 81) to thank him for his '*Eid ul Adha*' message that was circulated on social media. I said that,

> 'Your message would have gone a long way to build bridges if broadcasted on national TV, as well as the national press, where Muslims are constantly subjected to negative profiling in one form or another. Derogatory comments have not helped, but each time exposes Muslims to even more racial hatred and ridicule from the extremists looking for scapegoats to vent their anger after reading such articles. In the spirit of your '*Eid ul Adha*' message, I beg you to listen to the ordinary people, Muslims and non-Muslims if we really want to tackle racial hatred, social harmony, discrimination, and radicalisation to build bridges across the social divide'.

I received an unsigned reply on 11th September 2019 (letter 82), acknowledging my letter on behalf of the PM. It is either an irony or just pure coincidence that the final communication date was 11th September 2019, from the Direct Correspondence Unit on behalf of the present PM, Boris Johnson. It was twenty years ago before 9/11 on 4th April 2000 (letter 3), when I wrote to Tony Blair to highlight various concerns. Unhappily, nothing has changed; I was ignored and treated with contempt then as I am today, and the problems remain the same, and in some cases have got much worse. I cannot say whether it has made any difference writing my letters, except I have no regrets. All I can say is that at least I tried to serve public duty, although not in an official capacity, but as an ordinary person, my record speaks for itself.

On 18th September 2019, Boris Johnson posted on twitter that "I've been PM for 57 days, part of my job is to talk to people on the ground, and listen to what they tell me about the big problems, and it doesn't matter whether we agree or not," when he was confronted by the father of a sick child about cuts to the NHS by the Conservative government. I felt encouraged by his positive attitude and decided to write letter 83 dated 19th September 2019. I said:

> 'I am encouraged by your tweet, but at the same feel despondent because it contradicts my experience when I wrote an open letter to you on 9th August 2019, and your office did not even have the courtesy to acknowledge it'.

As expected, I heard nothing further.

I have highlighted the numerous times over the years, since 1997 when I have brought up wide-ranging concerns to the attention of five PMs, cross-party political leaders, MPs, government ministers and eminent people, and the political class have not bothered to reply, let alone listen seriously. I have further counted that in all, but for a few instances, I have always been ignored or shunned, very often not even as a matter of courtesy sent an acknowledgement, let alone a reply. A few times I have been given a long-winded patronising reply. I harbour no resentment, just twenty years of frustration by not being given a chance to change life for the better, saving disharmony and suspicion, as well as hatred between and amongst communities. I feel that apart from being denied my democratic right by my constituent MP, who is paid by the tax payer, including myself, my contributions would have helped address real life issues affecting not only his 72,999 constituents, but others nationally. Occasionally I continued to draw attention of cross-party MPs on pertinent issues to benefit others, because I thought it was improper for an MP to shun responsibility. Meanwhile I was left with the following three dilemmas as 1 of 73,000 Woking constituents, either forfeit my democratic right, follow what I was told by my MP and not bother him, or to move home to another constituency, hoping for a more sympathetic MP, or stand for elections, which is what I decided to do in June 2017.

Regardless of all the negative experiences, it would have been easy for me to give up. Even though I am not a career politician or a party activist, I have always believed in public duty. I also feel that as an ordinary person, it is important to exercise my democratic right like any other citizen, through the established channels. I feel privileged that I have been able to persevere, in spite of all the obstacles, and that I did not get deterred, if anything, it made me more determined to do something. This is because I do not want to be robbed of my democratic right. That is what has kept me going all these years, even at a personal cost and sacrifice. I did not take a defeatist attitude then, and will not now.

10

Lawmakers, Double Standards and Hypocrisy

In any society or country, however big or small, influential or not, a culture of double standards and hypocrisy does not help build confidence and respect. The ordinary people get the impression that there is 'one rule for one, and another for everybody else' when the 'establishment' themselves break the laws, or only speak out when they fall foul of the laws they have made. In similar instances of injustices, an ordinary individual or a family would have to endure so much heartache, delays, obstacles or left on their own to seek justice, whether it is a car accident, murder inquiry, miscarriage of justice, compensation, extradition, illegal imprisonment or even a big public scandal like Grenfell, Windrush, Hillsborough and many more. It does not help when double standards and hypocrisy is blatantly obvious in high-profile murder cases like that of Saudi Arabian, Adnan Khashoggi's stitched-up trial, despite the US, Britain and the West knowing about it, and did not seem bothered about human rights violations, because they did not want to jeopardise their lucrative arms exports to Saudi Arabia. So, what chance of justice can mere mortals expect? For example, the many recorded or unrecorded less high-profile cases, such as 'ethnic cleansing', rape, child abuse, civil rights etc. do not see the light of day, because of lack of media interest, until the situation worsens.

It is true that natural disasters, political crisis and conflicts have been going on for centuries, and such events will continue in some shape or form. It is also true that political deception amongst politicians is nothing new, as this has also been going on for centuries. But, not to such a level, because it has now spread like cancer, with politicians believing that making laws puts them above the law. What is new and significant today is the present suffering, disputes and disasters occurring in full view of the public, due to the advancement in technology that allows what is happening to be instantly scrutinised. In the past, everything was covered-up and confined to the privileged few and their cohorts, and by the time others found out, the privileged few and their cohorts had left, resigned, retired or even passed away. Today, we are now able to witness the actual abuse of political power, lies, and greed within our public institutions that is occurring at a greater pace than in the past. On one hand, the public are told that law enforcement is the centrepiece of a democratic government, yet on the other, when it affects the political class, they go to extreme lengths to pick and choose which laws to respect. Such abuse of democracy is now played out in the full glare of the social media and 24-hour TV news channels, which does not set a good example for the public. Politicians get accused, taken to court for breaking laws passed by the Mother of Parliament. Politics has sunk to an all-time low, and become vile and unscrupulous. What sort of example are we setting the future generations, and those countries we are trying to encourage to embrace democracy?

Democracy should not be about people joining this or that protest group or political party, but should be more about making politicians accountable for their actions to restore trust, not make a mockery of democracy and public institutions. They are very happy to be in charge and enjoy the perks, yet when they get found out, they are quick to abandon the sinking ship in the midst of a mess they created, leaving the public to face the consequences of their actions. We have also witnessed similar shenanigans from councillors at the local level playing party politics, at the expense of the taxpayer for self-serving interests, by voting or abstaining against motions, as if politics is a game, instead of serving public duty, for which they are paid well for.

In 2019, in order to get elected, we have seen our politicians stop at nothing, even if it means breaking the laws of the land and telling porky pies. They have led the nation into a constitutional crisis to woo voters with a populist agenda, pedalling insulting and divisive statements, like 'people versus parliament'[7] and 'enemies of the people'.[8] Such selfish behaviour of pitting one group against another only serves to cause more resentment and further alienation. It also encourages the public to emulate such behaviour. Whatever the political belief, one should set a good example for others to follow and make a difference, but to do that, politics needs to open up more to the ordinary public, to reflect empathy of real-life issues and burning injustices, not just speech-making, then

---

[7] Financial Times: 'people vs parliament' election 26th September 2019 https://www.ft.com/content/5cd109c6-df82-11e9-9743-db5a370481bc
[8] Daily Mail: 'enemies of the people' 4th November 2016 https://www.dailymail.co.uk/news/article-3903436/Enemies-people-Fury-touch-judges-defied-17-4m-Brexit-voters-trigger-constitutional-crisis.html

to go back on what they said after they have been elected. Instead, modern-day politics has become confined to self-serving party interests. The job of an MP or a local councillor is no longer a voice for the people, such as putting national and local interests first, but more to do with the fear of de-selection, or missing out on a plum position, by not sucking-up to the party line. It seems when privileged individuals get caught with skeletons in their cupboards and face prosecutions, for example tax evasion, sex scandals or other malpractices, it affects them less than the average person. They even manage to make a comeback to politics if found guilty, or avoid prosecution, by hiring the best lawyers that money can buy; whereas, the ordinary people, without the financial clout, face the full consequences of breaking the law. In fact, politicians still manage to get elected into high public office, despite major doubts about trust that makes big news headlines, even during an election campaign. The powerful establishment elite when caught in the 'tangled web of deceit', without shame or remorse tell any lie(s) they can contort to spin their way out of trouble, treating the public as mindless idiots. It has become normal for politicians to lie without flinching an eyelid, but the lawmakers are wrong, because all they have succeeded in doing is to make people feel more disenfranchised by their arrogant and contemptuous behaviour. Equally worrying is that with such blemishes on one's character, which everyone knows about, what sort of example does this set for the country's reputation? Those in high public office should surely be squeaky clean to some extent, and not to be prone to legal challenges and blackmail that may affect national security.

Lawmakers are quick to react to avert crises, especially in the middle of a general election if it will affect their chances of getting re-elected. Prior to announcing the general election date in November 2019, Downing Street took prompt emergency action to head off winter pressures in the NHS, amid growing fears that a healthcare crisis could derail the election campaign. It led the PM to hold regular meetings with the head of NHS England. This was because of the mounting evidence of long delays, due to an acute shortage of doctors and nurses, and long waiting times at A&E and GP surgeries. In the process, the British Medical Association issued a highly critical statement, saying it should not take a general election to prompt the government to act, and warn the public that the NHS was in a 'perpetual state of crisis.[9] What this shows is one of many similar examples of hypocrisy, when in power, successive political leaders do not pay much attention or care to listen to the real-life consequences of their policy decisions on the ordinary public, which they have control over.

The same can be seen in other public services too, where the public have seen a drop in standards, which is a direct consequence of ill thought short-term knee-

---

[9] The Guardian: 'General election: Tories act to prevent NHS crisis hitting poll hopes' 2nd November 2019
https://www.theguardian.com/society/2019/nov/02/tories-act-to-prevent-nhs-crisis-hitting-election-hopes

jerking solutions. In the process, this is just exacerbating the situation for the future, costing more to put right, whether in the NHS, education, crime, welfare or housing. What is equally baffling is where do politicians suddenly find the money to fulfil these pledges, which have been neglected over the years. Here are a few examples from a long list of eye watering promises: £3b to farmers, 40 new NHS hospitals, £95m for regeneration of Northern towns, £14bn boost to schools, build new railway lines, 20,000 police officers - on top of wasting taxpayer's money on cancelled ferry contracts (£50m), dredging Ramsgate harbour, lorry parks and more. Not to be outdone, Labour pledged free broadband and dental checks, a four-day week, to plant millions of trees, create green jobs, clean up the environment and much more! Regrettably, the lawmaker's enthusiasm and awareness of reality faced by the ordinary people, usually just lasts until Election Day. It is as plain as ABC that the political class are not bothered to honour the pledges they have made, as long as their interests to get elected are served. When the nation is faced with disasters like Covid-19, it is the public who pay for the lack of investment in the NHS and social care for short-term political gains affecting innocent lives, and billions of pounds wasted on emergency temporary measures costing the taxpayers, money which over the years could have been invested wisely. In the process, the frontline public service workers place their lives at risk, because of the shortage of Personal Protection Equipment and inadequate testing, due to inadequate planning. Although politicians tested without delays, minimising their risk or flouting the lockdown rules to suit them.

Hypocrisy has also become more noticeable amongst lawmakers when they become victim of the laws passed by them in parliament. Then they are very eager to criticise austerity, only to change their tune later on, when it affects them. The MP, Nigel Evans was quick to speak out after being cleared by the court, expressing regrets for supporting cuts to Legal Aid Sentencing and Punishment of Offenders Act (LASPO), which cost £130,000 to fund his defence, and he was shocked to realise he would not be able to recover the legal fees after his acquittal. He said, "If I had my time again, I would stand up and argue against the implementation of LASPO. It's wrong, completely wrong, to remove people's right to have legal representation, and now I've gone through this, I can see that clearly.

We're definitely talking about justice being denied, as a result of LASPO."[10,11] He went on to say, "My experience of being falsely accused, and losing my life

---

[10] The Guardian: It's completely wrong': falsely accused Tory MP attacks legal aid cuts 27th December 2018 https://www.theguardian.com/law/2018/dec/27/its-completely-wrong-falsely-accused-tory-mp-attacks-legal-aid-cuts

[11] Evening Standard: 'Nigel Evans: people cleared of crimes should have 'reasonable' legal costs paid back 14th April2014 https://www.standard.co.uk/news/politics/nigel-evans-people-cleared-of-crimes-should-have-reasonable-legal-costs-paid-back-9258768.html

savings to defend myself, proves that was a road to Damascus moment for me. I'm a changed person now, in terms of LASPO and sympathise with all those who now have to go through the legal system without expert help, support and advice." He added, "I'm not just talking about those accused in criminal courts like me, but everyone affected by LASPO. Such as, parents going through the family courts, tenants fighting landlords, patients fighting hospitals, and so on. LASPO is clearly not working. It needs to be overhauled." The MP's plight was quickly echoed by prominent MPs, as well as the Chairs of Home Affairs and Commons Justice Parliament Select Committees.[11,12] What this shows is that MPs are prepared to change their minds when it affects them. What about the effects on the public when the pendulum of thoughtless unnecessary cuts to public services gets swung too far, by voting in favour of short-sighted austerity policy decisions considered as needless expenditure taken on impulse, which happened in 2010 to cut down government budgets.

MPs see things somewhat differently when they have tested the effects of their own medicine. What they fail to grasp is that they are in a special position and have a voice in parliament to make changes that will help support the public. There are lots of ordinary people who have also gone through legal ordeals, charged or sought justice, and forced through the same heartache and stress, only to be found innocent or failed to seek justice after being through the mill. The ordinary public do not have a voice, and it is too late by the time their plight and pleas of help gets heard. Lawmakers are quick to claim foul play when they are affected, but do not raise an eyebrow when less high-profile people get affected by the ill thought laws passed by them! Are ordinary people not entitled to a review of the system at the lower end, so that they can also get justice and do not suffer unfairly, or their lives put at risk? Why should Chairs of Parliamentary Select Committees make calls for a review of laws, only when it applies to cases involving politicians, celebrities or the wealthy? There is nothing wrong with the idea of a review, because it is impossible to get legislation right first time, as the lawmakers will be quick to claim. Of course, no one disputes that! However, there should not be an outcry when MPs and celebrities fall victim. The opportunity to call for a parliamentary review must be applied equally across the spectrum, not only when it suits them.

It reflects strange and worrying times that our lawmakers support legislation on a whim, unaware of the consequences of their actions upon constituents or others, until they feel the first-hand effects of the laws that they had voted in favour of. In fact, most MPs lack empathy with the ordinary people, especially the disadvantaged, such as the poor, sick and disabled. They vote for self-serving party interests, not the people. What is more, when you hear them speak, they

---

[12] Mail on Line: 'Tory MP who spent his life savings defending himself against false rape claims calls for legal aid cuts to be reversed' 28 December 2018 https://www.joe.co.uk/news/nigel-evans-legal-aid-213654

give the impression they are an authority on the subject they are discussing, but in reality, it is just eloquent bluster of word twisting to stay in power. What the lawmaker should reflect on is that Nigel Evans, just like other MPs were content to vote in favour of the law. There is equally a huge catalogue of instances where people have been denied justice, because of cuts to the legal aid budget. Eminent barristers have raised concerns of how the cuts over the past decade have restricted access to funding in both the magistrate's and crown courts, affecting the masses, without any reservations from politicians, until it affects them.

I have already mentioned my two personal experiences to seek justice, and why I had to give up in my quest to bring the injustices I had suffered, not only by me, but also affecting many others out into the open, instead of getting brushed under the carpet. On both occasions, I had requested politicians to make representation to the Parliamentary Select Committee for an inquiry into the monopoly wholesaler, and workings of a public organisation with Priti Patel and Jonathan Lord, both falling on deaf ears, demonstrating that MPs should put themselves in the shoes of the public, and see how they would feel when affected by the decisions made by them, or when they deny their own constituents their rights, which happened in my case. MPs should not be in contempt of the democratic process, and should speak out when real-life injustices occur, not only when it affects them. It will serve well to be reminded of the footage from the newsreel documentary of Winston Churchill, weeping after he heard about the sinking of HMS Prince of Wales by the Japanese, which showed that when a leader can show sorrow and empathy, it will not lower him in the eyes of his people. MPs should put people first before their own self-serving egos.

Theresa May and Margaret Thatcher also showed emotion and wept when they got forced out of Downing Street by scheming men in the Tory Party, as reported in the news. Neither was evicted from Downing Street by the voters, but the tears they shed were not for the hardship and suffering they had caused the poor, because of government policies they oversaw as PMs. It was more to do with the shameful and cruel way they were driven out of office by their own Tory MPs. In fact, in 2002 Mrs May has gone on record referring to the Tory Party as the 'nasty party.[13] Theresa May who was the Home Secretary and later became the PM presided over policies, such as the Windrush scandal, bedroom tax, 'Go Home' vans that inflicted severe hardships and suffering on disadvantaged people. When she became PM, she referred to 'the burning injustices' in her inaugural speech, pledging to address discrimination by setting up the 'Race Audit'. Nothing has materialised, other than reinforcing what was known before, namely inequality based on race, creed and sex. In contrast, Tony Blair, Gordon Brown and David Cameron showed no remorse or emotion, not

---

[13] The Guardian: 'Nasty party warning to Tories' 8th October 2002
https://www.theguardian.com/politics/2002/oct/08/uk.conservatives2002

even an apology for the policy failures that caused misery, suffering and illegal wars when they left office. Except David Cameron was humming a tune after he resigned, perhaps relieved he will not have to clear up the Brexit mess or face any consequences, due to his actions and failures.

Lawmakers think they are born to rule, and people like them are superior and above the law. When a scandal breaks out, which affects them, such as the fraud claims that happened during the recent 2019 general elections, Brexit Party politicians were quick to call for an inquiry, never mind even if it turns out not to be the case. After all, they are known to be economical with the truth when it comes to self-serving interest like UKIP during the 2016 EU referendum. Political parties are not saints and renown for breaking elections rules in one way or another. They rush out and blame each other for breaking electoral rules, saying it raises serious questions about the integrity of the general elections and democracy. Often forgetting how desperate and corrupt they have become to get onto the gravy train at whatever cost, or using whatever means.

Why is bribing voters with false pledges a lesser crime, and not worthy of investigation, as well as attempting to cheat the electoral system and pervert our democratic system? Why were alleged Tory offers of peerage to the Brexit Party candidates not to contest during the 2019 general elections not a bigger crime? If it turns out to be true, and it is if, it means somebody was fabricating the truth to get elected, and should have been investigated before, not after the election, and dealt with severely to prevent future damage. If the allegations were false, it meant that the Brexit Party had distorted the truth, and should be made to pay through their nose for wasting police time, costing the taxpayer, money which could be well spent elsewhere. It is about time politicians are made to pay for their dirty tricks to restore trust in democracy and end deceit. A crime is a crime, and should be investigated irrespective of who is affected. If the law enforcers wish to investigate someone or a group, they should also look at investigating themselves on how they conduct their business. The common person would not even receive a visit from the police when a 'genuine crime' has been reported; instead they are issued a crime reference number for statistical purposes, which in most cases will not merit further investigation.

Free and fair elections are one of the most sacred principles of any democracy. The West is now facing an unprecedented threat to democracy in the modern era. Serious concerns of meddling have been raised in France, Ukraine, the US and Britain. It has come in various forms, such as phone hacking, dark money raised to influence elections, cyber-attacks, or radio phone-in programmes by President Trump, rendering democracy dysfunctional, by depriving the ordinary public the right to vote for a democratically elected government. Not calling out any form of meddling is hypocritical. The most powerful leaders in the world should know better, not to interfere in EU referendum, and 2019 General Elections in the UK to influence the result, and let British people decide themselves what is good or bad for them. Politicians should be mindful and shun such practices.

Unlike in the past, hypocrisy has now become more common in society. It also does not help when acquaintances or aides of the elite class are happy to enjoy the perks for a better life-style, such as promotions or honours, and keep quiet when they witness malpractice. So are more relaxed, by turning a blind eye to the improper behaviour they have seen, heard or personally experienced, as long as they are the beneficiaries. They only come out of the woodwork after being sacked from the job shouting from the roof tops of how badly they have been mistreated by their master, or what they have witnessed them do. The aides then go on to sell their story to the tabloid press to express feelings and regrets for not speaking out about their behaviour sooner, speaking of personal relationships, potential conflict of interests, how they were shocked by the use of an offensive word, how they were groped, how they were sexually harassed and bullied. In short, how they covered-up for their masters. Such incidents have led to a very confusing situation and mistrust, whereby it is difficult to distinguish fact from fiction, and whom to trust.

The British people have seen similar double standards and hypocrisy, when Harry Dunn, aged 19, was killed on his motorbike in an accident on 27th August 2019 near RAF Croughton, Northamptonshire, involving a car travelling in the opposite direction driven by the wife of a US intelligence official, who promptly claimed diplomatic immunity and fled the UK to avoid police investigation. What happened next was unbelievable. Something one would not expect from the most powerful and 'civilised' country in the. The actions of the offender show how those in power or their sub-ordinates abuse diplomatic immunity. To add insult to injury, the grieving family were subjected to insensitive comments by the most powerful man in the world with the responsibility to uphold law and order. Donald Trump ridiculed the gravity of the situation, by saying that wrong-way driving "happens," defending the offender. Even a request from the British PM to reconsider granting immunity to the suspected American woman failed to resolve the diplomatic wrangle. It does not give hope for humanity when the most powerful political leaders do not practice what they preach. There are many everyday cases of constant struggle for the ordinary public to even seek or get justice, and in many cases, they just give up without even trying.

When the lawmakers behave with such arrogance and ignore the law of the land for self-serving interests, how can the public have trust and faith in getting justice? It is an insult to the judiciary system. If there are any important lessons to be learnt from this sad episode, a public inquiry should be held by the government quickly. One thing is for sure, if it had happened to an American citizen Donald Trump would be screaming for justice, and our PM would have readily obliged, so as not to upset our 'special relationship' with America, especially post-Brexit, due to negotiating trade deals. This does not set a good example for others to follow, and if less 'civilised' countries had behaved in the same way, the US would have been quick to impose economic sanctions, or sent drones to kill defenceless civilians.

Our politicians have created a situation of double standards, hypocrisy and self-serving interests instead of bona fide scruples. It seems to the ordinary public that it is alright to kill or murder somebody, and just walk away claiming diplomatic immunity. If that was not enough, when lawmakers get caught violating laws, they escape with a slap on the wrist. The public have witnessed scandals by the bucket load, yet see politicians getting away scot-free. On the other hand, the public are told no one is above the law. It does not stop the legislatures to test the laws passed by them to the limit, to see if they can get away with it, and if found guilty after costly legal battles paid by the tax payer, it makes no difference, because they are able to continue with their life with the same perks, as if nothing has happened.

Playtime with year old Naamah in makeshift shop playground.

Week-end staff Toby and Lindsay, quality control inspectors hard at work.

Origin of two for the price of one. Multitasking drafting letters to politicians while attending to business (1990s).

State of the art 'patented' food mixer in full production.

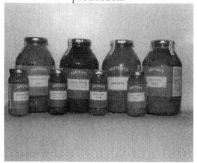

Assorted pickle range retail and catering size

Pond materials and transport (2000).

Pond construction using voluntary efforts.

Project accomplished - completed pond.

SIR Profile

Voices in the wilderness: but now, thanks to the SIR, independents have a chance to have their views heard

COMING OUT FROM BEHIND THE SHADOWS

SIR is heading for the top of the class, and a strong campaigning voice is emerging. Jac Roper reports

Dr Hassan Akherali is a very modest man. He insists no photographs. He prefers to be the man behind the movement – the Society of Independent Retailers (SIR) – which a couple of months ago could have been accurately described as an underground movement.

But now SIR is beginning to emerge (C-Store, June 2). It has had a small write-up in The Times, and behind the scenes the name has appeared on hundreds of letter-headings sent to all manner of authorities. Its members are beginning to air their ideas regularly on the Dawn Trader programme run by Spectrum Radio.

And Akherali the thinker – the doctor of philosophy who dreamed up the idea – now thinks it is time for action. Akherali did not set out to be a retailer. In his large immediate family, which included some 30 cousins, in Tanzania, he was the only academic.

After a lifetime of competing for and winning scholarships he finally gained a doctorate at Manchester University in marine biology, got a research grant then settled down to write books.

Then ten years ago he met Femi, a businesswoman, and got married. For the last nine years they have run a smallish London c-store at Woking in Surrey. Together they have experienced first hand the multitude of frustrations faced by independent businesses.

He started writing letters to the Prime Minister's office about five years ago. He began questioning news wholesaling practices at the same time. Eventually he solved most of his own retailing problems but realised, while listening to Dawn Trader, that many retailers still faced the same problems.

"I realised I wanted to give them the benefit of my experience. And I realised that if you have a purposeful voice you'll not be taken for granted when it counts."

The raison d'être for SIR is quite simple. According to Akherali, although there are a lot of other federations, associations, lobby and pressure groups, none of them have succeeded in bolting the stable door while the horse is still inside. They all react after the damage has been done.

"Everyone says they are committed to helping independent retailers, Banks, Government, the various associations and federations. But most just take them for granted. I want to focus the energy of the independent sector. We must get geared up because nobody else is going to do it for us."

He says it saddens him that independents don't have the time to spend fighting all the problems they face. "They have to be accountant, delivery man, health & safety officer, security guard, cleaner. They are working 80 to 90 man hours a week. On top of that they have to

follow Government policies, tackle wholesalers, then find time for their families. Leisure! What's that?

"They are tired, drained... so their efficiency dips. Bureaucracy is the killer – a drip, drip, poison."

As he warms to his subject, he says that the independent sector is being used as a cheap labour force and as unpaid civil servants. The penalties of dealing with the demands of the law, regulations and red tape are high.

"Depending on turnover, the cost of compliance with the law is between £5,000 and £15,000 a year. It's around two and half per cent of turnover. Costs are escalating quicker than profits."

So what can SIR do about all these problems that others cannot? Akherali says that commitment is the answer. And that is all he requires from other retailers: to belong to the movement. With enough commitment the voice will be loud, clear and influential. Morale will be high which will bring its own benefits.

So far he has around one dozen

20 Convenience Store June 16 1995

members who have invested a lot of their own time and money in writing and sending letters and faxes to Government, to the news wholesalers, to the authorities, to various watchdog committees and so on.

The group also has between 200 and 300 members who belong but who spend less actual time working on issues.

He acknowledges that eventually, as the group grows, he will have to ask for fees.

"What we want now is a network of professional voluntary members who will take on the extra work of writing to MPs. We want quality input. There's no force, but let's be realistic. When the need arises, there will be a fee for membership. At the moment we are taking everything out of our own resources."

Membership so far has come not just from convenience store operators and newsagents but also from pharmacists, key cutters, electrical retailers, sandwich bar operators – any and all you might find in the High Street and local shopping parades.

Akherali thinks the groundwork is now almost complete. "We have got the right name – one that gives pride, recognition. And we are now working on the constitution. We are ready...and we are almost prepared."

SIR's policy

Harish Sedani (pictured above)

The main objective of SIR is to take preventive action, to be influential when policy which affects the independent is being made, rather than reacting after the damage is done.

The group's letterhead reworks a motto from the musketeers: One For All, All for One.

All it asks of members is commitment. It does not ask that you resign from any other group you may belong to, in fact it hopes to work with other groups such as the ACS and the NFRN.

■ Anyone interested should contact East London retailer Harish Sedani at his shop: Seji Enterprise, 69 Wilton Way, London E8 1BJ. As we said in our last issue, a stamped addressed envelope would be appreciated by this no funds operation.

What he thinks

About ethnics being overqualified. "In life there is no such thing as being overqualified. Learning is a continuous process. Anyone who knows it all should be dead because that is when learning stops. Life is full of vacations and you can be overqualified for a vocation – so you move on, or diversify, use your experience to learn something different.

About the lottery: "So much disappointment. One in 14 million wins. The rest are losers. They face the week with this disappointment and usually the first thing they see is their independent retailer."

A feature in trade journal.

News

SIR gets to sit round the table at Westminster

Jac Roper deputy editor

Convenience Store EXCLUSIVE

A delegation from the Society of Independent Retailers (SIR) began the first in a series of meetings with MPs last week in an attempt to get in at the policy-making level on the major issues affecting independents.

The group of five retailers, led by Londis retailer Dr Hassan Akberali who founded the movement, stayed an hour at Westminster all told, spending half of it in a formal meeting with Tory backbencher Sir Rhodes Boyson.

This was followed by two unprompted meetings with Labour MP Jim Dowd and Conservative MP Niranjan Deva.

As a result of the latter meeting, SIR will be going back to the Houses of Parliament this week to tackle one specific issue close to its heart. Akberali told *Convenience Store!*

"It was brilliant. We came out with far more than we had bargained for. The meeting with Deva will be to discuss the Restrictive Trades Practice Act as it applies to newspaper wholesalers."

The group left a discussion paper with Sir Rhodes which focussed on four big issues:

O Economic problems.
O The monopoly of newspaper wholesalers.
O The revitalisation of town centres.
O The business rates and the cost of compliance with red tape.

The meeting this week (June 26) with Deva will be followed by another with Labour MP Keith Vaz. A date has yet to be set for this meeting but Vaz has offered to co-ordinate with several other MPs to ensure their attendance.

The meetings have come about thanks to the tenacity of the SIR network, which operates without funds and relies on the commitment and efforts of its members.

In the course of its four months existence, SIR has already lobbied ministers, MPs and individuals with some 300 letters; had several consultations with the DTI and sub-

In conference: Dr Hassan Akberali spent a successful hour at Westminster talking to MPs

mitted evidence to the Office of Fair Trading on the unfair selection of lottery outlets.

The group, subject to financial reserves, plans to carry out two research projects to discuss the strengths, weaknesses, contributions and future of the independent sector. This will be the first of its kind commissioned by individuals actually working in the trade.

LETTERS

WRITE OF REPLY

Cash and carries cashing in on cigs

Something to get off your chest? Let us know. Write to The Editor, *Convenience Store*, William Reed Publishing, Broadfield Park, Crawley, West Sussex RH11 9RT, or fax us on 01293 610320

Time to clear ambiguities in 1996

The New Year has started with just as many issues not resolved as the Old Year had solutions for. The issues and concerns pertaining to small family businesses have been definitely posed for the last five years.

The agenda for 1996 requires retailers and their respective trade organisations to recapture the lost ground with practical plans and participation at policy making level to secure their commercial interests and needs. A 1996 shopping list for small retailers should explore avenues to provide solutions to help rid themselves of chains that restrict progress and diversification of their businesses.

The Government and trade politicians must be made aware of how various regulation and legislation in the name of free markets favours big businesses with unfair monopolies – hindering the survival of small family businesses.

For example:

O A clear demarcation in the definition of small businesses to identify the needs of small family businesses with practical policies.

O A review of the present franch-

Dr Hassan Akberali: "time for retailers and trade organisations to recapture lost ground"

ponch of Unfair governing UK competition policy allowing abuse of powers by monopolis-tic businesses – such as town wholesalers and Cartels – and enforcement of Britain's absurdly long-winded and expensive competition vetting process by toothless regulatory bodies.

O Practical participation in the deregulation of secondary legislation initiatives and help with the cost of complying with red-tape and bureaucracy.

O To minimise the detrimental affect of out of town shopping centre and traffic restrictions.

O Also included in the shopping

list for 1996 is the retailer's right to expect his wholesaler's invoice and returns credit to be correct. Despite today's hi-tech scanning, mistakes are still being made too often. Nobody knows how often, or to what extent retailers are being affected.

The sector is hoping and expecting progress in other outstanding issues to which solutions do exist. What the retailer requires most in 1996 is practical programme to put action in process.

Hassan Akberali,
Chairman,
Society for Independent
Retailers,
Shepherds Bush,
London W12

I have dealt with the same cash and carry at Watford for many years and was disgusted when they put their cigarette prices up just two days after the November Budget.

They maintain that they are all for the independent retailer and yet they raise their prices as quickly as this – just sheer greed to get more profit. I knew we knew about the Budget and that cigarettes were certain to go up, but small businesses cannot afford to stock up with a large amount of cigarettes.

All we asked was for the cash and carries to hold their prices for a reasonable time to enable us to compete with the bigger stores. We now have a situation where two large companies in this town are still selling cigarettes at 18-20p below the old price. So as far as I'm concerned I will buy mine from them until they put their prices up, so the cash and carry loses out anyway.

I would like to suggest that the manufacturers price all their cigarettes before a budget so that no one can profit out of Budget increases.

(Name and address supplied)

■ Editor's note: Please refer to *Convenience Store* December 15, page 9

The waiting game

Due to the number of letters received, some have been held over for the next issue of *Convenience Store*. Letters are published on a first-come, first-printed basis. In some cases, letters are abridged.

Press reports from the 1990s

Dr Hassan Akberali

Independent ✓

Society for Independent Reformists (SIR)
An independent voice for Woking

- » Do you want to make a difference and make your vote count?
- » Are you tired of broken promises from all levels of bureaucracy?
- » Do you want real democracy to work irrespective of age and class?
- » Are you tired of the tribal party politics of blame, spin, divide and rule slogans?
- » Would you like to live in social harmony and fulfil your aspirations?

Grass roots understanding of trust and accountability

My whole background is based on an understanding that politicians, service providers and stake holders perform civic duty built on trust and accountability above anything else, who must act as role models to uphold the moral, welfare and social fabric of the society.

I am passionate about what the public would really like our politicians to do, namely address real life concerns for all, not different rules for those with media, legal, lobbying and financial clout who when caught claim denial or blame others for failure.

The best way to send a message to the establishment elite is to elect a local Councillor who will put the residents above party-political allegiance and self-serving interests. I believe those who live and work in Knaphill are best placed to share in the decision-making process.

What difference will a Reformist MP make to Woking constituents?

We believe those who live and work in the Woking constituency are best placed to share in the decision-making process affecting their future.

A vote for Dr Hassan Akberali on the 8th June is a promise to transform the process of democracy and accountability starting in Woking as an example to national politics.

Anyone can get in touch to participate in open door democracy.

We offer a chance to speak on your doorstep or at a meeting in your area to discuss local and national issues.

A vote for Hassan is a vote to throw open the door to real democracy. As a Woking MP I'll put hope, social harmony and fairness at the heart of everything I do.

I have always written my own letters and election leaflets. These for General and Local Elections in 2017, 2018 and 2019 reflects I have held consistent views in my lifetime. I thoroughly enjoyed direct interaction with the public during the campaigns and maintained contact ever since.

11

PM's Inaugural Speeches

The pledges made in the PM's inaugural speeches on the steps of Downing Street only remains a dream for the ordinary public, as the elected PM once steps inside one of the most powerful addresses in the world, and soon gets detached from them and out of touch with reality, making a mockery of their victory speeches, as empty arrogance and broken pledges. All past five British PMs, since John Major, went to universities, and four of them attended the prestigious Oxford University. It shows a lack of political leadership and conviction that they are just mere intelligent amateurs, more concerned about their own agendas and self-interests in their pursuit for power. In the process, their actions have had serious affects, caused shambles and far reaching damage to the country and breakdown in social harmony, the consequences of which are still faced today. We must not forget that they all entered politics to serve public duty, and the people pay their wages. The voters looking in from the outside are appalled by the cosy little games played in Westminster. What the public cannot stand is political hypocrisy. Nobody can keep all their promises, because of the changing priorities and risks involved, so why make pledges which cannot be honoured? Across all political spectrums the truth no longer is sacred.

The following highlights just one example of the major failures in the case of each PM from a long list of many, and raises serious questions about their political judgement and conviction. The policy failures still echo while the ordinary public endure continued hardships.

Tony Blair presided over the illegal Iraq War in 2003, the effects still being felt by the Iraqi civilians, which has also led to a steep rise in radicalisation and terrorism in Britain and elsewhere. Whereas, Gordon Brown's "no more boom and bust" mantra amounted to nothing, except led to the coalition government to impose severe austerity measures, with cuts in public services, affecting the poor and disadvantaged. Whereas David Cameron, in order to curtail the rise of UKIP for self-serving Tory party political interests offered the 2016 EU Referendum that resulted in Brexit and divided the country, and it is still unsure what future trade deals to expect from the EU and other countries. Theresa May under her charge created a hostile immigrant environment, not only in the Home Office that severely affected the lives of the Windrush generation, but also hatred on the streets for ethnic people with the illegal immigrant 'Go Home' van posters. The nation now eagerly waits for the 'sunny uplands' promised by Boris Johnson, who was elected in 2019. He has portrayed himself as a knight on a white horse pandering to a selective audience with a 'populist political agenda', while alienating ethnic and non-ethnic people. In spite of all these and other major policy failures, they have all escaped scot-free without being held accountable for their broken pledges. The opposition leaders of the time have been no different in their deliberations, like their contemporaries, blaming everyone else except themselves. It is hard to see them as good real-life role models for the young, as well as the old to emulate.

I am relating personal efforts, experiences and difficulties faced by a 'man in the street' within the context of all the PM's inaugural speeches despite the pledges made by them over the last twenty years. Since 1997 all five PMs in their victory speeches on the steps of Downing Street have said the same thing expressed differently, and that is to create a fairer society built on enterprise, and social justice with big investments in public and transport services. In a nutshell, saying they will provide the people with an inclusive and an open government that will work for the national interests. Politicians will say anything to stay in power! They pretend to be believers and doers, saying what voters would like to hear, by using all the tricks of the trade. I will go further. The main gist except for choice of words in speeches is no different other than politely, not openly, recriminating the outgoing PM for not looking after people's concerns, while the successor speaks with bluster and optimism.

I have summarised all five PM's respective victory speeches on the steps of Downing Street, which was no different from that given by Tony Blair[14,15,16] in

---

[14] General election victory speech, 1997. Tony Blair (Labour) www.britishpoliticalspeech.org/speech-archive.htm?speech=222

[15] The Guardian: 'Tony Blair's victory speech' 8th June 2001
https://www.theguardian.com/politics/2001/jun/08/election2001.electionspast1

[16] BBC News | UK | Election 2005 | Tony Blair's third term victory speech outside No 10 on 6th May 2005
news.bbc.co.uk/1/hi/uk_politics/vote_2005/frontpage/4522185.stm

1997, 2001 and 2005, Gordon Brown[17] in 2007, David Cameron[18,19] in 2010 and 2015, Theresa May[20,21] in 2016 and 2017, and for that matter from Boris Johnson [22,23] in 2019. After nearly a quarter of century, the pledges remain more or less the same, which I can liken to a revolving door or a merry-go-round.

They all started by paying tribute to their predecessor, and they all acknowledged and knew too well the responsibility and trust the British people had placed on them. They relished the challenge and were grateful to the public for the opportunity of standing in office. They recognised it was also not a mandate for more of the same broken pledges, but a mandate to get those things done in our country that desperately needed doing for a better future for all and public services. They promised to govern in the interests of all people, the whole of Britain. What else was promised by politicians was to restore trust in politics to give people hope that politics should always be about service to the public. A government rooted in strong values, the values of justice and progress for the good of society. They all claimed a united Britain, one nation where ambitions of people are matched by a sense of compassion, decency and duty towards others. Simple values, but the right ones! They all got a second bite at the cherry, by being re-elected as PMs, except for Gordon Brown.

They all felt an even greater obligation, after re-election, to tell people very clearly the difficult choices and tasks facing the country, and how they would try to work their way through them, as well as recognising the purpose of each and every change needed to create an honest and open society, a better nation at ease with one another. In a way they wanted to create a country where not just a few people are at the top, but for every one of our citizens to get the chance to fulfil their true potential.

They even mentioned of their experiences during the election campaign that gave them a chance to go out and talk to people for week after week, whilst listening and learning something about the British people, so they were able to

---

[17] UK | UK Politics | In full: Gordon Brown¡**Error! Marcador no definido.**'s speech - BBC NEWS 27th June 2007 http://news.bbc.co.uk/1/hi/uk_politics/6246114.stm

[18] The Guardian: 'The transcript of Cameron's speech outside No 10 Downing Street as prime minister' 11th May 2010
https://www.theguardian.com/politics/2010/may/11/david-cameron-speech-full-text

[19] BBC News | UK | Election 2015 | David Cameron's victory speech outside No 10 on 8th May 2015
https://www.bbc.co.uk/news/uk-politics-32661073

[20] The Independent: 'Theresa May's first speech to the nation as prime minister - in full' 13th July 2016
https://www.independent.co.uk/news/uk/politics/theresa-mays-first-speech-to-the-nation-as-prime-minister-in-full-a7135301.html

[21] BBC News | UK | Election2017 | Theresa May's victory speech outside No 10 on 9th June 2017
https://www.bbc.co.uk/news/election-2017-40223959

[22] UK | UK Politics | In full: Boris Johnson - First speech as PM in full BBC NEWS on 24th July 2019
https://www.bbc.co.uk/news/uk-politics-49102495

[23] BBC News | UK | Election2019 | Election results 2019: Boris Johnson's victory speech in full on 13th December 2019 https://www.bbc.co.uk/news/election-2019-50777071

get a very clear idea of what the British people now expect from them in their second or third term. They spoke of their love for the country being the main reason they entered politics with a belief in public service, having a vision that the best days are yet to come. They roused the public to help them build a more responsible society in Britain. One where we do not just ask what are my entitlements, but what are my responsibilities, explaining they shared the same sentiments as the public, such as cleaning up the expense scandals, reforming parliament, and making sure people are in control - and that the politicians are always their servant, and not their masters. In essence, honest about what the government can achieve with real change, by pulling everyone together and building on some clear values of freedom, fairness and responsibility, where we can all exercise our rights and responsibilities, not only to ourselves, but also to our families, communities and others to build a more responsible society.

The politicians mentioned their commitment to the union, not just between the nations of the UK, but between all citizens, whoever we are and wherever we are from, by fighting against the 'burning injustices' that if you are born poor, you will usually die early, and tackle discrimination based on race, creed, sex, age and class, pledging to lead a government driven not by the interests of the privileged few, but by the under privileged, by giving them more control of their lives, and think of the needy when making government policies, to lead a government that will put fairness and opportunity at the heart of everything, where no one and no community is left behind, allowing prosperity and opportunity to be shared by all right across Britain.

They spoke of their mission, a strong purpose, a steadfast will, a resolute action and service to meet the concerns and aspirations of our whole country. They recalled the reasons for standing on the steps of Downing street, because of opportunities they had received, and wanted the same chances for everyone, as they recognised changes were required to build a brighter future for the nation, which cannot be met by 'old politics'. So they pledged 'new politics' that would mean they listened to the people, reaching out beyond narrow party interest to build a government that uses all talents, by inviting men and women of good will to contribute their energies in a new spirit of public service to make our nation great again, because they were convinced no weakness existed in Britain today that could not be overcome by the strength of the British people. They spoke confidently about focusing on a strong economy, jobs, living wage, affordable housing, immigration, crime, justice and most importantly investment in our public services, especially the NHS, welfare, education, transport network and much more, including reform. On top of that, they recognised the needed to start building the economy of the future, based on application of technology, skills, talents and education, ready for the 21st century, as they knew that we could only compete in the future on the basis of skill and ability, not low wages.

Despite such mouth-watering spending sprees in all areas, they pledged to deliver a balanced budget and bring down the national debt.

The chosen politicians recalled words and personal promises that have stayed with them since childhood, and their political career, which mattered a great deal to them. At the same time other pledges were made, without raising any doubt in people's minds that they will guide the country through some difficult times, such as crucial Brexit negotiations with the EU, but they would look after British interests to deliver the will of the people, in addition to cracking down on the ideology of Islamist extremism, radicalisation, anti-social behaviour, giving the police the powers they need to keep our country safe. No ifs or buts.

Going by the forgoing account, it would appear that the job of the present occupant, Boris Johnson, would be a walk in the park, a piece of cake, as all problems facing the nation should have been resolved by his predecessors, but seems not, because his speech was the longest, with full of bluster, sounding more like a speech at an Oxford Union debate. He blamed everyone was wrong. He not only pledged the same as his predecessors, but much more, everything under the sun, as if he has found the 'magic money tree'. Whilst ignoring the fact that balanced budgets promised by his predecessors by 2015 had not yet been met, instead national debt has increased to £1.78 trillion and rising, with severe austerity measures since 2010 that are still in place in 2020. So much for trust in politics and accountability! Let's hope he breaks the trend of the last four PMs, otherwise what levels of national debt will we leave for future generations, and what legacy? It is still early days, and I sincerely wish him well in his future endeavours and vision for the country. The jury is out!

It is equally amazing that despite recognising and admitting their mistakes, politicians go on to make the same mistakes and ignore real-life concerns of ordinary people, even after learning lessons! Have we not heard similar chants before? It is also surprising that they did not know the values of the British until election time. A contradiction in itself, because MPs claim they entered politics to serve public duty, and make life better for the people! They all recognised the need to go out and meet people and listen to them, but when people try to engage, they call them bigoted,[24] or ignore them altogether. The most common theme in all the speeches that PMs relate is to trust, accountability, fairness, justice, hope and a level playing field, and being servants to the people. All this is forgotten as soon as they enter through the door of Number 10 Downing Street. All their pledges and listening mode disappears into hot air, except those privileged to have access to them, while ignoring ordinary people.

---

[24] The Guardian: 'The Gordon Brown and Gillian Duffy transcript' 28th April 2010
https://www.theguardian.com/politics/2010/apr/28/gordon-brown-gillian-duffy-transcript

I have summarised the main message and pledges publicly made in various victory speeches over the last two decades since 2000. It was in 1992 that I had raised real-life concerns with pro-active solutions at no extra cost to the tax payer, which I have emphasised in detail. It is remarkable that after nearly three decades, the political leaders have still not learnt lessons from their costly public inquiries and listening exercises, except how to pass the buck and blame others. It seems like the same 'old politics' dressed up in sheep's wool. Is it any wonder that the public do not trust them! Let me make it clear again, it has never been my thinking that I have answers or the solution to everything, then or even now, but what I can say is that many of the concerns I had raised were root causes, which needed fixing. It is heart-breaking! I wish I was given a chance and listened to, because, some of the things I had to offer would have made a real difference to our society. It would not only have saved the tax payer money, but prevented undue suffering and loss of lives, which has alienated some communities even further. If anything, the situation has worsened, costing the tax payer even more money, with further resentment and uncertainty.

It was in 1992 when I had raised a number of issues relating to unfair trading practices, newspaper wholesale distribution and a lack of a level playing field, which affected small businesses then, and the same problems still exist today. These issues have come back to haunt us, with derelict high streets, town centres and Northern towns, which is part of the underlying causes of anti-social behaviour and crime. I had written to Tony Blair in 2000, and again in 2005, with a similar underlying message on social cohesion with more emphasis on community spirit. It was before 9/11, the effects that are still felt today, and nothing has improved as such, except appeasement politics and window dressing, without addressing underlying reasons of inequality. I had highlighted serious concerns that have since become the focus of government, with costly knee-jerking policy initiatives, in one form or another, as they are seen to be doing something without addressing the root causes, just exacerbating the situation further. I also tried in 2007, 2008 and 2009 when I felt encouraged by Gordon Brown's inaugural speech to build a government that uses all the talents, as previously pledged by David Cameron and Theresa May of "new politics" and accountability to address the 'burning injustices'.

At times I do feel frustrated because of the indifferent attitude by the 'establishment', especially when they pledge one thing and do the opposite. I am a passionate man with strong convictions when I know I can make a difference. However, such attitude and a lack of empathy on the politicians' part have not helped. Not only has it inflicted more pain, hatred and suffering towards law abiding Muslims and other ethnic people, but also has made them less likely to engage. This is not the right way to address the burning injustices.

Is it any surprise that the trust in politics is at its lowest ebb? People can no longer be fooled, particularly when successive PMs have openly admitted in their speeches that there has been a lack of trust, accountability and social injustice for over a period of two decades. The Conservative leader, Boris Johnson, faced humiliating moments of laughter from a studio audience when asked if the truth matters in this election, he insisted, "I think it does," provoking chuckles from the audience at the 2019 election debate at ITV Manchester in 2019. Labour leader, Jeremy Corbyn faced similar laughter after he repeatedly refused to reveal whether he personally believed the UK should leave the EU or not. The truth of the matter is that the crazy pledges made by politicians will have no effect on them, as they are never held accountable when policies go pear shaped. After all, they are not the ones who will suffer! Is it any wonder the national debt is rising due to unaccountable politicians? To add insult to injury, when things go wrong, the people pay for their mistakes by paying more taxes, and having to put up with cuts to public services, even bailing out greedy bankers during the 2008 financial crisis. Unlike the 'establishment', if an ordinary person falls on hard times, they and their families face the consequences. It is worth noting, if people ran their domestic budgets in the same way as the politicians, they would go bankrupt, which begs the question, why should people believe and trust what the PMs pledge in their inaugural speech?

The extravagant pledges made by politicians to woo voters have a negative effect on the population, as they give misleading impressions that all problems will be solved in five years, if they are elected to form a government. Why have they waited so long, inflicting pain and suffering on the very people whose lives they are meant to make better? At the moment, it is perceived that breaking laws or pledges to gain power or greed is acceptable, as long as one does not get caught. When politicians fail to deliver those extravagant pledges, they blame their inevitable failure on some mysterious 'establishment', which makes people even angrier.

It is this sort of politics that ultimately divides a country - rich against poor, poor against poor, religion against religion, race against race, North against South, London against the rest, people against parliament, Brexiters against Remainers, and old against young. It is a dangerous ploy to make pledges to entice voters by using headline grabbing pledges to increase spending in schools, hospitals and high streets, targeting marginal seats that have been neglected over the years, which voted leave in the 2016 EU referendum without addressing the real-life concerns of the people.

12

Easier Said Than Done

Autobiographies, biographies or memoirs are mostly, if not always are published after an individual attains great success and eminence in a particular field with the intention to inspire ordinary folk to achieve success if they work hard. These are usually written by professional authors on behalf of the dignitary or by the individual himself, who has an immense grasp of writing, and the book launched with the usual publicity fanfare. It is very rare to find one written by an ordinary person narrating what they have managed to achieve in their own small way. Even if they do, they find it difficult to find a publisher willing to take a chance on them, because they do not know if it is worth telling, unless the author comes across somebody famous prepared to publicise their cause. Like the humanitarian work of Mother Teresa that came more into limelight after her unique bond with Princess Diana.

Let me make it absolutely clear, it is not my intention to referee on the works of very illustrious individuals, who have made significant contributions for humanity. Something which an ordinary person like me cannot even contemplate to achieve, not even a little bit in comparison to them, except for having a dream to fulfil aspirations abiding by the rules set by the lawmakers in society, which the rest of humanity have to accept and follow. Over the years, I have read quite a few biographies of eminent individuals who have played prominent roles in science, civil rights movements, journalism, sports, politics and business whom I have always regarded as great icons and role models. It is because I have always been keen to find out what inspired them to achieve such greatness, and if I can learn a thing or two from them, as it is never too late to learn, or do something useful for humanity.

What comes across is most intriguing. They all share some similarities. What led them to greatness was a specific tragedy, discovery or multiple crisis, and most of all the dedication and sacrifice. In science it was a simple observation they made, which has stood the test of time. In the field of sport, it was a means to get out of poverty, bullying or hardship. For a civil right activist, it was injustices they faced as a child or in adult life that led them to stand up for worthy causes, which they fought with great acts of unselfish sacrifices to bring about change, such as human rights, poverty or standing up against tyrants. However, in a few cases, doubts have also been raised, and a difference of opinion exists as to what their actual motives and methods were to achieve their goals. Some critics have raised serious questions - not from me, as I do not claim to be an expert or an authority - based on the cover up of certain events in their life.

The same could be said about biographies of a few political leaders I have read. They write about their great achievements and what led them to enter politics, which was to serve public duty to make life better for others, by addressing injustices. In their memoirs, they also focus on examples of political deception and behaviour of others, giving the impression that they were saints, and did nothing wrong. Rarely, do they admit their own failures. If anything, apportion blame onto others for failures, by becoming armchair specialists, and end up as after dinner speakers with lucrative contracts, by lecturing others on what to do and what not to do. In contrast, the biographies I have read of a few wealthy people, soon became apparent at the start that what led them to make lots of money was when they faced extreme hardships, such as starvation, homelessness, humiliation, injustice and so forth, in their childhood. Such events made them determined to acquire wealth to get out of their poverty-stricken life.

However, my main purpose of this memoir, from a lay-person's perception is about hope and reality. This account is written within the context of the world of wealth creators, millionaires (billionaires) and politicians' inaugural speeches mentioned in the previous chapter. Because the impression one gets from their biographies and rousing talk protected by speeches is how virtuous and ethical, they are, and the great emphasis they place to uphold scruples. They also lecture to the public that they too can achieve great success, by aspiring to anything they want to in life. Basically, the world is their oyster! Whereas, the wealthy narrate the driving force behind their motivation citing examples of the dire straits their parents faced or how their widowed mother had to struggle to raise them and other siblings when they were orphaned. It is under such extreme conditions that they knew exactly what had to be done, and decided to pull their socks up to escape hardships, and get out of poverty by making lots of money and not face hard times ever again. I would say there is no doubt, none whatsoever that such sentiments and aspirations are not unique to the wealthy, and shared by all individuals, in one form or another. Whether, it comes to earning a square meal or colossal banquet, gaining basic literacy and numeracy skills, or a university degree and a roof over their head, or live in a mansion. It all boils down to opportunities and being in the right place at the right time.

But what the wealthy and the politicians forget is that poverty is relative, one can say a lot against and little in its favour. It also depends on which end of the poverty spectrum, duration, or regularity one has fallen victim of. There are inevitably times when respectable members of the ordinary public have also fallen on hard times in one form or another for short periods, and parents gone without food, eaten less, homes repossessed or faced evictions, and even walked to save on bus fares, so as not to deprive their children. However, hunger can never be compared to those who face extreme poverty on a regular basis, when someone does not know where their next meal will come from, or have to rely on food banks and charity on a daily basis over a long period of time, or for the rest of their life. It is only once the basic hunger for food is met that humans can than spend time in their quest in search of contemporary knowledge, education, civic duty and justice to seek a better life, and not fall victim to those who preach hate. This is no different to the atrocities faced by those unfortunate people in prisoner of war and concentration camps during the two World Wars. In such circumstances, the foremost thing on their minds was a square meal, not education and other opportunities. We have also seen images on TV of the starving orphans and their mothers from the warm comfort of living rooms and expect them to do something about it. But, unlike millionaires, they lack a stable environment to do that, something which should not be forgotten, but remembered. It is also true that people will appear to befriend you when you are wealthy, but precious few will do the same when you are poor. If wealth can be a magnet, poverty can be a repellent. Yet, poverty can also often bring out great acts of heroism and daily feats of survival amongst those faced with such adversities inflicted upon them, during conflicts or natural disasters.

It is not denied in any way the achievements of the wealthy required a lot of great sacrifices, and visionary decisions had to be taken. But when reading biographies in between the lines of wealthy philanthropists, including those of eminent people in science and sports, it transpires that in most cases they have had some helping hand of one way or another, or have had a lucky break. In the case of political leaders and civil activists, they have all had support, such as moral, financial, followers with many of them having graduated from famous universities, or some even attended famous public schools. Quite a few, also practiced professionally as journalists, lawyers, doctors, bankers, they were/are not leading impoverish lives and cannot be described as the Mother Teresa(s) of our time sharing the pain of their followers on a daily basis. When they did suffer, it was stage managed to maximise publicity, making sure to capitalise from the event. It is patronising and an insult to suggest otherwise, and lecture others that we can all achieve success, if we work hard and make sacrifices to succeed in life by aiming high, which is what my ancestors had managed to do, but something, which I think a victim of war, discrimination, child abuse or sexual exploitation would find very hard to swallow because of the suffering inflicted by the action of someone powerful.

What is most noticeable when reading the biography of the famous forensically (not openly admitted) is that they have also received some help, direct or indirect, such as financial, guidance, contacts, from one if not a few individuals, and in some cases even motivated or spurned them onto the right path. Even if none of the foregoing happened, it may be because of luck, destiny and blessings. It is vitally important to appreciate and show humility that success, apart from hard work, sacrifices and suffering, needs luck. It also helps if one is in the right place at the right time, with basic skills to take advantage of opportunities when they come along. What the present lawmakers and the 'establishment' omit to mention is that in order to grab opportunities, going by their own track record, one must also be greedy, ruthless, selfish, and less accountable, because they did not all become successful or wealthy by just being honourable, honest and fair. I would say, you do not become wealthy and powerful by being generous and soft natured.

What further becomes apparent in the biographies once wealth, political or social ambitions have been acquired to the very highest level, is that it is usually followed by establishing charitable foundations and trusts. These are either in their own name, or that of a beloved, for good causes to help the poor and the needy in the fields of education, health, social care, and welfare or refugee camps. Without doubt these are extremely worthy acts of philanthropy, although, raises the following question. Why not share their wealth by investing in their employee's future first? Such as pay a decent living wage or provide amenities, such as accommodation, education and health facilities like some well-known philanthropists did in the past, not by pushing people into a race to the bottom, and the individual then has to rely on state benefits to supplement their income for survival. In a way, the taxpayer subsiding their workforce, because of the low wages paid by the wealthy businessmen or those on zero-hour contracts. If that was not enough, unlike the ordinary public who pay their fair share of tax, the wealthy benefit further by not paying their full share of tax because of various tax avoidance schemes, allowing them to exploit loop holes to invest their profits in off-shore tax heavens, money which could have been spent to improve public services when needed most by the public.

There is nothing wrong with making money. It is greed and how you make it that matters. If wealth was invested and shared wisely in the first place, it would not result in extreme hardships for the poor, who then require charitable acts from the wealthy later on. It does not mean that one should not be ambitious, or success should be discouraged, and not believe in charity; of course not, but it is more to do with fairness and reality. When thinking about it, it is poverty that often brings out the true generosity in people, as people do not like seeing fellow humans suffer and go to their aid in their hour of need. It is noticeable that the wealthy embark on their charitable acts to help the disadvantaged after making vast fortunes, which does qualify for tax-relief, whilst, in the process conveniently forget their own circumstances and poverty that led them on their path to achieve riches in the first place! Likewise, political leaders will announce foreign aid packages after inflicting suffering on defenceless civilians, the real victims of wars.

It beggars belief why embark on senseless destruction and killing either directly or encouraging others, and then follow it by giving foreign aid to 'rebuild' lives initially, instead of preventing such atrocities from happening! What this shows is that there must have been ulterior motives. It is an insult to preach to those born in refugee camps and deprived neighbourhoods informing them that they too can become doctors, lawyers and millionaires, by working hard, without addressing the root causes that have put them there.

13

Role Models and Accountability

H uman society relies on role models right from birth, and throughout one's life. A child in early life learns good and bad habits from their parent(s), followed by peer groups, service providers, such as teachers, police and community members, not forgetting social media, TV, politicians and religious leaders. In a way no different from the animal species, such as primates, birds, potter wasps, male Hippocampus' (seahorse) and so forth. The parental role plays a crucial part to equip their offspring with the right skills to give a realistic survival chance, to progress in life. It is also known that social learning from others in humans and non-human primates plays a crucial role for the effective functioning of communities.

Role models are an important component of human society. There was a period not so long ago when a majority of our politicians, religious and community leaders including professionals - lawyers, bankers, doctors, teachers, civil servants, police, estate agents, accountants and the like - were treated with the greatest of respect. It was because they set the standards, which they adhered to, upholding the social and moral fabric of human society. They behaved honourably in its truest sense, but for some reason in the aftermath of war, cracks slowly started to appear in the system. Insatiable greed for power and money reared its ugly head above the pulpit, and gradually but surely this has continued. Now, lies, smears, abuse, misleading information, spin and damned statistics has become the norm for many politicians and their associates.

The public now recognise that politicians in the main cannot be trusted and respected, because they are not at all honourable. People have also lost trust in government statistics, despite showing that the majority of us are living happily, but equally see the rise in the working poor and homelessness in a country with the fifth largest economy. While the forgotten disadvantaged sectors of our society have to rely on foodbanks and charities, whose responsibility it has now become to look after. Those who are better off can have a clear conscious, as it has become an accepted practice and an easy option to donate money to absolve responsibility to help the disadvantaged.

The main purpose of mine is not to question the merits of various laws or judgement made by policymakers, I just want to give a true record of contempt, and the reality faced by a member of the public, so the 'defenders of society' can adopt a pragmatic approach based on reality, when formulating policies in the corridors of power. This is why I would like to focus on the underlying reasons behind the failures of some well-meant past policy initiatives costing millions, if not billions of pounds wasted without achieving the desired objectives. It is also the responsibility of politicians to listen and engage with their constituents, not only during election time. It seems that after they are elected, all they do is sit in their ivory tower, without paying any attention to their electorates, and enjoy the perks of the job. The same could be said for MPs who have chosen politics as a political career, should also be required to undergo compulsory induction courses, which were specifically drawn up in 1995 after the sleaze scandals that embraced the seven ethical standards to guide their behaviour in public life, which are accountability, selflessness, integrity, leadership, objectivity, openness and honesty.

The most important role for MPs above anything else should be to serve their constituents in the 'Mother of Parliaments'. For example, if a constituent falls victim of the legislation, or is let down by a public organisation meant to serve and protect the citizen, then (within reason) it should be the duty of an MP to help and guide the constituent, not shun duty. If MPs listened more to the public, it would restore trust and fairness in democracy. Hostility, insults and disrespect between politicians seen during Prime Minister's Questions on live TV also does not help, as it spills out onto the streets, encouraging the public, to imitate such 'uncivilised' behaviour. At times, a gesture of politeness amongst the political class would go a long way to solve division, instead of showing contempt and arrogance. We also need to ask why a fewer proportion of the population is turning up to vote? Is it because nearly half of Britons feel only anger towards politics and politicians? Why is there a drop in voter turnout, particularly among the under thirties? Is it because the majority lack any respect, and feel furious towards the political class? When the public are asked for a single word to describe how they feel about politics and politicians in general, they say they are 'angry' or 'bored'; whilst only some felt 'inspired' by British politicians and their politics. Such indifference amongst all age groups reveals how politicians and their constituents are generations apart, and not talking to each other.

A society has functional components, in terms of vocational aspirations; it is made up of three broad categories: business - a multi-million-pound enterprise, a street vendor; professionals - politicians, priests, doctors, police, teachers, and a labour class - manual or non-manual. For a business person, the vocation revolves around making profit, whether millions or pennies, with the sole goal to make money to build a business empire. There is nothing wrong with that, as it provides employment, not only for themselves, but also others. In their quest for wealth, it is up to the entrepreneur to uphold scruples on how they go about making money, such as pay the workforce a decent living wage and looking after the welfare of their employees, as well as paying their full share of tax. Failing that, they will pay the penalties for their actions and deeds, such as a disloyal workforce, strikes or get prosecuted for fraudulent tax avoidance and other employment violations. In the case of a manual or non-manual worker - a cleaner, miner, white or blue-collar worker – they sell their labour to make a living, and their wages are fixed and paid by the employer (state or private). In contrast, professionals enjoy the privilege of studying particular skills, allowing them to specialise in fields in order to gain expertise to serve and benefit humanity in areas such as: justice, health, education, welfare, politics, civic order, research, inventions and religious guidance, upholding the ethical and social fabric of society. In the process, the state or society rewards professionals with a better salary than a labourer. In the past, having a vocation gave them great contentment and immense pride of being a professional, as they were held in high esteem by the public. The vocation provided more satisfaction, in terms of serving humanity, rich and poor, with less emphasis on income and greed, because the professionals maintained all aspects of the proper functioning of society, with sound ethical standards. No doubt there were instances in the past of abuse and greed amongst professionals, but unlike today, these were few and far between. Anyway, those few greedy ones were generally found out, and faced public humiliation, as well as from their fellow professionals for letting the side down, and disqualified from working in their particular field again.

Unluckily, two of the most crucial components in the professional category, namely the political and religious class have embarked on a path to acquire excessive wealth over the years. They have made their noble roles into a very profitable career, by remaining answerable only to themselves, until they get found out, but even then, manage to escape the consequences. One would say there is nothing wrong with that, but the main difference is that it is under the wrong pretext, as politicians say that their main interest is to serve public duty, not monetary gain. Whereas the religious brigade preaches to the masses that greed tops the sin list, if not number one, and must be avoided at all costs. Obviously, the level of greed and perks amongst politicians and religious people varies according to the hierarchy and status in which they are in. Also, not all are involved in various scams to milk the system.

But the behaviour of some career politicians and religious priests has led other professionals to follow suit, resulting in demands for higher pay. Many also find time to engage as private consultants whilst employed in their full-time well-paid public service posts, yet at the same time complain that they are overworked and have less time to properly examine NHS patients. However, except for a few bad apples, most NHS staff remain true to their profession, but it has led, not only doctors, but also teachers, as well as other professionals leaving public institutions to work in private establishments, because some professionals equate reward as a monetary gain, not job satisfaction. Such as, witnessing a pupil succeed, see a patient get better, prevent crime, serve civic duty, provide justice and so on. Compromising and trading the gift of intellectual excellence, to uphold the moral fabric of society, as a means to make money to lead a life of luxury, like millionaires.

Our politicians as the 'defenders of society' are happy to enjoy the perks of being in charge, but quick to absolve responsibility, quick to shun responsibility after the illegal Iraq war, EU referendum results and so forth, leaving the public to clear up their mess. The public has also witnessed politicians happy to lead the nation into constitutional crisis and break laws of the land, like proroguing parliament to woo voters with a 'populist political agenda', and pedalling insulting and divisive statements to stir up emotions for self-serving egos. It is true that lying and greed amongst politicians is nothing new. It has been going on for hundreds of years, but not to such an extent for some politicians believing that making the laws of the land gives them absolution of those laws, as witnessed in the number of public inquiries. We have to ask what examples are they setting in our public institutions. This is setting a precedent for the ordinary public that greed gets rewarded, when they see politicians lying and fiddling expenses without facing serious or any consequences. They also see religious leaders involved and engaged in unscrupulous activities. The old tested scruples of role-models founded on the basic concepts that the 'defenders of society' perform civic and professional duty to serve the public are no longer adhered to and easily abandoned. It is the same within the business sector. The public witness scandals, greed and a race to the bottom, such as tax evasion, pay disputes, violations of workers' rights, while top executives earn huge salaries and bonuses.

This is what the third largest component of society (the public) witness when they look up to these role-models. The public see nothing but a drop in public standards in all walks of life, and either emulate their behaviour as normal, thinking after all what they are doing must be right, so why not follow. To the public it seems a natural practice, as we see in our own homes that children will pick up good and bad habits from those around them, especially the bad habits. The desire to get rich quickly with the least effort and scruples has spread to the rest of society, just like cancer. Everyone wants to make a fast buck in the shortest possible time. In fact, one often hears people saying that if they won the lotto, the first thing they would do is give up their job and go on a spending spree. In the past, the significant majority believed in earning an honest hard day's work and job satisfaction, now it has become a dread to go to work.

We now face a situation whereby professionals and management work with less conviction and duty, equating their role to monetary gain, which has led to the ensuing breakdown in the ethical fabric of the society. It has resulted in the masses emulating greed and unscrupulous behaviour practiced by their superiors, who are meant to be the gatekeepers for the well-being of society. Instead, greed has now become normalised, to the extent that it means to succeed in order to lead a celebrity lifestyle, greed is good and acceptable if one can get away at the expense of the common good of society. If greed and a drop in work ethics was not enough, the 'defenders of society' get promoted or nominated for knighthoods and honours for recognition of their services for doing the job that they get handsomely paid, with good perks, and less accountability when things go wrong. For example, a doctor, nurse, civil servant and others in the limelight receive honours for delivering a royal baby and other such acts. Really, rewarded for doing their job! The average woman does not see or have a consultant gynaecologist at her bedside as she delivers her baby. Most of us, if we are lucky have to suffice with a midwife, who is run ragged. For the elite, it seems everything they do gets easily noticed and appreciated, for the average Joe in the street, they have to work hard for years, and most of them do not get recognised. Even if the average Joe gets nominated, they start at the bottom of the pile with a low-ranking title. A token gesture handed out in the name of transparency to keep them happy, so they can continue to believe in hope, fairness and democracy, even if theirs maybe a far worthier cause then some celebrities.

The honours system is meant to recognise people who have achieved something in their life, and committed to serving and helping to enhance life in Britain. What is difficult to comprehend, is that quite often people get recognised for getting sacked from government, public office and disgraceful scandals, such as fraud, extra marital affairs, perjury and more. A system they have milked for years, at the expense of the taxpayer. The main reason politicians, chief constables, civil servants and the like get honours is to keep the secrets within their elite circle of friends is because they all know too much, and so are dangerous, and treated as potential loose cannons. How can we forget Jimmy Saville, Rolf Harris and Jeffrey Archer, to name a few? The honours system has rapidly morphed into rewards for services rendered to those in power, whoever they may be, with an impression of having a rigid selection criterion. Many of those on the list are millionaires in their own right, and are amply rewarded throughout their affluent lifestyle. The honours system should look further afield and recognise those who have gone above and beyond their line of duty to help others without financial gain. Film stars, rock stars, business people have had their recognition, success and financial rewards paid in the form of tax cuts and other perks. While in the real world, the charity food banks and hot meals for the homeless that are prepared by volunteers are on the increase, because of austerity, low wages, high rents and government policy failures. Those MPs who retire or do not get re-elected, get generous re-settlement grants, pensions or are rewarded by ending up in the House of Lords, being rewarded for their failures with even more perks! Besides, most have built a nest egg and have consultancy jobs lined-up, so then go on to act as advisors for big businesses on how to take advantage of loop holes, by lobbying and influencing the lawmakers they were once a part off. The same could be said about celebrities, who can get their contributions noticed easily because of useful contacts and media coverage. Whereas, for the regular person in the street not in the public eye, need to rely on lady luck for their years of hard work to get noticed by an influential person, or celebrity to recommend them. It is equally noticeable that the awards system is to entertain celebrities. For example, during the Pride of Britain Awards, ceremonies held to commemorate the public for brave acts, those in the audience were mostly the rich and famous applauding at recipients with no sign of many ordinary people, as if the event is organised for the celebrities to dress up and have a night out, and get noticed as philanthropists. Such scenes are no different from the past when the gladiators performed in front of nobility.

*****

There is no doubt that there is a distinct lack of accountability in public office. Do not take my word for it or for the matter that of the ordinary public. It speaks volumes when successive political leaders, despite recognising lack of accountability in public office have failed to honour their own pledges to shift power to make politicians more accountable. In 2010, David Cameron pledged to instruct Whitehall departments and public institutions to publish government policy business plans, setting out what they intend to do, and how voters can hold them accountable. David Cameron had claimed it will help reverse the trend and decentralise power in Whitehall, away from the 'Westminster Bubble' and encourage ministers and officials to govern for the long term. It has yet to see daylight.[25] Looking back, it has had a reverse effect, because more political chaos

---

[25] 'Missed Targets and Not Quite Accountable: The Reality of Whitehall Business Plans' 28th November 2011

and lack of mistrust in the democratic process is resulting in short-term knee-jerking policies with detrimental long-term financial cost, suffering and loss of lives. Not to be outdone by others, team Boris on 2nd January 2020 revealed 'seismic' changes planned for the civil servants, forcing them to sit regular exams to prove they are competent to work in Whitehall.[26] So, what happened to the pledge on MP's seven ethical standards course promised in 1995? By contrast, recent successive governments have left a bigger mess and more long-term uncertainty for the country, in terms of economy, environment, security, national debt and social harmony with less power shifted to the people, resulting in even a greater shift to the politician's default position hoarding more power. The public, also fail to see why they should have to pay for the continuing mistakes of politicians and other the 'defenders of society' acting on top professional advice paid for by them. Why should the public have to suffer for their major policy failures? Why are politicians and their advisers not held responsible for their failed policies?

Having just recovered from the dishonesty of MPs expenses and sleaze of the 1990s, along comes illegal wars, greedy bankers, NHS blood transfusion scandals, Windrush and many more, which finally resulted in people venting their anger by voting for Brexit, because of years of frustration of being let down by the 'defenders of society'. There is a limit to how much the public can tolerate. The British bulldog spirit is not one of violence by nature, but controlled and determined. However, over the past few decades we have witnessed a greater leaning towards violence and drunkenness to vent anger. Though this should not be an excuse, but is reality. It is equally worrying for ethnic people, who have made UK their home, as past world history often reflects civil unrest, often ending in the persecution of minority groups as easy targets. We are seeing an increase in hate crimes because of fascist leaders or government(s) covering up their failures by targeting minority groups like that was seen during the World Wars, or in recent times such as 'ethnic cleansing' in Myanmar, India, Bosnia, Burundi, Israel and elsewhere. In the UK, police records also show an increase in hate crime directed towards ethnic people, not only during the 2016 EU referendum and Brexit debate, but also when political leaders have made speeches, or write newspaper columns with a 'populist political agenda' attacking minority groups.

Despite the lack of accountability recognised way back in 1995, 2010,[25] and as recently as 2020,[26] public concerns and cries of help by the ordinary public still get ignored until a disaster, event or scandal happens, causing immense damage

---

https://www.instituteforgovernment.org.uk/news/in-the-press/europhile-peer-behind-article-50-sparks-fury-after-he-says-we-need-more-migrants?page=112

[26] The Telegraph: 'Thursday morning news briefing: Civil Service revolution revealed' 2nd January 2020 https://www.telegraph.co.uk/news/2020/01/02/thursday-morning-news-briefing-civil-service-revolution-revealed/

to property, suffering and/or loss of lives. The public has suffered horrific consequences. Unfortunately, it is only after major disasters that MPs get stimulated to organise cross-party committees to investigate the causes behind such dreadful policy failures. These efforts usually end up with a conclusion of outrage that such miseries are taking place in modern times, in a country with the fifth largest economy in the world. While the government's standard response in these situations is that it is working on the inquiry findings to improve the system, so they can prevent it from happening again, at the same time, scapegoats are found and hung out to dry, and those responsible get away with it scot-free. Even if forced to resign for misconduct in public office, the politicians can return in another capacity to make more mistakes without ever be held accountable for the suffering they have caused.

To add insult to injury, those guilty at the top of the decision-making process are just moved aside or retired, without facing any penalty of wasting millions of pounds of taxpayers hard earned money on failed costly projects and wars. Learning lessons from expensive public inquiries has become a lucrative business for lawyers. Legal public inquiry costs should be laid against all parties, who knowingly and willingly seek to thwart policies. This has also been shown when top civil servants and advisors criticise the failings of government policies, only when they become victims of the system themselves.[27] They then rush to give press interviews describing how unfair, complex and unprofessional the policies affect the poor. They use big words like "Kafkaesque" - meaning weird, oppressive and unconsidered in lay-person's language - to express the profound shock at the administrative failures, which penalises disadvantage and disable people.

The public face a colossal task to get heard, concerns often falling on deaf ears, and only after loss of lives and suffering are given the impression that they are being heard. But in reality, I do not think so. Instead of politicians and the 'establishment' leading from the front, shun responsibilities and pass the buck onto their subordinates. Instead of leadership, politicians rely more on a managerial style, called the 'sofa-style government',[28] with a culture of blaming others. If politicians would only listen to the public's concerns, and not brush these under the carpet, it would not only expose irregularities in public life, but also save lives and public money.

We have elected politicians and executives failing in their duties, whilst squandering public money on un-costed vanity projects. The defenders of the

---

[27] The Guardian: 'Former watchdog chief labels disabled benefits process a 'hostile environment' 6th October 2018 https://www.theguardian.com/society/2018/oct/06/former-watchdog-chief-labels-disabled-benefits-process-a-hostile-environment
[28] UK | Politics | Curtains for Blair's 'sofa cabinet'? - BBC NEWS 15th July 2004 http://news.bbc.co.uk/2/hi/3895921.stm

culture of less political accountability brigade, namely the 'establishment', are often heard jumping on the band wagon that such responsibility will deter 'political talent' entering into politics and go elsewhere. Ministers have a highly paid top team of professional 'expert advisers' at their disposal to guide and enable them in all aspects of the decision-making process, so why can they not be held responsible for the decision-making process? There is no excuse why they should not be held accountable, especially when politicians' wishes have been met, because the job is very well paid, and must have attracted exceptional talent, because most of them have entered politics as a chosen career. Many have an impeccable education background, as they have attended well-known grammar, public or private schools and world-renowned universities. Therefore, you would think highly qualified to execute duties more responsibly and professionally. The last five British PMs since 1997 have attended prestigious academies, four attended Oxford University, and one would expect with such an education pedigree, the nation would benefit immensely from their intellectual talent, impeccable integrity, ability to grasp facts with sound judgement, trained to analyse facts, aided by an equally clever team of expert advisers, they should not put a foot wrong when making decisions. Instead, there is a drastic increase in the number of public inquiries and legal challenges with examples of severe abuse of democracy, illegal wars, Brexit negotiations failures and more. Such failures raise the question of their decision-making ability, because their conduct in public office contradicts what one would expect from a graduate from such a respected establishment. What the public object to most, is the outrageously dishonourable and disrespectful mishandling of events or situations with the audacity to act as if they have done nothing wrong, and acted within the law, which we all know, is not true!

No one denies that politicians are infallible, after all they are only human, and we all make mistakes, but what has been puzzling recently is the rapid rise in mistakes made by them, usually followed by denial and apportioning blame onto others. Is it because politicians and their top public executives are fully aware that they will not be held accountable, and in the worst-case scenario, if blamed they can always resign or move to another post, and/or even make a comeback later when the dust has settled? The public just wish former political leaders and minsters; having done untold damage, not only to this country, but also to world peace, would just fade into obscurity and stop behaving as armchair pundits, abstain from preaching the rights and wrongs to others, but examine their own record when in office, because the suffering they have caused due to their actions still exists today. In normal life, people would get fired for not doing their job properly, without payment, or even go to jail for serious offences. But despite blunders, our politicians continue in their jobs, and if they resign, sacked or do not get elected, get rewarded in the future for their failures. As for some they enter a gentler, less demanding, more dignified role that awaits them in the

House of Lords, the board of companies or charities with equally good perks, others even end up on handsomely paid lecture circuits, advising others how to govern or write newspaper columns, and even get knighted for their work.

Politicians have also been involved in some other mind-boggling scandals and decision-making disasters, but remain unaffected. Such instances are where the Iraq inquiry raised serious doubts about the grounds upon which the government of the time had allied itself, scams involving property deals, violation of electoral rules by individuals and political parties, breach of 'anti-money laundering' laws, Westminster sex scandals where MPs, Members of Scottish Parliament, Assembly Members and politicians in high office accused of misogyny, sexual harassment, perverting the course of justice, bullying and assault, altercation with police, traffic violations, renewable energy heat incentive scandal, breaking ministerial code, and even an admission in public of drug use, which has no detrimental effect on the career or ambitions of politicians in a leadership contest, as well as covering up party donors and their tax status, on-going expenses fiddles, ferry contracts, rail timetable chaos, legal aid cuts, part-privatisation, employment tribunal fees, Brexit negations and many more fiascos costing the tax payer, to the extent democracy was tested to destruction, without any accountability in the irritable, burning and deeply divisive aftermath of the 2016 EU referendum, which was held for self-serving interests to settle old party feuds.

The public has also witnessed expensive policy failures whereby government lawyers and advisers negotiated the EU Brexit withdrawal agreement, with strict 'red lines' followed by slogans 'no deal is better than a bad deal' to satisfy Tory EU rebels, which they rejected, only to willingly support a re-packaged Brexit deal with a few minor changes as 'oven ready', costing the tax payer significantly and causing uncertainty. After three years of wasted negotiations, the government's impatient approach to get Brexit resolved is extremely worrying. It seems lessons have not been learnt from our past short-sighted hasty decisions, dividing people for self-serving political interests, the effects of which are still being played out right in front of us, for example Hong Kong, Kashmir, and the Middle East, we can only hope we do not create a similar situation in Ireland, and just like their predecessors, they will just swan-off to write biographies and newspaper columns to advice others what to do. It is increasingly clear that the divisions over Brexit will dominate and define domestic life for many years to come, with a 'populist political agenda', pitting one group against other, only to be followed by costly inquiries to learn lessons after inflicting suffering and loss of lives.

We also see anti-social behaviour in public places increasing, which cannot be tackled entirely by extra police officers or more laws being made. We need to nurture positive relationships, mutual respect, empathy and trust. It is fashionable for the lawmakers with a 'populist political agenda' to demand tougher laws to curtail the rise in anti-social behaviour, or question the 'common sense' of the ordinary people at the time of disasters, like Jacob Rees-Mogg did in 2019, during the Grenfell fire public inquiry. Instead, what we need more than anything else are pro-active solutions, starting with good role-models in public life with a deeper insight of real-life problems, with less egos and more accountability from those holding positions of power and responsibility in society. Their behaviour in public life over the past decades has fallen far short, and they are not doing anything to rectify the situation, which is now getting entrenched, not only amongst the adult population, but also the future generations at an early age. A drop in public standards has started to take its toll at a much faster rate and needs to be rectified to restore trust, before it exacerbates further.

We need to ask what legacy we can expect to leave for future generations, when both parents and children constantly witness bad behaviour of greed, lies, arrogance, unaccountability and breaking the laws of the land by the 'establishment'. What we have to remember is how small society and the planet has become, because a young person growing up at home, or in a remote place of the world can watch good and bad behaviour of role models in a split second. Television and social media have shrunk the world, and in the process have become a great weapon for eradicating ignorance, promoting good scruples, but at the same time it can also have a drastic effect on children when they witness bad behaviour of political leaders played out in the open.

14

Building Bridges: Discrimination and Social Cohesion

Some of the government initiatives like the 'Race Audit', 'Social Mobility', 'Task Force', 'British Values' and 'Big Society' followed the successive PM's speeches, but failed to address the inherent issues, wasting the tax payer's money, millions of pounds that could have been invested wisely to improve public services. Social cohesion can only be achieved without an 'US' or 'THEM' attitude. What took place in the past has happened, big mistakes were made, but humanity benefitted from many good things too, such as advances in technology, education, health, welfare, travel and much more, albeit by some and not all. We cannot keep on dwelling on past mistakes, and who should be held responsible for what. Instead, we need to address the current mess; otherwise, the future generations will blame us for wasting time. It is best to heal and let us all move on towards a brighter future. We all have better opportunities now, more than ever before, let us unite all our unique skills and build a better world, rather than 'you did this, you did that' syndrome. We will all be affected by climate change if this is not tackled soon, and need to realise that present day atrocities, sufferings and poverty will get much worse, which will fuel more anger, envy and hatred. Of course, we need to talk and remember past issues, but in a 'civilised' manner, so not to increase racially and religious motivated conflicts. We are now in a new century, and the events that happened generations ago cannot be changed, and most of us were not even born then. The older generation and politicians need to stop dreaming about the colonial past, and embrace the fact that the younger generation have other priorities, different to those of the last century. After all, it is their future we need to think off!

Britain reflects a land of multicultural society. Some of the progress can be attributed directly to the fundamental goodwill and decency of the British people. It is also to do with what is visible about the vast majority of ethnic people, in terms of respecting the law, hard work, enterprise and family values. I have always believed that the UK is a blessed land, because religious worship is freely practiced here by many people of different faiths. We need to work towards a peaceful co-existence, and this can only be achieved by recognising all faiths, or those of no faith, everyone has their own point of view on many issues from marriage, abortion, divorce, financial matters and much more, but whatever the feelings or differences are, we must all obey the law of the land. In fact, loyalty to the land of dwelling has been enshrined in all faiths, showing compassion towards fellow humans, regardless of sex, creed race or class. These principles are at the heart of every serious religion, in order to gain a peaceful existence. They also recognise that hatred only breeds more hatred.

I have always regarded myself a proud British citizen, because I have decided to call it my home, just like I would have called Tanzania my home, if I still lived there. Britain is a great country, and its people have good virtues. However, it is compulsory for all British ethnic and non-ethnic people to respect each other, and live in harmony in our multicultural country. My main criticism of those who believe otherwise would be, if you disagree why live here? Over the past hundred years, human beings of all cultures and faiths have faced atrocities, such as discrimination and persecution. It is even happening now at home, and in many other parts of the world, and in some way, we are all guilty to allow this to happen. Like me, many others are proud to be British, choose to live here, and thrilled to be a part of Britain, just wanting the best for the country and its people. The concerns I raised twenty years ago, from April 2000 onwards have sadly come true, because of failures in government policy initiatives. It has done more harm in terms of integration between ethnic and indigenous people into the mainstream British way of life, fuelling anger and resentment, and alienating communities. This is because in the past, when formulating policies relating to ethnic people, too much emphasis has been placed on politics of appeasement and reliance on certain individuals claiming to be the 'gatekeepers' of ethnic communities. Ethnic people need to engage more and can no longer afford to take for granted the goodwill of their host community. For this to happen, they need to overcome negative profiling of stereotyping and prejudice of non-ethnic people towards them. It is necessary to place greater emphasis at the grass roots level, in both ethnic and non-ethnic communities, to reach out and heal misconceptions and differences. All too often we are made to believe that government and public bodies operate under the democratic principles of fairness to realise the aspirations and dreams of all, yet the public see no signs of this. In all honesty, what the public see is that we have become a world and society where:

We have more rights, only accessible with frustrating and exhaustive efforts
We have more courts and mechanisms for justice, if one has financial clout
We have more parliamentary democracy, easy for those with right contacts
We have more laws, and those obeying penalised more than the lawmakers
We have more politicians listening to advisers than ordinary people
We have more policy initiatives, but accomplish less
We have more career politicians with less real-life values and common sense
We have more experts and ideologies, but fewer problems solved
We have more inspection targets, with less resources for public services
We have more charities with politicians tackling fewer underlying issues
We have more food banks and homeless in fifth richest nation in the world
We have more commissions for human rights, but people still suffer
We have more biographies and speeches made, but less real-life principles
We have more journalists but less scrutiny of right/left wing extremism in politics
We have more millionaires investing off-shore, than pay fair share of tax
We have bigger government budgets, and less accomplished policy pledges
We have highly paid politicians with lower morals, and less accountability
We have been to the moon, but cannot cross the street to help neighbours

It is about time real-life experiences of ordinary people leading everyday lives were taken on board by the government. I am not at all advocating that the advice from Whitehall officials, ethnic leaders and entrepreneurs is improper, no not at all! Except like our politicians, they are also out of touch with reality, and have stopped listening to the people. When they reach fame and eminence, they rely on advisors or assistants, who in some cases, have their own agenda or ambitions. I am aware the present situation is a reflection of the present times, but we cannot afford to ignore reality. We have got to do something about it! Solutions do exist, if we are prepared to search with conviction. We need to address the dilemma of not listening to the public, which has become the main stumbling block in realising certain government objectives. I fully appreciate, because of time constraints, it would be impractical for the PM and ministers to listen to each and every person, so have to rely on advisors. However, we need to break away from the politics of the past and govern for all, not only those who are loud and get their voice heard. What has lacked in the past is a direct interaction between ethnic and non-ethnic communities. It has resulted in people leading isolated lives, and being suspicious of one another. We need to encourage interaction at the local level between churches, mosques, synagogues and temples, to enhance civic duty. Organising interfaith community-based projects and social events would help bring local neighbourhoods together, with a better understanding and respect of each other's religious ethos and culture, instead of living in fear of one another. This would help promote the importance of living in peace, because it will encourage everyone, young and old, to engage with one another. Such an approach would encourage ethnic and non-ethnic communities to benefit from direct interaction.

As humans, we need to treat each other with mutual respect, whether a politician or not. It is inhumane to treat animals badly, so why treat fellow humans with less dignity. If we open up to each other, such a strategy will work, as well as working as a deterrent against those who preach to cause division and hatred. People will become less suspicious of each other, allowing greater interaction and harmony, by asking questions and learning more about one another. If an individual leads an isolated confined life, they could get brainwashed easily, by mixing with undesirable elements in society, and believe in propaganda aimed at causing hatred and division. Whereas with positive reasoning and interaction, people would see for themselves that we all believe in similar shared values, such as our desire for equal rights, and to make a living to provide a better future for our children. Learning and communication are vital, and it is our duty to stay in touch with each other's society, because isolation not only serves to corrupt one's values, but is not good for one's mind and health. This is nothing new! Loneliness has no age barrier, and can have detrimental consequences, such as depression, social anxiety and paranoia.

Discrimination has not helped with the integration of ethnic people into the mainstream British life. Especially when ethnic people consistently face negative everyday experiences - all frequently associated with racism - in the press or hear Chinese whispers in schools, neighbourhoods, and workplaces that they are not welcome in the UK. It also does not help when politicians, in their quest for power, use ethnic people as cheap election fodder with 'dog whistle' politics of targeting minority groups for their own failed policies, resulting in shortages in public service and affordable housing. In 2013, the illegal immigrant 'Go Home' posters were not a clever way of dealing with the issue of immigration. It caused a lot of hurt for the families entitled to live in this country, and who do so as proud British citizens, and like me, objected to the tone of the campaign launched by the Home Office. So, it is not surprising that the general public treat immigrants with hostility, attacking women dressed in a certain style, because of the derogatory manner they get portrayed, either by the press or some politicians.

I can speak from personal experience, when it comes to dealing with the hostile environment of pain and financial cost inflicted by the Home Office on genuine British citizens of ethnic origin, at times we are left to feel like second-class citizens. I have never advocated an open-door immigration policy, but just fairness. The default position adopted by the Home Office officials is one of suspicion. It is based on the assumption that all British citizens of ethnic origin are illegal, with only one motive; to claim and live on welfare benefits.

*****

In September 2006, I had compiled a visa application with full supporting documents, and posted the package for my mother and sister to lodge at the visa processing in Mombasa for a six-month UK Visitor Visa. I had clearly explained the circumstances behind the visit, which was to allow the family to mourn together, following the bereavement of my father in March 2006 in Kenya, followed by my brother-in-law in June 2006 in Reading. It would have also helped my widowed sister with two young children (one autistic), to come to terms with after their sad loss. My mother received a phone call from the British High Commission inviting them to attend an interview in Nairobi at very short notice, which was about three hundred miles from where she lived. I had already explained in the letter that my mother was elderly, and it would be difficult for her to travel a long distance by bus. I then had to phone the High Commission to explain the situation further, but they remained adamant that she had to attend. I then tried to request for them to hold a telephone interview, which was also declined. By the way, there was a British High Commission office in Mombasa where they could have been interviewed, but the officials in their wisdom decided against this. The visa was refused on some ridiculous grounds, such as they may not return to Kenya, and may claim welfare benefits, or my seventy-nine-year-old mother and sixty-one-year-old sister may try to get jobs here. I lodged an appeal challenging the diabolical reasons. It was heard on 2nd February 2007 and the hearing lasted less than an hour, as the Home Office had reached a decision on unfounded grounds. The appeal was upheld. I fought the appeal myself to avoid the expensive legal costs, because justice comes at a price! It took six months to get a simple Visitor Visa from the time it was lodged. It is difficult to describe the lack of compassion on the part of the High Commission at a time of bereavement, bearing in mind it was not for sightseeing. Even if it was, they had no right to stop them from coming. But I know it happens, because of the mindset of the Home Office and extra hoops ethnic people have to go through to satisfy them. By the time the visa was granted, we had all lost interest, as we had come to cope individually with the sad loss of our two close family members. Since, I had already spent so much time, effort and money, I decided they should come for a visit after all. They arrived in April 2007; a year after father passed away, and more importantly, did not claim benefits or find a job, and returned to Kenya after their visit.

*****

This plainly highlights the obstacles faced by ethnic people, and also raises the question whether people from Australia, Canada, New Zealand and elsewhere, of non-ethnic origin would face similar obstacles? I know many examples like mine, and personally volunteered to help others defending two appeals, with successful outcomes. I have raised such discrepancies in government policies, and the attitude of the Home Office many times with politicians, but as usual, these concerns fall on deaf ears. To add insult to injury, in 2013 the Home Office sent vans with hostile posters. We also know of the suffering caused to the Windrush generation, and the hostility of the Home Office environment towards them. The resentment towards immigrants will make no difference, even if the current Home Secretary and her predecessor are both ethnic. What needs addressing is the general attitude towards ethnic people. During the 2019 election campaign, the PM advocated there was a Muslim Chancellor (now ex) in his cabinet, as proof that Islamophobia does not exist in the Tory Party, let alone in other public bodies, but this will not wash, because I, like many others know what it feels like to experience discrimination. The government, by remaining in denial and ignorant of such racial issues does not mean that discrimination has been eliminated, and boasting about a token of ethnic people in public life, does not mean that the ordinary ethnic people do not face discrimination. In real life, it is ethnic Muslims who have to run the daily gauntlet of racist verbal abuse and physical attacks. Let us not forget that the ex-Chairman of the Tory Party has gone on record to say that Islamophobia does exist in the Tory party. Often when the question of racism, antisemitism and Islamophobia gets raised during debates, politicians are quick to condemn this, and then it gets forgotten until it is raised again. This has also become the norm for politicians, when they get found out about their racist behaviour, or when challenged by the public or the press they are quick to claim that they are not racist, and know many ethnic, black, Muslim and Jewish people. Of course, we all know people from different backgrounds, but knowing someone and living their experiences on a daily basis is another thing. It is this mind-set that we need to tackle, if we really want to make further progress in achieving social harmony.

Politicians are quick to grab headlines when they think it will raise their profile to get elected, and when it suits them, they make sure that they are filmed in the company of the ethnic people, dress to look like them and sound 'cool', or do something silly. They are then happy to post this on social media. Some politicians will also insult ethnic people for their dress code in well-paid newspaper columns to boost their campaign to woo voters, grabbing any opportunity to raise their profile during election or EU referendum campaigns, until it backfires. They then become restrained and apologise for the suffering and pain they caused to those they attacked, but then having the cheek to blame and patronise others for construing the facts, because they have not read or listened to their full article or speech. This also raises the question about their judgement when making important decisions on behalf of the country, whether they can be trusted to honour their promises, or mean what they say.

There have been times that some right-wing tabloid press, political group or politician who are quick to comment on news item(s) of incidents, events or civil unrest involving ethnic people with an undertone in their report of Islamophobia and hostility towards immigration. When challenged about their coverage or views, they then jump on the band wagon to defend that 'the point here is about free speech, which has now got reduced to a stage where no one can innocently say anything'. They even go on to say that 'their views reflect that of the majority, or their words are construed, as they did not mean what they said or wrote'. Politicians then try their utmost to defend themselves, by mentioning procedures they have set-up to address Islamophobia, antisemitism and other types of discrimination. Just empty words, to give the impression that the party is a broad church and the few bad apples will be dealt with, after the internal disciplinary process has taken its course. Really!

Sometimes, instead of directly facing journalists or the public, politicians will send an ethnic spokesperson to do their dirty work to defend their actions, making desperate claims to justify that they are a son of an immigrant, that the politician holds no such racist views. This happened when Kwasi Kwarteng, an ethnic Business Minister was sent on 18th February 2020 to do the rounds within TV studios and radio stations to pacify Andrew Sabisky's past remarks, as 'offensive' and 'racist', who resigned after being appointment by Boris Johnson and his advisor.[29] Not to be left out, Priti Patel our ethnic Home Secretary was also sent to do the media rounds the next day on 19th February, to defend the PM following the comment made by Rapper Dave at the Brit Awards about Boris Johnson's judgement to hire Mr Sabisky.[30] She said the comments where "utter nonsense," adding, "I don't know what those comments are based on. It's wrong to make judgements about individuals when you don't know a particular individual, as in the case of the PM. He's not a racist at all, and I just think those comments are highly inappropriate." This raises three questions. Why do organ grinders send ethnic ministers to get them out of the hole? Is it one of the roles of their appointment to do the PM's dirty work? Why should the PM hide and not defend himself, after causing controversy? A few handpicked ethnic ministers may be good for illusion sake, a charade which one can easily see through. These are past practices of divide and rule, best left behind where they belong, as the painful lessons of our colonial history, which we must not need to practice or re-learn. What the political leaders do not realise, is that unlike the ordinary public, they do not have to face real-life consequences in neighbourhoods, workplaces and schools with chants of go home, or monkey noises on football pitches. Unfortunately, politicians, after making bullish remarks in newspapers or speeches, such as Muslim women look like 'letter boxes', black people with 'watermelon smiles' and gay men as 'tank-topped bum-

---

[29] The Guardian: 'Andrew Sabisky: minister urges review of No 10-hiring process' 18th February 2020 https://www.theguardian.com/politics/2020/feb/18/andrew-sabisky-no-10-hiring-process-needs-looking-at-minister-kwasi-kwarteng
[30] Daily Mail: 'Priti Patel steps in to defend Boris Johnson branding claims he's racist as 'utter nonsense' after rapper Dave hit out at the Prime Minister at the Brit Awards' 19th February 2020 https://www.dailymail.co.uk/news/article-8019615/Priti-Patel-calls-rapper-Daves-claim-Brit-awards-Boris-Johnson-racist-utter-nonsense.html

boys' to name a few, then decline offers to engage in proper face-to-face debates with those they have insulted, or blamed for their failed policies or actions.

It is true that significant progress has been made in the last century to address blatant and traditional forms of discrimination through the Suffragettes, Apartheid, American Civil Rights, and other campaigns. Equally true is that more people, especially in the West, enjoy far greater civil, welfare, marital and employment rights than ever before. But what we are seeing now is an increase in various subtle forms of discrimination based on race, class, sex and age, not only directed towards ethnic people, but also towards non-ethnic. It pains me to see we are still spending so much time dividing each other, rather than working on shared values, by focusing on strengthening links, built on the positive aspects during the British colonial rule. Instead of learning lessons from the past, we are brushing them aside, ignoring aspirations and realties. Whether we admit it or not, past memories of evil practices do exist, albeit to a lesser extent. In reality, Islamophobia, antisemitism and 'ethnic cleansing' are modern versions of apartheid for self-serving political interests, based on nationalist and 'populist political agendas'.

Throughout the history of humanity, democracy, capitalism, free market, socialism, communism and other ideologies came into existence to give hope, with pledges to make life better for ordinary people. Such expectations on the surface seem plausible, and working with achievable prospects for most, as long as the progression proceeds without major obstacles, so that dreams and aspirations are met, whatever they may be. It is only when a member of the public faces difficulty, and tries to put into practice the pledges of hope and fairness made in election speeches, do they realise what those pledges actually mean, in terms of accountability, transparency, justice and democratic rights, because all those pledges become a distant reality, except for those individuals with financial clout, media help or campaigns led by influential individuals, celebrities, charitable agencies and trade organisations.

Ethnic people also get blamed for shortages in public services, increase in crime and more. Therefore, ethnic communities, unlike non-ethnic people, face a double whammy from both blatant and subtle forms of discrimination in public life. We also see non-ethnic people fall victim to the subtle forms of discrimination, not based on race or creed, but upbringing, in terms of schools attended and social etiquette, such as dress code, accent and eating manners. However, the outcome of the EU referendum was more to do with the North-South divide, due to the failed fifty-year policies of past successive Tory and Labour governments, to address the real-life concerns of ordinary people. In fact, the shortage in hospitals, housing stock and schools is not the fault of ethnic people, but more to do with political failures. For humanity to function effectively in a 'civilised' manner, we need governance and politics to bring out the good in the people and nations, not by using divisive politics, by bringing out the worst in people, which is unforgivable, undemocratic and unacceptable. Let politicians remain true to their vows and pledges.

The question of social cohesion is about justice and social inclusion for the rich as well as the poor, and it should not be only about race. Even marginalised and deprived communities who happen to be non-ethnic must also be included in our vision of social cohesion. We need to go much deeper than just persuasive speaking or writing if we want to tackle radicalisation, social cohesion and social mobility. How to underpin them all is as old as those values that bind humanity, such as how we live together and respect one another, and how we can put back into the communities in which we live. In Britain, we have been here before. In the last century Britain has done more than its fair share to provide refuge to the dispossessed, whether during conflicts between Catholics and Protestants, the fallout from which we are still living today, the integration of Eastern European Jews, or coming to the aid of Ugandan Asians. We have achieved those goals through a combination of a steadfast faith in our institutions and values, such as freedom under the rule of law, diversity, and above all tolerance, because society, including the minority community, stood together as one, even during two World Wars. There is no reason to believe we cannot do the same today, and our approach should be the same, determined, not defeatist. Although we need to be worried about the debate on radicalisation, Islamophobia, social harmony and social mobility, with respect to an agenda based on right-wing nationalism. We must not fall under the illusion that the problems can be solved simply by the top-down, quick-fix state action, by legislating our way out of problems. The most powerful weapon against radicalisation and hatred would be to place real hope and fairness right at the top of the agenda.

Social cohesion has been further exacerbated for ethnic and non-ethnic people from disadvantaged households, as they are left behind, because of the 'retreat' of successful Britons from areas where ethnic people live, limiting cultural integration, which ought to make us anxious. This is not good news! Not only does it prevent social cohesion, in terms of less familiarity with various cultural codes, such as income, lifestyle, customs, but also hinders progress leading to more problems of employment, as most jobs come through the non-ethnic majority, and contacts of knowing someone. This will mean that a growing ethnic population will get more isolated, and by lacking connections, will reduce access to most jobs and other networks. For example, in Canada studies show that immigrants in cities, such as Toronto and Vancouver have a larger immigrant population earning less than the national average than immigrants in smaller, less diverse cities.[31] Also the findings in 2019 by the British Integration Survey shows that Britain is becoming more segregated.[32] It is extremely serious, and we should not ignore such trends and sleepwalk into segregation. It poses great threats inflicting pain and sufferings on humanity, especially on the peace loving 'vast silent majority'. In the era of globalisation and great technological advance, we all have to respect each other to achieve greater things, not by living in fear of each other. We need to find a middle ground, not destroy shared human values with a divide and rule agenda, and in order to feel safe, it is necessary to recognise each other's values and contributions, anyone who abandons hatred, will serve humanity well, and this country will be a safer place for us all, as well as for future generations to live.

Most government initiatives, however well-meaning, lack direct engagement at the most basic level. Such interaction is most needed to deliver results, and prevent atrocities from happening in the first place. Since 9/11, we have seen costly high-powered policy initiatives started to prevent extremism to strengthen communities. These initiatives launched and announced, aim to bring together expertise and experience of eminent ethnic people, except those who are affected most by policy failures at local, national and international level. In fact, the reason past policy initiatives have failed is because eminent people fail to recognise the actual needs of ordinary ethnic people, as they rely on advisers for information, who know little about the actual real-life issues and feelings, and facts can get construed by inaccurate and tarnished prejudices. No different from the way non-ethnic people feel ignored by the politicians. Of course, state action is necessary, but legislation is not the only answer, as it is not only insufficient, but extremely expensive to effectively administer. We need politicians to be good role models, and listen to real-life concerns at a basic community level. To the vast majority of humans at home and abroad, social cohesion means people of different faiths and backgrounds living together in harmony in their search of common goals of hope and fairness, with a sense of belonging and shared values. Unfortunately, the politician's policy of a 'populist political agenda' has undermined our nation's sense of social cohesion with emphasis on what divides us, rather than what brings us together. Politicians believe that they can legislate all forms of discrimination, and expect those affected to seek justice through the courts, which is not the right way to address social cohesion. It is not as easy as it looks, because lawyers do not come cheap. Also, no amount of compensation will alleviate pain or bring back lost ones, because of the suffering inflicted by the actions of others. Let us not forget, the government is equally guilty when it comes to breaking laws, or putting obstacles in place, when implementing

---

[31] Ethnic Enclaves in Canada: Opportunities and Challenges Residing Within
https://www.researchgate.net/publication/327752315_Ethnic_Enclaves_in_Canada_Opportunities_and_Ch
allenges_of_Residing_Within
[32] British Integration Survey 2019 – The Challenge https://the-challenge.org/impact/reports/the-british-integration-survey-2019/

immigration and welfare benefit laws. They are also equally keen to use phrases like "we're all in this together." But are we really?

Having been bought up in a multi-cultural environment with many happy memories, it has always come naturally to look at people as fellow human beings. I was born and went to school in a small town of Tanga with many pleasant memories of growing-up in a multi-cultural environment, like others of similar age. It never crossed my mind, as I grew older to look at people as belonging to a different race, creed, sex or class; it was only when I came to the UK that I learnt various names for referring to different races of people. I still see people the same way today, as I did in the past that we are all the same, with an overwhelming hope and desire to fulfil aspirations in a stable family unit and social cohesion, to realise one's dreams. Let us truly commit ourselves to foster sound social cohesion, because we all cherish leaving a better legacy for the future generations. Too many have suffered, but continue to hope for love, fairness and freedom.

The only times I have been made conscious of my ethnic origin has been directly by a few people, or when required to declare my ethnicity on forms, or heard people like myself referred to differently by politicians and in the media. In fact, during my interactions with people, even when I was canvassing for their votes, I did not see them as a different colour, creed or class. Overwhelmingly, I can say that I only saw people treat each other with respect and trust, sharing the same hope and values. I am optimistic, because I have experienced first-hand signs of British compassion and that just needs to be harnessed in a positive way, to make an even kinder and loving society for all to live in. I believe there is still goodness left in the British people, which I have witnessed on my travels during the elections, but we cannot afford to be complacent and take it for granted, allowing political chaos to hijack the inherent British virtues. I believe in social cohesion that unites people and communities. Nationalism is about flag waving, fear and dividing, but we can have national pride without the populist politics of nationalism.

I love Tanzania; it is a great country and I have fond memories of growing up there, as well as for the education I received. But if you asked me whether I could ever live full time in Tanzania now, or could have gone to any other country for further education, the answer would be "No," not because I love Tanzania any less, but because Britain has been good to me, and is my true home now, and has my full loyalty, but Tanzania will always remain my motherland.

15

Radicalisation and 'Ethnic Cleansing'

I will now focus on another subject I have tried to tackle over the last two decades with Prime Ministers, cross-party politicians including my constituent MP. There is no doubt that human suffering from natural disasters is beyond the control of mankind, but what is unforgivable is when the West inflicts unnecessary inhumanity, carnage and suffering on vast populations of defenceless civilians of one particular faith under the wrong pretext of democracy, the 'war on terror', and then criticises the innocent followers of the faith with an untruthful label as radicalised Muslims. Disappointingly the word radicalisation has wrongly become closely associated with Muslims and frequently used by certain political leaders in the West and other countries, with their own divisive 'populist political agenda' for self-serving interests. If truth be told, it is nothing new. We have been sleep-walking through it, more so in the last two decades, with our heads buried in the sand, due to the actions of a few Western political leaders conspiring with the leaders of the wealthy Middle East countries who have rich oil reserves, claiming to be the custodians of Islam, and the West has no qualms doing lucrative business by exporting lethal weapons and supporting conflicts. Something I have been trying to highlight well before 9/11.

In fact, if the word radicalisation is applied with honesty, the 'populist political agenda' adopted and preached by certain political leaders, whether democratically elected or not, in the West, India and elsewhere is no different, however differently we try to dress it. What past history reflects is that if left unchecked can have serious consequences, as it did in the 20th century, which led to the rise in fascism and WWII. Equally worrying is that the two blatant traditional concepts, namely right and left-wing politics have evolved into many inter-linked subtle forms from this. Because of this, the subtle variants of the two extreme forms of radicalisation will be almost impossible to tackle outright, by tinkering at the edges with short-term solutions as it has been done of late. Instead of learning lessons from the past two World Wars, we still witness people being persecuted because of their faith, race, class and sex. Whereby, our 'learned' leaders in the West subtly pursue right-wing 'populist political agendas' based on nationalism to get elected, continuing to stay in power to cover up policy failures, under the pretext of democracy. Many voters when interviewed on TV during the 2019 general elections openly admitted they are not going to vote, because they do not trust politicians. The majority of the general public can be fooled no more! They are no longer oblivious to the blatant forms of fabricated lies spouted shamelessly by politicians on a regular basis just to get elected to serve in the highest ranks of public office. If the 'civilised' politicians in the West have stooped to such low standards, how can we expect others to behave any differently?

In a way, the form of radicalisation adopted by certain political leaders in the West and elsewhere is no different to that practiced by some politicised 'religious' leaders of all faiths, who instead of the 'normalised' political mechanisms are using faith for their own self-serving interests in total contradiction of all religious, agnostic or atheist doctrines practiced in the world to-day. Regardless of whether a true believer of any faith, the basic principle for everyone is to respect all life, as well as plant and animal life, even the physical environment that allows life to thrive, and if we do not, we have seen the consequences. So, what right has any individual got to take the life of a fellow human, especially by a 21st century, whether they are a religious or political leader, who respectively are not the original forbearers of the creator's divine message(s) or custodians of humanity.

How can any present-day religious leader(s) make bold claims that their interpretation of Holy Scriptures allows them to inflict such atrocities? Just the same as what right has a political leader(s) got to claim that they are custodians of humanity, and decide on whom to wage war on, and take innocent life in the name of democracy, or other political ideologies? The increase in radicalisation is more to do with men's ambition to rule others, as political or religious leaders, and adopt whatever methods to achieve it. The same can be said for political leaders, whether elected democratically or not, will stop at nothing to reach their goal, even if means taking the citizens of the nation to war. In fact, both religious and political leaders advocating such divisive radicalised ideologies, are never seen in the frontline leading the cause, except from the safety of their heavily guarded hideouts.

They are both forms of radicalisation, and no different. Both inflict hardship and loss of lives. The elected leaders for five years have claimed a democratic mandate to do what they like, especially if they secure a landslide victory, a sort of 'legalised form of dictatorship', while the unelected ones do it without a democratic mandate, but with the rule of gun, and a promise of a better after life. I would say why believe them, because there will be nothing to worry about if one has lived a life of good virtue, as the Creator would have wished us to live, not one of greed, destruction and lies. So why should the word of religious extremists, just like the democratically elected political leaders be believed, when time and time again, they are known to break pledges and behave differently from what they preach.

Politicians are keen to jump on the bandwagon by targeting minority groups. They are quick to declare multi-culturalism as a failure, without blaming themselves for their policy failures. All they can say in their controversial speeches is that we need a tougher stricter approach to tackle Islamist extremism and terrorism, without giving any pragmatic solutions. While conveniently forgetting to mention in their televised speeches or well-paid newspaper columns, the role they have played in encouraging radicalisation, such as supporting conflicts, exporting arms and divisive politics. In their quest for power, PMs then have the audacity to criticise and tarnish others for their own mistakes. David Cameron blamed non-white communities for 'passive tolerance' of unacceptable practices in a speech in Germany on 5th February 2011, claiming that such an approach had only served to help radicalise young Muslims, and urged a new 'muscular liberalism' that would promote British values more forcefully.[33] This is simply not true, because when ethnic people like me try to engage, they get ignored, not only by him, but four other PMs, cross-party politicians and own MP! He should realise he will not address real-life challenges by preaching and making divisive speeches.

Politicians should understand the extreme pain suffered directly or indirectly by law abiding ordinary Muslims, who witness vile actions conducted by the dictators, rebels or rulers in the Middle East - the self-appointed custodians of Islam - deploying arms supplied by the 'civilised' West to boost export trade and jobs. Muslims also witness relentless offensive persecution of the Faith of Islam by the media, depicting standard TV images of Burka (face veil) clad women and bearded men, doing nothing else but praying and chanting slogans 'Allahu Akbar'. Not to be outdone, it does not help when eminent political leaders write

---

[33] BBC News | UK Politics: 'State multiculturalism has failed, says David Cameron' 5th February 2011 https://www.bbc.co.uk/news/uk-politics-12371994

nonsense in newspaper columns, attacking Muslims by implying they make no contribution towards humanity, except carnage. Surprisingly, a 'free press' will not even bother to check facts before publishing such 'humbug', and are prepared to fork out five thousand pounds for writing these articles. When challenged, the author in question Boris Johnson, pleads innocence, as use of 'colourful language' claiming his article has got blown out of proportion, and when challenged in an open debate, they go into hiding to avoid their lies being scrutinised, and instead send one of his ethnic Ministerial appointees to diffuse the situation. Surely this is not what they were taught at the prestigious educational establishments they attended, namely not to take part in public debates after making false allegations!

It is not Islam, but a blend of various factors playing a vital part in the rise of extremists aided by the West, now prophesying Caliphate (someone who considers themselves as politico-religious successor and leader of the whole Muslim community), justifying their atrocities in the name of Islam. In the process the followers of the faith get tarnished as radicalised Muslims by a disingenuous label by the Western politicians and media, however hard they try to convince that not all Muslims are terrorists. For most Muslims, the realty is different. As I have mentioned what my eleven-year-old was taught in the history lesson 'that the events in New York and Washington were because of Islam', which is completely untrue! Because the word Islam derived from the Arabic root 'Salema', meaning Peace, which matters a lot to the vast majority of Muslims. It is also equally important not to refer to countries or Kingdoms as Muslim states, since these states have no mandate (democratic or otherwise) over Muslims. They are not custodians, just followers of the faith, like any other Muslim. In fact, they have their own political, posh lifestyles and egoistic agenda, while innocent Muslims and non-Muslims suffer the consequences of lethal weapons supplied by the West to the so-called 'Muslim nations', which then trickles into the hands, of the rebels, and ordinary civilians. Equally, Russia, Iran and Syria to name a few, are complicit in such atrocities, and like the West, are not helping by waging wars to settle internal political, tribal and family disputes or ambitions to control foreign countries, accept inflict more hardships on their civilians.

It is an added irony that the same 'civilised' nations in the West turn a blind eye to worse, if not similar subtle atrocities taking place elsewhere, without tarnishing those faiths or countries. For example, in the aftermath of the 9/11 atrocities caused by Saudi militants, the US attacked Iraq, Afghanistan and Libya, engaging itself in many covert hostilities under the pretext of the 'war on terror', a result of many present-day crises. When it comes to Saudi Arabia or Israel causing tensions in Yemen or Gaza, despite international pressure, the US dismissed these concerns, due to strong lobbying and lucrative arm sales, claiming that they are acting in self-defence. We have already witnessed genocide when hundreds of thousands of people were killed and millions displaced in Rwanda, Myanmar and Bosnia, resulting in the killing of one man, not for what he has done, but because of what he is. Showing that this can lead to a campaign of 'ethnic cleansing' where one neighbour turns on another, encouraged by leaders with a 'populist political agenda', based on nationalism, leading to suffering and poverty and being denied opportunity, because of his race and creed. What begins with the failure to uphold the dignity of one life often ends with a calamity for entire nations and humanity.

In the last two years, China is almost unnoticed by others, whilst they have built the largest network of imprisonment camps in the world. There are more than one thousand camps in the Western region of Xinjiang, where roughly one to two million Muslims have been detained with the official aim of eradicating the 'virus in their thinking', and reports of torture, killing, rape and suicide, have been reported.[34] Also Palestinians are being mistreated by the Israeli state, in the city of Hebron, where a form of 'apartheid' is taking place. Palestinians are not allowed to walk the streets and even the planned Israeli settlements in occupied lands are deemed illegal under international law.[35] Despite such lucid admission by British politicians, ordinary Muslims continue to face daily struggles. A similar situation also exists in India, whereby democracy has been used as a tool to sanction people. Hindu nationalism, encouraged by the Indian PM, Narendra Modi, has resulted in the persecution of Indian citizens of Muslim origin, and they are subjected to atrocities such as 'ethnic cleansing', because of new 'anti-Muslim' law,[36] which has also led to attacks on Muslims in streets and their mosques. However, Mr Modi's vile actions as Prime Minister of India, as well as a Hindu have not been used to stigmatise the whole country or the Hindu religion. Why? Well, this is because, since getting elected in 2014, Mr Modi is being mollycoddled by the US, Britain, Europe and the Middle East, so as not to ruin their chances for having a lucrative trade deal with India. Incidentally, Mr Modi had faced a travel ban imposed by the US and UK, because of the deadly anti-Muslim riots he presided over in Gujarat in 2002, leaving more than two thousand dead, including three Britons. The world has also remained silent over his actions in Kashmir.[37] The West ignores such blatant violations of human rights, and Israel, India, China and Myanmar are allowed to continue relentless pursuits of such repugnant practices. We have also witnessed social disharmony,

---

[34] The Spectator: 'The chilling stories from inside China's Muslim internment camps' 14th December 2019 https://www.spectator.co.uk/article/the-chilling-stories-from-inside-china-s-muslim-internment-camps
[35] The Independent: 'Israel's treatment of Palestinians in Hebron is 'apartheid', former Tory international development minister says 22nd November 2016 https://www.independent.co.uk/news/uk/politics/israel-palestine-hebron-apartheid-desmond-swayne-uk-government-minister-a7432091.html
[36] www.bbc.com › news › world-asia-india-50670393: 'Citizenship Amendment Bill: India's new 'anti-Muslim' 11th December 2019 https://www.bbc.co.uk/news/world-asia-india-50670393
[37] www.bbc.com › news › world-asia-india-49956960: 'Kashmir conflict: Woes deepen as lockdown stifles economy' 8th October 2019 https://www.bbc.co.uk/news/world-asia-india-49956960

when 'radicalised individuals' and groups, like Donald Trump, Nigel Farage, Benjamin Netanyahu, Ms Le Pen, Narendra Modi, Aung San Suu Kyi and the European Research Groups capitalise and claim democratic victory, with populist nationalist undertones of racial and religious hatred. For example, 'make America great again', 'Hindus for Trump', 'Trump for India', 'Trump for Israel', glossing over Trumps real motives to get elected, using whatever means. Politicians are here today, gone tomorrow! However, their divisive democratic slogans lead to an aftermath of suffering and killing, which does not affect them, but the ordinary people, worldwide, who have to suffer for years.

Such blatant violations have not evoked a single statement of condemnation in the West. The West is not even referring to these vile actions, conducted by 'radicalised individuals' of Hindu, Jewish and Buddhist faiths or nations, so as not to scupper their chances of lucrative trade deals. What example is the West setting? That it is 'civilised' to kill, and the crimes will be forgotten once elected as a leader of a nation. No one bats an eyelid when Muslims in war torn zones and refugee camps face daily squalor and hunger, with no chance whatsoever of a better future, which only serves as a breeding ground for more hatred and anger towards the West. We witness Muslims living the nightmare of being colonised, looted, tortured, dehumanised, murdered, brutalised, enslaved and occupied. Their homes and lands carved-up, then ruled by 'puppet regimes' imposed on them, controlled by the West and other foreign power. They face daily wars, drone attacks, destruction and death in conflict zones, as well as rape of Muslim women in India, China and Myanmar. Despite experiencing so many atrocities, Muslims are expected to live a normal life, and told to keep quiet and accept the pain. They do without a quibble, trying their level best to live a normal life. People of which other faith have we seen subjected to such blatant sufferings and abuse of human rights in the 21st century by democratically elected political leaders? If they were, then by now there would have been an uproar, warships would have been dispatched with talks of economic sanctions and other measures put in place without delay. The world's response to-date has been based on greed, not what inhumanity does to humanity. Is there no end to greed?

What we are witnessing is a rise in nationalism with right-wing and religious extremism within the pretext of democracy, fuelled by a few political leaders in the West and elsewhere. The trend reflects a worrying breakdown of respect and political dialogue in an increasingly divided way. It has allowed the treacherous influence of angry far right politics, changing the rules by encouraging bitterness at grass-roots level, attacking the very foundation of our democracy, and making it vulnerable. Radicalisation has accelerated to record levels, and is now more universal. Not only has it become common, so more difficult to detect, but is less sophisticated in its approach and training, such as using a car, knife, or machete, and with limited effort and resources, allowing large groups to recruit individuals as 'lone wolves' to carry out terrorist acts to cause maximum disruption and chaos, which happened outside the Palace of Westminster in London, as well as other places. We are also seeing an increase in solo terrorist acts by right-wing extremists, machine gunning down innocent civilians in America, Australia, Canada, New Zealand, Sweden and other countries. In Germany, politicians who openly support immigration of Muslim refugees seeking asylum fleeing wars in Syria, Afghanistan and Iraq, have increasingly been targeted. People have been killed by the supporters of far-right extremists, who are committing twice the crime than the extreme left.[38] In Britain, how can we forget the senseless murder of politician Jo Cox by a far-right radicalised 'lone wolf' extremist terrorist.

What is worrying is that in Germany; nearly half of all politically motivated attacks could not be attributed to any specific group, reflecting erosion of civil norms, a free for all, being a worrying scenario in Germany, Britain and other Western countries. What will happen if there are no immigrants to blame, Muslims or other minorities, just one race and people of the same faith? Who will the far-right politicians and media demean with a disingenuous label by referring as 'radicalised individuals' like the one they do to stigmatise Muslims? Who will the far-right politicians and media attack during elections and referendums, when easily identifiable targets no longer exist to blame for their policy failures? Let us face reality! The shortages in schools, NHS appointments, jobs and much more cannot all be blamed upon immigrants. Who will the people of one race and faith then attack in streets, neighbourhoods and workplaces? It will be the poor, disadvantaged and the weak, despite belonging to the same race and faith. Who will be next after them? Perhaps those less financially affluent or less qualified than others. Who will do the low paid jobs? The problem here is the same all over the world - elected representatives not representing the people who elected them - causing unnecessary division and bitterness. It is about time like minded politicians woke up, be wary and confront populist politics of nationalism, putting aside personal interests, and stop following like a flock of sheep those advocating divisive agendas of a few egoistical political and religious leaders, pitting one group against another for self-serving interests.

We should condemn persecution of any minority groups: Christians have also been targeted, as accusations of blasphemy have led to violence against them by militant Islamists. At least there was a ray of hope and human decency and justice was done in 2012, when a Christian girl, Rimsha Masih, was acquitted in a blasphemy case, once it was discovered she had been framed by a local Muslim cleric. We need more encouraging news such as this one. Some of the violence towards Christians was directly related to the American-led war in Afghanistan, so it had an expressly political motive, which is just the same as targeting

[38] New York Times: 'Politics of Hate Takes a Toll in Germany Well Beyond Immigrants' 21st February 2020
https://www.nytimes.com/2020/02/21/world/europe/germany-mayors-far-right.html

Muslims. There is no excuse to take an innocent life because of the actions taken by egoistical political and religious leaders. When Donald Trump announced the withdrawal of US troops from Northern Syria, he obviously cared little for the Syrian Christians, who were once again abandoned by alleged allies. He only left some troops to protect the oil fields, and not interested in saving human life. Christians also get persecuted in Myanmar, China and North Korea, where there is a Buddhist majority. This has led the Anglican bishop of Truro, Philip Mounstephen, to request a review of these countries, saying, "Christian persecution is not certainly limited to the Islamic-majority, and this is not a stalking horse for the Islamophobic far right, and nor does it give the Islamophobic right a stick to beat Islam with." Something, all individuals should heed that in our quest to live in peace, all faiths are united, not only in our desire to respect each other, but equally important in our need to do so in a multi-faith world.

In the West, democratically elected leaders are equally culpable in promoting radicalisation during elections and referendum campaigns with a right-wing 'populist political agenda' of nationalism. It may not be blatant, but exists in subtle forms via the Internet, in particular social media, promoting and inflicting hatred. Also, religious extremists glorify violence to attract and influence many people, and in some cases, succeed in radicalising them. It is no secret that young children can be trusting, and not understand prejudice, which can attract them to adopt and radicalise extremists' ideas that can become normalised, by viewing shocking or subtle content of violence. The present situation is surely the fault of grown-ups, the 'defenders of society', who in the name of democracy, freedom, hope and other paraphernalia, set the ball in motion with illegal wars, breaking laws, legitimising violence and using unscrupulous nationalistic political agendas to cover up their failures, and aiding the spread of radicalisation. It is the lack of political leadership and coherent policy that needs to be addressed foremost, to restore trust and confidence at the most basic level.

The lack of education can be a great barrier, as it does not only improve career prospects, but gives someone opportunity and confidence, opening their minds, and prevents them from falling victim to those who preach hatred. Also, just because someone is educated, does not mean that they are enlightened and tolerant of others; education is not the same thing as wisdom. Because wisdom is the combination of experience and knowledge, so a person needs both to give the ability to think and act appropriately and make correct decisions. There are some very educated people in the world, but they can lack wisdom, therefore can be useless and also full of hatred. We need to focus more on education, discipline and mutual respect from which flows everything - prosperity, decency, law and order. If we let troublemakers in classrooms become diligent students, our whole society and educational system benefits, including the pupils and their classmates. In many ways, disorder in society is often the result of what the younger generation learn and perceive as right and wrong, set by their role-models at home and those in public life. I would say the blame lies not entirely with the children, but with the adults who guide them in their early years. We need to ask why, despite great progress made in the last century in many areas to uphold peace and human rights, and the lessons learnt from the two World Wars, we still witness suffering and pain inflicted by inhumanity on humanity!

We need to ask, is it because for human aptitude to flourish, mere principles will be inadequate? Do we need a proper education curriculum and disciplined atmosphere to bring about awareness? The centres of learning and upbringing are those wherein abilities and virtues can develop, be enriched and blossom, so both the individual and society as a whole, share its fruits. We need interlinked centres of learning to tackle the root causes of the poisonous arguments and distorted ideas that a minority of radicalised adult extremists push forward, by targeting the young. Children need a stable home, where life and personality are first shaped, which has been happening for ages. Most human beings hold family life at a very high level of importance, and a miracle of the momentous act of creation. If an individual correctly provides for the upbringing of their family, making provisions for their learning, good manners and respect for others, this will take them all on the path of righteousness. Whereas, if an individual who is sinful, will cause harm and misery. For the believers of faith, places of worship should provide the root of spiritual fusion for the social well-being of individuals, as well as the wider community, not hatred. The place of worship should serve as the centre for spiritual leadership, whether religious or otherwise, and should not distinguish between spiritual and contemporary knowledge of the world, but build a bridge, and by acquiring knowledge; the scholar gains the experiences of the handiwork of the creator in the universe, in the world of soul, in the world of religion and in the world of humanity.

Most parents show interest and pay attention to what is being taught in their children's schools, but some just absolve themselves of all responsibilities. We also need to look at it from a different perspective, and learn by asking the right questions, such as how did parents in the past who never went to school, so were unable to help their children with homework manage? Why did their children not become radicalised? Why was there no such thing as radicalisation or hatred on the scale we see today? Are we missing something? Maybe it goes much deeper than just throwing more money at schools and changing the syllabus, or setting performance targets, which can hinder some children. We also need to look at the real-life pressures faced by parents today, could it be something to do with those pressures? Could it be because parents now have less time to spend with their children during their child's early formative years? If so, we need to address this and other aspects of a child's life, as well as their social mobility. Maybe we need to find ways to realise the full potential of women's roles within society, something men will never understand or are capable of fulfilling. A child's education – academic and spiritual – is much better served by women, as they are ideally placed to show good habits, which my mother and grandmothers gave me.

In the 21st century, people like to be seen as 'civilised', and believe wherever they are born that they should be given a fair start in life to fulfil their dreams. We have no choice which family or faith we are born into, and no one has been given a right by anyone to kill or attack other faiths. In every great faith, culture and tradition, one can find the values of tolerance, mutual understanding and respect for all life. What matters most is to respect life of a fellow human, as they also have similar aspirations for a better life. If we believe that, then what right have we to discriminate or inflict suffering on defenceless people based on faith, race, class, sex, or/and nation. If they are so despicable, why were they created? In fact, the test for us in the eyes of any divine power, has more to do with how we respect and get along with each other.

I believe if there is a place to go to after death, we will be pleasantly surprised that we may all end up in the same place, whether a believer or not, irrespective of one's creed, race and class. What matters most are the good deeds practiced in this life. We are born naked, and then given pledges of hope and fairness made by the 'defenders of society', as well as a level playing field, but for the majority of ordinary people, it becomes a daily struggle to make a decent living, pay taxes and bills, and abide by the laws enacted by the lawmakers in the name of democracy and freedom, for society to follow, despite factors well beyond their control, such as wars and exploitation. However, there is a common shared belief that the sacred soul departs the physical body. We leave empty handed, despite the wealthy placing material things in tombs or mausoleums, which over time becomes a distant relic, or fades, gets stolen, vandalised or even destroyed during conflicts. The war we must fight is one that forges new paths to peace, by questioning behaviour of those that do not. It will require Britain and others, including religious and community leaders to be brave in their convictions to say the things we do not say, and put an end to religious, political radicalisation and 'ethnic cleansing'.

16

Women:
The Unsung Heroes

When I started writing this chapter, I admit with honesty, after deciding a vague title, the first sentence I wrote was 'dedicated to the women in my life for their inspiration'. So, this chapter is in recognition of the women who have played a crucial role in my life, and as I have got older, my thoughts have turned more to the part my mother and other people have played in my life, which at times, we can all take for granted. I am also glad that apart from dedicating this memoir to them, the first four names in name index at the end, other than obviously mine, happen to be women who have helped me succeed in life. Call it a coincidence or fate, one thing for sure, is that it has not been fixed, as it would have been difficult to do so. The first name is my mother who nurtured me. My wife Femi is the next, after all she is not only the mother of my two children and a companion in my life, but has also played a big part in producing this book. I am glad it has worked out this way, as I truly believe we will see women play eminent roles in the 21st century, and clear up the mess created by men. I hope I am around to see the shared values of everyone come to fruition.

Quite often, I think about my parents and many others who have inspired me, whether in a big or small way, helpful or not. My mother, Batul, never complained about her life, and so nor will I about mine. Mother was from a large, poor, but happy family. She devoted her whole life to her family, relatives, friends, neighbours and strangers. She also played a huge part in my upbringing, especially in my education, and always prayed for my well-being. Perhaps the most disappointing thing in her life was that she wanted to go to school, but never did, as her parents could not afford to let her attend. She often told me about this, and that is why she was absolutely determined that her children would not suffer the same fate. She and her family, like most families in those days had a hard life, but she was always proud of her parents for their love and care that they had given her. Mother was always willing us to do well at school. Femi did the same with our children, especially during those difficult times, when she had to juggle her time helping to run the business and raise a family. It is no secret that most women, just like my mother, play a pivotal role in the development and shaping of moral values, particularly giving their love and tenderness, because of their unique quality to nurture life within their own body, and after birth. A mother's love for their child does not diminish, even when the child reaches adulthood and have children of their own. In short, a mother's love is true love, without condition.

My mother always fed her children first. I recall that when mother prepared meals she would always ask if we had any preference on what we would like to eat, and when serving made sure her children did not go without, or had less food than herself, even late at night she would ask if we had eaten. Honestly, I cannot recall asking her if she had eaten, but just took it for granted that she must have. Femi, like both our mothers instinctively does the same for all our children. Amongst some animals, we also witness female instincts become prevalent during feeding time, where a mother upon return to the nest, or after a hunt will assist their off springs to feed with tenderly love. Even if a male feed's the young, the difference between a motherly bond is more noticeable as being less aggressive than the male.

I understand the pain of anybody who has been through life deprived of motherly love, because of circumstances beyond their control. To those encouraging division and hatred, I can only say please let us not deprive the future generation of their mothers by waging wars, killing innocent civilians for greed and personal egos. Even, Boris Johnson recognised the judgement of his mother, when he mentioned in his maiden Tory Party conference speech on 2nd October 2019 in Manchester that he has to deliver Brexit, because his mother voted to leave in the 2016 referendum. At the same conference Chancellor Sajid Javid felt proud to see his mother sitting at the front, and she was overwhelmed by his success. Wonder how she felt when he resigned in February 2020 following the cabinet reshuffle by Boris Johnson. Prime Minister Narendra Modi's love for his mother is also known to all. It is his sheer love that even amidst his busy schedule, he meets her on all special occasions, whether it is the swearing-in ceremony or his birthday. This shows that even powerful men realise the importance of motherly love, and the role played by the women in their lives, and like to share their success with them, by singling them out at prestigious events. I hope politicians would give others similar opportunities, by learning lessons from various public inquiries held after major disasters and wars, legal or illegal that in the long run solves nothing, but just causes more misery and suffering, as well as wasting public money. The heart-breaking TV images of young motherless children or malnourished babies in the laps of helpless mothers in war zones should make them stop and think. So, let us give credit where it is due, and give innocent victims of war a chance in life, and not deprive children of their mothers' love.

We have seen examples, during hard times where women manage to cope well emotionally, more resilient and patient than men; however difficult it may be. In many instances, if a husband dies first, the wife generally lives longer, by adjusting their lifestyle. This happened to be true with my mother, and many other examples which I know of, with a very few exceptions. In my own immediate large family, there are many women who are still alive today, sometimes even fifty years after their husband has passed away. Not that they married young, or the husband died young. We often witness that when a wife dies first the husband soon follows, at times within a year or so. In my own family, when my paternal grandmother and mother-in-law passed away, my grandfather and father-in-law followed within a year, but when my father and nine uncles passed away, my mother and aunties lived for many more years. I have also noticed similar trends in my friend's circle, and other people who I am acquainted with. Such qualities show women are tougher than men, maybe not physically, but definitely within their character, and endure hard times with greater dignity.

A mother will also relinquish her own comforts for her child, at a personal cost. For example, Nazanin Zaghari-Ratcliffe, a British-Iranian woman with dual citizenship has been detained in Iran since 3rd April 2016. She has a daughter called Gabriella who lived in Iran with her grandparents for three and a half years, while her mother was in prison. Gabriella would visit her mother in the notorious Evin Prison, which comforted Nazanin. When Gabriella turned five, Nazanin felt that Gabriella's education was important and made the ultimate sacrifice, by deciding to send her to the UK so she could get a good education. However hard it must have been, she put her daughter's interests before her own, knowing that she would not be able to see her daughter for a long time. Only a woman can tolerate such mental and physical torture in the interest of others. This reflects the ordeal of a high-profile woman who was caught up in a diplomatic male-dominated political tangle. Just spare a thought for the vast silent majority whose plight never gets mentioned.

The importance women place on education is highlighted in a UNICEF report 'War hits home when it hits women and girls', which is about the hardships faced by women and girls (in particular) that are different from men, because of the gender division of roles and responsibilities that women have.[39] Despite facing handicaps in education and health, even experiencing rape and violence, women have shown greater flexibility and concern for a peaceful future, even when they have been displaced or involved in conflicts that they did not start, and had no control over. During the Eritrean struggle, the women fighting for national independence established a school curriculum, reflecting a strong commitment to social equality and women's rights. The classes were co-educational, and girls were encouraged to fully participate in all fields, particularly the technical ones. It shows a woman's natural instincts in search for a peaceful existence, a resilience not to give up hope, which befits their unique role to nurture, not destroy. While men would be keener to focus on army camps for military training, to inflict more suffering and destroy lives. Shame on men! Regrettably, a few radicalised women have followed males as their masters and subordinates, which I feel goes against a woman's nurturing instincts. Humanity has got to wake up, and the only way atrocities can get addressed is by having more policy and decision-makers who are women, not an 'establishment' dominated by male politicians.

Women face a never-ending cycle of injustices, not only in peace time, but also during wars and other conflicts. Women and girls are known to suffer disproportionately more, because of men's actions as existing inequalities get magnified.[40] A breakdown in social networks make women more vulnerable to sexual violence and exploitation. Young girls also fall victim to prostitution, following the arrival of peace-keeping forces. Women suffer during wars and its aftermath, not only because of atrocious violence inflicted upon them by men, but also have to agonise over the loss of their fathers, husbands and sons. If that is not enough, health services available in emergency situations are dominated by men, so many women and girls, for cultural or religious reasons, underutilise these services, despite their need for it.

During my childhood, my mother managed all aspects of domestic, financial and education affairs, just like my wife does today. With Femi having complete control over our finances, including giving me spending money, it is amazing that we have never been short during good and hard times! I, like my father have full confidence and trust in my wife. My mother and Femi have done a great job, far better than my father or I could have done. Most women seem to be better than men in such matters. Usually female professionals, MPs and political leaders show greater concerns and empathy relating to human values, environment, upbringing, culture, education and health, and seem to be less ruthless and more accommodating then men, because they think for the good of humanity. We see

---

[39] War hits home when it hits women and girls https://sites.unicef.org/graca/women.htm

[40] The Guardian: 'War disproportionately affects women, so why so few female peacekeepers?' 7th September 2016.https://www.theguardian.com/global-development/2016/sep/07/war-disproportionately-affects-women-female-peacekeepers-fiona-hodgson

women, with a few exceptions, who are the voice of reason in Westminster, local councils and elsewhere, in contrast to the rowdy and raucous behaviour of their male counterparts that could be observed at Prime Minister's Questions on 25th September 2011 on the return to parliament after prorogation. Also, when men try to be compassionate, during a time of lives being lost or senseless suffering, a lack of passion can be seen lurking underneath. Whereas female MPs, during parliamentary or public debates are more dignified, passionate, dedicated and better role-models than their male equivalents who come across as being selfish, troublesome, unscrupulous and dishonest.

It is true that during the previous agricultural model it was necessary for men to hunt and farm to provide food for their household. Men worked in the field, and the women stayed at home to prepare the meals, and take care of the household. Now we live in a 'civilised' society, no longer in a primitive farming dominated world of the past. When more workers were needed, no one argued that women should stay at home, as the industrial revolution asserted itself and needed more factory workers; women left their nurturing roles to participate in manufacturing goods. So why should men now argue whether women should be paid the same salary they are entitled to? If anything, they should be paid in their own right, not in comparison to a man's ability and salary. Let us not forget, an employed woman not only honours her work duties, but also does not relinquish her innate responsibility towards her children, family and domestic role. Something a man can never claim capable of achieving; however, superior he thinks he may be!

Furthermore, in the West, women were needed in the factories for the war effort; women elsewhere in the world lagged behind in fulfilling their full potential, and continue to do so, despite some countries being in the forefront of various civilisations, such as Mesopotamian, Egyptian, Chinese and many others. When the West developed bullets and guns, they invaded those countries, and as colonialists prevented both men and women to advance or benefit fully from the Industrial Age. Women have stayed submissive in the kitchen since the economy did not see a need for them in the manufacture of goods after the war. These differences have continued to exist, admittedly on a varying scale, but do exist in forms and shapes affecting women's rights everywhere in the world, even in the West. Throughout our life, we are conditioned to refer to the human race as the 'history of mankind', instead of the 'history of humankind'. How can men decide what women are capable of doing? Men need to realise that women are part of the economy, without defining their role or what they are worth, if we really want to make progress. This will allow us to move away from hate, conflicts and carnage, so let women play a prominent role in their own right for the good of whole humanity.

It is about time women grabbed the initiative themselves to define their role to be important and worthy. Women's worth should be recognised as a 'standard model', because when women try to compete against men, they generally lose out. This makes it more difficult for them to fulfil their full potential based on their own unique innate and distinct qualities to serve humanity; unlike men who are more gung-ho to inflict undue suffering, by triggering wars and disharmony. Men have a lesser grasp of the basic home economics, lacking empathy to comprehend real-life hardships, and the effects of failed government policy on the people. In contrast, women are more astute in such matters, as they try to juggle family budgets on a daily basis, making sure their family does not go without the bare necessities. At times it is disheartening to see well-known female political leaders like Margaret Thatcher, Theresa May and Aung San Suu Kyi who all started off with well-meant policy initiatives and political convictions, only to succumb and fail, when they tried to emulate or pacify their testosterone male dominated counterparts. Equally it is heartening to see female politicians beginning to challenge male dominated politics, and bring their unique ethics and inherent instincts of a better understanding of human life and needs. Let us hope they are allowed to develop their full potential of unique set of skills and humanity does not have to wait too long to benefit from it.

Based on personal experience, during my election campaign I found women more engaging and abreast of reality, and understandably worried about the future, because of their inherent nurturing role. Women were more willing to help and honest in their commitment to vote. How humbling and privileged, who says goodness is on the way out? Such attitude gives hope, and if harnessed, can restore trust in our democracy. Women also tend to give their honest opinions, without avoiding the question, often reflecting widely held views of the public. For example, a constituent of Boris Johnson was asked about him by a Sky news presenter, and her reply was "don't ever mention that name in front of me, that filthy piece of toe-rag." What is noticeable is that she conveyed her feelings in a more effective dignified manner, without physical combat and/or social hatred, similar to 'Bristol Brenda' in 2017 and Gillian Duffy in 2010. I found women of all ages more pleasant, polite and engaging, offering help to distribute leaflets and displaying posters. It was apparent during the Brexit debate that female MPs were more passionate and concerned about future generations, whilst the PM, Boris Johnson, referred to the security threats as 'humbug' discarding employment and insecurities lightly with a blasé attitude, which was also the feeling of the male dominated European Research Group made up of Tory EU rebels. Of course, there are female politicians and individuals who adhere to uncompromising self-serving egos, feministic views and are not good at their jobs, just like there are male chauvinistic politicians and individuals.

If that is not enough, women tend to be more prone to direct or subtle forms of male chauvinism and the culprits claim it is part of the rough and tumble of political combat. For example, Margaret Thatcher and Theresa May were hounded by men and forced to resign early. It only serves to exacerbate hostility towards women by men. In contrast, Boris Johnson was given an easy ride by the European Research Group who claimed he had negotiated a better Brexit deal, which was no different in substance than the one brokered by Theresa May that they and Boris Johnson voted against. Such hypocrisy does not set a good example for the rest of us, when male politicians behave in such a manner for their self-serving interests, because this can be taken as acceptable practice to treat all women in this way.

What makes men respect and have a high regard for their mothers, wives, daughters and sisters, but treat other women as less equal? Concerns about various inequalities are frequently raised by women's organisations, as well as politicians in Britain and abroad. We claim women have equal rights, but then at the same time find that women are not entitled to the same pay, even at times penalised when they have to fulfil the most crucial role in any human society, to raise a new life. Ethnic women also face added obstacles when employers base their decisions on the written information available on their CVs, since names identify their ethnicity, so they can get discriminated against. Why is this allowed to happen, despite men recognising the important roles played by women to raise children?

We have also witnessed the repulsive acts of sexual harassments by 'powerful men' in the West, such as a President boasting of his sexual prowess and a royal, HRH Prince Andrew having to deny these allegations. How can we forget the sexual abuse of thousands of women by soldiers and officials of well-known charities?[41] All along, defenceless women have remained dignified, despite falling victim. We can only hope their suffering will not go unpunished and justice is served, by holding those guilty accountable for their actions, whether Nobel Peace Prize winners like Aung San Suu Kyi, Presidents, PMs or not. At least for now some victims of the movie tycoon, Harvey Weinstein, after his denials and prolonged legal battles have finally got justice. What is so sad is the length of time this took, allowing him to go unpunished for such a long time, due to his wealth, so he could manipulate legal loopholes to his advantage. Same old story for the less wealthy victim(s)! Let us hope it is not long before other culprits are brought to justice too.

---

[41] The Independent: 'Oxfam was told of aid workers raping and sexually exploiting children in Haiti a decade ago' 16th February 2018 https://www.independent.co.uk/news/uk/home-news/oxfam-latest-sex-scandal-prostitution-rape-children-haiti-warned-2008-save-the-children-a8214781.html

No wonder we have noticed a drop in moral standards in public life towards women. Those in position of power should know better, and need to behave properly towards them. We often hear instances of women's spitefulness towards fellow colleagues. In a way such behaviour is no different to that of alpha males, and goes against the grain of the natural female instincts, because some women in power feel obliged to emulate men's behaviour for personal gain. In some cases, even encouraged by men to do their dirty work, like ethnic ministers sent to answer tricky questions on racism from the press.[30] For most female politicians, they are concerned about education, the environment, health, crime, welfare and jobs, which always seems to be at the top of their priority list, as it is an instinctive response, as they address everyday family issues. They tend to be more passionate on domestic issues than their male counterparts, in their role to serve public duty.

In 2018 we celebrated one hundred years when women were given the right to vote, not the full franchise, but a start in recognition of common humanity. Prior to the 19th century, women in Britain were treated as inferior citizens to men. For example, married women over thirty had to wait until 1918 to vote. Why were women held in such low priority in the eyes of the male lawmakers? This was more to do with sexism that dominated the Western society, because everywhere women started from an unequal status. In English law, the movable assets, e.g. clothes, furniture and earnings of married women rightfully belonged to their husbands, even requiring their husband's permission to rent out or sell any houses or land they inherited. Women were not allowed to make a will without their husband's consent, and they were also not permitted to attend university, practice a profession, such as law or medicine, or hold public office. Men at this time could legally beat and rape their wives without any consequences, as long as he did not kill her. She also had to gain her ask her husband if she could bring guests home. Husbands were entitled to enter homes of his wife's next of kin to bring her back to the family home if she ran away, as she could not legally leave him. It was not permissible in court for wives to give evidence for or against their husbands. In some parts of England, an unofficial form of divorce existed amongst the locals, involving a husband selling his wife to the highest bidder for a nominal sum of a few pennies. Equal opportunity for women was not particularly relevant at the beginning of the 20th century, and still had some way to go. Even now in the 21st century, women still lack equality, not only in the West, but all over the world. Such differences will not get resolved because of the male bias, unless women are assessed as a 'standard model' in their own right, with their unique and different set of skills, not that determined by men to meet their mental, emotional and physical abilities.

How long do women have to wait and suffer to be recognised as worthy human beings with their own set of talents? Let us hope we do not have to wait another century to tackle relevant issues affecting their everyday life. If lawmakers are really serious, it is still not too late to tackle woman's rights, by asking the correct questions as to why differences still exist. What we need is a change of attitude from the top, not new legislation, simple solutions with the right checks and balances to prevent men from exerting too much power, making effective use of existing laws to empower women. There is a distinct vacuum of leaders in the world today, and world leaders who are capable of leading from the front to get things done for the whole of humanity. Instead, we have unaccountable male politicians getting elected with troublesome 'populist political agendas' inflicting hatred and illegal conflicts. But I remain optimistic that it is just a matter of time until we will see the rise of true women world leaders.

I believe you can tell a great deal about a person's character and leadership qualities by the way they treat another fellow human being in a time of a major crisis. I also think that when someone merits praise, it needs to be said. Especially when they share the pain, they have suffered by the people around them in their hour of need, which should be based on natural instincts, and not political point scoring or deception. This is how I felt about Jacinda Arden, when I offered my heartfelt condolence and prayers for her courage and leadership during the darkest hour in the history of New Zealand on Friday 15th March 2019, following the Christchurch tragedy. I wrote to her on 31st March 2019 (letter 78), saying that I was humbled and grateful to the Almighty, ever since that fateful day when the whole of humanity, irrespective of race and creed, was dealt a severe blow.

> 'You showed nothing but formidable leadership, vision and courage, during the Remembrance Day service on 29th March 2019. You spoke eloquently about the ugliest viruses, such as extremism, violence and racism, which are an assault on the freedom of humanity. I agree with you when you said "we cannot confront these issues alone, none of us can … The answer lies in our humanity. But for now, we will remember the tears of our nation, and the new resolve we have formed."

You have shown a spirit of leadership during challenging times, with heartwarming words of wisdom, lifting not only the image and people of New Zealand to new heights, but also giving hope to the whole of humanity. You have made strangers like myself, and many more your best admirers. I hope it is not long before the Nobel Peace Prize is bestowed upon you, unlike other so-called leaders openly touting for one, who should first learn that actions speak louder than words'.

I received a touching reply (letter 79) from her office, thanking me for my kind words.

In Jacinda Arden, I believe we already have an individual showing great leadership during challenging times, with steel and determination, lifting the hopes of humanity during the shocking mosque shootings in Christchurch and White Island volcano, two tragic moments faced by New Zealand in the same year. Her leadership was in stark contrast to her male counterpart, who faced anger from people in neighboring Australia during the bush fires. Boris Johnson was also widely mocked during his belated visit following the floods in North England, as he failed miserably to use a mop during a ten minutes photo opportunity. We also have budding young women coming through the ranks in Malala Yousafzai and Greta Thunberg. I strongly believe the next real leader(s) to serve humanity will be women, who will clear up the mess created by greedy and egotistical men.

As a man, son, father, brother and nephew, I believe most mothers and women have divine, distinctive and instinctive virtues, qualities that are alien to men. If we look back and think with honesty, we will find most women have played a unique role in our lives at home, work and neighbourhood, whether in a professional or a non-professional role. If only men would admit that we are not that superior to women, and instead learn to harness their nurturing qualities most of us have benefited from in one form or another, and not take women for granted. It is unfair to compare a woman's unique values based on man's abilities defined by him, a faulty assumption, preventing women to fulfil their role as human beings. We all know what evil men are capable of, and something is not better just because a man does it. I believe women are worth even more, because only they have the credentials, chemistry and personality to be a nurturer. For me, as a Muslim, Islam actually speaks of the importance of respecting and honouring our mothers, even more so than our fathers, because under her feet lies heaven. There will be no advantage for humanity if women simply copied males.

The challenge now for the whole of humanity should not be one of total domination, but one of recognition, self-containment and empathy that all world problems cannot be solved entirely by the all-conquering alpha male. Men need to recognise that the hunter, gatherer, agricultural model is no longer relevant and/or significant today. The natural female instincts of nurturing life are ideally more suited to create social harmony and save the environment from self-destruction. After all, we often refer to our planet as Mother Earth or Earth Mother, a personification and embodiment of nature that focuses on the life-giving and nurturing aspects of women. We cannot escape the fact that Western society, in so many ways has still fundamentally remained sexist, preventing women to reach their full potential. Let us hope we rectify such inappropriateness without any more delays. I believe influential women, including our mothers, wives, daughters, sisters and nieces, as well as men will rise to the challenge of doing things in a just way, and not through hypocrisy and empty patronising words.

17

Stronger Commonwealth:
A Hope for Mortals

My earliest and most vivid memories of the British are from when I was a boy, I used to visit the British Navy ships calling at Tanga harbour; I was in primary school at that time. I also benefitted from quality education, which has served me well most of my life. Like many others in the Tanga area, I grew-up watching British films, British Pathé News, and listening to the BBC World Service. I remember family elders speaking highly of British justice, bravery, civil service, craftsmanship, inventions and machinery, such as the sturdy second-hand fleet of Albion FT101 Lorries used in the British Army, which were bought by the family to transport timber logs from the Usambara Mountains to the sawmills. So, the UK was the first and only destination of choice to pursue my further education. This was not nostalgia, reminiscing of romantic times on my part, but appreciating the good moments from the colonial past and learn from the bad mistakes for a better future by not repeating them.

The last century saw two World Wars, and after WWII world leaders endeavoured not to repeat the same mistakes, as a result international organisations and laws were specifically enacted on the principle of the equal worth of every human being to prevent conflicts. This has to continue, although it has not been an easy or a painless process, requiring patience, determination, and all the will to seek peace, even when all the signs point to conflicts. However, daunting the task may seem, a long-term peaceful existence is in the interest for the whole human race. An attack on one human being is an attack on humanity.

We inherited the political, as well as the scientific and technological power in the last century, and if we have the will to use and put them to good use, it will give us the hope and chance to vanquish poverty, ignorance, and disease, and live in peace. The ills of the present century are the result of past mistakes and mistrust, and if not addressed will continue to be a curse. It is necessary that all social forces, countries, the private sector, institutions of learning and research, and civil society in all its forms must unite their efforts in the pursuit of specific, achievable goals. Today, the world looks like a muddled place, with conflicts and crises popping up everywhere and unfortunately will get messier if allowed to continue, unless more work is done to stop the juggernaut of greed and war that is inflicting pointless suffering on defenceless civilians, which happened when half the Western World was dragged into a war with Iraq over the 'weapons of mass destruction' on the bogus evidence concocted by the CIA. On arrival, there was nothing except the death of over three million civilians and soldiers.

The Commonwealth, as the name suggests, has great potential to become a brotherhood of nations. Even today, after all the mistakes and horrors from the past colonial history, there is still the possibility of seeing a better future because of a deeper awareness of the bonds that unites and grips, young and old, when we see pain suffered by fellow human beings, during manmade and natural disasters. In our hearts there exists a profound awareness of the sanctity, dignity and needs of everyone, regardless of race or religion, and we need to look beyond the framework of countries, and below the surface of communities and nations that a peaceful existence belongs to each and every member of those communities. After dismantling the British Empire, I believe there was a missed opportunity at that time to bring the newly Independent ex-colonies even closer by working together, not sharing the burden, but sharing the decision-making in the true spirit of the Commonwealth Charter that was established in 1931. This charter recognised the need for peace, security, democracy, human rights and broadened economic opportunities, as a compelling force for good, and as an effective network for co-operation, for promoting development. I feel passionately about the Commonwealth, and believe that it is not too late to grasp new opportunities by working together, if we forget past differences. As a purposeful body, the Commonwealth can lead the way in the world for the good of all humanity. I believe with lots of effort, hard work and visionary political leaders, we can turn it around and become a powerful force.

South Africa is a shining example of this. Nelson Mandela has already shown us how to do this relatively smoothly, so why should we not learn from the great man himself! In a decade he transformed the country from a racist, undemocratic, oppressive state, to a multi-ethnic democracy dominated by the African majority, not with a disruptive democratic political agenda practised by a few present-day Commonwealth and other leaders, but with forgiveness and inclusion. No doubt South Africa still has enormous problems with poverty, AIDS, crime, some pockets of racism, but the cruel, humiliating and shameful signs of apartheid (universal labels of 'whites' and 'non-whites'), prisons for political protesters and shameful laws have all disappeared. But sadly, we are witnessing a return of such detestable practices in certain other countries where politicians are using the pretext of democracy as a legitimate tool to inflict suffering on the minority citizens. These power-hungry democratically elected leaders are behaving as dictators, by abusing democracy after having used it as a vehicle to get to a position of enough power and passing severe laws to strengthen their self-serving populist political agendas. I am not deluded to think it will be easy to follow in Mandela's footsteps, but I believe once proclaimed with trust, a purposeful Commonwealth will become a reality, and this is where education will serve to play a great role.

It is odd how even now, when the name of Mandela gets mentioned, it feels special, saintly and dignified, unlike the famous quote of Enoch Powell, when he said that "all political careers end in failure." Mandela was a special and rare breed of political leader, who does not fall into that category. He endured twenty-seven years of imprisonment, which he once referred to it as, "a long holiday for 27 years." He preached, but most importantly practiced reconciliation and forgiveness himself, serving as the symbol of the struggle against apartheid, forging a democratic government, and he governed as the first South African president elected by national suffrage, irrespective of colour. He did not loot and deposit the nation's wealth in foreign banks, but stepped down from power when his term ended, unlike others who have to be forced to resign because of improper conduct, or stabbed in the back by 'political colleagues'. No one else in Africa, perhaps in the world, even in the 'civilised' West can match that record. Let us hope one emerges soon within the UK, but judging by the present crop, we can only remain optimistic that we do not have to wait long for a visionary leader to emerge and take the baton of the Commonwealth towards its rightful destination. I think political leaders owe it to humanity, the people owe it to themselves, and if we all work together and put differences and hostilities of the past behind us, then we should be able to live in a peaceful and prosperous world.

This is why in 2014 I felt compelled and undeterred by past failures. I persevered following various depressing TV images depicting atrocious acts of rape, carnage and suffering of human beings worldwide. I wrote on 21st August (letter 46) to cross-party Tory, Labour and LibDem politicians, including David Cameron, Jonathan Lord, BBC on-line and other national newspapers, which totalled about twenty or more letters. I entitled them 'Why a sudden unfolding of crises in Iraq and elsewhere? An urgent need for political and diplomatic solutions – not greed and double standards'. I only heard from one person, an assistant of Sir Ming Campbell (letter 47) that he will bear in mind what I said. I mentioned:

> 'It is important to understand the extreme pain suffered by ordinary law-abiding Muslims worldwide who have witnessed the vile actions of dictators, activists, or Kingdoms deploying arms supplied by the 'civilised' world to boost exports, and the offensive persecution of Islam with negative tabloid headlines and TV coverage. The 20th century was regarded as the most disastrous period in the history of mankind. For the first time, unlike past conflicts, the entire world population was affected by two World Wars. The Third World found it equally hard to embrace alien concepts. Now the West has adopted a new strategy to leave behind a legacy of starting conflicts, not on their own doorstep, but on foreign soil, followed by charitable aid. Not forgetting that most are past colonies with military or civilian leaders who gained power through a military coup, or dodgy elections with Western support. Britain can play a significant role to find ways to enforce a watertight international treaty, a protocol that involves all major and secondary arms manufacturers to regulate the strict sale of arms. Britain never expected to lose the Empire or relinquish it so quickly, and lost a huge opportunity to reorganise the international body, like the Commonwealth. It is still not too late for Britain to play a leading role to strive towards a peaceful coexistence, but has to play the role of an honest broker, so that we have a world, not dominated by one all-powerful superpower, especially after the end of the Cold War (non-military hostilities). Why do I say that? Because part of the causes of the present problems are from the colonial past, but respect for HM The Queen as Head of the Commonwealth is unquestionable, and will continue even under HRH Prince of Wales. As a nation, we have a lot of goodwill and values to stand against injustices. We also have a better record of social cohesion and shared values, because of the past colonial era, and proven ability to address minor and major difficulties head on'.

It can also be argued that the political turmoil of the 20th century has largely disillusioned us of the notion that the world has reached some sort of utopian 'end of history', as we are in an unprecedented era of peace and progress, with perhaps less likelihood of a Third World War, because of a growing consensus that war between the super powers is unthinkable, due to their weapons. It may sound like an optimistic idealist narrative, as we see ourselves today living in a safer and more prosperous environment than our ancestors, and suffering less cruelty. Why I say this is because when we look from a high enough vantage point, violence, except in few places, is in decline after centuries of hostilities. Our lives are reshaped in every aspect; even spanking our children is now seen as a cruel act, especially in the West. We think we are more 'civilised' and have come a long way from our 'uncivilised' predecessors and comrades from other parts of the world, because of our steadfast moral values and democracy to uphold justice in all aspect of life. So, it goes against our grain to inflict suffering and carnage on other fellow human beings, and we find that the silent majority of people, throughout the history of mankind have shared similar 'civilised' values, namely through hard work and respecting each other, as 'world citizens'.

This is no different from when my ancestors embarked upon their perilous journey in search of a better life. We even see it happening today, people searching for a better life for their families. It is equally true that in the past we also inflicted pain on others, but what is different is the type of suffering, and its overall effects. For example, all forms of deplorable acts, such as apartheid, war, religious bigotry, political intolerance, class bias, slavery and other forms of barbarism that took place over the past millennia were entirely different, in terms of its magnitude and pretext seen today. In the past, such atrocious acts were blatant, with clear separation of boundaries and foes. Today, they are concealed and subversive, carried out in the name of democracy with double standards, inciting hatred amongst people and nations, or tarnishing a whole faith as radicalised Muslim terrorists. The scale of suffering by innocent people as collateral damage in the present-day far outweigh those of the past, in terms of numbers, as well as having longer lasting consequences, a result of prolonged bullying, threats of economic sanctions and use of lethal weapons.

What is different in the 21st century? Firstly, such heinous acts are not inflicted in blatant forms, but more as a right to defend, as 'war on terror'. In reality, we see countries use the excuse to carry out subtle targeted acts of 'ethnic cleansing', no different from the blatant persecution and apartheid of the past , which the 'civilised' nations turn a blind eye to if it is against their interests, depending on who is inflicting suffering on whom. Secondly, the blatant evil acts and practices of the past have been minimised, because of the civil and human rights laws. Thirdly, as humans prefer to be referred to as 'civilised', the deep rooted 'uncivilised' blatant forms of discrimination based on race, creed, class and sex goes against the grain, and becomes more subtle. Therefore, it is more difficult to eradicate, control or detect, as highlighted by public inquiry findings held after major disasters. Fourthly, if anyone feels subjected to discrimination, we can always seek justice in courts, whether they can afford it is another matter. The 'defenders of society' constantly remind the public that democracy works on the principles of 'a level playing field', and we can achieve anything, whether true or not is another matter. Lastly, the cumulative effect of all illegal wars, conflicts and other disasters, apart from the loss of lives, suffering, collateral damage and vicious cycle of revenge, results in spending billions of pounds by Western governments in foreign aid to rebuild broken societies at home and/or abroad, something which could have been avoided in the first place, as we are blessed with international bodies, technology and resources to monitor such atrocities.

If we are really serious, we can greatly minimise, if not eradicate poverty, illiteracy, famine, disease and violations of human rights that still exists. If tackled sensibly and with conviction, a lot of loss of lives and suffering can be alleviated, and prevent individuals undertaking perilous migration journeys in search of a better life, reducing immigration to the West. Technological, social, cultural, educational, medical, political and other advances over the centuries has shrunk the world to such an extent that globalisation has made it possible to change our lives, giving people the freedom and opportunities to do what they want. This also allows people to move freely, giving them a range of comforts, products and lifestyle from different parts of the world in the shortest possible time and effort, which is mainly enjoyed universally, but not by all. Even in Britain, the fifth largest economy in the world, homelessness and poverty is still on the increase, but those fortunate enough to enjoy comforts, have not known or experienced hard times, and take it for granted; it has always been this way. Only when we see horrible images on TV or social media do we realise it is not true for many fellow humans, and quickly forget this until the next cycle of events. But for the vast population of the world it persistently continues, facing hardships, pestilence, disease, wars, famine and misery on a daily basis, with no means to escape.

One can continue to remain deluded, or pretend that the massive destruction and carnage cannot happen on the scale seen previously in the last century, by believing pledges made by some powerful 'civilised' men that the vast sums of money invested in weapons is only for 'self-defence'. If so, why sell it to others to encourage conflicts? Why not settle disputes in a 'civilised' manner through international organisations and laws, which were specifically created after WWII to monitor, control and limit possible conflicts. By using these initiatives, we can leave a better legacy for future generations. It is about time politicians focused on the root causes with practical initiatives, not uncontrolled arm sales, a lack of coherent foreign policy, double standards and greed to end the cycle of conflicts, crises, murders and suffering. Britain can play an important part in restoring world peace, because present conflicts are over boundary disputes from the colonial legacy, such as Israel/Palestine, India/Pakistan and Hong Kong, creating instability in those regions, affecting world peace. I hope history does not repeat itself in Ireland, with short-sighted hasty decisions by politicians in their rush to 'get Brexit done', which may result in a border of some form. The clock on our colonial legacy cannot be turned back. Others will say this is not our problem any longer, and it is best to keep quiet, so not to jeopardise trade deal negotiations with the US and India, or exporting arms to Saudi Arabia and others. Some would be happy to let these 'uncivilised' people fight it out amongst themselves, even if it means annihilating one religion, race or a nation. I will argue the vast majority of British people do not actually share or believe in such ideologies. With ever increasing unfolding humanitarian disasters, we cannot afford to turn a blind eye to the root causes, by selling lethal weapons to other nations, who claim they are just defending their borders.

I believe humanity is crying out for a visionary political leadership. Something has got to be done to stop the endless cycle of atrocities. This cannot be achieved by blaming each other, and who will give in first. No one wants to be the first to lay down their weapons, because they feel it will leave them in a much weaker bargaining position. Of course, there has to be equality, not just arrogance, if we follow that path, we will never find peace. Humanity working as one has managed to settle many past conflicts in the last century. Who would have ever thought conflicts like the two World Wars, Vietnam War, Northern Ireland and Bosnia, would get settled? But they did! Conflicts in Kashmir and Palestine can also be settled through political will, peaceful negotiations and 'people power' just like before. These examples can be seen with the Berlin wall being pulled down, and the Soviet Union breaking-up, and republics like Russia and others becoming sovereign nations. The Soviet Union got dismantled, and apartheid in South Africa was settled on the basis of logic, so common sense prevailed, showing that such acts of segregations are 'uncivilised'. This was only accomplished through visionary and iconic leaders, such as Mikhail Gorbachev and Nelson Mandela, who both saw the reality of the situation in their respective countries.

We need true leaders, not career politicians with self-serving egos to fill the huge vacuum in leadership in the world today before it is too late, and I am optimistic we will. We already have a leader in Jacinda Arden, who showed leadership when her nation faced challenging times. We can hope she will take charge of the baton to lead the Commonwealth, as a great icon of the 21st century. I further believe it is 'people power', seen during climate change protests that will bring about the of political attitude, demanding a different approach of finding a way to live together, solving new challenges facing humanity. We are already seeing encouraging signs of integration, as people realise beneath our skin, we are all the same, and given time, there will be greater respect and acceptance for each other, even if there are occasional flare-ups. Britain with immigrants of every nationality, and its rich colonial history can lead the way in a pragmatic way, helping solve the present crises, because of Britain's past industrial era experience, and learning by the mistakes from the colonial rule. We are ideally suited to make further progress, before it worsens. We already have in place an international club of fifty-four nations, with huge natural resources, and human talent headed by HM The Queen. In Jacinda Arden we already have another visionary who is determined, having similar virtues as Her Majesty, which will develop and establish the Commonwealth to fulfil a more pragmatic role. We also have to inspire future generations to think of the

Commonwealth, and make sure their voices are heard and counsel heeded, and not ignored.

Once we could look to the authoritarian forces of communism, and few dictators acting as a buffer to keep much of the despair of the poor and homeless in check. But now we cannot, because of the end of the 'Cold War' and people like Saddam Hussein and Idi Amin have long gone, also due to TV and social media people's hopes and expectations for a better life have risen. This has now left the world and British PMs at the mercy of the US as the most powerful nation in the history of 'mankind', with an array of unimaginable resource to wage wars. This has put Britain in an awkward situation, at times trying in vain to dissuade the US from preventative independent action, like the illegal Iraq war. However, with Donald Trump who knows what can happen! On one hand he gives the impression he is against engaging American troops, or acts as 'a world policeman', whilst on the other hand, with his confusing foreign policy it is difficult to predict what he will do or tweet next to insult, blame or declare a trade war with. Only time will tell if he will keep his promise of a functional trade deal with the UK after Brexit, and the consequences of this, remains to be seen.

The Iraq war uncovered that it was more to do with oil and greed than a 'war on terror', exposing Britain's 'special relationship' with the US as a one-way affair. Britain's role in the 'coalition of the willing', left Britain with the responsibility of being in Iraq with no authority, and it is hard to see any future British PMs going to war on such terms. This is why it is even more imperative for Britain to regain its position as a beacon for hope, fairness and justice, which has been lost by yielding to America and the tribal politics of divide and rule, during Brexit, which has only served to undermine our position on the world stage, a position once served to guide nations. Britain has always been a great multilateral, working together with other countries, and was looked upon as the clever person in the room, people looking to us to see what we had to say. Regrettably over the last sixty years, Britain's status has been undermined by the lack of leadership and double standards. Our politicians have lost the trust of the people, and made Britain a laughing stock in the world. Britain gave justice, hope, education and more to the people of the Commonwealth and the world, but at home people are struggling. Yes, there were some very dark moments, but lots of good also happened during the colonial rule. But it is also about learning from history, even part of that history some might regard as painful. Learning about the British Empire is the intrinsic part of any Commonwealth citizen, and should not be learnt as a means to seek retribution, but a platform to build a better future. No one pretends that the British Empire was without its faults, we have all experienced it in some form; of course, many have had far worse experiences than others, and people still suffer in some parts of the world from the colonial mistakes. But we can only heal the wounds by moving forward, not by more carnage, by harbouring resentment against the past morals and values of the British Empire. Although we have progressed, and a lot of wrong has been put right and changed. If we do not improve our understanding, evolve and learn from history, we are still in the same position, harbouring hatred.

What good is history if it does not enable someone to see the true picture and learn from the past, we will not be controlled by myths and/or illusions? There is a lot of history an average British and Commonwealth citizen does not know about, or even care to find out. Just like politicians, those who do not want to learn remain blinkered with their own racist ideologies and prejudices, 'learnt' from only listening to propaganda. If the Commonwealth functioned more in the line of 'what it says on the tin', as the name suggests, we will be nearer to solving conflicts and perilous migration journeys. Our participation and role in the UN, World Bank and International Monetary Fund, needs revisiting. It should not stifle the growth of poorer nations, so that the West can thrive. Not forgetting the ongoing purge of natural resources from Third World nations that still continues. Just like it happened during the colonial era, but now under the pretext by deploying various 'civilised' financial institutions and mechanisms, such as the International Monetary Fund and the World Bank that still controls their destiny. Over the years the nations have chosen their own destination, and politicians are suspicious of each other; not only in the UK, but in the whole Commonwealth. What is at stake here is the interest of humanity, both at home and abroad. It may not be possible to bring all the nations of the Commonwealth on board at the same time, but we can start the process by setting a good example, leading from the front with clear intentions, not exploitation, but mutual benefit, so that all can progress, even if it means initially starting with one or two countries, we can then build on this for others to see. Once people see the conviction, integrity, vision and benefits, others would hopefully soon join. A unified Commonwealth will harness and unleash its great potential, manpower and natural resources for mutual advantage, addressing people's expectations of hope.

It is true that trust in politicians is at its lowest ebb, so that is what should be tackled first, as a top priority. In politics, there is great suspicion and realisation that your friends are never your friends for life. Your friends will use you and some may dump you later, but that is just the way it is at the moment, because of the rot that has been allowed to set into political and moral standards. For instance, over the years the UK has been happier to support and overlook the behaviour of ruthless dictators and Kingdoms, but what the ordinary public are looking forward to is a new style of politics, moving away from the old style, which is based on greed, envy, mistrust and conflicts. Surely if people start seeing changes in their living standards, others will get inspired and follow, and if not, people will demand a change from their own politicians, like the humble beginnings seen during the Arab Spring - a series of anti-government protests, uprisings in response to oppressive regimes and low standard of living - which sadly failed to gain momentum, because of double standards of mistrust in politicians, saying one thing and doing another.

The reason why I believe in a stronger Commonwealth is because of the unusually British characteristic of not wanting to belong to Europe, and also at times feel uncomfortable supporting the United States' agenda, but do so out of no choice to appease, because of past historical ties and common language. I can understand why, because it is in the British blood, just like my disillusion towards the arrogant and selfish American attitude that they are always right, and also putting American interests first above anything else. Nothing wrong with that, but others also matter and they cannot always be right. Traditionally, the British usually side with plucky underdogs Robin Hood, Oliver Twist, not Goliath, Trump, Modi and Netanyahu.

I was against joining the EEC in 1975, and voted to leave in the 2016 EU referendum. On both occasions my decisions were not based on the lies steered by the politicians on both sides of the argument, if anything I voted to leave despite UKIP's racist anti-immigrant poster! Why? Because both decisions of mine were based on the firm belief that the UK would be far better-off, with a closer transparent trading treaty and diplomatic ties with the Commonwealth. The Commonwealth nations and Britain share a unique bond, and has the potential to become a robust force, capable of better trade deals worldwide. It can also lead the way, developing a stronger unified international voice of reason and justice to tackle poverty, conflict, migration, illiteracy, health, global warming, environmental issues and other disasters, not only for the good of Commonwealth citizens, but for the whole of humanity. Think about it, if the US had not become a confederation of fifty individual states, it would not have reached its superpower status that it enjoys today. By combining the force of the whole Commonwealth, we can make a huge difference based as equals, hope and fairness, without an 'US' or 'THEM' attitude. In life, we all have to give and take and with the right adjustments, not everything will suit everyone, but on the whole, we will be productive Nations, but life changing endeavours take time to build, it may take fifty or hundred years. It took a long time to build the British Empire, but less to destroy it, because of the short-sighted decisions made by the political leaders of the time.

I think that both the bright and dark moments should be taught as a subject in school openly, so the future generation can learn from the good and bad history of the Commonwealth. If taught with honesty and in the spirit of exploration, just like our own family ancestry, history can explain so much and should unite, not divide. But we have to be prepared to learn with an open mind, free of prejudice and envy, free of harboured grudges, as well as a willingness to build for the common good. The ordinary British people, if we think about it, also did not escape the atrocities of conflicts. Even in Britain, which was effectively 'deprived and exploited' when lands were confiscated, and sons and husbands recruited to join armed forces during both World Wars, with no compensation for their suffering and loss of life. Britain can play a major role and lead the way in serving humanity, but first we need to put our house in order so that we can be good role models for others to follow. Education means not to be afraid to discuss, reason, respect and even agree to disagree. The British Empire is quite fresh in the minds of quite a lot of people born in the 20th century. I have no disillusions, having benefited and suffered from blatant and subtle effects of some of the colonial practices, but it will soon get forgotten, and it will be shame not to capitalise from the good things that happened. This has been one of the main reasons why past achievements from civilisations - such as Abyssinian, Egyptian, Greek, Roman, Babylon, Inca were forgotten, and many people in those countries still face poverty and conflicts. They all disappeared, just living behind ancient physical constructions, most now in ruins, without capitalising from the moral, cultural and economic advances. So, by salvaging the good things from the British empire is imperative, before it too late.

We need to look to the future, learn from past mistakes and build on good things from the shared history developed from Commonwealth bond and the respect for HM The Queen. One thing I can say with great confidence about the British – regrettably not politicians – is that they have far better benevolence, virtues, justice, standing-up for the under-dog, honesty and selfless acts of charity to help the disadvantaged, far outweighing anything elsewhere that I have experienced or seen, even when growing up in Tanzania. I am not saying differences do not or did not exist; of course, they have and always will, because man is destined to fight, even with his neighbour and family at the slightest provocation. Another important British characteristic is that people never shirk one's responsibility, but help and address the problem when it matters most. We have already seen British values not to succumb to bullies during the two World Wars, and other conflicts. On the 29th November 2019, during the cowardly terrorist act on London Bridge, we saw the emergency service and ordinary public helping victims; they did not run away from danger.

We can achieve anything we set our minds on. We have seen similar endeavours in local communities during the Covid-19 outbreak, the public coming to each other's aid. We also realised the crucial role played by the ethnic people in all walks of life, especially the frontline low-paid and high-risk occupations public service jobs, such as the NHS, cleaners, carers, transport and shop workers, as coronavirus deaths amongst ethnic people were starkly over-represented by as much as 27%, as it was confirmed that ethnic minorities in

England were dying in disproportionately high numbers compared with non-ethnic people. We owe all workers who have died at work during Covid-19. If there are two important lessons to be learnt by the politicians from the aftermath of the coronavirus, as well as past pandemics, is to realise the strong bonds that runs through the Commonwealth, and the important role played by the ordinary people, irrespective of creed, class and race. Politicians should also not leave solving problems to the last minute, because of the lack of investment in public services, which only makes matters worse in the long run, and more expensive to tackle.

We all live in hope to lead a better life and do our best, even those mere mortals who are suffering because of other people's actions. This is no different to my ancestors fleeing famine in search of a better life in the 19th century. The only difference is that it was a natural disaster, which forced them to uproot their lives. Today's real borders are not between nations, but between the powerful and powerless, free and fettered, privileged and humiliated. The whole of humanity gets affected, because of the actions of one against another. In times of crisis, like during the Covid-19 outbreak, mass religious and social gathering was prohibited, with countries on lockdown alerts, even the very rich with all their wealth and powerful leaders with strong economies and lethal weapons were left defenceless by Covit-19. But it was because of individuals, such as key workers and public and private sector employees who came to each other's aide to save other fellow human beings and not conflicts. This is what having faith in humanity is all about. What this shows is how vulnerable humanity has become, and if we learn lessons from the past and present, then we will be able to build a brighter Commonwealth in its truest sense, but if we do not learn now, when will we?

18

Restoring Trust in a
Dysfunctional Democracy

The ideological victory battle of democracy and capitalism over communism and socialism has coincided with widespread voter dissatisfaction. It relates to the two main aspects of democracy. Firstly, once elected raises concerns when decisions are made by politicians without further voter engagement, until the next election. A democratic shortfall of a kind, as some political decisions are invariably constrained by those of a non-democratic kind, based on self-serving interests without further voter and media scrutiny, or happens after it is too late. Secondly, it is to do with the acceptable political 'civilised' metaphors, such as bung money, donations, favours and lobbying. In other words, called 'corruption', the 'uncivilised' similes reserved for Third World nations. While such problems arise in any form of politics elected or not, this has become a major concern in democratic regimes. Democracy has been hijacked more now than before by individuals, or lobby groups with financial clout, as highlighted by the 19th century Baron Rothschild who said "I care not what puppet is placed on the throne of England to rule the Empire ...the man that controls money supply controls the British Empire. And I control the money supply." This has now become the norm, for moneymen to dictate to politicians, who just obey their masters without political convictions. Also the 1980s mantra, 'you cannot buck the market' has not helped, allowing powerful multinationals and individuals to do what they like, and seen as they are doing nothing wrong.[42] The power of money allows individuals to manipulate the 'free market', tax

---

[42] The Independent: 'Leading article: You can't buck the market' 6th April 1998
https://www.independent.co.uk/voices/leading-article-you-cant-buck-the-market-1154872.html

avoidance, media outlets or honours list, as long as it is within the law, failing the people because of greed, as well as government rewarding banks by bailing them out at the tax payer's expense, which was seen during the 2008 financial crisis, just adds insult to injury. The same could be said of unaccountable politicians making pledges funded by borrowing and squandering valuable resources adding to national debt, instead of investing wisely in public services. Such behaviour has resulted in faceless moneymen running the show, to get their politician of choice elected, as the outcomes of elections are determined by divisive 'populist political agenda' and the party with most money to spend on advertising are able to mobilise votes. In reality, the moneymen pull the strings, and the world leaders are like puppets on a string just obeying their masters.

Democracy relies on an honour code, imposed during elections at the ballot boxes. A simple contract fulfilled by the marking of a cross. This is an unspoken agreement by those who take part that once elected they will cherish and abide by its principles. The majority, if not all of its participants will act in good faith, and not undermine democracy's constitutional foundations. But enemies of civil liberties have found novel subtle ways to undermine democracy. They conduct information warfare against open societies, which cannot always be enforced. The findings and implications of past interference during elections and referendums in the UK and other democracies still remain unresolved.[43] They are undermining the very democratic processes that has brought them fame, by resorting to despicable forms of political trickery to hang onto power for self-serving egos. Democracy is also being undermined by influential individuals using social media to make huge financial gains from currency and stock market speculations, based on disinformation, populism and polarised political opinions to influence electorates to vote for a certain political party, and use the same technology to disburse money as donations by special interest groups, or individuals to fund flashy election campaigns. The use of unscrupulous methods has now become more common, and these methods have replaced the culture of letting voters make an informed decision, based on facts. Bad people are rubbing their hands with glee. Big mistakes are being made. Will we wake up before it is too late? Democrats must hope that MPs will collectively put the country and people before party and self-interests to uphold 'the will of the people'.

The evacuation of Tory MPs ahead of the December 2019 general election, which was entirely made up of MPs who voted to remain in the 2016 EU referendum is worrying. It will be a great loss, not only to the party, but the nation. It included some senior and young talent, men and women with great experience. Equally, in the Labour party, some famous names left to join another

---

[43] Financial Times: 'Russia and the UK general election' 21st November 2019
https://www.ft.com/content/82b93560-0c59-11ea-bb52-34c8d9dc6d84

party, and like few Tories, who stood as independents, did not get elected. The migration provoked concern that both the Tory and Labour parties will shift further to the extreme right or left, with the loss of prominent voices from the party. In the process, the two main parties are becoming more tribalistic in their politics, by stoking hatred and civil unrest, with a 'populist political agenda' relying on party loyalists to vote for them. It is a recipe for disaster at a time when voter turnout during elections is falling, because of indifference, which is rife, due to public disenchantment with politicians. This will compromise democracy, as it will result in a government elected by a minority section of the country's population; although democratically speaking, a so-called 'majority'. What is happening in Britain today shows how extraordinarily quickly the rot can set in. Our political honour code is breaking down, with few remaining good men and women who sit in parliament, who can only watch the horror unfold. The most frightening thing is that we do not yet know where this road will end. It is entirely conceivable that things will get worse before they get better. What started with the 2016 EU referendum campaign, unleashed a decades-long Tory civil war into the open, which has now ended with a PM who thinks he has the divine right to invalidate our sovereign parliament, as a political campaign strategy. Yes, it can be argued that the PM was elected through a democratic mandate, and can be voted out at the next general election, but the worrying part is what damage will be inflicted on the ordinary people when he is in power, especially at a time when the opposition Labour Party is in total disarray. These underlying aspects and consequences need to be resolved to restore trust in democracy, to make it work in the 21st century.

Democracy has had a good run in countries, allowing it to flourish. It has given people unfettered civil rights, often taken for granted from birth. It has also seen off fascism, communism and most forms of dictatorship. We have also gone to the length to wage wars, whether legal or not, fund and arm opposition forces to rise against a government, or a ruling party in foreign lands, to impose our much-cherished democracy, as well as making it an acceptable practice. Whether in government or opposition, it has become an acceptable practice to blame everybody else when policies fail and remain unaccountable, but claim credit when they work. It is an easy get out of jail card, but in reality, such misuse over the years has caused resentment and mistrust in democracy. For instance, during the 2016 EU referendum the public were told lies that Turkey was about to join the EU and 80 million Turks would invade the UK, with even more lies painted on the red campaign bus by the 'Vote Leave'. Whereas, the 'Vote Remain' distributed leaflets costing the tax payer £9 million with more lies, informing that each household will be £4,300 worse off by 2030. How did the Chancellor George Osborne know? If he could predict that far ahead, why did he not put his intellect to good use solving today's problems!

Such propaganda divides people, and lies fed by the ultra-rich individuals or political parties only serves their own short-term objectives, to retain power and get richer. It does not help to restore trust in politics. In the process, it undermines trust in the democracy, making the public perceive politicians, not as great patriots to serve the nation and its people, but more to do with protecting their own self-serving interests. The state of our politics has gone from bad to worse, turning into a ghastly circus. It is not politics per se that has left democracy and the country in such a mess, but the quality of individuals that the political parties nowadays attract. Politics has always been a fairly murky business. However, the current crop seems worse by a country mile. They will do anything to satisfy their own egos, and in the process their behaviour gets copied by others in society as a normal thing to do, in order to succeed in life. When politicians defy their electorate's views, and deny them democracy, they must not forget that the decisions they make, as a backbencher MP or a minister in a government; greatly affects people's lives. After all, they are there to make life better for them, not worsen a situation.

Internationally, as a prominent member of the UN, North Atlantic Treaty Organisation, Commonwealth or other organisations, it has become even more difficult for Britain to be taken seriously, particularly when under closer examination people witness subtle and direct breach of basic democratic principles. Those with financial, legal, media, and lobbying clout and have friends in these fields, tend to get heard more than those without. Such influence(s) shows that they are no different from the unelected leaders and dictators in other countries. This is because modern democracy seems like a form of 'legalised dictatorship'. Once politicians are elected, they are then a law onto themselves, until the next election, when the cycle of pledges, deceit and lies gets repeated all over again to get re-elected 'democratically', in name only. I am sure critics will line up to point out that various parliamentary mechanisms are in place, to keep politicians under check and accountable, because governments can be challenged with the 'vote of no confidence' by the opposition and the Recall of MPs Act 2015 gives voters' powers to recall an MP for misconduct. Journalists can also closely scrutinise politicians, whether or not this is effective is questionable, because the press has been tarnished as 'fake news', in a very 'clever' way by politicians like Donald Trump, and now eagerly copied by others, as well as the public. Besides, it is up to the PM if they would like to be scrutinised. Judging by the recent ban on some journalists and reluctance to give interviews, it will be difficult to hold politicians accountable. I am also fully aware that an ordinary constituent can always exercise their democratic right by contacting their MP, but in reality, it is also questionable whether all the foregoing mechanisms and checks are taken seriously, and actually work. Bearing in mind the political deception, bung money (bribes) paid to minority group(s) for parliamentary votes, or offers of plum jobs, by going into a coalition government, along with offers of peerage and much more. If they get found out which is rare or too late, due to them swanning off to write their biography, moved to other lucrative posts at the end of their tenure, or resign on full pension and other perks.

Politicians will do anything to stay in power, and use any possible means to cover-up their failings and conduct in public office. Such political deceit, lies and lack of accountability has existed since the foundations of modern-day self-government were established. However, unlike in the past, these malpractices cannot remain hidden indefinitely, forgotten or brushed under the carpet, because of social media and 24-hour news. So, people can no longer be fooled, however hard, or by whatever means the politicians deploy. Unfortunately, it seems politicians continue to remain oblivious, despite a dramatic rise in civil unrest and public discontent in recent times like Brexit, extinction rebellion, Grenfell, Windrush, Universal Credit, besides increase in knife crime and terrorist attacks. They must have witnessed the unrest and suffering, and should ask themselves why? How many costly public inquiries sanctioned by them have been held to learn important lessons, some are still ongoing? Those completed, have concluded that a lot of suffering and loss of lives could have been averted, if the public pleas for help were listened to, and not ignored. How can politicians ever forget the laughter generated during the live ITV debate in 2019, when both Boris Johnson and Jeremy Corbyn were asked if they could be trusted. They should be fully aware of the mood in the country, and if they really care about politics, then without wasting time, they should change and start listening to the people to restore trust in democracy before it is too late.

Democracy in its purest form should allow, or at least give everyone an opportunity to speak or be listened to by those elected, and should not feel out of reach. The majority of the electorate should not feel that democracy is reserved for those with hierarchy importance, or those who shout and protest the loudest, or those who appease their own party members. It is now up to politicians themselves to restore trust, hope and fairness in the truest sense of democracy. It is appropriate to revisit democracy and capitalism models, which has served us well in the past, but as I have highlighted it needs updating for the 21st century, owing to technology progressing, and people's expectations.

In the past, communities were smaller, and it was possible for politicians to listen to their views, if they wanted to. It is no longer possible to ignore people, because the public are more aware of their rights, and constantly reminded by politicians in their speeches that they have learnt to listen, and that the people have a right to voice their opinions. Politicians cannot afford to ignore or spin a yarn indefinitely, after making pledges, because the chances of eventually getting exposed are far greater nowadays. The rudimentary awareness in democracy in various parts of the world, such as the Arab Spring (anti-government protests) in some countries, although not successful, was an encouraging victory. The protests managed to raise people's hopes and aspirations to benefit from the global economy, irrespective of race, creed, class or colour, and become a part of the democratic process that has dramatically increased the possibility of peace and social justice in the region(s). Nevertheless, the rudimentary beginnings of the Arab Spring need to be nurtured. Their dreams are not farfetched or naïve, but universal human instincts to provide a better future for their families. What it showed was that it is impossible to continually suppress people. Same is equally true of nations, whether developed, developing, or Third World countries. Unfortunately, what we also witnessed was double standards, and abuse of power. While America, in the name of democracy, takes on the role of 'world policeman', then on a whim treats one nation with kid gloves, pouring everything into it, including the 'kitchen sink', but once their purpose is served, or after making a bigger mess of a situation, they just bugger off, as seen in Afghanistan, Iraq, Iran, Kashmir, Palestine, Yemen and elsewhere, except in the case of Israel and Saudi Arabia.

What is now becoming even more fashionable for political leaders in countries with a great record of democracy is to inflict suffering on its own citizens. In Kenya, India and elsewhere, different communities lived in social harmony for so many years. Kenya and India were shining examples of post-independent countries in Africa and the sub-continent, where people from various backgrounds lived in peaceful co-existence. A lesson on the merits of secularism: the principle of separation of the state from religious institutions, not only for its citizens, but also for the rest of world. Today, we witness politicians encouraging people of the nation, with divisive 'populist political agenda', for self-serving interests. People of same race are at loggerheads, killing each other or living in fear because of tribal, religious or caste differences, and neighbours who had been living next to one another for many years, are suddenly becoming sworn enemies.

In the West we can see the same thing happening, thank goodness, but not to the same extent. Britain, known for its Mother of Parliaments, and America founders of democracy and liberation are two countries with a great record of human and civil rights, standing against fascism; even though some political leaders have shamelessly embarked on a 'populist political agenda' in order to get elected, no matter whatever the consequences. They blame immigrants for shortages in housing, jobs, schools and hospitals, or anybody else except themselves. In the process, they are doing untold damage to humanity, by creating tension and civil unrest, played out on the streets in the name of democracy and Brexit. We see a union of four great nations, England, Northern Ireland, Scotland and Wales in turmoil, at the verge of breaking point. The Tory

Party claims they are the Unionist Party, but have no qualms to stitch others up to satisfy their own rebels in the party. At the root of all this is ego, politicians thinking they are God. What is equally worrying is that the rot in the world order has become deeply engraved because of divisive 'populist political agenda' preached by unpredictable leaders, under the pretext of democracy. We all know that politics has always been a dirty game; this is not a new thing. What is different now is that it is played in the open for all to see. This has led not only world leaders copying each other's election strategy to gain power in the West, but also elsewhere, with greed and ego becoming an addiction to them. They are also willing to go to any lengths to hang onto their power once they have it. We have seen what has happened in some African, South American, Asian, European and Middle Eastern countries, and no one can do anything about it. Even the UN is powerless! It is because no one can take a moral high ground to tell others of their wrong doing, or abuse of human rights, illegal invasion of countries, carnage and 'ethnic cleansing'.

Sadly, as in all conflicts, disasters and crises, human or natural, it is the innocent and the poor at the bottom of the 'food chain' who suffer the most. Also, it is the poor who inflict most pain on fellow human beings, by carrying out the orders of their leaders, because one very rarely sees the political leader or ruler in the front line in wars and civil disorder, or dying from starvation, because of their actions. The powerful and the rich remain protected and well fed. In the worse scenario, the leader just leaves the country, and returns when it is safe to do. It is the mere mortal who suffers the consequences of their leader's actions. The leaders will not be seen protesting on the streets as they are not affected by their own policy failures, or face shortages in public services and affordable housing, as they are treated as a priority, such as during the Covid-19 pandemic. The only time they are seen out and about talking to the public is during well managed stereotype election campaigns, under the tightest of security, and if and when journalists get a chance to confront them, some make a quick exit, whilst others try to seek refuge in the 'fridge'.

Ordinary people have been appalled by the present state of affairs in the oldest democracy in the world. Who knows where it will end, unless we somehow pull ourselves back from the brink and find a way to rekindle a respect for the democracy and constitutional principles, we once held so dearly? It is now an opportune time for both democracy and capitalism to evolve further, to keep pace with people's optimism, to be a part of the democratic process that reflects 21st century needs. Not an unaccountable patronising political system dictated by few individuals or groups with financial, media and legal power to influence politics. The two-hundred-year-old party-political system has not been fit for purpose for the last few decades, and we now have a breed of Oxbridge and private school educated career politicians. It appears that Parliament likes it that way, so that those in the 'club' can leech thousands in expenses, and other fiddles. Nowadays it seems it is not about serving the people, but profiteering from them. If we think about it, nothing of substance has been achieved for decades since the formation of the NHS and the social housing building programmes after WWII. If we look closely, the state of both are on its knees, as more is taken out than put in, which could be cured in an instant by proper investment, right political will and belief. But politicians do not have the stomach to do it as it involves commitment. They know they only have to bumble along, doing nothing, and sucking up the tax payer's hard earned money, along with empty pledges, as they could be out in five years. The public has already witnessed a Westminster on the brink of a constitution crisis during the Brexit negotiations disaster, with some disillusioned Tory and Labour MPs rejecting tribal party politics, pushing them to form an Independent group. Although it was refreshing to see some MPs coming to their senses, but the public had already suspected that self-serving party-interests was taking place, which led to tribal political allegiance leading to a rise in nationalism, populism, social unrest, extremism, racism, nepotism and more. The whole thing stinks!

In a healthy democracy, we need greater participation from the population, with higher turnouts during elections. Instead we face voter disengagement, especially amongst the young, leading to a declining sense of efficiency within politics locally and centrally, a situation where the electorates think that the main political parties are all the same, greedy, and are not like us, so it makes no difference who gets voted in. The best way for the electorates to 'take back control' of democracy, in its truest sense, is to exercise their hard-won voting right, by those who fought for it in the past through war, mass movements, or legislative battles. A huge turnout at elections would be good place to start, because low turnouts suit tribal politics, allowing it to flourish, encouraging complacency and unaccountability amongst career politicians in 'safe seats'. A huge voter turnout would help clear out a few cobwebs to prevent complacency amongst career politicians, who rely on low turnouts to get elected, which gives them an advantage, as they can rely on their army of party registered supporters to come out to vote them in.

Not only do ordinary people suffer, but so does the government from a lack of effective leadership, as politicians fail to take responsibility. There was a time before Margaret Thatcher that politicians were held to account, but she changed all that because of the many scandals in her various cabinets. There is a distinct lack in political leadership which has worsened further in the last few decades, not only in Britain, but worldwide. Instead of political leaders, we now have a fair share of managers. The rot in Britain started when Tony Blair became PM, because he promoted a relaxed 'sofa government' to liberate ministers with fewer committee and cabinet meetings,[28] ending up with more advisers, and settling government business over coffee and liaising the 21st century way, by email, a somewhat less direct style of interaction with fellow politicians. This seems to have encouraged career politicians to have less contact with their electorates, as they live in their ivory towers, out of touch with reality. Since the turn of the century, we have just elected managers, not MPs, because of a distinct of lack of choice of politicians with leadership qualities. Successive governments have only been interested in the top-down reorganisation of public services, such as the NHS, education and welfare with unaccountable management hierarchy. Such reforms result in retiring the top-brass with attractive pensions and financial compensation packages, costing the tax payers a fortune. After which only to return to take similar posts elsewhere, or get hired as advisers to government. Governments have only been interested in tinkering with the education syllabus, concerned with performance targets at the expense of the child's future, rather than the quality of education. Only for the next government to change it again and the cycle repeats itself with billions wasted. It is unbelievable to think how the ordinary person would survive if we squandered our hard-earned wages in the same way, but then why should they worry? It is not their money, just like when they conduct illegal wars; it is not their lives at stake, but that of the ordinary person! The country desperately needs leadership courage and energy, not by charm by utterly inexperienced young men armed with education from well-known academic establishments, with only a sense of entitlement to run family estates.

Time and again we are beginning to witness the consequences of the first-past-the-post system that was introduced in 1888. This system elects' politicians with the highest votes, and a government with the highest number of MPs from the same party to replace a complex system favouring the wealthy land owners and old-fashioned politician,[44] which may have worked at that time, because people had far more pertinent priorities to worry about. In 1888, women did not even have the right to vote. Also, people did not enjoy many civil rights, so why would they be interested who governs them. But it is different in the 21st century, when the expectations of people have changed, not only in terms of aspirations, but their complete outlook, because of travel, human rights, diet, jobs, leisure, and many other things that have changed the world we live in. For the majority of ordinary people, the division along old party-political allegiance is not as distinct as before, but more confusing, because we all have to work whether rich or poor, so we are all working class and owning property (small or a mansion) that means many of us are land owners. Society has moved on so much beyond recognition, and the public's values and priorities have changed drastically, not always necessarily along wealth or worker's rights. Also, in the past, for most

[44] The Sun: 'What is first-past-the-post voting system? when did the UK start using the electoral system the winner takes all' 12th December 2019 https://www.thesun.co.uk/uncategorized/3752882/what-is-first-past-the-post-voting-system/

people, education, home ownership, environment, health, leisure and so forth were a lesser priority. It meant political views amongst the privileged were more distinct on those lines, easily reflected and divided along party lines. In the 21st century the division along party lines are not that distinct, as there are more affluent, educated and 'upwardly mobile', people enjoying better standards. As a result, we have a population with a range of priorities, then along the specific traditional political lines, and the parties have lagged behind. Conflicting views held within the political parties does not help, causing further doubts in the public's mind. The electorates have reached a gridlock in democracy, and needs a pragmatic system allowing the public's real-life concerns to get heard, and not ignored in the midst of tribal politics. Perhaps more interaction at the basic level is needed, not only along party lines but more widely, and looking at proportional representation models to enhance public participation in democracy with conviction politics, not self-serving party-political interests.

The current situation has also led to a situation encouraging too many MPs to vote along tribal party lines, instead of relying on their own judgement and needs of the electorates they are meant to serve. Of course, no one is disputing that in a debating chamber there is strength in numbers, but the public would be better served if those debates relied on agreement, rather than a few vocal voices with a bluster of oratory debating skills dictating the agenda. The quality and conviction of politicians is on the decline. Most MPs are passengers on a party ticket not selected on merit, but whether they will kneel on party lines, like a flock of sheep and do what they are told. "MPs will do what they are told to do," is what Boris Johnson said of the 630 Tory candidates, during the 2019 election. What it means is that within any constituency, those who did not vote for his party will be ignored. In 2019, the Tory Party's share of votes was 44%, so 56% did not vote for them. The turnout was 67%, so 33% did not even vote for any political party. This means a lot of people's views remain unrepresented. People will say this is democracy, and there are always losers and winners. Yes, but it does not mean we should not look at other options before it gets worse. As I have said, in a thriving democracy we need to look at ways to engage voters to increase turnout during general and local elections, which will also bring out the best in our career politicians, as they will realise they can no longer afford to be complacent, by taking the electorates for granted, and get elected on low turnouts.

I suppose, based on such personal experience of the political class, MPs referred to as 'Honourable Members' means loyalty to themselves and their chums, namely the old world of the 'establishment'. Power to a politician, a wealthy entrepreneur or a celebrity is an aphrodisiac, and ultimately gives them power and fame. Yet, wealthy people with their hand on heart can say that their top priority to donate to political parties and charities has nothing to do with hobnobbing or recognition. Ask anyone of them how they feel when singled out in a crowd, or how they feel when they get ignored? Ask them how their ego is boosted when recognised, or deflated when overlooked? So, they are lying when they claim that the top priority is to help the poor, or make life better for others. The 'establishment' needs to be honest for them to serve public duty, and not their own interests.

Despite whatever one is made to believe, in a thriving democracy we all have equal rights. Supporting a political party with money is an important element of politics, whether in a democracy or otherwise. It goes without saying that politicians will think first about their big wealthy party donors, whilst the rich expect to get the red-carpet treatment, and very often appointments are fixed over an informal phone call, or word of mouth, without having to put pen to paper, because the donors expect a quick response. Those for whom the system works will defend it to the hilt, there is nothing wrong with that, it happens all over the world, money gets recognition, and it will continue to do so. Throughout my unsuccessful ordeal in my dealings with politicians to raise real-life concerns, I have always realised that it was not going to be easy for the ordinary 'man in the street' to run for public office, and without any money it is very difficult to get heard. Preaching to others is one thing, but putting it into practice is another. Politicians and wealthy people should put themselves in the shoes of the ordinary public. How would they feel if they wrote to a fellow dignitary and got ignored, and not even as a matter of courtesy was sent an acknowledgement letter? They should remind themselves how quickly they respond when a fellow eminent person writes to them, and remember how often they have not even bothered to reply, let alone acknowledge the efforts made by an ordinary person. They should be mindful of anyone, whether a multi-millionaire, a famous individual or not, all need acknowledging. It does not cost anything to them, except it is the public who pay for their arrogance and contempt. After all, politicians are handsomely paid by the tax payer to perform public duty, as well as it being common courtesy to reply.

In the past, politicians came through the ranks at local level, serving apprenticeship in communities, gaining real-life experiences in the field and progressed to national level. Not university degrees in politics, philosophy, law, media, economics and the like, followed by 'fast track' political internships and promotions based on loyalty to the 'establishment'. Today, it seems to be about egos, claiming expenses, a good salary, and power to milk the system and control others. I am sure the beneficiaries of the system will strongly disagree with this, all I can say, the record speaks for itself; politicians need to find out for themselves by listening more to the feelings of the ordinary people. I believe this can only happen if there is a big change of attitude, a change which can only be brought about by 'people power', electing politicians with scruples and a conscience.

With the sackings, defections and resignations of MPs seen in 2019 in Tory and Labour confirms there is no room for thinkers and intellectuals in both parties. A dilemma that has led to a void in leadership potential, already exacerbated by the 'sofa government' mentality from the past encouraging a lack of healthy democratic debate, and complacency has left a distinct vacuum of critical voices in local and central government to scrutinise policy, spending and borrowing decisions. This is not good for the electorates and not good in a healthy democracy, as openness, consultations and disclosures are far better, and practical in serving public duty. We are also witnessing the worst examples of tribal political allegiance, not only in Britain, but also in some of the former colonies as we are seeing signs of the beginnings of a steady rise in the mild forms of extremism, on the right and left of the political spectrum. Such as Tory EU rebels' revoke article 50 petition and momentum groups, as well as in other well-established democracies in Kenya, India, Israel and the US (to name a few). Such divisions, only serves to divert attention from real-life concerns facing the ordinary public, often succeeding in scuppering political agenda by bringing down leaders and governments, by holding them to ransom, leading to chaos and squandering of financial resources. Such mild forms of extremism are no different from that seen in the past that led to WWII and Afghanistan in the 1980s with the Taliban (encouraged by the West), which later spread terrorism like cancer elsewhere. It led to the whole faith getting tarnished as Islamist terrorists. Is it not how past tyrants started? Who will we deracialise or blame next?

The public are often reminded that to attract the best calibre of people to enter into politics, MPs need to be paid well. As a result, we have seen a huge increase in their salaries and other perks. But it is not entirely true, because the main stumbling block to attracting talented politicians is tribal party-political structure, and its process to select prospective candidates. To get selected, the potential candidates have to be more compromising and submissive to the demands of the party hierarchy, or face threats of deselection, ruining their promotion prospects. We have witnessed politicians elevated by turning on the charm and knowing how to please the boss, as well as possessing the skill of not answering the question. So instead of promoting excellence, the old tribal party loyalty stifles intellectual ability and ingenuity to serve public duty. This is reflected by an increase in the number of U-turns and public inquiries, an indication of incompetence, or a sign of shackled politicians deprived to think for themselves, or what is good for the people and country. The collective responsibility means no one can be held accountable, and no one has to own up to their mistakes. It allows them to blame and pass the buck. Surely the Tory Party as firm believers of a 'free market' and competition should be able to see that it stifles talent, through the weakness of the party loyalty structures. Competition is healthy and efficient, just like private businesses as opposed to nationalised businesses, but then the breed of politicians has changed, and no one wants to rock the boat, and stop the gravy train. The mind-set in British politics needs revisiting before tribal politics becomes a bigger threat, in the early stages during Brexit.

We need to rectify the situation before the 1968 'Rivers of Blood' speech by Enoch Powell becomes a reality, not because of immigrants, but more to do with the politicians and their 'populist political agenda' driving a wedge between people, communities and social harmony. Such blatant exploitation in the name of democracy, pitting one group against another, can lead to venting anger and hatred on ethnic people, who will become easy identifiable targets, despite well-spoken local or posh English-speaking accents and dialects than those of Caucasian origin. Career politicians have broken the public's trust in democracy, which takes years to build, seconds to break, forever to repair, and the work to restore trust in democracy should not be delayed any longer!

19

A Role for all to Play

We can continue with the blame game. Nations blaming nations, politicians blaming politicians, people blaming people, faiths blaming faiths, north blaming south, rich blaming poor and tinker at the edges for short-term gains, individually or collectively. It is time for politicians, nations and humanity to come together, work with honesty for a better world. In my view, people are inseparably linked in this globalised world, and we cannot just rely on individuals, organisations or governments to look after national interests. We all have to play our role for the benefit of humanity. In fact, we depend upon each other even more now, because of the current unpredictable burning state of world politics, and cannot afford to take things for granted. I never stop thinking what is around the next corner, because life is all about dealing with the events, consequences, and if possible, finding a way out. To this day, I believe we are all born equal, with shared values to succeed in life. It is unfair how political and economic systems make us unequal. In some parts of the world, less fortunate people face the consequences of conflicts that were fought on their lands by foreign powers, orthodox extremist religious and political groups. I feel people can work together to win for humanity as a whole, if we all pull together and play our part.

My family ancestors, like many South Asians who migrated to East Africa from the mid-19th century onwards would not have been successful, let alone survive, without the goodwill and charitable deeds of fellow human beings on the way, and when they reached their destination. Because of this, they did not wait until they had amassed significant wealth before they helped others, in whatever capacity they could as a businessman, or as labourers. Crucially, they did not forget what it had been like to be poor, and helped people in their actual hour of need. Even if it meant just providing a meal and/or shelter to help them get established. As my family and others prospered, they took every opportunity to share their wealth to benefit the needy. Not only Asians, but everyone, just like Cadbury and many other families. What past philanthropic acts did was to invest in the infrastructure to improve lives of people while employed, so families would not have to rely on charitable acts to make ends meet.

The Akberali Hassanali family took every opportunity to share their good fortune to benefit others, especially the indigenous people of Mombo, because they believed in acts of philanthropy. The family built a school, mosque, health centre and other public amenities, as well as building living quarters for their employees. The family also cultivated land allocated to the Mombo Women's Group for planting rice. In 1966, the family donated a fully operational sawmill at Mbwi, in the Handeni District, by forming an African co-operative of workers managed by Abdi Hassani. The sawmill was opened with a ceremony attended by President Julius Nyerere, making it the first act of its kind at the time. In later years, I also had the opportunity to make a small contribution in public life to others' lives in the UK; I would say that I did not learn from anyone, because it is in my genes, which came from my father and mother.

There is nothing wrong in being very successful and extremely wealthy, especially when somebody has worked hard for it, but why wait for charitable acts, until vast wealth has been amassed. Instead treat others the way we would like to be treated, and practice the old saying that 'charity begins at home', by investing in the wellbeing of the workforce. This does not mean that the job creators should abandon sound business principles and not enjoy the luxuries of life, because money helps us to get noticed. Also, there is no alternative for money, as it is needed by everyone, rich or poor. But it is more about business ethics, and how those profits were made in the first place. I understand that people do not get rich by being nice, but there is a limit to excessive greed at the expense of others. For instance, if profits were ploughed back by paying workers a decent wage when needed most, they would not have to rely on foodbanks and welfare benefits. It would also help everyone if the wealthy paid their fair share of tax, instead of hiring expensive lawyers and accountants to exploit loop-holes and avoid paying tax, as well as investing in tax free havens. Incidentally, the costly professional fees are then written-off against the tycoon's tax returns as expenses. The public who pay tax at source are dealt a twofold setback by the wealthy businessmen, a double whammy of first paying the workforce less wages, and then re-claiming expenses to avoid paying their full share of tax. Charitable acts are also tax exempt, resulting in further loss of tax revenue for the government to spend on public services. It would be better if everyone paid tax equally, instead of having complex systems for the wealthy to exploit, and then act as philanthropists (saviours of the disadvantaged and the poor). In fact, the charitable acts by the very wealthy is the same as handing back the money taken out of the public purse, through tax avoidance and paying low wages to the public. Why have loopholes in the first place to encourage tax avoidance? The government is at fault, not those exploiting the laws. In the end it costs much less if resources are spent wisely, then there would a less need for charitable acts. Concerns have also been raised on the increase in the practice of well-known celebrities accepting thousands of pounds for backing charities.[45] While ordinary people performing philanthropy free-of-charge without costing the tax payer anything, as demonstrated by the newsvendor that Bill Gates mentions[1] and many others. Small acts of kindness go a long way when needed most.

Politicians have also abandoned their main democratic pledge that they 'entered politics to make life better for others', instead they have embarked on self-serving egos and party-political agendas, compartmentalising and dividing people. The root causes of civil unrest and international tensions in the 21st century will not be like those faced during the two World Wars in the last century, a carnage to save civil liberties against fascists, but an age of explosive populist politics of nationalism, pitting one group of non-ethnic people against another, which was seen during Brexit. Politicians were exploiting the sentiments of people, who felt left out and ignored for years. People were led to believe that they were protecting their hard fought 'civilised' democratic rights, to 'take back control' for a more prosperous future. The politicians have succeeded in achieving their own self-serving interests by delaying future civil tensions with false political pledges, with disruptive right-wing populist political agendas during election campaigns adopted from foreign countries. Such as that used by Donald Trump, to entice voters by causing resentment against civic institutions with false allegations: such as 'drain the swamp' meaning the 'establishment' and 'lock her up' referring to his opponent Hilary Clinton, and pandering to ethnic groups with slogans like 'Jews for Trump', 'Hindus for Trump'. We saw similar trends in the 2019 UK elections, like 'Parliament against People', 'Hindus for Tories', 'Jews against Labour', and 'Palestinians support Labour'. However, we will have to wait for the outcome of Brexit negotiations and what effects it will have on people's daily life. I wonder who in the future will take the blame for the shortages in public services. One thing we can be sure of is that it will not be the politicians, so who will pay the consequences for their mistakes? It is about time we learnt lessons that we have an obligation to our future generations, and not self-serving party interests by pandering to the extreme right or left wing of the political spectrum. We the public need to engage by holding politicians more accountable, more so now than we have done in the past. The rich also should not continue

---

[45] Channel 4: 'Dispatches quoted almost £60,000 for charity…https://eastieoaks.com/2020/03/08/channel-4-dispatches-quoted-almost-60000-for-charity-promotion-with-caitlyn-jenner/

with excessive greed at whatever cost, extracting what they feel worth taking at somebody else's expense.

The present cocktail is truly explosive. Why? Because more than ever before it has allowed the depressed, suppressed, lonely and disadvantaged, not only at home but also abroad, who now understand the full extent of material wealth enjoyed by some, at the expense of others, while they face the consequences of illegal wars, injustices, global warming, poverty, foodbanks and homelessness. It gives those facing these injustices the impression that we are not serious of the unfolding events, breeding a culture of 'US' and 'THEM', and they see no hope in our public institutions to solve the important real-life issues facing humanity, becoming targets for those seeking to cause division. As technological capacity to better our lives to inform each other grows, our horizons shrink and memories become short lived, because of the excessive, and at times less relevant worthless, unverified information and scams. The situation is further exacerbated with the advent of satellite TV. As the Western channels feed more concepts and images of better living standards to the rest of the world, we in the West are presented with less reality of the world, and how their lives are affected because of our actions. Whereas those fortunate ones in the West, witness events covered on TV and social media with great intensity in the comforts of their living rooms, only to quickly disappear as it appeared with the development of another news item, and feel those in need of help at home or abroad as somebody else's responsibility. We all need to play our role to restore trust in our human society by leading from the front, by being good role-models for the young, not just empty boasting. Our outlook is actually narrowing, despite an ever-increasing appetite and technological advances to transmit news from the farthest and remotest corners of the world. We have to ask who is seriously tackling the plight of the ordinary human beings at home and across world. An easy option would be to shun responsibility, by blaming politicians and others. We should also not tarnish all politicians with the same brush that they are not doing their public duty and not fit for purpose, because we need politicians to govern us.

Let us embark on a true mission and serve humanity in a productive and enriching way, to lead a dignified and scrupulous life. Not by encouraging situations that lead to poverty, and then go out of our way to help the needy, as a charitable cause, as it would be far better not to entrench people in a life of poverty, misery and suffering in the first place, which gets them hooked on handouts. We need to restore hope, trust and fairness, and address failings in our dysfunctional democracy; otherwise, it is only a matter of time that the homeless, whether at home or abroad, will become more resentful. It will not involve nations at war in an overwhelming Third World War kind of way, but disenchanted citizens venting anger and hatred in never-ending stabs, creating civil unrest and migrations to escape poverty, conflicts and effects of climate change, which will render our daily lives even more insecure. As seen during Brexit and other crises, revenge will start on easily identifiable minority groups based on race, creed, sex or class, making them more susceptible to attacks in their homes and neighbourhoods. In the absence of easy targets, the disadvantaged non-ethnic people will become vulnerable to more austerity and hatred towards each other. A direct result of differences based on class, privileges and social mobility.

In an environment where politics is becoming brutally nationalistic and politicians less accountable for policy failures, the political journalists should play their impartial role, and spend more time scrutinising government policies to give deeper insight and explanation of political deception to the public. Voters rely on journalists to guide them through their political leaders' conspiracies to distinguish between what is true and not. Quite often journalists and the 'free press' are quick to pick breaking news to get exclusive coverage, with hot eye-catching headlines or celebrity stories, which makes good TV to boost audience figures, but then just move onto the next story, without pushing further, when certain stories need to be investigated, so justice takes place. With such fluid change of news coverage, it leads to abuse of political power, because politicians are fully aware that their failures will quickly get brushed under the carpet. Hostilities and suffering inflicted upon the poor will soon get forgotten, and remain unresolved, until the next time when the situation flares up again to merit coverage, and the endless cycle of suffering is allowed to continue. Very often, journalists ignore news with less popular headlines affecting lives or achievements of the ordinary people. This undermines democracy, with people losing trust in the 'establishment', because it lets off those responsible for their suffering. Journalists should not allow themselves to be used to spread 'fake news' by peddling lies and smears in exchange for favours from political leaders for perks, such as places on state visits, honours and news exclusives. Reputable political journalists should also not allow themselves to be exploited, as propaganda channels for political leaders. They should exercise proper scrutiny, as anxieties grow about the spread of 'fake news', which is unmoderated and unaccountable on social media sites, used by politicians and others. Some journalists for their own vested interest would argue that the media has been lobbying politicians and their advisors for news exclusives for decades, and has become an accepted practice, but that does not mean it is right, and we should continue doing it, especially when they know it is wrong. They should not become too compliant in their eagerness to receive inside information, and report without challenge, as we saw during the 2019 election, when reputable journalists reported an untrue account of a so-called physical attack outside an NHS trust, which is unacceptable behaviour, and so does not give the public much faith in the news they read.

There comes a point when the only thing for people is to stand-up to the very public institutions put in place to serve them, which have let them down. Civil unrest not only destroys social cohesion, but also ruins lives. A time will come when people can no longer remain silent, and if left unchecked will have serious consequences, such as increasing incidents of public riots. In the 21st century we have no excuse, but engage in a positive way to make a real difference as to how we are governed, and not to be taken for granted by the political class. Throughout political history, we have witnessed pledges made and broken to satisfy the greediness of politicians in their search to gain power at whatever cost, but not at the rate seen today, which has led the political class to stoop down to very low levels. Judging by the mood of the country, the ordinary public are not going to allow common sense, morality, decency and British goodwill downgraded by being lied to by politicians, who lack moral virtues.

We need to heed the lessons learnt from past mistakes, with frequent public inquiries. The overall findings of many public inquiries indicate the 'establishment' do not listen to the concerns raised by the ordinary public. If their cries of pleas and help were listened to, this would have eased a lot of pain, suffering and loss of lives. This is the reason why people feel politicians are out of touch, and have stopped listening. The present situation goes beyond party politics and trade unions. The issues are more fundamental, so we need to ask ourselves, what kind of society we wish to live in? A society that works on the basis of competition, winners and losers, or do we value people, and want to provide equality and care for all who need it, gaining economic security for all. Do we feel comfortable when sexual harassment, elderly leading isolated lives, food banks, homelessness and crime rate are all on an increase? We must ask ourselves, as a 'civilised' society, do we have the right to live without the fear of becoming a victim, and ending up as a government statistic of the circumstances imposed by the 'fittest', who think it is there divine right to survive by ruling others. We must also ask whether we share a common set of values that act as a platform for all governmental policies, discussing openly such 'fundamentals', and perhaps explore the idea of a real constitution that not only encourages citizens to contribute in a 'civilised' society, but also protects them regardless of colour, creed, age, gender, class and/or where they were born.

I am optimistic that it is still not too late to rescue the situation, changing it for the common good, and I passionately believe we will rise to the challenges facing humanity. Why am I optimistic? It is because the experience I gained from the direct interaction I had with people during the elections have been very enlightening. I treasure those moments! It was reassuring that despite the present-day post-Brexit turmoil, mistrust and disillusion in politicians, goodwill and kindness at the local level has continued. We have seen people help each other during floods, terrorist attacks and other hardships, followed with generous charitable acts. But underneath, one can sense people feel the anxiety and uncertainty of the legacy we will leave for future generations, in terms of global warming and security. I share the public's sentiments, and know how they feel, as I have mentioned, I have been through similar experiences in my attempts to contact politicians without success. I have also learnt that people, just like me, are not demanding or expecting miracles to happen, but feel the present problems could be avoided, if we trust each other. I think politicians should show empathy and interact more with electorates. In a thriving democracy, it does not matter who initiates the debate, as long as what matters gets resolved and achieved. Ignoring people's views and concerns constantly, only worsens the situation, and more expensive in terms of suffering and money to put it right. In theory, it is one thing for politicians to encourage the public to engage in the democratic process, and ignore the voter when they take the trouble to do so, once elected.

We must also not forget or take our freedom for granted, and should be grateful to those who sacrificed their lives for our freedom, civil rights and the right to vote, which I am sure we do not. For example, in 2019 I called on an elderly voter, who said he was fed up, and not going to cast his vote because of the current state of politics and Brexit. I informed him that I felt the same way, and that is why I decided to contest as an independent, because politicians are too busy looking after self-serving egos and party interests. I mentioned these elections affected local issues and party politics has infiltrated at the local level, with politicians failing to serve public duty, and politely went onto say that he should not give-up his 'right to vote', and exercise it on election day. The gentleman sternly reprimanded me, and said that I have no right to tell him whether he should vote or not, it is his civil right to do what he wants. I apologised profusely. Fully appreciating what he had said, but I was not forcing him or anyone to vote against their wishes. I was only highlighting that it was his generation that made great sacrifices for the freedom we enjoy today, and it is in our hands to bring about change, if we believe politicians are not fulfilling their obligations to the electorates.

In another incident, after pushing an election leaflet through the letterbox when there was no reply, a lady came running after me to hand it back, saying she is not interested in voting, because all politicians are the same. She went on to inform me that it is only during the election process that politicians are seen to make promises, and once elected, they are not to be seen until the next election. I reasoned with her, explaining that I was not a career politician, and it is for the same reasons that she had brought up that I had decided to do something about it. I continued to enlighten her that at the same time I was also enjoying the experience of meeting fellow residents, whether I get elected or not.

This made her change her mind, and she said that she would use her right to vote. These were isolated incidents, and on the whole people remained engaged.

I also feel optimistic with a sense of satisfaction knowing there is a new generation growing up interested in politics, because they understand the new challenges facing them in the 21st century. For me it was not until I was forty-one that I started dabbling in politics, even now I consider myself a novice. Since we are talking about getting involved in politics, it only seems right to mention the anxieties of our young people who feel that their concerns on global warming are not listened to, and they are now starting to understand the betrayal of the older generation, because of some major government policy failures that will affect their future. It is encouraging that they are doing something about it, making sure that the eyes of all future generations are upon those failing them. The young have decided to draw the line, and given an ultimatum to the decision-makers that they will never forgive, and not let those responsible to get away with the threat of global warming facing the future of the whole planet. We can sense real change coming, and humanity waking up. Although regrettably in a confrontational manner costing the tax payer, as they are expensive to police, but necessary to make this change. The best way to harness such enthusiasm would be for the young to engage directly in the democratic process, by making sure to register once eligible to vote. They need to be made aware at an early age that the future of democracy, just like that of climate change, is in their hands. We need to find ways to engage both young and old to participate actively in politics and public duty, in a unique way to harness both talents. The older generation have the benefit of experience of what they have seen and how things have gone wrong for them in the past; whereas the young are showing interest and vigour in their future and that of the planet, which needs to be encouraged. It would also help alleviate some of the blight of modern society, such as loneliness, mental health, anti-social behaviour, social mobility, and social harmony, by bringing awareness through quality education at an early age, with subjects like civic studies in the school curriculum, so they can learn the importance of public duty. The main aim should be to give an overview of topical political events at local, national and international level of social interest, to encourage awareness with well-informed discussions for a better understanding of the problems facing the world. This would then yield impressive results, in terms of a well-informed worthy society, not easily swayed by hatred preached by religious and political leaders with a populist agenda, targeting vulnerable audiences for their own personal gain.

There is no doubt the political dialogue has got to change, which can only be brought about by voting for a politician committed to serving public duty. Unluckily, there has been an increase in hatred towards them, and by venting our anger against them is not going to help address real-life concerns, because we need governance and public institutions for the effective functioning of our public services. If politicians are failing in their duty, then it is up to the people do something about it. The responsibility falls on the people to elect politicians who will serve by listening to the electorates, not those with self-serving interests.

20

2017 Election and Public Duty: 1 of 73,000

While growing up in Tanzania during colonial times and after independence, politics was something above most young people's brains. Our main ambition was to focus on getting a good education to succeed in life. As far as I can recall, the meaning of politics was not clear, as I had focused more on science subjects from an early age. I never got an opportunity to study politically oriented subjects to generate interest, except when I was taught current affairs in school for a year. I still recall a lesson on the UN by my teacher Mr Jani who taught us that the Secretary General at the time, U Thant, should not be addressed as Mr Thant, because U in Burmese means 'Mister'. I started reading newspapers when I was about twelve years old, not to generate interest in politics, but more to improve my reading, something a wise elderly Parsi family friend, Mr Wadia advised my mother I should do, because knowledge and information were to be found in books. After school, I would go to his place to collect old copies of the Tanzania Standard, National Geography, and Readers Digest after he had finished reading them himself. In 1970, at the age of nineteen, it was in Dar-es-Salaam when I met politically minded students who would discuss communism, capitalism, socialism and apartheid in South Africa. For me, it was nothing more than just banter, part of university student life. It was a strange disjointedness of activity, by potentially angry students, which at times felt quite unnerving; giving me an impression that politics could be dangerous, getting people into trouble, and it was best for me to keep away, which I did until 2017. This is when I decided to contest an election at sixty-six years of age. I had no epiphany, no singular revelation, and no moment of truth to become a politician as such. Perhaps it was because of a steady accumulation of thoughts, based on an ever-increasing feeling that the communication I had entered into with cross-party politicians and successive PMs was just falling on deaf ears. It seemed that the ever-growing crop of career politicians were detached from the public and self-serving interests was more important than their constituents. One thing for sure was that I have never been inclined to join any political party or protest group. It is because I have been brought up with a belief that in a society it is the duty of the learned professionals, such as teachers, doctors, police and judges, as well as religious and political leaders, who are the 'defenders of society', to uphold welfare, moral and social values of society and the nation as a whole.

As I have said, I cannot pinpoint a specific moment in time when I became politicised, not even as an activist or a politician, but it was more to do with serving public duty. Maybe, it was because I was involved earlier in a voluntary capacity, and perhaps as mentioned previously by Jonathan Lord in his letters 21 and 58, I felt that as 1 of his 73,000 constituent I was denied my democratic right. I do not dispute whatsoever that Jonathan Lord has the responsibility for 73,000 people in his constituency, and I do realise that I am not the only one, but what is worrying is the casual manner by which he had denied my democratic right, and who knows how many others he has done this to. So, it could be possible that all these factors were at the back of my mind or in my heart. As usual I got up early on Thursday 20th April 2017, and the first thing I told Femi was that I was going to contest in the snap general election on 8th June that Theresa May had announced two days before on the Downing Street steps. I must say, I have never considered myself a politician even to this day, except heeded the advice given by my MP to contest election(s), if I wanted to get heard. I had no experience of contesting elections, but remained undeterred or daunted by the task. I had no funds, supporters or advisers, not even a minuscule of infrastructure enjoyed by the established political parties. All that was in my favour was that I wanted to try my level best, because if I believe in something, then that is enough to motivate me, as I do not like having any regrets. Before making my final decision to contest for the parliamentary seat of Woking, Femi and I decided to seek advice. She suggested Reverend Denis Robinson at Gordons, the school attended by both my daughters. We all held him in high regard, so I went to see Denis. The first thing he said was that he was going to stay neutral because of his vocation, which I was aware of and fully respected. I said it was more to do with whether I am mad to even consider contesting in the general election. All he said was, "Hassan you are on a journey of discovery and listen to your heart, and I will pray for you." It was good enough for me, and the more I thought about it, the more I felt I had to do this so I did not have any regrets. I am sure the prayers of Denis, my mother and others have helped in many ways, for which I am truly grateful and humbled. I also went to see a good friend of mine, Jon Davis, a local printer whom I have known since 1996. He encouraged me, and messaged me after the election, saying, "Well done and you should be proud of doing what lots of people only talk about – that is stand up for your beliefs – you have also made friends, earning much respect from many." It is true, although I lost; I made many friends and enjoyed meeting people.

My logical decision to contest in the 2017 general election did not deter me, even though I had never been politicised from birth, or attended any political speeches or studied politics, nor noticed that my life was restricted by political events. For me, there was no contradiction, only to serve public duty, because I was first and foremost a human being standing for a cause I believed in. I was also not inclined to join any political party or a protest group. I felt politics was a system of compartmentalising people, pitting people against people, exacerbating the situation, instead of serving public duty in its purest form. I was determined to bring democracy to the doorstep, a common criticism I shared with the people I met when I was canvassing, based on personal experience about politicians that were elected, and were not to be seen until the next election. My election campaign was based on simple credentials on one fine early morning; although, I had never been a politician, never been a member of any political party, never joined a protest group, and never looked at people as being 'US' or 'THEM'. I was entering a new and challenging path on my own, a path to win votes, to serve public duty and get democratically elected, in the truest sense 'by the people, from the people, for the people', the outcome of which I did not and could not know. I started as a total novice, without any experience, except for my determination and conviction of wanting fairness and justice on a level playing field.

Even though I did not have any experience, manpower, money or other resources, what I did have was the drive and the will power. I began in the only way I knew how. I first sought views from my family, followed by neighbours, Simon and Suzanne Lee-Smith, Phillip and Anna Anderson on either side of where Femi and I live, and others down the street, and anybody else who knew me. In true British tradition of 'supporting the underdog' they were all very positive about my suggestion of running in the general election, and admired my get-up-and-go attitude to take on-the-big-boys. I was also fortunate that I could read, write and make new friends, in addition to having 'old' friends I could talk to. I was not afraid to learn or admit if I did not know something. I was prepared to learn by asking questions. Besides, I had the humility to accept that I was not going to change the world single-handily, nor did I attempt to reinvent politics, or displace party-affiliated politicians, which I mentioned clearly in my general and local election leaflets and thank-you newsletters. I focused my whole campaign on personal experience and the general public's feeling that politicians and service providers should perform their civic and professional duty for the stake holders, based on trust and accountability above anything else, and not self-serving interest, and act as role models to uphold moral, welfare and the social fabric of society. It was so satisfying that I succeeded, because after the election the posts from the residents reflected that I came across as an 'honest person' on the Knaphill Community Facebook page, something that is far more important to me than money, or power.

Once I had decided to contest in the 2017 general election, one thing I was fully aware off was that there would be a lot of walking, knocking on doors, speaking and writing involved, but before all that, I knew there had to be a registration process of some sort, and I had to learn the election rules. But I did not know whom to contact. Over the years, I had heard on the news about the Electoral Commission, holding inquiries into the violation of election rules by political parties and candidates, relating to expenses, donations, advertising and other scandals. I thought that would be a good place to start. I spoke to Zoe Armstrong, a very helpful official, and I wrote on 12th May 2017 (letter 61) to Chris Hinde, who was the regional manager of the Midlands informing him that Zoe Armstrong had gone the extra mile to help me. He replied (letter 62)

> 'It is always pleasing to receive positive comments on staff, and I am grateful to you for having the time to write to me'.

I took the trouble to write, because it is easy to complain. I believe in giving credit where it is due. I asked Zoe what I had to do to contest in this election. The first thing she asked is if I belonged to any party. I told her no, and have no experience in such matters. She informed me that it would be best if she sent the election rules guide. On receiving the package, I discovered there were so many formalities involved. As a beginner, without an election agent or party infrastructure, I had to learn quickly. I made my way through the information pack, and realised most of it was not applicable to me, as I was the only member. To cut the story short, I called Zoe, as I did not have the time to go through the list of questions I had prepared, with the election only four weeks away. After a few more phone calls I got the gist of what I had to do. I decided not to register the SIR logo, as there was no time and money to get it done. I also decided not to use the Royal Mail postal service for leaflet distribution, as I did not have the manpower to get proofs of my leaflet approved on time either, or get leaflet bundles collated, and dropped off at their distribution centres.

Despite the handicaps, I remained undeterred and decided to go ahead. As advised by Zoe, I phoned the election office in Woking Borough Council and spoke to Charlotte Griffiths, another helpful official, with whom I would have further dealings in the 2018 and 2019 local elections. She guided me through the registration process. Armed with my nomination papers, I was registered as a bona fide candidate on 4th May 2017 for the 8th June 2017 general election. I gave my first press release 'Quartet aims to become Woking MP', which appeared in the local newspaper, Woking News and Mail on 11th May 2017, which was the beginning of a long relationship with the same local newspaper. I have continued writing letters to the editor on wide-ranging topics, as well as appearing in their coverage of biographies and election features. With less than four weeks to go to the Election Day, I had to write the election leaflet, and get them printed, then delivered on time to some 40,000 Woking homes. I asked our friend Jenny Wilkinson to help. Jon Davis continued to play his part in getting the leaflets printed at short notice, and always at the end of the phone to give encouragement. It was equally true of David (Bro), who thought I was mad to waste money, but admired my convictions, and kept in touch to give moral support. Later Bro confessed he was very concerned about the physical well-being of his little brother, because of the public's general hatred towards politicians. He thought I might be prone to being attacked when delivering the leaflets. He was pleased when I said, "Not as such, except for a few minor instances of verbal offensive insults, but thank God nothing physical." As an early riser, I would start delivering the leaflets very early in the morning and in-between leaflet delivery attend to various matters, like replying to letters from well-wishers, make phone calls, or write speeches. Femi and Naamah helped me when they got home from work until late in the evening. I was lucky to recruit some of Naamah's friends, neighbours like Robert Ayres, Naar Thamshuhang, Seb Smith and Sophie White, and a good friend of mine, Michael Jackson, yes that is his name! I also got random help from people to deliver leaflets in their streets, and mothers on the school run. In three weeks, we managed to deliver some 20,000 leaflets, not to all homes, but about half.

I worked hard with my small army of supporters, thoroughly enjoyed knowing and meeting potential constituents. An important part of being an MP is to meet people from all walks of life and ages, not only during elections, but even after they have finished. I felt honoured and privileged to be well received, and the experience would serve me well later in my 2018 and 2019 local election campaigns too.

*****

Monday, 22nd May 2017 was another sad day for the British people, especially in Manchester, a place which will always remain close to my heart. On 23rd May I wrote the following letter of condolences to Andy Burnham, the Mayor of Manchester.

Dear Mr Burnham,

I am horrified by the horrendous events in Manchester last night. Today the whole country will grieve for the innocent people who have lost their lives.

We have once again seen the worst of cowardly acts and the best of humanity in yesterday's Manchester terrorist attack. Few people are intent on harming and ending life, while countless hundreds of others, including our emergency services tirelessly did their utmost to maintain and protect the lives of those they may not even have known. Our gratitude to you all for the brave instinctive behavior and immense courage of resilience.

This and similar cowardly acts are meant to dishearten and defeat us; they are meant to take away our resolve, and aim to lead us into a spiral of revenge. However hard they try; it will not destroy our precious way of life and democracy. Despite evocative attempts to corrupt our hearts to hatred, we on the contrary have seen acts of unwavering sacrifices, selflessness and compassion.

Our thoughts and prayers are foremost with those who have lost loved ones, those who are injured and those who will carry the trauma of what they have experienced in their darkest hour.

Manchester is a vibrant beautiful city. I have 12 years of very fond memories of the lovely people of Manchester. We will not allow your sacrifices to be forgotten'.

I received the following courteous reply from the Mayor's Office.

'Dear Dr Akberali

Thank you for your kind words – I will ensure these are passed on.

Best Wishes

Karen'

*****

On 25th May 2017, I was invited by Woking College to attend my very first hustings to address potential voters, which commenced at 2pm. I was preparing my notes to cover various issues that I thought some of the sixth form students would raise as first-time voters. Around 10am I had a call from a panic-stricken Femi. She had been hit from the rear, whilst she was waiting at the traffic lights at junction 12 slip road going onto the M25. I tried to calm her, as she did not know what to do. She asked if I could come and help. I found out she was not seriously hurt and the highway patrol was at the scene, and the car was towed away to a vehicle centre near Reading. I told her not to worry, and arranged a minicab to bring her home. I kept in touch while preparing for the hustings. It was a relief, because at about 1.30pm she phoned to confirm she was on her way home. At the hustings I met my MP Jonathan Lord, for the first time since writing to him on 8th May 2010 (letter 19). Although Jonathan Lord told me not to waste his time, I introduced myself, because this was the first time we had met. After that, we encountered each other again at the next hustings, organised by the local newspaper, Woking News and Mail on 1st June 2017. I also met James Brierley, the Green Party candidate with whom I have become good friends, his wife Angela and two children, in addition to meeting other candidates. I still enjoy a good rapport with Will Forster (LibDem) and Troy De Leon (UKIP), because they live in Woking. I met them a few times on different occasions.

In the 2017 general election I came last with 200 votes. I had funded my own campaign and set aside a small budget for printing and £500 election deposit, which I lost. But it was one of the best investments I had ever made, not only had I made new friends, but also what was to follow afterwards. Although I did not win, I learnt from my one-to-one interaction with the people of Woking that I had a lot in common with them, only reinforcing what murdered MP, Jo Cox, who eloquently said, "We are far more united than the things that divide us."

In my thank you message to the supporters I wrote:

> 'The campaign has enriched my life, widened my circle of friends and renewed hope for the future. One of my main goals was not having regrets by not trying to bring democracy to the doorstep, after a quarter of a century of disappointing and patronising experiences from our career politicians. Tomorrow, one adventure in my life will close and new ones will begin. When I got up on that fateful morning on 20th April, I was walking alone and wished I could reach the 'end of the road', but when family, neighbours and supporters joined me, I now wish the 'road never ends', and somebody will continue the journey to bring hope, fairness and real democracy! Together we have come a long way. I also remember my late parents for instilling the importance of education in me, as it has served well to engage in civic duty. I would like to thank my family and my wife Femi, who is my best friend for all her support, and putting up with me'.

*****

I had previously written to Mr Burnham after the heinous cowardly act in Manchester to give him support, and less than a month later on 3rd June 2017, the people of our great nation had suffered another terrorist attack, but his time in London. So, I wrote a similar letter (63) of condolence to the London Mayor, Sadiq Khan on 4th June 2017, and received a reply (letter 64) from his office thanking me for writing.

*****

In 2018, I stood for the elections as a local councillor candidate in the ward of Knaphill, a Tory stronghold. I came second, losing by about a thousand votes, ahead of the LibDems and Labour parties. In just over a year I had learnt a lot. So, during the May 2019 local elections my campaign was more purposeful and exuberant. I focused by engaging even more with Knaphill residents on their doorsteps, high streets and outside schools, instead of doing the normal thing of just dropping leaflets off once, and not engaging with the public, I went around Knaphill twice to deliver leaflets to each and every 4,500 households, and engaging with the public, which I thoroughly enjoyed. I was fortunate in two aspects, not only was I a bit more experienced this time round, but I also had more political knowledge. This was evident because I began to attract attention from local Independent councillors, most notably John Bond. He brought to me his formidable experience, providing me with a great moral boost, with his generous support. This time round, I also gave the Tory party candidate a good run for their money. To the extent a Tory loyalist confided in me that they got worried, and about three weeks before the election doubled their efforts to catch-up, because I was setting the pace and the agenda for the campaign. I also fell victim to the dirty tricks deployed by big political parties, when they feel threatened that they might lose. A false complaint was made, and I was accused of breaking polling day election rules, which was not upheld. It was disheartening to experience first-hand what one hears on the news of the behaviour of politicians, and the lengths they will go to secure victory. I came second, cutting a two thousand Tory majority in 2015 to one hundred and fifty-two. Again, I was really humbled by the warm messages posted on the Knaphill Facebook page by residents, thanking me for contesting, and encouraging me not to give up, but to persevere. On top of that, I received messages of support from the chairman, John Butler, and Rebecca Ward of the Knaphill Resident Association Community.

I think that I share similar values to most people, wanting to control our own destiny, but at the same time, fully respect we are part of a country, society, community of the larger world. Our problems may seem distinctive, special and even requiring urgent addressing, but they are not unique, and if we focus with a belief and conviction, we can alleviate those hardships. It is our duty as 'world citizens' to serve for the greater good of the world, by learning lessons from past mistakes. So, I was prepared to put to good use my real-life experiences, means and energy for the good of the people. I worked hard with patience and compassion during the three election campaigns, having a great time on the way, meeting people, and listening and learning from them all the time. I was touched by the offers of cups of tea, people welcoming me into their homes, or just stopping to have a chat in the streets, or outside schools. I was affected by the goodness amongst the people whom I met, which if harnessed positively by the political class, would not only serve this great country well in the future, but would also be good for the humanity as a whole, instead of having division and hatred.

I was humbled when people said they could talk to me, because they found a sympathetic ear with someone who shared similar values. I had a mother saying that her daughter recognised me, and told her "that's the same man on the poster across the road from us." In a similar incident a child waved at me from a car when it stopped at the traffic lights at top of the hill in Knaphill. The mother opened the window and told her daughter, "There's that same man in the photograph in the leaflet delivered to our home." It would be impossible to show my gratitude in words or list names, all I can say is that I still feel emotional writing such memories, and I hope by speaking broadly and mentioning a few names, I am addressing all of them personally, and feel as if I had known them all for a long time, actually all my life. I met Annie and Steven Wheeler outside the polling station, and offered to look after their lovely dog Massey, and we have kept in touch ever since, just like the Sarwals (Jay and Mita), Mario Valentino and many others. Many offered prayers and delivered leaflets, come rain or shine. As before, some helped with the layout of the leaflet, displayed posters, and willingly offered to distribute leaflets, including mothers on their way to school. These are the many moments I will always treasure in my mind. It would be dishonourable to say I did not come across hostility or prejudice. Of course, I did, but fortunately I can count those on one hand. Even being able to recall where they occurred. Maybe I was lucky not to have encountered extreme forms of physical or racial abuse, as experienced by some unfortunate politicians, or perhaps it is a reflection of the people of Knaphill, and I feel proud that it is my home town. These are fond memories that money or ego can never buy.

In June 2019, after the local elections, I distributed a newsletter to each resident's home to thank everyone who voted for me, alongside those whose trust I failed to win, but also gave a warm welcome on their doorsteps. It gave me an opportunity to discuss and share their real-life issues, which have been ignored over a long period of time. In my newsletter I suggested it would be a shame to let it all go to waste and forgotten without exploring pro-active measures to resolve the publics concerns, before it is too late. The main reason for contesting for the first time on 8th June 2017 was to bring democracy to the public's front doorstep, and engage with the voters on a regular basis. In my newsletter I therefore proposed formation of a Knaphill Village Forum Facebook page, and requested thoughts and help. I was delivering the newsletter to people's homes one fine Sunday morning, and not long after this, I met Rebecca Wheelan on a walk with her family and husband, Damian. She willingly offered help to set-up the Facebook page with her friend Jo Walker, and act as administrators of the group, together with Naamah. It is such support like this, which has overwhelmed me. Even though I did not win, the goodness and warmth still exist in our society, despite the recent rise in the 'populist political agenda' of divide and rule, adopted by politicians.

During all my three election campaigns in 2017, 2018 and 2019, I travelled by car to different destinations, and parked my car. Then I covered a lot of miles on foot, meeting people explaining on a one-to-one basis why I decided to contest as an independent candidate. I had no sophisticated means of mass communication, so this was the obvious strategy to adopt to win the support of people individually. I started on lonely impossible quests to contest against a sitting MP and local councillors in one of the safest Tory seats in the country, and members of a well-financed political party, with all the party infrastructure and volunteers at their disposal. In contrast, my campaigns started at home with the support of my wife and neighbours acting as proposers, seconders and nominees. I was my own campaign manager, agent and handled everything needed to run an election campaign. I never thought for a second I had a chance against Jonathan Lord or Tory Councillors, but I was passionate to serve public duty for fellow human beings, so that I could put something back into society, because Britain has been very good to me, and has been my home since 1973 when I was just twenty-two. As I mentioned, I had not been involved in politics at all, but the rapid rise of crises and political events in the 21st century left me despondent, as it has with so many people, making us feel that we have wasted the best years of our lives trusting in vain selfish people to do the job of governance, as elected representatives. It seems that democracy has now been hijacked by career politicians, funded by rich individuals and businesses, with self-serving egos and party interests above those of the people they pretend to serve. All they have done is turn politics into nothing but a racket, costing the tax payer significant sums for failed policies, illegal wars, conflicts and unaccountability.

I have always taken challenges in life head-on, not in the sense as to gain power, wealth or status, but more to do with not having regrets later on in life for not trying, when I feel something needs to be done. I know this is something people would find difficult to understand, but do not get me wrong, I am not saying wealth, materialistic possessions and ambition are not important, of course they are, even to me, but as far I am concerned, they are not everything, and I am not saying others are wrong, if they believe otherwise. I also understand one can do much more for others by being wealthy. I cannot explain the sort of drive I have to change things when they are not right. The restlessness has pushed me to new challenges that are right out of my comfort zone, not in search of more wealth or power, but more to do with helping others by serving public duty. I feel privileged I have been able to pay back some of the British goodwill in my own small way, during my wide-ranging vocational career. Some might say there must be a motive, but I can say, with a clear conscience that if I had a motive, there have been many instances when I could have made more money or gained status, if I had not stuck to my principles. I have even turned down offers from well-known political parties to contest future elections as their candidate and told it will improve my chances to get elected if backed by them following my performance during the three elections as independent candidate. It is because I am more content with what I have achieved, by working hard. When I look back, I do wonder how I managed to survive a certain period in my life and not faced bankruptcy or serious consequences, because of such and such incident. I believe I have been lucky to fulfil my ambitions, because God has looked after me, by listening to my mother's prayers.

What is disheartening is the attitude of elected politicians towards the electorates. In the 2019 general election, Jonathan Lord received about twenty-six thousand votes, leaving a silent majority of about forty-seven thousand as collateral damage. In fact, I was not wasting his precious 'time', but raising vital real-life concerns affecting all British people, and not only for his 72,999 constituents. It defeats the purpose of the whole democratic process, and fails in its main aims when a constituent cannot do that. It is one thing to be told of a level playing field, another to confront it on a regular basis. Reality serves a dual purpose; it liberates one's practical experience, and it also offers a tremendous psychological boost to go out and actually meet the voters. They should be bit more sympathetic and helpful towards all their constituents.

Sadly, my experiences with Jonathan Lord is no different from that I have experienced from Tony Blair to Boris Johnson (inclusive) and cross-party politicians, or those in charge with the responsibility to serve public duty. Is it any wonder the general public feel excluded and disfranchised by the political class? The public also face similar handicaps from both the print and broadcasting media, as they are only a poor shadow of reality. Their information is important, not because it is meant to reveal the truth, but because it does not disclose the biases and perceptions of news coverage of those who produce the newspaper and those who read it, so not a 'free press' as such. Also, politicians often invent fake stories to manipulate their favourite journalists, who oblige so as not to miss out on perks. The journalists respond with eye catching headlines, only to apologise later after inflicting damage on others. I have often noticed that the 'free press' will not even publish responses from those who are the subject of the vile attacks and lies spouted by politicians, when victims try to put the record straight. And, when questioned, politicians like Boris Johnson defend their insults directed at certain faiths, by claiming 'use of colourful language'. Wonder if any ordinary person would get away with such behaviour, especially when there so-called 'colourful language' has caused physical harm to those they have insulted in their columns, or by their actions! It seems like a default position adopted by politicians to avoid giving an honest answer, ignoring or wearing out the public with a bureaucratic reply, until a disaster happens, causing suffering and loss of lives, only to be followed by expensive public inquiries at an enormous expense to the tax payer, to learn lessons.

For me, running for the elections was more to do with the truest sense of democracy. I remain undeterred, even now. I suppose all the work I have done, and the material saved over the years has helped me in way to reconstruct the main bulk of the facts for this memoir. It has served me well to give an accurate reality check of hope faced by the majority of people. It was a question of my integrity as to why I would lose one particular reply from the minister and save all the other letters after having taken the trouble of writing in the first place. I therefore requested Jonathan Lord for the minister's reply, he had referred to in his reply (letter 58), which he point blankly refused; as he may have thought that he had already sent it. Why would I ask if I had it, when I have saved replies, even those few handful ones including those unsigned postcard replies received on very rare occasions going back as far as 20th January 1992 (letter 1).

I used to think it was a waste of time to discuss politics and religion, and shun such confrontations. Now I am of the opinion that with religion I have a choice not to follow if I do not agree with the teachings, and when the time comes, it will be between the Creator and me; whereas my thinking towards politics has changed drastically, based on personal experience. I have realised that by being disenchanted with politics is not going to help, but to the contrary. If we think about it, by not engaging directly with politicians or indirectly by not voting, everyone's life gets affected on a daily basis. Whether we like it or not, the lawmakers are making political decisions on our behalf, such as with tax, public services, wars and even the quality of air we breathe. So, here is my admission as to why I decided to enter politics in 2017, it was because of Jonathan Lord. In fact, I was also told by a reliable source from within the local Tory Party during the 2019 local election that I was becoming a serious threat to the defending Tory candidate in the Knaphill Ward, and they blamed Jonathan Lord, and told him so for stirring me up. Looking back, I am glad I contested the 2017 election.

During the 2017 general election, my eldest daughter Naamah had registered for a postal vote, as she was living with us at the time. When she opened her postal vote, she felt so proud to see my full name on the ballot paper, but equally also to see her grandfather's and great-grandfather's name. I shared her sentiments, knowing how my parents felt when I was progressing in my academic career. I must confess, as I have been taught under the British education system, I am something of an Anglophile. So, when I saw my name on the ballot paper I thought of democracy, and the 'mother of parliaments'. The very model of education, justice, and get-up-and-go never-say-die-attitude in me and my forefathers, is no different to the British values. History also reflects the dark times during the colonial rule that helped to inflict a malicious injustice on fellow human beings. The consequences of those decisions are still felt today in some parts of the world, where we turn a blind eye by allowing political leaders to practice a modern version of those policies, in the name of democracy. While, we abhor those dark times of British imperialism, we should also never reject the trappings of progress made during that time.

I sincerely hope we can learn lessons from the past, and rectify the situation to alleviate suffering and loss of lives still occurring in the world today. It was with this ambition that I contested the 2017 general election, to serve in the British Parliament to make a difference, not only at home, but to serve humanity elsewhere. Though, this did not happen in 2017, and 2018 or 2019 at the local level, I now hope to continue my quest to serve public duty, if not as politician, at least in shape of this memoir. The desire and fire in my belly, which continues to burn has been to achieve everything that I possibly could, with whatever talents and support I could get. I have been fortunate to enjoy opportunities, but I will always stand up for what I believe is right, and defend in whatever field I am working, be it business, education, community and welfare. In a way, my conviction to make a contribution to put something back in a small way into the country and society that I have also benefitted from. If we think about it, it is the basic instinct shared by all humans, which we need to nurture and allow it to develop to its full potential. I have always said that the respect I have for people is in my genes, which has come from my Akberali Hassanali ancestry, because they practiced such values as 'world citizens' nearly one hundred fifty years ago. I hope I have made them proud in my own small attempts to serve public duty.

I have also learnt an important lesson, not to isolate myself, but to maintain firm contact with people, which I was adamant to do on the door-steps during all my election campaigns and afterwards despite not getting elected because of my belief and trust in the people, and not the politicians as they do not have a monopoly on political wisdom, as proven by the outcome of some of the decisions taken by them. Just like other voters, I have tried more often to engage in the democratic process, and heard more truth, honesty, courtesy and sanity from people outside parliament than some of those inside. I decided to continue knocking on doors and listening to the people because I know exactly what it feels like not to be listened to. I am glad I did, as I have learnt a lot and met some lovely human beings along the way. I know no other way. I make mistakes, everybody does! Nobody is perfect! I believe in not letting anyone down. I will try my best to help, especially when people place their trust in me.

Epilogue:
Shared Values

I n my memoir I have focused on a lay-person's perception of hope and reality, which otherwise would have been lost to posterity, and is from the perspective of an individual that has not achieved great fame or wealth, but grateful for what I have achieved. I feel proud to dedicate this memoir to my late mother, who had the foresightedness and her 'eureka moment' to instil in me hope and the value of education, enabling me to help humanity, in my own very small way. I thought because of the politician's attitude towards me, I had missed my moment to serve public duty, when I tried hard to raise real-life concerns, but to the contrary. I am an eternal optimist, and hope this memoir will serve to send an important message of encouragement to others, not to give up their belief in humanity, and encourage our politicians to start listening to restore and stimulate British values, such as goodwill, courage and innovative skills to overcome adversity.

I started by quoting Bill Gates, which ended with "people need to understand that the truly rich are those who possess a rich heart, rather than lots of money. It's really very important to have a rich heart to help others." I hope my memoir will serve to give politicians a deeper insight into the ordinary people's experiences of hope and reality, not the old cliché 'to learn important lessons from expensive public inquiries, at a great cost to the taxpayer. As human beings, we are all born to aspire to give a better life to our children, with a fire of some sort in our bellies; most of us succeed in some way to achieve that goal. But sadly, there are a vast majority of people who just lead a life in hope with a hunger to survive and succeed, but denied the right to fulfil their dreams, because of the actions of others in their quest of their own self-serving egos.

I have been brought up to respect parents and elders, and as long as I have respected people, communities and society, I have not been troubled by the laws of man or God, and if I sin with the later, it will be between him and me. I believe that human suffering occurs because of the actions of others, when the pledges of hope and reality become meaningless, an elusive dream for the ordinary public when they try to put them into practice, only to find out that some are more equal than others. This is not anything new, and has been going on for centuries in some form or another. What is different now is that this has become of a common occurrence, whereby pledges are made and broken, as well as various inhumane atrocities carried in the name freedom, hope, fairness and democracy by politicians without being held accountable.

It was only when I began to take interest in politics, not as a politician or as a political career, but to serve public duty, was when I learnt that the disenchantment I felt was equally felt and shared by the public at large, which led me to enter politics. I firmly believe the spirit of justice, fairness, morals and goodwill still exists amongst the British people, in spite of the divisive populist political agenda adopted by politicians. It is this sort of shared values that makes the human race outstanding. This has made me more determined to serve civic duty, so that I (we) do not take democracy for granted, which our forefathers gave their lives, and Britain can play an important role in the world as a beacon of hope, a place for good education and justice, not a place inciting hatred.

I have come full circle, as regards to whatever dreams I may have had. For example, some of us may be entrepreneurial, or others more successful than our fellow humans; but for the vast majority, it is just survival with the resolve to do their best, not to give up, but try to endure whatever circumstances they have been dealt by others. Throughout human history we hear of remarkable journeys made to shape fortunes and lives, just like the pioneering achievements of those who crossed the *kalapani* (black waters) of the Indian Ocean in a dhow. I dread to think how many did not make it, and how they felt witnessing fellow human beings dying or suffering right in front of them. Just like today, when we hear about lives of people lost in refrigerated trucks or drowned in the sea, who embark on similar perilous journeys. The sad thing about that is there is no need for it to happen in our globalised 'civilised' world, if we pull our resources together for the benefit of humanity as a whole. I am sure the parents of my great-grandfather were not the only ones to send one of their sons (not sure if they had more) with Omani Arabs, to search for a better life, let alone a nearby place with a different language, culture with very little means of communication or family contact. It is a tribute to their persistence and will to survive, not only make it, but set-up home and a business empire, built homes, not only for themselves, but also for others, as well as embark on philanthropic acts to better the lives of others.

I was born surrounded by motherly love and hope-in every way any new born would know. I had no worries, as long as I had someone to nurture and protect me on my journey. I had nothing to fear, provided I obeyed and learnt from family members, elders and role models, such as friends, teachers, doctors and many others. I would say that I always believed in hope, fairness and reality that depended upon working hard, and not taking anything for granted. It was only when I started to communicate with the lawmakers (politicians) that I realised after a long time it was not that straight forward what I was made to understand that in a thriving democracy we are all equal, because of a level playing field. The more I sought help, guidance and support from my elected politicians or even interacted with them, the further it became apparent not to even expect an acknowledgement. I was left despondent as I was made to believe to expect a better standard of scruples from those in authority, responsible in setting rules, laws and standards in public life for mere mortals like me to obey, learn and follow. As I indulged more with the political class at all levels, I realised it was a futile exercise, and that their behaviour was not 'honourable' at all. I did not get deterred, and persevered in what I believed was not right, not that I feel anymore virtuous or self-sacrificing than the next person, or have the solution or an obsession to put everything right in life, not at all! I passionately believe in trust and respect for authority, especially those blessed and endowed with power to change society for the good of all humanity. As time progressed, I learnt that I was not the only one, but many people felt the same as I did, so I decided to do something about it in 2017, to restore trust and accountability in my own small way. Although I did not succeed, I will keep on trying. If I fail to win the trust of the public, I hope my memoir will serve to inspire and motivate people not to give up or lose faith in humanity, in order to make politicians sitting in their ivory tower aware of the reality faced by the people.

I was a novice, as far as politics was concerned. Yet I have always believed that human beings need each other, and rely upon one another to face the problems of society, for the good of the whole nation. I engaged with politicians with absolute integrity and total dedication to contribute positively, with the sole purpose to focus on ways to improve social harmony in our multicultural country, with no ulterior motive, which I did in only one way I knew how, by being direct and honest about everything. The consistency and sincerity of mine is reflected in the numerous original correspondence of the views and stance I expressed in the very first letter I wrote in 1992 to Sir John Major, and the very last letter to Boris Johnson, and other PMs and cross-party politicians. It is in black and white, with nothing made up, and the contempt shown in return. What it highlights further is that the ordinary public may not be career politicians or top-notch policymakers, but at times worth listening to, as they may have less costly but more effective solutions, due to a better understanding of real-life issues. In my election leaflets I reflected the views catalogued over twenty-eight years ago. It formed the basis of my campaign, 'education is the wealth of the individual and the nation', as well as the reason I stood as an Independent to serve society, not party politics or self-serving interests, as mentioned in my letter to John Major, way back in 1992.

The present hostility and catastrophe of entrenched party politics fanning division over Brexit, and other populist political agenda, will dominate and define domestic life for many years to come. Nevertheless, I remain hopeful from what I have learnt and experienced when campaigning, meeting and talking with people face-to-face, because the British people are astute and fair-minded with plenty of 'common-sense', contrary to that claimed publicly by Jacob Rees-Mogg. I think the mood of the nation has changed drastically, especially the lack of trust in politicians, which people can see through, particularly female MPs and voters. I found women more engaging and concerned about the state of affairs affecting all aspects of life. I can see women playing a very important role in the 21st century, rescuing democracy and serving humanity as a whole, to stop the divide and rule politics of today. Why do I feel optimistic? Because it was women who helped me set-up a forum group to discuss local issues. It shows commitment at the grass roots level.

Just as my family ancestors worked hard in Tanzania to provide a better future for their families, I hope my endeavours will serve as an inspiration for my children, grandchildren and other individuals like me in the UK or elsewhere, not to give up hope, but do their level best to achieve their goals. At the same time, I will continue in my endeavours, as the fire still burns in my belly to fulfil any wildest ambitions of mine in one form or another. I hope when my children, their husbands and my grandson embark on their journeys, this memoir will serve them as a starting point where we come from. Such as what our ancestor's vision was for a better future, and shared human values as a 'world citizen'. But for me, I will continue to focus my energy to serve public duty, so I can put something back into human society and the country that gave me opportunities, which I have benefited so much. To achieve all that, I will remain optimistic, and believe in human endeavour, hope and shared values, and if I interest a wider audience, that is an added bonus.

Acknowledgements

I could not have even contemplated starting, or for that matter finishing this book without acknowledging the people with whom I have been closely associated with during my life.

First of all, I remember my parents, teachers and friends, who helped and supported me, during my formative years. The book has been especially difficult because of many false starts in the past, but once I started, my immediate family Femi, Naamah, Husein, Ummehani, Mustali and even my grandson, Taher, have driven me on, helping in many ways. Some of the key chapters were re-written when I spent some quality time in the great company of Taher, when I visited Doha.

Writing the first draft was the easy bit, once I got motivated by the story of the newspaper vendor. Finding someone to help get it published was the hard part. I approached many people for guidance and assistance. Either I did not hear further from them, or was informed that I had to be famous to generate market demand. Others quoted colossal amounts for their editorial expertise, well beyond my small budget, a financial risk I could not take with my life's savings, in case the book was a failure.

I even approached Bill and Melinda Gates Foundation. In my letter 84 - 27th December 2020,

'I apologised for taking the liberty to encroach on his valuable time but felt necessary to write after reading his newsvendor experience. I explained how it inspired me to finish my book and the difficulty I was facing getting professional help, because of financial constraints, and also being an unknown entity. I asked if opportunities existed within the Gates Foundation, as the book will inspire others. I went onto say that I did not have publishing experience except determination to put in the effort as I do not expect things to happen'.

I want to thank my old school friend Zahir Dhalla for his valuable guidance, whom I have not met since 1969, except kept in touch occasionally via e-mail. I contacted him as he has often published on Amazon, and without hesitation, Zahir helped in the truest sense, a friend in need is a friend indeed. I also want to thank Julie De Souza, who lives in Manchester, for prompting me to publish on Amazon when I met her in Doha. What a small world? I am grateful to Shamus Bedi, who has expertly captured the story in his design of the book cover and the map.

I hold nobody responsible for any failures in my life, just extreme gratitude for the opportunities they have given me, and those who feel I have failed them in some way in the past, please accept my humble apologies; and for those whom I have been of some help, please multiply tenfold to help others, wherever they may be!

And, finally, looking back at what I have written, the book could not have been written without real-life experiences and coincidences reflected above and elsewhere, which truly compliments the book. It is fate that it has happened this way, giving more credibility to the title '*Hope and Shared Values: A reality check*'.

Dr. Hassan B. Akberali
June 2020

Appendix

A selection of original correspondence in chronological order from a huge collection of few hundred written in my own time and expense referred in the book. The contents of the letters cover a wide range of real-life issues and concerns I have raised, a detailed perspective of reality faced as an ordinary member of the public. Unless, indicated, in all cases except a handful of one-line acknowledgements and long-winded patronising replies, all my efforts have been ignored. The letters are originals and nothing has been altered. I hope the reader will accept my apologies for the mistakes in places, such as grammar, spellings and punctuations, which I am aware but not altered so as to retain authenticity as genuine correspondence.

(1) Letter to John Major.

20th January 1992

'Dear Prime Minister,

I must apologise for taking the liberty in writing directly to you and taking up your precious time. With great respect to you, your colleagues and advisors, the reason I have been led to write to you personally is due to the recent reports relating to the depth of the recession which have appeared in the media after Christmas. It has been my personal strong belief since August 1991, that the recession is very deep and will prolong for much longer than originally envisaged. I also predict that the end will be in June/July 1992, even then the economic recovery will be insignificant and slow due to the weak financial position of a number of small businesses. Since my main concern for writing to you relates to the fate of the small businesses rather than party politics therefore, please excuse me for forwarding the copies of this letter to Rt.Hon. Neil Kinnock and Rt.Hon. Paddy Ashdown.

Admittedly, the UK recession is linked to the worldwide economy however, our intrinsic factors contributing to the recession are deep rooted and to some extent continues to persist irrespective of the extrinsic factors. As an owner of a small business, I would like you to consider the main points listed below, which I believe has hindered the UK economy in the past. Some drastic measures are needed in order to revive the incentives and confidence within the small business community.

It is of prime importance to the Owners of small businesses to succeed and survive due to the very nature of the business investments, e.g. personal equity, savings and sacrifices. Therefore, such businesses are better providers of stability and continuity within the economy as a whole. In contrast, certain other businesses dictated solely by shareholders or profits are here to-day and gone to-morrow. It is now widely acknowledged by your Government that the small business community is the true provider of jobs and growth in the UK economy. For example, from 1985 to 1987, businesses employing fewer than 20 created 500,000 jobs against just 20,000 by the others. It is again possible to repeat and sustain that economic transformation brought about by small businesses however, urgent Government help and action is required in terms of restoring meaningful incentives and un-loading the burden of some complex regulations imposed on small businesses.

The complex multi-tier VAT system based on differing marketing levels is complicated to enforce, costly to administer and susceptible to default, possibly losing the Treasury significant revenue. I have prepared a prototype based on a simple single-tier VAT system showing significant advantages and gains over the present multi-tier VAT system. The advantages are reflected in terms of reduced administrative/operational costs, relatively fewer mistakes due to the reduced list of VAT applicable/non applicable items, less chance of under-declaration or default. The surplus financial benefits to the Treasury from the proposed single-tier VAT system, may than be utilised either to decrease the actual VAT rate or passed over to various Government Departments. I would gladly submit, if you wish, the draft prototype for your perusal.

Many small businesses, with no protection like Limited companies, are forced to operate on very tight budgets and restricted manpower. Quite often such businesses are managed, with great sacrifices, by husband and wife with children. The burdens placed on such businesses are immense and widely varied, ranging from the actual managing of the business to observing various regulations, e.g. VAT returns, PAYE, health/safety, legal aspects. These un-paid responsibilities consume significant time and are expected to be carried out as a professionally qualified person or else face server penalties and humiliation. Alternatively, a qualified person is hired at a significant cost to observe these responsibilities.

Business Rents/ Rent Reviews based on the present system of comparable evidence is hypothetical and leads to inflationary pretentious rent settlements, benefitting only the Landlords and the body of Chartered Surveyors. Realistic reflection of Business Rents/Rent Reviews would be more beneficial to all the parties concerned.

At this juncture, I would like to cite our personal experience on the above point. Our last rent increase, reviewed in 1989, rose by a staggering 80% despite contesting the original exorbitant demand of 110% increased. However, the whole exercise cost us £2500 in various fees. We are determined to survive the present recession by employing a number of measures and sacrifices. Unfortunately, our next rent review is in 1994 during the period of much expected economic boom and we are greatly concerned that all our present sacrifices will count for nothing.

It is about time that the wider aspects of the Uniform Business Rates are considered in detail with particular emphasis on their effects on small businesses. Councils should consider it a privilege that Businesses by operating within their respective Boroughs are creating employment/prosperity and therefore, Councils should be made to attract and not penalise the business community. UBR is a major un-productive and un-controllable business overhead for which, for example, trade waste is not even collected. The complete abolishing of UBR will revive businesses, making them more competitive. There are a number of economically easier ways to generate the shortfall in the income from the UBR to supplement Council budgets.

In 1991, a record number of businesses have been declared bankrupt and existing businesses including ours, have lost money. Due to professional costs, we have not pursued our bad debts from three Limited companies declared bankrupt hence, further weakening our financial position. Unfortunately, at least one company that we are aware off, continues to operate the same business under a differently named company. Therefore, it is questionable whether the figures for bankruptcy or new businesses reflect a true and complete situation.

The economy in the UK is increasingly controlled either directly or indirectly by a few, namely Financial Institutions and Multinationals with monopolies. Such a control undermines the overall economy, at times with detrimental effects on the nation. The consequences on small businesses are even severe in relation to supplies, costs, terms, cost of business premises and bank charges.

Present laws and regulations are meant to be observed irrespective of individual status. Recently, it is more apparent that there is deliberate flaunting of laws, e.g. Sunday trading, by companies or individuals with immense financial or influential powers. Any financial penalties if imposed, will be insignificant in relation to the actual benefits of flaunting. Such penalties on small businesses or individuals in a similar predicament will affect them more in terms of financial hardships and personal ruin.

A firm and continuous control of inflation is paramount. However, the complete reliance on higher interest rates, although necessary at times, is an easy option achieving temporary objectives but at a significant cost to the nation, e.g. lack of investment, job losses, business failures, repossessions. Priority should be given to the longer-term objectives by tackling inflation at the root level in order to maintain realistic business overheads.

Historically, it is worth reviving the derogatory quote made to his surprise by Napoleon that "Britain is a nation of shopkeepers……". As a nation, we are capable of numerous achievements provided the right incentives exist within the economy for both big and small businesses.

In the past on numerous occasions stop/start measures have been taken to regulate the economy. It will be a great pity, if the present hardships and sacrifices of the nation due to the recession and high interest rates are made to account for only a temporary period of economic recovery. It is about time that a fresh start is made to base the economy on a firmer foundation by tackling the root problems presently existing in the UK. Another fallacy in order to satisfy the critics, before completely achieving the aims, would be to artificially kick-start the economy either by lowering of the interest rates or devaluation of the pound. Furthermore, any budget tax cuts should be delayed, instead the budget surplus should be utilised to make some of the changes outlined above, making it more beneficial in the longer term. Lastly, a setting up of a committee complementing the CBI to directly monitor the atmosphere and confidence within the small business community will also be advantageous.

Finally, I would like to wish you a successful year and sincerely hope, that your personal success will be shared by us all.

Yours sincerely',
cc. Rt. Hon. Norman Lamont, MP
cc. Rt. Hon. Cranley Onslow, MP'

(2) Letter to Cranley Onslow.

28 October 1994

'Dear Mr Onslow
Re: The National Lottery

As the owner of a small newsagency/general store in this town, I write to you on behalf of small retail units everywhere concerning the above and the possible avenues that its establishment could open up for the proliferation of unfair trading practices. This is not to say that we do not approve of the Government's decision to launch a National Lottery- far from it. However, we are alarmed at the granting of exclusive rights to the Camelot Group plc, to organise the project which has already resulted in their adoption of unpublished criteria for the appointment of lottery agents.

A parallel situation had existed for many years in the newspaper distributive trade which, we were relieved to see the Government has at last seen fit to improve after £10+m enquiry by the Monopolies and Mergers Commission. An equitable Code of Practice was recently announced by the then Corporate Affairs Minister, Neil Hamilton.

At a recent conference of the Association of Circulation Executives, Sir Bryan Carsberg, the Director General of Fair Trading, stating (inter alia) "I regard the refusal to supply as always raising a question requiring careful consideration" and that he remained unimpressed by the traditional arguments for restricting supplies (e.g. "the area is adequately served").

We are like mind. We believe that the market will decide the success or otherwise of a given product. For a principal to be granted a Government monopoly to market a product, and then allowed to manipulate the market structure to suit its own interests, is, we believe, wrong. By the exclusion **for not stated reason** of any willing small independent retailer from their distributor list, Camelot is effectively operating a restrictive practice and denying a free market for its product.

I ask you most urgently, on behalf of us all, to persuade those concerned to look into the selection criteria adopted by Camelot. Our own listing would broaden the basic scope for selection and include the following general safeguards.

*Selection criteria to be approved by the Office for Fair Trading and clearly set out a matter of public record.

* All applications to be acknowledged rather than ignored as has been the case in some instances.

*Unsuccessful applicants to be appraised of the reason(s) for their being turned down.

*Introduce competition by allowing another Group to organise a rival lottery.

We, as a body, are obviously concerned that we have not been considered as potential agents for the sale of lottery tickets. Our livelihoods are already on the line. We face increasing competition from multiples, the supermarkets, the petrol stations and the rising burden of Uniform Business Rate. I also a copy of the letter received from our newspaper wholesaler, already highlighting the proliferation of unfair trading practices.

On behalf of us all, I seek your co-operation in bringing this situation to the attention of the Minister or whomsoever else may be concerned as quickly as possible. At this point in time the matter can still be re-addressed and hopefully made more fair without incurring enormous costs as was the case for newspaper distribution. We look forward to your support in this matter."

Yours sincerely',

(3) Letter to Tony Blair with short curt reply and heard nothing further:

4 April 2000

'Dear Prime Minister

Following my letter of 29 February 2000 and acknowledgement of 3rd March on your behalf from Zulma Fernandez of the Direct communication Unit, I write to you once again with reference to the implementation of government policies for ethnic communities.

The past and present history of the UK reflects a land of immigrant activity. The recent progress can be attributed directly to the fundamental democracy, goodwill and decency of Her Majesty's successive governments and her subjects, together with what is salient about the ethnic communities in terms of respecting the law, hard work, enterprise and family values.

Despite well-meant initiatives from successive governments the second-class status of the ethnic people continues because of institutional prejudices and racism in the neighbourhood, schools and workplace, recently highlighted by government and independent inquires. Sadly, such attitudes and practices will continue to exist despite passing laws and spending millions of pounds to rectify the situation because attempts only serve to benefit to those involved in advising the government and administrators of the various schemes.

It is extremely important to bring all cultures to be an important part of the mainstream politics and life in the UK based on mutual respect rather than alienating and compartmentalising communities and cultures by setting up specific initiatives. I believe this has done more harm than good to the ethnic communities by generating resentment within the indigenous population with consequential negative effects.

Why is it many initiatives that have been in operation for years within various government departments and the civil service including Business Link for ethnic communities and their businesses across the country has failed to make an impact? Whatever their aims, most schemes do not seem to serve the purpose of integrating ethnic people into the mainstream. Secondly, many schemes are bureaucratic oriented and reign supreme by becoming a burden acting as a deterrent. Instead of positive participation it succeeds in wearing out an individual without achieving the desire objectives.

As recently as last week, The Rt. Hon. Mo Mowlam on her visits was trying to encourage ethnic children to consider a career within the Civil Service by showing them a video of six Asian civil servants. After all these years, the London Mayoral candidate The Rt. Hon. Frank Dobson during his campaign was appalled by the level of graffiti, racism and unemployment embracing ethnic communities. He has promised to rectify the situation when elected.

In order to have a deeper insight into insight into the subtle mechanisms that an individual has to overcome in order progress. I believe that only personal experience can appreciate the practical dilemma. Otherwise, promises will remain unfulfilled and resources wasted.

I also believe that in comparison to other countries, we in the United Kingdom have successfully fostered a wider cultural diversity in terms of harmony and mutual respect. We need to take further advantages of these gains by overcoming racist prejudices and handicaps faced by the ethnic people. Not least, the contribution by the ethnic communities and their businesses on the economy, social and cultural fabric of the UK has been enormous despite practical difficulties. Only isolated groups know with the majority of the indigenous population having a stereotype impression that ethnic communities having a peculiar lifestyle relying on handouts. Unfortunately, such resentment then filters through the vocational responsibilities of the indigenous population with serious consequences on the career, commercial and social prospects of the ethnic people.

A realistic approach with less emphasis on bureaucracy and completion of complex forms would serve well because ethnic people are more practical and less administration minded. An area that needs to be explored further in the formulation of existing and future government initiatives directed towards improving the quality of life for the ethnic communities and their businesses.

I sincerely hope the above is of some benefit to advantage of the available resources and existing infrastructure. I look forward to from hearing you'.

(4) I received the following reply from the DCU and nothing further from anyone.

4 May 2000

'Dear Mr Akberali

The Prime Minister has asked me to thank you for your recent letter.

Mr Blair hopes you will understand that, as the matters you raise are the responsibility of both the Department for Education and Employment and the Department for Trade and Industry, he has asked that your letter be forwarded to those Departments so that they may reply to you direct on his behalf'.

Yours sincerely
Jan Taylor'

(5) Letter to Tony Blair.

6 September 2005

'Dear Prime Minister,

Further to my previous attempts of 4 April 2000 of writing directly to your goodself on various issues, I sincerely hope on this occasion despite your heavy time schedule you will get a chance to personally read this letter upon your return from China and India.

Since 1990, I have raised a number of issues pertaining to the small family retail businesses at governmental level with cross-party politicians. To-date, all such and other efforts have been voluntary using personal initiatives and I am pleased to say that a number of ideas and suggestions have come to some fruition for the benefit of the sector.

Moreover, I have always passionately believed that the UK is a blessed land because of the religious worship practiced freely by a significant number of different faiths and therefore, no lasting harm will come to this uniquely blessed land of ours. We will overcome natural difficulties and always rise above man-made obstacles.

I have often wondered as to why some well-meaning government policies and initiatives directed towards ethnic communities by the Labour and the past Conservative governments has prevented progress within certain ethnic communities and hindered integration into the mainstream.

Despite well-meant initiatives from successive governments, certain sectors of the ethnic community still continue to feel being second class citizens, which at times has been exacerbated by stereotype prejudices by grown-ups in neighbourhoods, workplaces etc, which gets imprinted on the innocent minds of children.

It is also equally important for ethnic communities to realise that it works both ways and by becoming an integral part of the UK, they will not get easily swayed or fall victims of the tiny minority with an unscrupulous agenda who either promote or preach, racial or religious hatred.

It is important that all cultures become part of the mainstream based on mutual respect rather than alienating communities and cultures by setting up specific initiatives. For certain ethnic communities, it has caused more harm than good and causes resentment within the mainstream population with consequential negative effects. We have to strive towards making the situation better so that common sense prevails and various communities co-exist in social harmony.

In the past, I have addressed areas that need closer scrutiny when formulating specific policies and measures including projects e.g.

- A need for a subtle emphasis to implement initiatives.
- Initiatives for ethnic people would be better served if incorporated when formulating mainstream policies e.g. health, home affairs, economy, heritage, education, defence, and not in isolation as an afterthought.
- Overcoming prejudices with less emphasis on specific initiatives.
- Progress undermined due to patronising initiatives, bureaucracy and red-tape.
- Central Government regulations based on practicality.
- Pro-active as opposed to knee-jerk reactive policies, measures and projects.

Since the sad and tragic event of 7 July, I have felt even more to be a part of the Public Life to make positive contribution within the Government policy-making machinery to overcome the present and future concerns facing our country within the context of ethnic communities and multicultural UK.

Since 7 July, in order to make the UK safer place, quite rightly your goodself, the Home Secretary and various government ministers have been engaged in positive debates with representatives from the Muslim faith who shout the loudest. We need to include the input of the vast silent majority from the UK Muslim community whose involvement and views continue to remain unheard.

I believe that the government needs to pursue long-term policies, measures and projects that are pro-active and not reactive in areas such as religious curriculum in schools and madrassas, public relations and professional involvement so that all communities become a part of the mainstream and not get alienated. It will serve as a deterrent against individuals or organisations with their own motives or political agenda. I am also of the firm opinion that either later or concurrently, a similar practical approach can be successfully adopted for other communities so that they do not feel left out and thus achieve a positive multicultural society at peace with one another in the UK.

I am of the firm belief that in comparison to other countries, we in the UK have successfully fostered a wider cultural diversity in terms of harmony and mutual respect.

I sincerely hope the above information is of some benefit and that we take advantage of the available resources and existing infrastructure."

Yours sincerely',

(6) Received the following reply from the DCU.

'The Prime Minister has asked me to thank you for your recent correspondence.

I regret that this is not a matter with which Mr Blair can help.

J Miles'

(7) Letter to Kenneth Clarke.

5 September 2005

'Dear Mr Clarke,

I was extremely pleased to hear the news last week that you have decided to stand for the Conservative party leadership contest. I strongly believe that because of your worthy consistent convictions, you will make an ideal leader both in opposition and in government as you will always lead from the front.

In the recent past, we have had leaders who have led mostly through consensus and appeasement whereby, policies and measures whether in government or opposition have been reactive rather than pro-active.

I am a British citizen with an ethnic background and a practicing Muslim and have lived in the UK since 1973. I am of the firm belief that in comparison to other countries, we in the UK have successfully fostered a wider cultural diversity in terms of harmony and mutual respect.

I have outlined areas that need closer scrutiny in terms of formulating specific policies in various communications and meetings, e.g.
- A Need for subtle emphasis to implement initiatives
- Initiatives for ethnic communities to be a part of the British mainstream
- Overcoming prejudices with less emphasis on specific initiatives
- Patronizing initiatives, bureaucracy, and red tape undermines progress
- Government regulations and initiatives based on practicality
- Pro-active as opposed to reactive policies/measures/projects

Since the sad and tragic event on 7th July, I have felt even more to be a part of the consultative policy unit. I fully appreciate that once you have been elected you will quite rightly engage in consultation with a number of religious organisations and ethnic communities in order to make the UK, a safer and better place. However, I entreat your goodself that we need to include the views from the vast majority especially from the Muslim community whose views have been and continue to remain silent due to a lack of practical representation.

I have interacted on regular basis when the Conservative party was in government. I have also had the pleasure of meeting your goodself in the House of Commons in 1995, other conservative Ministers and cross-party MPs. I enclose copies of two letters, which indicates that I have continued to do so even when the Conservative Party has been in opposition.
I look forward to hearing from you and wishing you well in your quest to become the leader of the Conservative party."

Kind Regards.
Yours most respectfully',

(8) Brief extract from the letter to David Cameron.

31 December 2005

'Dear Mr Cameron

Re: Practical implementation of polices to encourage further integration of ethnic communities

Let me take this opportunity me take this to wish you a prosperous and a very successful New Year in all your endeavours as a Leader of the Conservative Party.

I trust that under your leadership, the Conservative party will be a voice for change, optimism and hope by adopting a positive, constructive and reasonable approach when formulating new ideas and polices when holding the government to account.

We need to ask, why some well-meaning Government policies and initiatives directed towards ethnic communities by the present Labour and the past Conservative Governments has prevented progress within certain ethnic communities has hindered integration into the mainstream.

I wish you well and look forward to hearing from you."

Yours most respectfully'

(9) Received the following reply.

22 February 2006

'Dear Dr Akberali,

I am writing on behalf of David Cameron to thank you for your letter of December 31st. I do apologise for the delay in replying, which is due to the enormous volume of correspondence he has received since becoming Leader of the Conservative Party. I know David would wish me to thank you for your kind words of congratulation and support.
I read your letter, and I think the best thing is if I copy this correspondence to Sayeeda Warsi, who is Party's Vice Chairman with responsibilities for cities. I will then ask her to get in touch with you directly."

Yours sincerely
Sue Dennis
Office of the Leader of the Opposition'

(10) Letter to Stephen Pound.

20 June 2007

'Dear Stephen

Re: Two Recent News Items of Relevance heard on the Radio

It was good to see you on Monday, 18 June, at the function to commemorate the long-standing bond between Britain and India, and thank you for your kind introduction to various dignitaries.

Just a short note to highlight some aspects of the points I have covered in the letters to Jack Straw and Hazel Blears (encl.), which I have also raised passionately over the years with Tony Blair and John Major. It is quite a coincidence and fitting what I had covered in light of the two news items below.

1. News Item on Tuesday, 19 June. A survey highlighting that ethnic communities especially of South Indian origin are losing out on government initiatives because of red tape and lack of awareness.

2. News Item on 20 June (today). Department of Trade and Industry have launched a special initiative to help small Asian family businesses to raise finances for investment.

The first news item is least surprising and it will continue to be the case unless if the government puts in place pro-active rather than reactive measures. I have given the reasons in Sept 2005 in my correspondence to Tony Blair and more recently to Jack Straw and Hazel Blears.

The second news item, based on real life experiences, I believe will have similar consequences, namely it will not reach those who need it most but benefit those who know how to apply for grants. Moreover, it will alienate ethnic communities further from the mainstream and cause resentment within the indigenous population. Once again, I have covered these points in my various correspondences."

Kind regards
Yours most respectfully'
encl.

(11) Letter to Gordon Brown.

16 May 2008

'Dear Prime Minister,

Re: Community Cohesion - A need for specific practical policies for the Integration of ethnic people into mainstream politics and British way of life

"I had written to your goodself last year after you succeeded The Rt.Hon. Tony Blair and gave your address on 27 June 2007 outside 10 Downing Street to accept the invitation of Her Majesty The Queen to form a government.

It was firstly to congratulate you on your well-deserved appointment.

It was also because I fervently believe I have a lot to contribute to the further well-being of our country so as to leave a better legacy for our children and therefore, I had to write when I heard your acceptance address in which amongst other things you mentioned that "As I travelled around the country and as I have learned from the British people- and as Prime Minster I will continue to listen and learn from the British people .... And this need for change cannot be met by the old politics...... So, I will reach out beyond narrow party interest and invite men and women of goodwill to contribute their energies in a new spirit of public service to make our nation what it can be..."

Unfortunately, I did not hear from you or your office. I hasten to add that I have also written to the Justice Secretary, the Communities Secretary and the Home Secretary highlighting various issues. Once again it is with deep regret, I have to say that as yet I have not heard from their Office or even received an acknowledgment. I am in regular contact with Stephen Pound, MP for Ealing North, and have highlighted a number of constructive policy issues.

I have always regarded myself fortunate to be a citizen of the UK because it is great country and its people have good virtues. However, as a British Muslim of ethnic background, I believe that we cannot afford to be complacent or take things for granted following the recent events and those of the past years, as it is threatening the true harmony of our multicultural society and British way of life.

In the past 15 years, I have made successful and significant contribution to the public life in areas pertaining to small family business and ethnic communities. Moreover, a number of my concerns have unfortunately come true because of personal fears in relation to certain governmental policies which have done more harm than good in terms of integration of ethnic communities into the mainstream British way of life. It has also been exacerbated further because it has caused resentment amongst the indigenous population.

Over the past years, multi-million-pound grants have been made available to ethnic communities but unfortunately it has been wasted and failed to achieve the desired objectives. Instead, it has fuelled anger and resentment amongst the indigenous people, thus alienating communities.

It is because in the past, when formulating policies relating to ethnic communities, too much emphasis has been placed on politics of appeasement, spin, sofa style leadership and reliance on certain individuals claiming to be the bastions ethnic communities. It is about time that the experiences of the ordinary people leading everyday life were taken on board.

I am by no means advocating that the advice from Whitehall mandarins, ethnic community leaders and entrepreneurs is improper, but at times they can be misinformed because they themselves get out of touch with reality on reaching their respective eminent positions and have to rely on advisors or assistants, who in some cases have their own agenda or ambitions. I am aware that the above is a reflection of the times we are living in.

It is the above dilemma that at times has been the stumbling block in realising certain objectives of various Prime Ministers. I also fully appreciate because of time constraints; it would be impractical for the Prime Minister and his government to listen to each and every one, and therefore have to rely on advisors. But as you have said, we need to break away from the politics of the past and govern for all and not only those who are loud and get their voice heard for wrong reasons.

Despite well-meant initiatives from successive governments, certain sectors of the ethnic community still continue to feel being treated as second class citizens, which at times has been exacerbated by stereotype prejudices by grown-ups in various neighbourhoods, workplaces etc, which then gets imprinted on the innocent minds of children.

It is equally important for the ethnic community to realise that it works both ways and by becoming an integral part of the UK, they will not get easily swayed or fall victims to the tiny minority with an unscrupulous agenda who promote and preach racial or religious hatred.

I have outlined a number of points in my various correspondences, and in addition have prepared a salient summary of the objectives based on practical experiences. I hasten to add that I do not claim that I have a magical potion or panacea to all our problems but I can confirm that a number of things raised in the past 15 years have come to fruition.

We have to remind ourselves that majority of the ethnic individuals are decent law-abiding citizens but like everything else, irrespective of one's background, we need laws and regulations to protect us from a few bigots who are determined to create problems for us all.

A Need for Specific Policy Objectives for Community Cohesion and Harmony:

- To encourage ethnic communities to be proud British Citizens
- To overcome prejudice in public life e.g. government departments
- To project ethnic communities in a positive way and not stereotyped manner
- To overcome and prevent radicalisation of young British born Muslims
- To address the problem of illegal and unscrupulous immigration
- To address reasons for failure of good past government policies/ initiatives
- Religious schools and education curriculum
- Recognition and involvement of ethnic professional women and men

Obviously, the above is a salient summary of points which needs to be developed with substance. I believe that if I am given the opportunity, I can make a practical contribution based on real life experience to realise the desired objectives. I sincerely hope that on this occasion you will get a chance to see the contents of my letter and I look forward to hearing from you.

Yours most respectfully'

(12) Letter to Gordon Brown.

10 June 2009

'Dear Prime Minister

I write once again to express views of an ordinary British citizen hoping on this occasion my letter will be brought to your personal attention and that I will at least receive an acknowledgement if not a reply from your goodself.

I had written to you previously on 16 May 2008 and attach a copy of that letter "Community Cohesion – A need for specific practical policies for integration of ethnic communities into mainstream politics and way of life."
In light of the recent tumultuous events, I am extremely pleased that common-sense has prevailed within the Parliamentary Labour party. I fervently believe you will build on your strengths to restore hope and faith in our democracy and lead us out of recession which is affecting daily lives of ordinary British families and individuals.

Moreover, it is equally important that in the name of democracy extreme fascists' parties do not succeed further than their achievements in last week's European elections because of apathy and resentment by the public towards politicians and the Labour Party.

As a parent, I dread to think the legacy we will leave behind for our future generations bearing in mind that in the last century a significant number of British, Commonwealth and Allied lives were lost the two World Wars to prevent the spread of fascism.

It is also a great pity that certain cabinet ministers have resigned because of personal agenda by not full-filling their public role with diligence instead they are directing their energy to undermine your authority. But I think it is their loss and our gain. Incidentally, I had also written to both the Communities and Home Secretaries without any fruition, not even an acknowledgement.

As it is commonly known that "a week is a long time in politics" I am equally convinced and confident that "a year before the next general election in 2010 is a long time" in which to alleviate difficulties suffered by the ordinary people by getting the country out of the recession and address current apathy.

I strongly believe I can make a positive contribution if given a chance to participate in public life for the well-being of our country in these areas in a transparent and constructive manner with a simplistic approach.

- Community cohesion by not alienating ethnic people from the main stream.

- Immigration with particular emphasis on illegal immigrants so as to make a positive contribution to the economy, tax revenue and reduce the drain on public services.
- Savings in the public sector without affecting quality of service or cuts in public services.

I confirm I have also sent a copy of the letter to Stephen Pound, MP for Ealing North.

I sincerely hope on this occasion you will get a chance to see the contents of my letter. I look forward to hearing from you or your Office.

Yours most respectfully'

(13) Reply from the Direct Communications Unit.

30 June 2009

'Dear Mr Akberali

The Prime Minister has asked me to thank you for your recent and enclosure.

As you can imagine, Mr Brown receives thousands of letters each week and regrets that he is unable to reply personally to them all.

I have been asked to forward your letter to the Department for Communities and Local Government so that they may reply to you direct.

Yours sincerely'
Mrs S Caine'

(14) Letter to Sayeeda Hussain Warsi.

23 October 2009

'Dear Baroness Warsi

Re: BBC Question Time 22 October 2009 – You Rose above Petty Politics

I write with great pride to congratulate you on your brilliant, intellectual and graceful performance on BBC Question Time worthy of a statesperson.

I strongly believe that the BBC's decision to invite Mr Griffin was right because in a democracy - which we in the UK proudly cherish and at times take it for granted - it would be wrong to stifle debate, especially when this great country and its colonies fought two World Wars with immense sacrifices and loss of lives to protect freedom and basic human rights.

It is debatable whether it was the right format because of unfair hostility shown towards Mr Griffin before and during the program which prevented discussions relating to actual policy issues. It is with this in mind that your input was extremely significant as the Rt. Hon. Jack Straw of the present government and Mr Dimbleby by not challenging Mr Griffin on policy issues has increased the profile of BNP because of public sympathy.

It is equally important that in the name of democracy extreme fascists' do not succeed further by exploiting apathy and a feeling of hopelessness due to the resentment of the British people towards failures of the main political parties in addressing real issues.

I fervently believe that all mainstream political parties have a responsibility to listen to those who turn to the BNP or future groups with similar beliefs. It is now an opportune point in time that political parties relinquish the politics of appeasement and address the actual issues based on pragmatic policies to live a better future legacy for our children.

Over the years, multi-million-pound grants have been made available to ethnic communities but unfortunately it has been wasted and failed to achieve the desired objectives. Instead, it has fuelled anger and resentment amongst indigenous people by alienating communities.

It is because when formulating policies relating to ethnic communities, too much emphasis has been placed on politics of appeasement, spin, sofa style leadership and reliance on certain individuals claiming to be the bastions of ethnic communities whilst discarding experiences of ordinary people leading everyday life.

I am by no means advocating that the advice of Whitehall mandarins, ethnic community leaders and entrepreneurs is improper, but at times they can be misinformed as they get out of touch with reality on reaching their respective eminent positions and rely on advisors or assistants, who in some cases have their own agenda or ambitions.

I fully appreciate it would be impractical to listen to each and every one. But we need to break away from the politics of the past and govern for all and not only those who are loud and get their voice heard for wrong reasons.

Despite well-meant initiatives from successive governments, certain ethnic groups continue to be treated as second class citizens, exacerbated by stereotype prejudices of grown-ups in various neighbourhoods, workplaces and get imprinted on the innocent minds of children.

It is equally important for the ethnic community to realise that it works both ways and by becoming an integral part of the UK, they will not get easily swayed or fall victims to the tiny minority with an unscrupulous agenda who promote and preach racial or religious hatred.

We have to remind ourselves that majority of the ethnic individuals are decent law-abiding citizens but like everything else, irrespective of one's background, we need laws and regulations to protect us from a few bigots determined to create problems for us all.

I entreat your goodself to address actual issues which matter to us all and the conservative party needs to abandon the politics of appeasement. I sincerely believe I can make a positive contribution in terms of how and why the areas highlighted above need to be addressed.

I look forward to hearing from you.
Yours respectfully'

(15) Letter to Sir Humphrey Malins.

2 October 2009

'Dear Sir Malins

I am your constituent and write to your goodself as my constituent MP.

I was subjected to discrimination and victimisation at my place of work. I followed all the internal disciplinary process and lodged a claim with the Employment Tribunal based on the advice by the Woking Citizen Advice Bureau. I was subsequently dismissed because of my claim. The trail was scheduled on 9 November 2009 for a ten-day hearing. To-date, I have managed all the requirements without professional help.

I took my wife to the pre-hearing review on 28 September 2009 and the Respondent's legal team tried to get the claim struck out without fruition. However, the Employment Judge advised me I Should hire the services of a Solicitor because the hearing can be a dauting experience for a layman in terms of preparing statements, witness cross examination etc.
I have tried various solicitors and I cannot afford their fees on my present earnings of £140.00 per week for a 20-hour week.

I have approached various agencies e.g. surrey Law Centre, bar-Pro-Bono, Legal Aid Agency, solicitors as well as philanthropic individuals for help, and unfortunately, I am not eligible because I am not on any benefits. All such activities also cost money e.g. phone calls, letters, travel which at present very difficult to meet as they all add up.

It seems no help is available to those who do not believe in claiming benefits or are prudent in terms of owning a property, not going on holidays etc and survive by making personal sacrifices.

The Respondents have legal clout and access to public funds paid for by the tax payer. I am also finding it difficult to find a permanent job because of the present economic climate, age and the stigma of a troublemaker because of my Employment Tribunal claim.

Incidentally, I have advised by the Legal Aid staff that I should approach my MP for referral to them because of my circumstances.

I look forward to your esteemed guidance as avenues available to people like me in order to seek justice who do not believe in claiming welfare benefits.

Yours most gratefully'

(16) Letter to Sir Humfrey Malins

9 November 2009

'Dear Sir Malins

I write to seek your esteemed guidance and support to bring to the attention of the Minister responsible of the public body like the CWGC of the underlying issues relating to discrimination based on the evidence gathered of the flawed internal disciplinary process.

In order to address the miscarriage of justice I had no choice but to lodge a Tribunal Appeal but reluctantly accepted an out of court settlement because of legal stress and intimidation.

I also humbly request your goodself to bring to the attention of the Minister whose portfolio covers accessibility for disadvantaged individuals to seek justice from an independent body but cannot do so because of intimidation and lack of support. I appreciate there are Trade Unions but this relates to underlying working of a Public body.

I entreat your support so that such practices are not allowed to continue and prevent it from happening to others.

I look forward to hearing from you.

Kind regards
Yours sincerely',

(17) Reply from Sir Humfrey Malins after a few exchanges with the Clerk.

23 February 2010

'Dear Dr Akberali

I enclose a copy of this letter I have received from the Clerk of the Defence Committee. I will be in touch when I have heard from Robin James. In the meantime, you may be aware I am retiring at the election and Parliament is likely to dissolved in a few weeks' time. I am sure that my successor, who may be the excellent Conservative candidate Jonathan Lord, will be very happy to take on your case but I will need your written authority to pass on your file to my successor if that is what you would like me to do when the time comes.

Yours sincerely'

(18) Letter to Humphrey Malins.

24 February 2010

'Dear Mr Malins

Thank for your letter of 23 Feb 2010 with the enclosed copy from the Clerk of the Defence Select Committee.

I am pleased to note that the concerns I had raised in my e-mail of 22 Feb 2010 of the forthcoming elections and the dissolving of the parliament together with your retirement have been put to rest that my efforts will not get brushed under the carpet.

In light of the above, I hereby give my written authority to pass on my file to your successor Jonathan Lord who may be the excellent Conservative candidate to take over from your goodself.

In mean time I look forward to hearing from you when you have heard from Robin James.

Finally, it would have been good to have heard from the Clerk of the Defence Select Committee in the first instance when I had written in November 2009 to have been informed accordingly which would have alleviated the unnecessary delays.

Thank you once again for your esteemed guidance and support.

Best wishes'

(19) Letter to Jonathan Lord after his election victory on 6 May 2010.

8 May 2010

'Dear Mr Lord

Congratulations and reference letter dated 23 Feb 2010 from Mr Malins

I write to congratulate you on your election victory as the Member of Parliament for the Woking constituency and also take the opportunity to introduce myself with reference to the letter dated 23 Feb 2010 from your predecessor Mr Malins.

As requested by Mr Malins, I had given him a written authority on 24 Feb 2010 to pass on my file to you as his successor.

I sincerely hope that having waited since November 2009, my efforts to bring to light the workings of a public organisation and the difficulties faced by ordinary people will now get addressed especially in light of the promises and pledges made during the recent general election to vote for change, "The Big Society", accountability and transparency in order to make the democratic process more accessible for the ordinary people.

I fully appreciate that the formal opening of the Parliament will be after HM The Queen's speech. However, I would be most grateful for your esteemed guidance and support on the matter as I have been waiting patiently for a long time and in the process suffered because of the workings and treatment of ordinary people by a public organisation funded by the tax payer.

I look forward to hearing from you.

Yours sincerely',

(20) Reply from by Jonathan Lord.

10 May 2010

'Thank you so much for all your good wishes.

It was a really terrific result in Woking - achieving 5,000 additional Conservative votes compared to the last election, and securing over 50% of the vote overall.

I will try to write back about the other issues you mention when I have a spare few minute.
Thank you again'!

(21) Final reply from Jonathan Lord after a few exchanges between us.

30 November 2010

'Dear Dr Akberali

Thank you for your email and letter of 25th November together with enclosure.

Firstly, regarding the Jobcentre plus – I understand what you say.

Secondly, Whom you should approach about other issues – you have done the right thing in raising with me, your MP and others in authority, but if you feel so strongly about local or national political issues, you are always at liberty to stand for election yourself or to get involved in appropriate charities or pressure groups."

Yours sincerely
Jonathan Lord'

(22) Letter to John Bercow.

6 December 2010

'Dear Mr Bercow

Re: Access to the Democratic Process – Real life handicaps of ordinary disadvantaged people with no financial, legal, lobbying or media influence

I have approached Mr Lord as my MP under the Parliamentary Rule to make representations on my behalf.

I write to your goodself in desperation in light of the recent reply received today from Mr Lord, asking me to stand for election (overnight with my background) or join protest groups so to raise matters of important nature affecting me within the context of coalition government's policies relating to freedom, fairness and responsibility.
I enclose copies for your perusal dated 30, 24, 10 and 8 Nov from Mr Lord with corresponding attached letters of mine dated 25,11, 9 Nov, 18 Oct and 14 Sept.

I would greatly appreciate your esteemed help or direction to access the democratic process as I can expect no support relating to the following policy matters raised with Mr Lord (inquiry issue going back to the time of his predecessor Mr Malins, CBE).

- Welfare benefits and Employment Opportunities – Government's attitude towards the unemployed and lack of support purported by the government.
- Accountability and transparency example set by PM's Office - Not even an acknowledgement (re: Letter to Mr Cameron dated 30 July 2010).
- Request for a Parliamentary Select Committee Inquiry – Waiting well over a year for a response.

I apologise for taking the liberty of writing and taking your valuable time.
Best wishes'.

(23) Reply from John Bercow's secretary.

10 December 2010

'Dear Dr Akberali

Mr Speaker has asked me to thank you for your letter of 6 December and to reply on his behalf.

The Speaker has asked me to explain that, although this a subject about which you feel deeply concerned, the nature of his position requires him to be politically impartial. He has no responsibility for the actions of Members outside the Chamber of the House of Commons; the way in which Members of Parliament choose to deal with their correspondence is entirely a matter for themselves. There is no Parliamentary or other body which deals with complaints of this nature against Members of Parliament.

Mr Speaker notes that you have already been in touch with your MP, Jonathan Lord, and can only advise that you continue to do so to seek guidance or to make your views known.

Yours sincerely
Renee Brownsey – Joyce
Secretary, Speaker's Office'

(24) Letter to David Cameron.

30 July 2010

'Dear Prime Minister

Re: Community Cohesion, Big Society and Ethnic Communities – An opportunity to galvanise and benefit from the historic ties of the Commonwealth as partners of choice.

I have written to your goodself previously in your capacity as the Leader of the Opposition and I sincerely hope that on this occasion you will get a chance to see the contents of my letter.

Over the years, I have also written to your three predecessors and others on a number of issues relating to the above because I fervently believe in the further well-being of our country so as to leave a better for legacy for the future generation.

It is nearly 3 months since your well-deserved appointment as the Prime Minister of the coalition government to reach out by inviting men and women of goodwill to contribute their energies in a new spirit of public service for better future based on freedom, fairness and responsibility.

I write once again in light of your recent successful State Visit to India. I share your vision India should be "a partner of choice". I have always been a strong advocate for need to galvanise the historic ties with the Commonwealth in a more structured way for mutual benefits. A strong Commonwealth would be more effective than the EU. It would also mean that we are not treated as junior partners by the USA or other emerging economies.

In the last 15 years, I have highlighted concerns which have unfortunately come true because of certain government policies which have done more harm than good in terms of integration of ethnic people into the mainstream British way of life. It has been exacerbated further because it has caused resentment amongst the indigenous population on understandable grounds.

A Need for Specific Policy Objectives for Community Cohesion and Harmony:

How to encourage ethnic communities to be proud British citizens.
- How to galvanise people of the Commonwealth as partners of choice.
- How to address unscrupulous immigration and the drain on public services e.g. health, education, and welfare benefits during austerity.
- How to overcome and prevent radicalisation of British born Muslims.
- Need to address religious schools and education curriculum.
- How to overcome subtle prejudice and discrimination in public life.
- Emphasis of government initiatives for ethnic communities better served if when formulating main policies and not in isolation as an afterthought.
- How to engage communities at grassroots level and not rely too much on loud middle-class national leadership organisations or individuals with their own agenda seeking to act as gatekeepers to the ethnic communities.
- A focus on government policies based on practicality and not patronising initiatives based on red-tape bureaucracy preventing direct involvement at the ethnic grassroots level with individuals having to rely on others.
- Government led emphasis to highlight significant contributions made in the various fields by ethnic communities in terms of what brings us together with less emphasis on what divides us.
- How to engage ethnic community into mainstream politics and civic role?

I have always regarded myself fortunate to be a citizen of the UK because it is great country and its people have good virtues. However, as a British Muslim of ethnic background, I believe that we cannot afford to be complacent or take things for granted following events of the recent years, as it is threatening the true harmony of our multicultural society and British way of life.

Over the past years, multi-million-pound grants have been made available to ethnic communities but unfortunately it has been squandered and failed to achieve the desired objectives. Instead, it has fuelled anger and resentment amongst the indigenous people, thus alienating communities.

It is because in the past, when formulating policies relating to ethnic communities, too much emphasis has been placed on politics of appeasement, spin and sofa style leadership as confirmed in the sudden rush of the publications of biographies. It beggar belief as to why the individuals did not follow their convictions based on accountability to public life in order to prevent economic and social misery to the country? In relation to ethnic communities too much reliance has been placed on middle class individuals or organisations claiming to be the bastions and not the ordinary people leading everyday life.

In relation to ethnic communities too much reliance has been placed on middle class individuals or organisations claiming to be the bastions and not the ordinary people leading everyday life. I am by no means advocating that advice of middle class ethnic leaders and entrepreneurs is improper, but at times they can be misinformed because they themselves get out of touch with reality on reaching their respective eminent positions and have to rely on advisors or assistants, who in some cases have their own agenda or ambitions. I am aware it is a reflection of the times we are living in.

It is the above dilemma that at times has been the stumbling block in realising certain objectives of various Prime Ministers. I also fully appreciate because of time constraints; it would be impractical for the Prime Minister and his government to listen to each and every one, and therefore have to rely on advisors. But as you have said, we need to break away from the politics of the past and govern for all and not only those who are loud and get their voice heard for wrong reasons.

Despite well-meant initiatives from successive governments, certain sectors of the ethnic community living in the inner cities continue to feel being treated as second class citizens, which at times has been exacerbated by stereotype prejudices by grown-ups in various neighbourhoods, workplaces etc, which then gets imprinted on the innocent minds of children. It is equally important for the ethnic community to realise that it works both ways and by becoming an integral part of the UK, they will not get easily swayed or fall victims to the tiny minority with an unscrupulous agenda who promote and preach racial, political or religious hatred.

Obviously, the above is a salient summary of points which needs to be developed with substance. I believe that if I am given the opportunity, I can make practical contribution based on real life experience to realise the desired objectives by asking the right questions for reasons undermining social cohesion not only within the context of ethnic communities but for the benefit of the whole society.

I look forward to hearing from you.

Yours sincerely'

(25) Letter to Nick Clegg.

18 December 2010

'Dear Mr Clegg

Re: Progressive or Regressive Government Policies? Access to opportunities and the Democratic process – Real life handicaps outside the Westminster bubble for the ordinary people with no financial, legal, lobbying, media or social clout.

I take this opportunity to write to you in desperation ahead of other options in wake of the reply from my MP, Mr Jonathan Lord informing me that he is not going to pursue matters on my behalf. Unfortunately, similar attempt of writing to Mr Cameron on pragmatic policy issues relating to immigration, radicalisation, etc has also resulted in contempt (see 14 Sept).

Mr Lord's only advice to me is that I should stand for elections or join protest groups, if I felt strongly about local or national issues. I have decided against standing for elections in five years' time or joining a protest or extreme group because I believe in peaceful democracy of electing an MP to represent concerns of ordinary people irrespective of party political and individual interests. In addition, I trust you will appreciate that unlike MPs or civil servants, I have no recourse to public or private money to fund such activities e.g. expenses, wages, pension, relocation grants when rendering civic duty. We ordinary people pay for expenses incurred privately or whilst rendering civic duty or contacting MPs in our own time.

Mr Lord has further advised that if I fail to find a job, I should consider charity work to help local people. I feel such comments are condescending and out of touch. Like the vast majority, I believe in charitable work. However, at present I find it difficult to meet basic expenses because of personal financial constraints due to being unemployed (see below). With respect, even the "Big Society" which is the political answer to all the problems created by the greedy few because of government failures (25 Nov) needs basic funds to function.

In light of the above, I hope you will appreciate, I have no alternative but seek your esteem support and guidance because of your important integral role in the government prophesising "New Politics" based on accountability and transparency as under the parliamentary rule there is no provision for ordinary constituents when faced with my dilemma. I enclose some copies of correspondence addressed to Mr Lord to give you a deeper insight.

Realities of the Unemployed – Stigma and irresponsible sound bites:

I am unemployed because of my treatment by a public body namely CWGC (see 14 Sept). I am looking for work without success and not refusing to work. I am not entitled to any welfare or housing benefits including Job Seekers Allowance because my wife has a full-time job although our total house-hold income is much less than the national income of £25K. We are managing with great difficulty on single income to pay all household bills including council tax, prescription/ dental charges etc. and extended family responsibilities.

The irony is that I have worked all my life and paid taxes. When I get unemployed for the first time because of my treatment by the CWGC, I am not entitled to any benefits. However, I would rather be employed than be on benefits. Moreover, as I am not a "claimant" I do not exist in the "claimant count" nor belong to the purported stigma of false universal statements by ministers that the unemployed are lazy leading a life of riley on welfare and housing benefits at the expense of others (see 9, 11 Nov). It seems there is one simple government rule which is to make it harder by hitting the prudent hardworking bottom 90% of the population and their families to pay for the mistakes of the unaccountable and greedy 10%.

Social mobility and the unemployed – Lack of adequate training and support:
It has always been a political desire to help unemployed find work to alleviate social misery. It is also basically accepted that social mobility condemns people because of where they were born, who their parents were and where they lived with less life expectancy, education and job opportunities of their choice. Despite concerted previous and present commitment to spend billions of pounds, it raises basic question as to why unemployment and poverty is on the increase despite various government schemes. We have to wait and see, whether, new initiatives amongst others e.g. pupil premiums, student scholarships for children from poorer backgrounds will be any different or will be compiled to history books as another failure.

It is most likely that there are other underlying reasons; I believe that the concerns I have raised with Mr Lord and Mr Cameron are well founded and the issues needs to be looked at more closely with pro-active approach based on genuine convictions instead of reactive measures relying on punitive threats of benefits withdrawal. It requires pragmatic solutions questioning convictions of various agencies and the management hierarchy who administer training and welfare schemes, programs or projects paid for by the tax payer. I am aware the government claims to pay private firms on results. We have heard such rhetoric before and paid the consequences.

Because of my practical experience of being unemployed, I believe it would be invaluable to have firsthand knowledge of the inherent difficulties which cannot be gained during formal stage-managed visits made by Ministers and advisers. It is disheartening Mr Lord despite agreeing with me following his impressive visit to Woking Job Centre Plus feels inappropriate to make representations on my behalf.

Political mantra and pledges for "new politics" to restore public trust:
We are constantly reminded by the coalition government of the challenges facing the nation to mend inherited politics and public finances with slogans e.g. "vote for change, we are all in it together, working together for national interest, the "Big Society", accountability, transparency, freedom, responsibility and fairness ....

I believe it feels no different as evident from my experience of taking the trouble to write to Mr Cameron and a lack of courtesy to acknowledge, even after requesting Mr Lord (see 14 Sept). It is with great sadness to conclude my experience indicates we are not breaking away from the deeply rooted politics of the past. It only deters ordinary people to participate if treated with contempt or rebuff especially when it is the proclaimed vision of Mr Cameron to encourage people from the "Big Society" to render civic role.

CWGC Inquiry - Need for political conviction and savings during austerity:
Because of my employment experiences with a public body CWGC, I approached the parliamentary select committee and Mr Lord's predecessor Mr Malins requesting an inquiry well over a year ago. I unequivocally state my quest for CWGC inquiry is not vexatious or an obsession. It is based on unquestionable integrity to unearth real life workings of a public body including failings of top-heavy unaccountable management and cover up at all costs.

I believe the inquiry into the CWGC will highlight workings of top-heavy management hierarchy structure and expose wastage. It will shed light into how savings of 20 % and up to 40% amounting to millions in just the CWGC can be made without serious impact on frontline services and jobs or minimal effects respectively. It will also give a deeper understanding of the workings and practical efficiency savings with minimal impact on front line services and jobs including social mobility in other public bodies e.g. health, education.

Mr Lord has advised "with regard to the CWGC, I fear we seem to have exhausted all the most obvious ways of attempting to get further investigations". I am not sure what he means by that as I have led all the initiative. I have also been sent a copy of the letter Dr Robin James, Clerk of the Foreign Affairs Committee, mentioning my "proposal for a select committee inquiry into the workings of the CWGC has been circulated to the members of Foreign Affairs Committee" (see 18 Oct 2010).

I hope you will press for an investigation in the event FAC decides against an inquiry. I fervently believe that the debate will unearth interesting findings within the context of freedom, fairness and responsibility political agenda of the coalition government.

I sincerely trust the above provides some extra information of real-life difficulties faced by disadvantaged individuals, and if incorporated -in time- may enhance political conviction at the forthcoming by-election in Oldham East to embrace and resolve policies for the good of the whole country.

I look forward to hearing from you and please do not hesitate to contact me if you require additional information or details. Finally, I wish you all a very happy Christmas and best wishes for the New Year and hope for best in terms of "New Politics" promised by the "Progressive" government.

Yours most respectfully,
Encl.'

(26) Letter to Nick Clegg.

13 January 2011

'Dear Mr Clegg,

Re: "New Politics" or same old politics dressed differently?

I write with deep regret as I have not heard following my letter of 18 Dec 2010 addressed to you, not even an acknowledgement as matter of courtesy.

During election campaign felt really good that at long last the nation will get deservedly clean politics of conviction following election campaign by PM and you to break away from the politics of the past. But it is no different as evident during PM question time, politicians apportioning blame onto everyone but themselves. After all, haven't we heard often when politicians claim they entered politics to better lives of others but it seems not to be the case where ordinary people are made to pay for the greed and mistakes of bankers, politicians and government advisers. The people are tired of politics of appeasement and a quagmire of broken political promises of the recent past.

Contacted my MP with no positive support of intervention, contacted PM and you unfortunately not even received a courtesy acknowledgement; therefore, it seems it is same old politics despite pledges for clean politics to hold politicians accountable to the electorate. It seems in modern politics and democracy there is no provision in the parliamentary rules for ordinary people faced with contempt, arrogance and indignation from their MP, PM and Deputy PM.

Both you and PM want to involve ordinary people with real life experiences outside the Westminster bubble (village) or individuals in ivory offices but seems it seems same old politics.

Yours most respectfully',

(27) Letter to Michael Gove.

14 January 2011

'Dear Mr Gove

Re: BBC Question Time 13 Jan 2011- A refreshing change to listen to politics of conviction instead of appeasement and broken promises under the cover of "new clean politics"

It was good to listen to your goodself and Mr Kennedy especially on the question relating to "English baccalaureate" tables. Unlike various recent examples in parliamentary democracy, you showed passionate dedication based on politics of conviction to better the educational standards of all irrespective of background, a clear example of the politician's most commonly used phrase "entered politics to better the life of people".

If the majority of the politicians and government advisers showed similar conviction to render civic duty it would eradicate a number of hardships and obstacles faced by ordinary disadvantaged individuals e.g. poverty, unemployment, opportunities, fairness etc.

I believe good education and health are the two most important requirements to equip future generation in order to give a good start in life to address social mobility and social cohesion. However, as demonstrated by you it requires sound practical policies to address the underlying root problems facing us in all aspects of everyday life. It also needs genuine conviction from professionals.

We expect our politicians to speak their minds to voice their honest opinions and not just empty words. Just because some people may disagree doesn't mean that others are not entitled to speak out for the good of the nation and not get ruled by knee-jerk reaction to the 24-hour media, spin and sofa style politics.

I further take this opportunity to highlight my unfortunate experience to date also in the wake of the comment made by you that it is extremely important to listen to ordinary people from "within ethnic communities" with reference to the question relating to the comments made by the Rt. Hon. Jack Straw.

Over the past few months, I have taken initiative in my own time to bring to the attention of my MP, Mr Jonathan Lord, Mr Cameron and Mr Clegg , a number of important issues based on real life experiences from "within" outside the Westminster village (Whitehall bubble) within the context of the "big society, we are all in this together, working together in national interest, alarm-clock Britain, accountability, transparency ......"

Unfortunately, Mr Lord is of the opinion that I should stand for election or join protest groups if I felt strongly about national or local issues. It is also with regret that I have not heard from Mr Cameron or his office, not even an acknowledgment as a matter of courtesy. Whereas Mr Clegg's secretary has ignored by saying it is the responsibility of the Dept. of Work and Pensions.

Mr Cameron on 15 Dec 2010 during PM questions in his answer to a question from a conservative backbencher on terrorist attack in Sweden mentioned that "we need to ask right questions about Islamist terrorism".

It is an irony when an individual takes the trouble of asking and attempting to provide solution to such questions, he faces contempt, arrogance and indignation of not even receiving an acknowledgement from PM's office!

In absence of support from my MP, I enclose copies of letters for your perusal and sincerely hope that you will use your esteemed political position and conviction including being an MP of the neighbouring constituency to mine.

I look forward to hearing from you especially on the points raised in the enclosed letters so that ordinary people with no financial, media, legal, lobbying or social clout can gain access to the democratic process.

Best wishes in all your endeavours.
Yours most respectfully'

(28) Letter to Simon Hughes.

17 January 2011

'Dear Mr Hughes

Re: "New Politics" or same old politics dressed differently?

I write to your goodself in your esteemed capacity as a Member of Parliament, Deputy Leader of the Liberal Democrats and most importantly the voice of reason championing everyday real-life difficulties of your constituents including ordinary people nationally.

I have written to my MP, Mr Lord and Mr Cameron on a number of real-life everyday concerns as an ordinary constituent and citizen. Mr Lord has informed me that he is unable to make representations on my behalf and I should consider standing for elections to gain access to the democracy process. Obviously, I feel disappointed because I was under the impression that an MP gets elected to render civic duty irrespective of party politics or personal interest.

In light of the reply received from Mr Lord and a total lack of response PM's office, I enclose letter 18 Dec 2010 written to Mr Clegg in his capacity as a Deputy PM to gain access to the democratic process. It is with deep regret that I have just received a patronising bureaucratic response (see reply) from his secretary avoiding the main concerns by passing the buck.

I fully appreciate that I am not your constituent and under parliamentary rules an MP can only make representations on behalf of their constituents however, there is no provision in the parliamentary rules for ordinary people faced with indignation, arrogance and contempt from their MP, PM and Deputy PM.

I, therefore, entreat your esteemed help on my behalf to bring to the attention of the coalition government real life experiences of ordinary people. It highlights that the voice of the disadvantaged in the society very rarely gets heard in stark contrast to the people with money. I fervently believe that if the coalition government believes in delivering the political agenda based on "freedom, fairness and responsibilities" listening to the views of ordinary people is important to bring to fruition policies which affect their lives most in terms of the high cost and high risk workings and failings of public organisations instead of relying entirely on self-interested individuals running various public organisations.

I look forward to hearing from you and please let me know if you require further information.

Yours sincerely',

(29) Letter to Nick Clegg.

5 February 2011

'Dear Mr Clegg

Re: Social mobility, opportunities and access to the democratic process - Real life handicaps outside the Westminster bubble for ordinary people without financial, legal, lobbying, media or social clout in the much-promised age of new politics, freedom, fairness, responsibility, accountability, austerity, transparency.

I have written to you previously on 13 January 2011. I received a reply on your behalf from Mrs Silver thanking on your behalf informing me that my letter has been passed to the DWP.

I have received a condescending bureaucratic reply from the DWP Correspondence Team with an unidentifiable signature without addressing the concerns raised with your goodself.

I write once again as it is extremely relevant the points raised by me with you, Messrs Lord, Cameron, Hughes and Gove as coalition government politicians following further evidence in the BBC2 programmes "Posh and Posher" and "Who Gets the Best Jobs" with reference to the above as it highlights the darker side of the root causes and real life difficulties.

The "Posh and Posher" programme shone the light by exposing unfairness of how politicians from all parties drawn from an even smaller social pool and networking contacts go on to run the country – and why it should matter to us all because of the wide-ranging consequences.

Whereas, from "Who Gets the Best Jobs", it transpired that one of the main reasons apart from money, contacts and family support hindering social mobility was a distinct lack of role models and mentors.

I think another factor hindering social mobility is constant frustrations from being let down by the system. I fervently believe my experience will give you further credible evidence as it is the living proof of the root causes of social mobility in various walks of life.

Over the last 30 years, the hopes and aspirations of ordinary people have been raised without fruition by politicians in terms of opportunities and fairness. It is the real-life folly of modern-day politics because of the politics of appeasement (sound bites) for short term gains and not conviction. In addition, there is a distinct vacuum of trustworthy role models exacerbated by greed accepted as a norm in life, the root cause preventing social mobility.

It is with the above in mind that I sincerely hope you will find time to read my letter unlike the contempt, indignation and arrogance shown by the coalition politicians and my MP.

According to parliamentary rules, I contacted my MP to make representations on my behalf on various matters including requesting why Mr Cameron or his office had not even bothered to acknowledge my letter of 30 July '10 after being promised change and new politics.

My MP has informed with blunt arrogance that I should stand for elections, join protest or voluntary charity ("the Big Society") groups if I felt strongly about local or national issues.

I have been left with a dilemma because the next election will be in 5 years' time and I have no financial backing of political parties, unions or rich tax exiles. Moreover, I am against joining a protest or extreme group as I believe in peaceful democracy through the ballot box by electing an MP to represent concerns of all ordinary people irrespective of MP's party political or individual interests.

It is disheartening especially in the wake of the answers given by Mr Cameron at PMQ's. For example, Mr Cameron on 15 Dec 2010 during PM questions in his answer to a question from a conservative backbencher on terrorist attack in Sweden mentioned that "we need to ask right questions about Islamist terrorism". It is an irony when an ordinary individual takes the trouble of asking and attempting to provide solution to such questions, he faces contempt, arrogance and indignation of not even receiving an acknowledgement from PM's office!

Moreover, as recently as 2 Feb 2011, a Labour MP when raised a question relating to the plight of a constituent's sick child, Mr Cameron replied that an MP should do his utmost to help constituents in all matters.

It is a bit rich and condescending for Mr Cameron to say one thing when personal experience of mine highlight's contempt shown by him, my MP and other members of the coalition government. It is far below anything expected from anyone especially the role models and the bastions of society holding important public offices prophesying social mobility.
Sir George Young following MPs expenses row on 3 Feb was reported saying "the political system is deterring people from less affluent backgrounds from becoming MPs and putting undue pressure on the family lives of existing parliamentarians".

It beggars belief whether politicians have a true measure of real-life experiences of ordinary people in terms of social mobility and employment. In reality, my MP has flatly refused to make representations but entitled to claim expenses and expects handsome remunerations whereas, ordinary people have no privilege to claim everyday work-related expenses but get affected by recession and austerity measures caused by politicians and greedy bankers.

I enclose copies of some letters to give a deeper insight of subtle and blatant obstacles faced by disadvantaged people. I will greatly appreciate if you will give me an opportunity to bring to your personal attention the real issues, culprits and impediments of social mobility curse.

I look forward to hearing from you and apologise for taking up your valuable time.

Yours most respectfully
encl.'

(30) Letter to Andrew Neil.

27 January 2011

'Dear Mr Neil

Re: The other side of "Posh and Posher"

Access to opportunities and Democratic process – Real life handicaps outside the Westminster bubble for people with no financial, legal, lobbying, media or social clout during the age of accountability, austerity and transparency

I write to thank you for the provocative film "Posh and Posher" shown on BBC2 on 26 January 2011.

I fervently believe the programme shone the light by exposing unfairness of how politicians from <u>all parties</u> drawn from an even smaller social pool and networking contacts go on to run the country – and why it should matter to us all because of the wide-ranging consequences.

In light of your brilliant programme, I write to you with hopeful expectations you would help me directly or accordingly to highlight the implications of our worrying politics and the decline of social mobility.

I am also an ardent follower of your "Daily Politics" and "This Week" BBC shows and thought it is now an opportune time to make you aware of the real-life difficulties for the ordinary people to gain access to the democratic process let alone standing for elections.

According to the Parliamentary rules, I contacted my MP requesting him to make representations on my behalf (see enclosed) and after a few months, I was bluntly informed that I should stand for elections, join protest or voluntary charity groups if I felt strongly about local and national issues. I have been left with a dilemma because the next election will be in 5 years' time and I have no financial backing of political parties, unions or rich tax exiles. Moreover, I am against joining a protest or extreme group as I believe in peaceful democracy through the ballot box by electing an MP to represent concerns of all ordinary people irrespective of MP's party political and individual interests.

I have also taken the trouble in my own time to write to Mr Cameron (see enclosed) mentioning a number of concerns relating to immigration, radicalisation of British Muslims, welfare, wastage of public funds etc with practical solutions to address such important issues.

As I did not even receive an acknowledgement from Mr Cameron's office and because of the stance adopted by my MP, I wrote to other senior members of the coalition government namely Mr Clegg, Mr Gove and Mr Hughes including The Speaker (see enclosed).

For all my efforts, I have only received very patronising and condescending bureaucratic replies from Mr Clegg's secretary informing me that my correspondence has been passed over to the DWP who have just written to thank me for writing without addressing the actual issues I spent significant time to raise to Mr Clegg (see enclosed).

Unfortunately, I have not yet heard or received an acknowledgement from Mr Gove and Hughes. I am not raising my hopes for answers to my efforts as I am resigned to receiving another patronising and condescending bureaucratic reply from their offices without them actually reading the contents of my letters.

In the wake of my above experiences together with the absence of a parliamentary process allowing ordinary people to access the democratic process (when bluntly refused by his MP to make representations), I would greatly appreciate if you would bring to the attention of the appropriate authorities the difficulties faced by ordinary people and also raise it with the politicians when they next flock to appear on your shows to score political points.

I entreat your esteemed guidance and support to bring to light important issues affecting ordinary people. I also hasten to add that issues raised in the letter to Mr Cameron are important and can be addressed with pragmatic results by listening to the real-life experiences of ordinary people from within the communities.

I look forward to hearing from you. I apologise for taking up your valuable time and sincerely hope my efforts will not be ignored as our bastions of society.

Yours most gratefully
encl.'

(31) Letter to Jonathan Lord.

16 February 2011

<u>By post and e-mail</u>
'Dear Mr Lord

Re: Multiculturalism warnings prior to the address by Mr Cameron on 5 Feb 2011

It is with great expectations I write to you once again hoping that on this occasion you will make positive representations on my behalf in the wake of the above.

I sincerely hope you will help overcome real life struggles and handicaps of ordinary people without adequate financial resources or contacts to gain access to our democratic institutions unlike sex offenders or prisoners who seem to get more representations for their rights.

You will be aware I wrote to you to make representations following my letter to Mr Cameron dated 30 July 2010. I had written because of Mr Cameron's vision of the Big Society to encourage individuals to make positive contribution for the good of our country and society. Unfortunately, his office to date has not had the decent courtesy to even acknowledge receipt of my letter despite requesting you to make representations on my behalf.

I fervently believe I can make a significant contribution in the various areas (see below) and beyond to realise the main policy objectives of the coalition government in the wake of Mr Cameron's vision of the Big Society.

Moreover, I would go further that substantial progress relating to immigration can be achieved in a matter of months depending on the will of the government. I hope you will agree that I can't be fairer in terms of accountability with a self-belief in my convictions.

However, just like his predecessors, Mr Cameron despite echoing reservations and concerns on 5 Feb 2011 in Germany, offered no solutions. I had written to Mr Cameron on 30 July 2010 because I believe we cannot afford complacency after 9/11 and 7/7 events, and we need to address it head on as it threatens true harmony in our society and British way of life.

I had highlighted the reasons for the failures of past initiatives from successive governments and the understandable resentment amongst indigenous population. We need to ask why various initiatives have failed to achieve desired objectives. Is it because of knee-jerk reactions for short term gains without thinking through future detrimental consequences?

The answers to my concerns are based on first-hand experience of a British citizen from within the ethnic Muslim community asking the right questions with strong belief in respect for the parent community and my faith. Just as we believe that it is not right to live on borrowed time and money, it is equally important to live a better legacy for our children.

Listed below are specific proactive cost-effective pragmatic solutions and not reactive measures of the past costing millions (wasted) for the mutual benefit of all communities. It will prevent imprinting of stereotype prejudices of grownups at work places and neighbourhoods on innocent minds.

- How to address unscrupulous/illegal immigration and the drain on public funds e.g. health, education, and welfare benefits during the present austerity measures?
- I hasten to add that the above will address the poignant reminder in the news today (16 Feb 2011) of the UK Border Agency letting immigrants into UK for profits.
- How to overcome and prevent radicalisation of young British born Muslims?
- How to address religious schools' curriculum?
- How to overcome subtle prejudice and discrimination in public life to prevent treatment of ethnic communities as second-class citizens?
- How to encourage ethnic communities to be proud British citizens?
- How to galvanise ethnic communities from the Commonwealth as partners of choice?
- How government initiatives for ethnic communities would be better served if incorporated when formulating main policies and not in isolation as an afterthought?
- How to engage communities at grassroots level and not rely too much on loud middle-class national leadership organisations or individuals with their own agenda seeking to act as gatekeepers to the ethnic communities?
- How to focus government policies based on practicality and not patronising initiatives based on bureaucracy and red tape preventing direct involvement at the ethnic grassroots level with individuals having to rely on others?
- How to engage ethnic community into mainstream politics and civic role?
- Government led emphasis to highlight significant contributions made in the various fields by ethnic communities in terms of what brings us together with less emphasis on what divides us.

I look forward to hearing from you together with your esteemed support on this occasion.

Yours most sincerely',

(32) Letter to Bernard Jenkins.

16 February 2011

'Dear Mr Jenkins

Re: Big Society-Contempt, arrogance and indignation from coalition politicians hindering participation

May I take this opportunity following your question at the PMQs today informing Mr Cameron of the launch of the Public Administration Committee inquiry into the Big Society.
I write with great expectations seeking your esteemed support that the members of the committee will take evidence with reference to the above summarised in the two examples of the enclosed letters including most recent letter dated 16 Feb 2011, "Multiculturalism warnings prior to the address by Mr Cameron on 5 Feb 2011 addressed to my MP, Mr Lord.

It highlights the real-life difficulties and struggles faced by ordinary people who passionately share the views that volunteering, charity and decentralising public services as positive values of a healthy society. However, putting into practice becomes an enduring obstacle race.

I wrote to Mr Cameron following the General Election within the context of his vision of the Big Society to encourage positive contributions for the good of our country. Unfortunately, his office to date has not had the decent courtesy to even acknowledge receipt of my letter despite enlisting help from my MP and other coalition politicians (see enclosed).

I sincerely hope you and your committee will examine real life difficulties and handicaps of ordinary people who fervently believe in making significant contribution in various areas (see enclosed) but struggle to make progress because of a lack of resources, support and contacts.

I trust you will agree that the plight of ordinary people would give the Public Administration Committee an opportunity to recognise the underlying issues hindering social mobility and various other aspects of public organisations. It would enable the coalition government to address the failures of the big state approach with something positive and effective.

I look forward to your esteemed support. I fervently believe that my experience will unearth the real handicaps facing the Big Society when it comes to accessing the democratic process.

With best wishes in all your endeavors.

Yours most respectfully
encl.'

(33) Letter to Keith Vaz.

26 February 2011

'Dear Mr Vaz

Re: Real life difficulties of ordinary public from indigenous and ethnic backgrounds

I write again with great expectations as an esteemed senior politician with great experience to highlight the subtle underlying aspects of various issues affecting all ordinary people with a greater effect on ethnic people.

I write to you not with the intention ethnic people should be treated differently from the mainstream but far from it as evident from the enclosed letters.

I relate my experiences as a proud British citizen of Muslim ethnic background to give a real-life perspective for the need of proactive policies at no extra cost but savings to the tax payer instead of knee jerk reactive measures and appeasement politics of the coalition government.

I fully appreciate an MP can only make representations on behalf of the constituent but I am hoping you will appreciate (from the enclosed) the difficulties faced by ordinary people to access the democratic process despite following the right protocol to bring to the attention of my MP and other coalition politicians. My diligent efforts are non-political and based on sincere convictions for the good of the society as a whole.

I look forward to your esteemed support in your added capacity as the Chairman of Parliamentary Home Office Select Committee because of the interrelated nature of the issues e.g. multiculturalism letter which falls within the remit of your committee members including the obstacles faced by close families of ethnic British citizens to obtain family visit visas.

I wonder if you think it would be worth bringing to the attention of Ed Miliband. However, I am sceptical whether he will get to see my correspondence unless if it is from you as evident by the contemptuous attitude shown by the coalition politicians despite taking the trouble of writing to them (not even a decent courtesy to acknowledge letters).

I apologise for taking your valuable time and if it would possible to meet to discuss in detail.

Yours most respectfully'

(34) Letter to Jonathan Lord.

9 July 2011

'Dear Mr Lord

Re: Opportunity for the coalition government to deliver promised "New Politics" to restore public faith

Recent events relating to the diabolical phone hacking practices of the media affecting lives of ordinary families of murder victims and brave soldiers once again vindicates the daily real-life difficulties faced by ordinary people with no financial, legal, social mobility or media clout I have raised with your goodself.

It is welcoming that at the Press Conference on Friday 8 July, Mr Cameron promised better scrutiny and accountability amongst politicians, media and the police and to end during his watch the cosy relationships which all political parties have flouted over the last decades with detrimental consequences on the democracy and individual rights.

In light of the above and within the context of the promised "New Politics" agenda of the coalition government to deliver fairness, freedom and responsibility, I once again entreat you to give credence to my request to highlight the workings in public organisations.

I fervently believe it will unveil similar practices of collusion, wastage of public funds and malpractice at whatever cost by the top-heavy management of the CWGC with detrimental consequences on the lives of ordinary people with no financial, legal, social mobility and media clout.
I once again attach copy of my letter dated 18 Oct 2010 Re: Reply from Dr James-FCO Inquiry into the workings of the CWGC for your close perusal.

I look forward to your esteemed guidance and support on this occasion as you will appreciate it will unearth interesting findings into the workings of public organisations which will further enable the coalition government to deliver the "New Politics" agenda.

I am also sending this email to Mr Mark Pritchard MP because I believe that he is a conviction politician.

Kind regards.
Yours sincerely'

(35) Letter to Ed Miliband.

15 August 2011

'Dear Mr Miliband

Re: Recent Riots and the Proposed Inquiry by the Labour Party

It was refreshing to hear that you are of the opinion that an inquiry to get to the bottom of reasons of the recent deplorable riots and acts of criminality should take into consideration real life concerns outside the Westminster bubble of ordinary people with no financial, legal, lobbying, media or social clout instead of age old practices of relying on the evidence of the so called unaccountable "experts".

Since the general election, I have written to my MP on a number of issues some of them summarised in the enclose copies of the most recent letters dated 10 Aug, 25 July, 19 July and 26 June, highlighting concerns and handicaps of ordinary Plebs.

Unfortunately, instead of making representations on my behalf, I have been advised if I felt strongly I should either stand for elections or join protest groups or a note of my comments has been made by him.

I also approached Mr Cameron and various coalition politicians Messrs. Clegg, Gove and Hughes including the Speaker and Mr Andrew Neil and others. The Speaker's office advised he can't intervene under parliamentary rules, whereas Mr Clegg's secretary informed I will hear from DWP (basically passing the buck). Sadly, with deep regret others have not even bothered replying or acknowledging receipt.

I trust my experience, echoes your 14 Jan 2011 speech "reputation of politics at all time low" after Oldham East & Saddleworth by-election victory. Moreover, following Mr Coulson's resignation on 22 Jan 2011, it was reported it would be great loss to Mr Cameron because he enabled Mr Cameron to connect with ordinary people. But in reality, it would be more effective if politicians would listen and respond directly to the efforts of ordinary people. It is an irony in Mr Coulson's case despite warnings; Mr Cameron gave him a second chance, a perk not available to Plebs without contacts.

I sincerely hope you will get to see my letter. I fervently believe politicians should listen directly to Plebs and not be influenced entirely by powerful individuals with social mobility, financial, media, lobbying or legal clout.

Yours most respectfully'

(36) Letter to Jonathan Lord.

15 June 2012

'Dear Mr Lord

Re: Immigration Announcement by the Home Secretary

I write to your goodself as your constituent to register my concern with reference to the above announcement by the Home Secretary to the Parliament this week.

It is most welcoming that the Home Secretary is considering tough new rules on the subject of dependent's entry into the UK. However, I would entreat the government does not enforce a blanket ban with stringent financial limits on ALL dependents and includes provisions for bonafide dependents of British citizens on the grounds of the extended family responsibility.

You know I am an ardent supporter of the control of unscrupulous immigration based on a firm but fair policies; however it seems the above announcement of a blanket ban on dependents based on stringent financial limits to control net migration targets set by the government is most unfair for bonafide British Citizens who have fully embraced and contributed to the United Kingdom.

I hope you will make appropriate representations to register the above concerns.

Kind regards.
Yours most gratefully'

(37) Letter to Jonathan Lord.

22 January 2013

'Dear Mr Lord

Re: BBC Panorama on Illegal Immigration Monday 21 Jan 2013

Thank you for your letter of 19 December 2012 sharing my frustrations and listing visa statistics to justify government's stringent immigration policies are working.

With respect, I believe government's tough stance does not tackle bad immigration but penalise and deters good migration without addressing the backlog.

In reality, one sees an ever-increasing immigrant population of over stayers in towns up and down the country, who have violated <u>ALL</u> original visa terms but now granted leave to remain in the UK (an effective amnesty to tackle the backlog). The scams are also readily witnessed in various ethnic communities with resulting exploitation.

I hope you will appreciate that the statistics are misleading and meaningless because successive government policies have consistently failed to address illegal immigration and the resultant backlog of bogus asylum applications of over 450,000 (the actual number is 2-3 million).

The 2011 census showed that 13% of the population was born abroad. It is actually much more about 30% of the adults or parent(s) born abroad bearing in mind the 2011 census will not have counted bogus applicants and their families. It will be reflected in the 2021 census by which time it will be too late and the bogus applicants will have been legalised by the UKBA and slipped through the net.

Over past months, I have raised similar concerns highlighted by The BBC Panorama of the problems faced by UKBA because of "ghost" (bogus) immigrants with genuine asylum seekers forced underground. I appreciate separating bogus immigrants from genuine applicants is a test for any system. However, I fervently believe it can be addressed if approached with pragmatic cost-effective solutions and determination before it is too late.

I hope coalition politicians will listen to the concerns of ordinary people instead of treating them as bigots (Re: Mrs Gillian Duffy 2010 election) and heed solutions offered by the Plebs instead of only relying on "experts" and expensive public inquiries to learn lessons.

I look forward to hearing from you.
Yours sincerely'

(38) Letter to David Cameron and a copy to Jonathan Lord.

25 June 2013

'Dear Mr Prime Minster

Re: New Task Force in the Wake of the Murder of Drummer Lee Rigby

I apologise for taking up your valuable time to write in support of the Government announcement to set up a cabinet-level taskforce in wake of the senseless murder of Drummer Lee Rigby by bigots claiming to be "bastions" of religion and freedom.

I also fervently believe the perpetrators will be brought to justice something which the bigots are denied by their own "spiritual leaders" who don't blow themselves up and go to paradise or lead impoverished life.

I hope this time we make real progress by listening to the concerns and real-life experiences of ordinary people and not repeat mistakes of similar past initiatives. I have summarised the main points and impediments under the following broad headings for your kind attention and the new Task Force: -

Britain a Blessed Land – Facts Ethnic Leaders Must Acknowledge
The past and present history of the UK reflects a land of immigrant activity. The progress can be attributed directly to the fundamental goodwill, democracy and decency of Her Majesty's governments and the British people, together with what is salient about the vast majority of the ethnic people in terms of respecting the law, hard work, family values and enterprise.

Sadly, over the years, the goodwill of the British has been cruelly exploited by ethnic leaders. Just like the indigenous population, the daily life of the silent law abiding bonafide proud British Citizens of immigrant origin is equally affected by the infiltration of unscrupulous immigrants in their respective ethnic communities.

Yet, I remain very optimistic for my adopted country because whichever political party is in charge, the resolute British common-sense in the end seems to prevail. We are blessed with a sound democratic process and the Mother of all Parliaments. However, the ethnic communities and their leaders should not take the goodwill of the British for granted because there is a limit to how much pressure one can bottle.

Moreover, I passionately believe UK is a blessed land because of the freedom enjoyed by people of all persuasions religious or otherwise to practice their beliefs, and therefore no lasting harm will come to this uniquely blessed land of ours. We will overcome natural difficulties and always rise above man-made obstacles.

The UK is the best country in the world to live, work and study. There is of course always room for improvement, and as long as we recognise these lacunae in our society and communities, and we are prepared to address them, all will be well.

Transparency and Onus Squarely on Ethnic Leaders – No Appeasement Politics
Britain is a pluralistic society and leaders of ethnic communities must be made to take the responsibility to make sure the congregation understand to respect the law and culture of the land, no matter how baffling it may seem.

After all Britain is not asking ethnic leaders to change their religion, if anything allowing them to practice with greater freedom and civil rights than their respective countries of origin, and should not expect everyone else to agree with theirs. If they believe they have a divine right than they should practice their faith with greater transparency and not behind closed doors or scared of public scrutiny. There is room for all religions in this life without anyone having the outright authority to claim they have got it right and others are all wrong!

In fact, much of the blame lies with successive Governments because, in order to be politically correct, they have mollycoddled self-serving ethnic leaders and rich business people by bestowing honours and eminent positions on them to act as advisers or gatekeepers for ethnic communities. Governments of all persuasion need to get tough with pragmatic solutions by placing a firm onus on the ethnic leaders to put their house in order relating to all aspects of daily life in the UK.

Naïve politicians seem to think that if they just show traditional British tolerance and a good liberal approach, ethnic leaders will eventually become like-minded. But the word "liberal" is not in these people's vocabulary but regard tolerance as weakness, and in the process have taken undue advantage of such folly for their own agenda under the Charitable Status.

Less Reliance on Ethnic Leaders or Individuals with Loud Voices and/or money
Let us hope on this occasion the task force will not entirely rely on the input from ethnic leaders and business people with loud voices who have their own agenda but consider all aspects of interrelated underlying factors relating to ethnic communities.

The ethnic congregations discharge their obligations through their male dominated leaders. The real culprits are not the youngsters or the ill-educated, who are easily persuaded, but evil-minded controllers who remain at large, spreading their poison by feathering their own nests financially, comfortable lives, power and ego.

Community Structure and Charitable Status
The intricate workings of closed-door policy and sinister activities under the Charitable Status needs to be understood and regulated with diligence by enforcing onus on leaders to declare and justify all aspects of their religious ethos.

At present, under the shroud of Charity Status, leaders are exploiting loopholes by serving only close-knit communities whilst closing doors on those who do not conform even if they belong to the same community. The financial transactions and structure need to be examined with greater scrutiny by making leaders culpable for their actions in order to operate under a Charitable Status.

Awareness, Fear and Changing the Mindset of Ethnic Communities
I understand the main focus of the task force will investigate and introduce new ways or powers to hold mosque committees responsible and encourage whistle-blowers to alert police. I gather that the task force will hold Mosque committees to account for the choice of leaders they make and empower those attending religious services a route to express their concerns.

It is the right approach but in reality, it will not happen as envisaged unless the Task Force acquires a sound understanding and workings of the deeply rooted religious, social and cultural constraints of ordinary ethnic people. It will also help the Task Force alleviate and address other serious issues akin to ethnic community.

Quite rightly, focus should be at the grassroots in particular on Asian men because the Asian way of life still represents a male-dominated society. They do not want to mingle with the host community so their lives revolve round their own kind and conversation always comes back to religion. This is the mentality even among the most educated and business circle of eminent Asians.

Most Asian men and women live in fear of being ostracised and social stigma if they speak against the leadership because the role of ethnic leaders and priests has been cleverly choreographed. It is not just spiritual but also takes on a social leadership. It gives them enormous control and influence upon the minds of their congregation and the way in which they conduct themselves outside the confines of their communities making the congregation more dependent under the direct of few individuals.

Representation and Democratic Rights at Grassroots
I believe it is going to be a daunting undertaking by Task Force to rely at grassroots to make changes. In the past similar well-meant government initiatives have come to no fruition because the vast majority of the followers have no access and rely on the message conveyed by the community leaders and their cronies.

However, on a positive note it can be achieved if stringent regulations are imposed on respective communities to enforce compulsory representation of democratically elected Asian men and women in committees. It will also extend the important role of parenthood to prevent indoctrination of the innocent minds of their children by the religious male priests. The appointment of neutrally minded men and women from within and outside will prevent extremist activities. It is extremely important that the Task Force does not rely on the male dominated religious leaders to appoint self-serving individuals or cajole public to reflect transparency.

Abolish Use of Outdated term "Ethnic Communities"

I have often wondered as to why well-meaning Government initiatives directed towards ethnic people has prevented progress and hindered integration into the mainstream. Despite well-meant initiatives, certain ethnic sectors still continue to feel being treated as second class citizens.

It has been further exacerbated by stereotype prejudices by grown-ups in various neighbourhoods, workplaces etc, which then gets imprinted on the innocent minds of children. It is also equally important for the ethnic people to realise that it works both ways and by becoming an integral part of the UK, they will not get easily swayed or fall victims to the tiny minority with an unscrupulous agenda who either promote/ preach racial or religious hatred.

The natural forbearance of the British will put up with so much, but a day will come when indigenous British will say they have had enough and it is this that should concern the future generations and children of bonafide immigrants. The ethnic grassroots need to be on their guard and should come forward as they cannot sit back and say I am innocent.

It is important that all cultures become part of the mainstream based on mutual respect rather than alienating communities and cultures by setting up specific initiatives. For certain ethnic communities, it has done more harm than good and caused resentment within the mainstream population with consequential negative effects. We have to strive towards making the situation better so that common-sense prevails and various communities can exist in social harmony.

Interaction at grassroots to Enhance Civic Duty and Social Cohesion

Interaction at local levels between twinned churches, temples, synagogues and mosques would enhance civic responsibility of ethnic men and women in a wider society. The organising of interfaith community-based projects and social events would promote the importance of living in peace with others in pluralist Britain. It will bring local communities in the neighbourhood closer with a better tolerance and understanding of interfaith relationship and respect for each other's culture and religion instead of living in fear and suspicion of each other.

It will also help connect people from all walks of life and encourage professional men and women in the fields of education, business, health, current affairs and other areas to play an active role to engage in various debates to break existing barriers.

It would provide a platform for men and women to participate in voluntary projects at local levels on their door steps and thus overcome the attendance barrier because of work and other constraints. Such an approach would encourage ethnic communities to be part of the mainstream and benefit from the direct interaction with Christian and other neighbours.

Unscrupulous Immigration and consequences in failings of the defunct UKBA
Thousands on visitor, family, student and work permit short visit visas continue to stay illegally as economic migrants and go missing with no intention to return. In the process, they have established families with 1-2 children (in some case more) later when joined by spouses on similar visas.

The unscrupulous immigrants with support of their leaders find with ease refuge in ethnic communities with illegal paid or unpaid jobs and pay no taxes (a blatant violation of visa terms). They speak no English and later, with the help of lawyers and other associates apply for "political" asylum claiming persecution back home on the grounds of Human and Family Rights, and become eligible to bring dependents.

The Task Force requires an understanding of how Ethnic Communities with Charitable Status support and mobilise illegal immigrants despite punitive penalties imposed on landlords and employers. The tighter banking regulations are no deterrent to transfer money as they use various methods to circumvent regulation.

Another area of concern brewing over the past years is pregnant British Women married to foreign nationals who come to the UK for delivery. This has two-fold impact, firstly a drain on the NHS by foreigners not having paid British taxes and secondly, the children have secured British citizens rights.

The 2011 census showed 13% of the population was born abroad. It is actually much more about 30% bearing in mind the 2011 census will not have counted illegal immigrants and their families. It will be reflected in the 2021 census by which time it will be too late as they will have been granted leave to remain in the UK.

Increase in illegal immigrant numbers has become a regular feature witnessed in ethnic communities. It is ringing alarm bells of the future consequences and repercussions amongst proud ethnic British citizens families settled 20-60 years. In some cases, they are outnumbered and overpowered by the illegal immigrants who have taken a stranglehold of the amenities in certain ethnic communities.

Understandably, there has been a large increase in anti-Muslim incidents since 9/11 and recently after the murder of Drummer Lee Rigby. It has also fuelled anti-sentiments towards immigrants and led to the popularity of UKIP, EDL and BNP who are capitalising on unscrupulous immigration created by the defunct UKBA (United Kingdom Backlog Agency). I sympathise with the resentment of the indigenous population because as other like-minded immigrants I feel appalled by the rise in unscrupulous immigration and treacherous acts in the name of religion.

Concerns Raised Pre and Post 9/11
I had raised similar concerns relating to ethnic communities and unscrupulous immigration following 9/11 and 7/7 by writing to Mr Tony Blair and Mr Gordon Brown including various cross-party politicians. Unfortunately, Mr Blair's office at the time acknowledged that he receives about 4,000 letters weekly and I should not expect him to read my letters whereas, Mr Brown's office thanked me for writing to him. As you know I have also written to the Mr Cameron which I attach once again.

Despite well-meant initiatives from successive governments, certain sectors of the ethnic community continue to feel being treated as second class citizens, which at times has been exacerbated by stereotype prejudices by grown-ups in various neighbourhoods, workplaces etc, which then gets imprinted on the innocent minds of children. It is equally important for the ethnic people to realise that it works both ways and by becoming an integral part of the UK, they will not get easily swayed or fall victims to the tiny minority with an unscrupulous agenda who promote and preach racial or religious hatred.

A Need for Specific Policy Objectives for Community Cohesion and Harmony:
- To encourage ethnic communities to be proud British Citizens
- To overcome prejudice in public life e.g. government departments
- To project ethnic communities in a positive way and not stereotyped manner
- To overcome and prevent radicalisation of young British born Muslims
- To address the problem of illegal and unscrupulous immigration
- To address the reasons for failure of good past government policies/initiatives
- Religious schools and education curriculum
- Recognition of ethnic professional women and men

I have spent significant thought and time on the above, and hope you will bring it to the attention of the Task Force and use in your deliberations with colleagues. I do not claim it is the panacea or a magic bullet to solve all difficulties but observations are drawn from real life to address issues faced by the society at large.

Please let me know if I can be of further help to the Task Force so we make real progress and prevent future atrocities and suffering.

I look forward to hearing from you.
Kind regards.

Yours most sincerely
cc. Jonathan Lord'

(39) Letter to David Wayne.

18 July 2013

'Dear Mr Wayne

Re: PMQ 17 July 2013 - Experience Shared by Ordinary People

I am not your constituent but I write to share similar real life experience raised by your goodself at PMQ on 17 July 2013 bearing in mind if an elected MP is treated with contempt by Mr Cameron, what hope ordinary people with no financial, media and influential clout can have or expect from cross party politicians and government advisers.

I had written to Mr David Cameron in the first instance on 30 July 2010, and to-date as a matter of common courtesy not even received an acknowledgement from his Office despite many subsequent attempts bringing to the attention of my own MP, Mr Jonathan Lord.

I also hasten to add that I have written to Mr Ed Miliband and just like Mr Cameron I have not heard from him. I have also written to Mr Blair and Mr Brown. At least, Mr Blair's Office politely informed me after a number of attempts that Mr Blair receives about 4,000 letters a week and I should not expect him to read all correspondence and Mr Brown's Office just thanked me for writing to him. I wonder whether I would have been ignored by Messrs Cameron, Blair, Brown and Miliband if I was wealthy financial donor?

I believe there are number of underlying obstacles and difficulties faced by ordinary people (Plebs) to get heard because modern day democracy entitles easy representation and access for those with financial, media (loud voices) and lobbying clout including friends and family contacts in high places.

I am also copying this e-mail to my own MP to give credibility I am not making it up, and also in case it is of any use in your deliberations with politicians with similar convictions who believe in the common good of the country and not only the privileged few.

Yours sincerely',

(40) Reply from David Wayne.

19 July 2013

Dear Dr Akberali

Thank you for your email.

I must say that I found the Prime Minister's failure to reply to the family of the blind couple particularly bad because he previously promised to examine all such bedroom tax cases.

Keep on trying.
Sincerely'.

(41) Letter to Jonathan Lord.

26 July 2013

'Dear Mr Lord

Re: Government's Illegal Immigrant Billboard Campaign

I write to raise concerns as your constituent and a bonafide British Citizen of "ethnic" origin with reference to the Home Office's decision to drive vans around London warning illegal immigrants to "go home or face arrest".

It is a cheap political stunt by the Government to appease a small proportion of voters away from UKIP, BNP or EDL by pretending we're doing something about illegal immigration, and in the process will lose chunks of indigenous and "ethnic" voters who will not be fooled by such cheap stunts.

The recent political gimmick is nasty and unpleasant politics of divide and rule at the expense of bonafide British Citizens like me and their children. It will only serve to cause more daily racial tension, hatred and abuse for law abiding "ethnic" individuals and their families at work place, schools, neighborhoods and public places.

These billboards must be dismantled and shredded quickly, and Government Ministers should listen to the real-life concerns and experiences of genuine British Citizens if serious about tackling illegal immigration and radicalisation. The proposed plan is disproportionate, distasteful and ineffective way to do it except it will further exacerbate social cohesion.

I don't believe using such messages will tackle illegal immigration despite assurances by Immigration Minister Mr Harper. It shows the Government has no understanding of the underlying problems and consequences or a coherent plan of action. Moreover, the proposed plan has one or two inherent problems and will take a long time. For example, official estimated illegal immigrants in the UK are 570,000 (in fact it is 1-2 million) and it will take a long time to make them aware or make arrests with two poster vans and dwindling number of Police Officers. I hasten to add we see continued increase in various ethnic communities of illegal immigrants despite recent strict immigration rules.

If Mr Harper and the Government is really concerned about tackling illegal immigration and promote social harmony then I implore him to listen to practical initiatives suggested to you on a number of previous occasions including points recently raised in my email of 25 June 2013 with reference to "the New Task Force in the Wake of the Murder of Drummer Lee Rigby".

I look forward to hearing from you and hope the Government will listen to the concerns of ordinary people based on real life experiences.

Kind regards.
Yours sincerely',

(42) Letter to Priti Patel.

27 March 2014

'Dear Ms Patel

Re: Newsagents and Monopolistic Newspaper Wholesale Distribution

I write to your goodself with reference to the above.

It is refreshing to hear on the news today that a Member of Parliament is willing to raise concerns pertaining to the everyday lives of ordinary voiceless people.

For years, Newsagents and their families have worked tirelessly unsociable hours for pittance, cheap slave labour, victims of crime and abuse, depriving them control of their commercial destiny because of an archaic wholesale distribution contravening all the basic principles of free market and competition.

In the 1990s, a certain section of the newsagents led a number of initiatives to highlight the actual realities faced by the newsagents. We led a number of successful campaigns with conservative and cross-party politicians. Unfortunately, it did not address the main problems concerning the newspaper wholesale distribution because of the powerful position enjoyed by the wholesalers.

An inquiry to get to the bottom of the monopolistic practices is long overdue as it undermines the basic commercial viability and family life of the newsagent. It is also an important small family business sector providing significant employment for hundreds of thousands of individuals (owners, family members and public).

I have significant evidence to highlight the actual practices of the monopolistic wholesale newspaper industry affecting the profits and lives of newsagents. It will be of great help in your campaign deliberations into the workings of wholesalers

I fervently believe my experience echoes your convictions and politicians need to listen directly to ordinary people and not be influenced entirely by powerful individuals with social mobility, financial, media, lobbying or legal clout.

I wish you success in your campaign which is long overdue. It will also raise the election profile of the conservative party.

Yours most respectfully',

(43) Reply from Priti Patel.

10 April 2014

'Dear Dr Akberali,

"Thank you very much for your email regarding the recent debate I initiated in the Parliament on the news supply trade.
I am grateful for your interest in this matter and would be very interested to review evidence you have gathered in relation to the wholesalers.

During the course of the debate, the Minister who responded suggested that new Competition and Markets Authority could re-investigate this issue and any you have may assist them to make this decision."

Yours sincerely,

With all good wishes' (written and signed personally)

(44) My reply to Priti Patel.
'Your Ref: W126662   24 April 2014

Dear Ms Patel

Re: Newsagents and Monopolistic Newspaper Wholesale Distribution

"Thank you kindly for the e-mail attachment of 10 April 2014 confirming your keen interest to review the evidence concerning the above.

I hope you will appreciate it would be impractical to address the significant volume of incriminating evidence in my possession entirely through correspondence.

The sensitive evidence was gathered over a period of time based on meticulous research as I felt I was going senile by wholesaler's antics of persistent unresolved invoicing errors relating to newspapers/ magazines returns credits.

Initially, it was like looking for a needle in a haystack but with perseverance I put in place a monitoring system to establish a clear link between visible/invisible administration and accounting errors encompassing vital areas with financial consequences on profit margins.

In the absence of formal contracts including legal or compensation redress within the "Newspaper Code of Practice" of 1990s, wholesalers enjoy a unique monopoly making healthy profits at newsagent's expense, and unlike energy consumers newsagents have no option to switch to another wholesaler for better service.

The wholesalers will refute the evidence as historical with claims they are operating a more efficient system. I have extreme doubts because in 2009/2010 I had an opportunity to examine various aspects of wholesale distribution. Despite cosmetic changes, the core accounting system remains susceptible to similar errors.

I look forward to your esteem guidance as to the best possible course to divulge information with safeguards to protect intellectual property of the evidence gathered using personal initiative."

With all good wishes.
Yours most gratefully'

(45) Follow-up letter to Priti Patel.

16 July 2014

'Dear Ms Patel

Re: Newsagents and Monopolistic Newspaper Wholesale Distribution

"It is with deep regret after waiting nearly three months; I have not received as a matter of courtesy even an acknowledgement of receipt of my letter if nothing else.

I hope you will not use the excuse of receiving hundreds of letters from constituents whilst presiding over a busy schedule following recent Cabinet reshuffle. Plebs also lead busy lives but have common courtesy to reply. I wonder if a rich party donor, a celebrity or a powerful lobby group would have been treated with similar contempt.

I took the trouble in the first instance to phone your Office to commend on the above initiative of yours, a national issue confined not only to a certain section of society.

Acting on advice from Benjamin, I wrote to you in my own time incurring costs as unlike MPs, I am not eligible to claim expenses. I took further trouble to provide information in my letter of 24 April 2014 as requested by your goodself.

I gave you the benefit of doubt and believed you shared concerns of ordinary people. The wider public look up to politicians as icons with paragons of virtues, whether traditional or "British" to uphold standards with a modicum of courtesy. I feel a fool for thinking that those who seek to run our country would seriously allow Plebs with no financial, media or lobbying clout to be a part of the process.

I believe your other weekly Radio announcements, PMQs and TV appearances are a bandwagon of sound bites seen to be doing something to entice Plebe votes and not genuine concern for their well-being.

It is the main reason why Newsagents face unresolved monopolistic practices enjoyed by wholesalers for the last 40 years with powerful lobbying and media clout including incestuous elite friends in high places.

Is it any wonder the chairman of the Committee on Standards in Public Life warned the Prime Minister to make sure politicians are aware of their duties to be honest, open, accountable and selfless or face lack of public trust and disenchantment with Westminster village politics and star struck politicians?

I hope you will understand why I feel aggrieved and insulted. I wish you well in your endeavours and now as a Minister not further disconnect with ordinary people."

Yours sincerely',

(46) Letter to the BBC on-line, national newspapers, cross-party politicians.

21 August 2014

'Dear

Re: Why a Sudden Unfolding of Crises in Iraq and Elsewhere? – An urgent need for political and diplomatic solutions, not greed and double standards

Further to my letter dated 5 August 2014, I write once again to your goodself with reference to the above under the following broad interrelated headings as it is not just a Muslim but humanitarian and international responsibility.

Nobody can fail to have been affected by the lugubrious TV images witnessed in Gaza, Syria, Iraq, Central African States, Ruanda, Ukraine, Burma, stranded Yazidis and other forgotten persecution of people in Sri Lanka, Kashmir or elsewhere, and now the appalling murder of James Foley.

The actions of ISIS and Israel are both wrong. One is a so-called democratic state unless you're an Arab and the other is a non- legal caliphate stealing land much the same as the West did in creating many Arab states in 1918, and with influential Jewish lobby creating Israel in 1948 which was Palestine. It is only a question of time; a bigger bully will come along. The US is looking to the Pacific not Europe, with China and Russia as big issues so Israel support won't be too high on US agenda.

If we are really serious calling ourselves a "civilised" race, and want to leave a better legacy for future generations, then it is about time cross party politicians took practical initiatives to end the cycle of crises witnessed after the illegal Iraq war by focussing on the following main root causes namely arm sales, a vacuum in coherent foreign policy, double standards and greed.

Peace would be possible if only the USA , UK and other arm producing countries stopped fomenting discord and conflict with direct or indirect sale of arms.

Let us not tarnish Islam as a Faith of Evil Radicalised Muslims and Terrorists
It is important to understand the extreme pain suffered directly or indirectly by ordinary law abiding Muslims in the Middle East and worldwide in witnessing vile actions of certain dictators, countries, dissidents, or Kingdoms, deploying arms

supplied by the "civilised" world to boost export trade, inconsistent Foreign policies, greed and double standards, and the relentless derogatory persecution of the Faith of Islam with negative tabloid headlines and TV coverage.

It is not Islam but the above factors playing a vital part in the rise of home-grown and other bigots prophesying Caliphate rule and conducting atrocities in the name of Islam, referred as radicalised Muslims by a disingenuous coined Western label, as Islam derived from Arabic root Arabic "Salema" means Peace.

In addition, the other root causes for the rise in dissidents waging atrocities in the name of Islam was the illegal Iraq war to depose Saddam Hussein under false pretences, incidentally coming to prominence during Iran/Iraq war blessed with US and UK support, not forgetting the role US played in the origins and rise of Al-Qaeda during the Soviet invasion of Afghanistan for self-serving interests.

Equally, it is important not to give dissidents or countries Islamic status, as they have no direct mandate of Muslims worldwide to act as custodians of Islam. The leaders of dissidents, countries and Kingdoms have their own political, financial and egoistic agenda, whilst innocent Muslims suffer consequences of the lethal arsenal getting into the hands of the dissidents from countries supplied by US and Britain, and then trickling into hands of the wider population with more suffering.

Britain has now adopted Kurds and decided to arm them. Let us sincerely hope, we are not stoking future crisis with short term solutions, and today's friend will become tomorrow's foe stigmatised by the West, Fox news and tabloid media as Radicalised Islamic Jihadists Terrorist Kurdish State (RIJTKS) once our short term interests are served, just as Assad, Saddam, Bin Laden, Mubarak, Amin, Mugabe etc enjoyed similar US and UK support, except Israel who seems to be doing nothing wrong.

We cannot condone actions of Saddam or dissidents; equally we need to condemn illegal actions of elected politicians. It would placate the situation, if Mr Blair admitted he got it wrong with the Iraq war. Instead, to add salt to injury, now Mr Blair as a Middle East peace envoy, struts around lecturing peace, perhaps advising leaders with colossal fees to buy more arms. It is just like handing keys to Mr Bush to protect world oil reserves, or Israel and dissidents to act as custodians of lethal arsenal.

In the West, we boast virtues of democracy, fairness, human rights, justice and press freedom. Now we see the very press and powerful lobby groups with financial and political clout in the US, Britain or Israel waging propaganda war affecting lives of ordinary Muslims for self-serving interests.

The silent majority of ordinary Muslim people feel unrepresented by what is not being said or done in the name of Islam; and do not want to feel disenfranchised. They too are concerned by growing anti-Islam sentiments, worried when criticism of the faith slips into the rhetoric that makes gross and distorted comparisons between the faith and motives of various dissidents as universally accepted by all Muslims.

But they also do not believe that criticism of the activities of dissidents is necessarily anti-Islam. They want to discuss the Middle East, Palestine crises and the massacre inflicted on civilians by Israel, its rights and wrongs, not because they do not believe Israel has a right to defend its citizens, but because they believe a global issue that impacts everyone and is worthy of a discussion and debate. They might vehemently disagree with the actions of dissidents, but they do not only want to talk about how to punish them. They also want to work out how the community can get behind peace, they want to know, in the aftermath of this bloody conflict, how they can speak up and support the voices of moderation on all sides of this conflict. But they know this will not be the topic of conversation, and therefore do not come forward as their voices are not heard. And the cycle of silence continues.

Vast majority of Muslims and wider British public is committed to create a society - one that respects differences of opinion, religious freedom and peace - we all have a job to do. Those invested in various conflicts, from whatever perspective they come, need to stand up, in partnership for which there is never an excuse. But we, need to take responsibility for saying what is not being said and stop double dealings. The war we must fight is one that bridges divides, forges new paths to peace, speaks up in support to bring the security, self-determination and peace which Palestinians and others deserve, and questions behaviour of ALL parties that will not. It will require Britain and others including   religious and community leaders to be feisty and brave in their convictions: to say the things we don't say.

Colonial Legacy and Present Crisis
Historians regard the 20th century as the most cataclysmic in the history of mankind because for the first time the entire population of the world was affected directly or indirectly by two world wars, one after another, that changed the face of civilisation.

The West would never be the same again but neither would the Third World. Soon after the colonial empire dissolved, the world was engaged in the storm of rage, confusion and uprisings. For Europe, practically centuries of complacency and supremacy were shattered. Suddenly alone, the Third World found equally hard to manage and embrace alien ideologies of democracy and Western concepts. The World could no longer be regarded as one single idea, one right colonial standard, and all other differences, mere uncivilised native discrepancies.

After the 1st World War which saw a senseless slaughter of young men by overrated politicians, diplomats and generals, Britain and France created a false empire of pro- Western countries, oil flawed and Arabs sold it to the West. Then we had 2nd world War, Palestinians were sold to the Israelis, the cause of the present Middle East.

The West, sold weapons to unelected tyrants and murderers in Syria, Saudi, Iraq, Iran, Gulf States without any democracy or basic human rights, with no ethical care but just greed for oil and export revenue from the sale of weapons: divided races and faiths because of the stupidity and ego of greedy Arab leaders unable to work it out. The tyrants then started funding conflicts and dissents in the name of Islam.

The illegal Iraq war also reinforced the perception that US - and often the UK too - display double standards when it comes to upholding the rule of law internationally. Those allegations have particular force on the Israel-Palestine issue.

Some of the chaos, we see in parts of the world, is partly a legacy of colonisation, the history of how colonisation displaced local cultures, leaving people culturally, and therefore intellectually as exploited and bereft as the resources of the lands they belonged. In addition, National boundaries were drawn hastily for quick exit strategy and convenience - later in Iraq and Afghanistan - based on geographical landmarks and in some cases plain straight lines. The West Indies seems to be the only part of Third World to escape unscathed from consequences of colonial boundary changes.

It would be naive to claim conflicts did not occur previously, and present or future crises can all be attributed to our colonial past. We have had millennia of crusades, conflicts and two World Wars, without whole races and faiths getting stigmatised as radicalised Christian, Fascist or Zionist terrorists.

However, present day crises are self-inflicted with third party interference and double standards, supporting groups or leaders for self-serving interest, and unlike the instigators of Crusader, Northern Ireland and two World Wars conflicts tarnishing a whole swathe of innocent followers as radicalised Muslims, terrorists and jihadist.

<u>A New Legacy of the Superpowers – Arm Sales, Conflicts, Crises and Aid</u>

In the later part of the 20th century, unlike direct colonisation by Britain, France and others, the World witnessed US and Russia embarking on cold war to gain entry into history books as superior powers by supplying lethal arsenal of weapons to various Third World states including Israel, causing further pain, hardship and genocide.

The world has seen events where not a single corner has escaped the lethal effects of arms inflicting pain and suffering; bearing in mind majority countries were past colonies whose leaders gained power through military coup or dodgy elections with Western support. If a Third World War happens, early beginnings seen in other forms; it will be the double standards of US administration acting as world policeman, maybe US wants to make sure this time they are on time by starting it.

In US and Britain, democracy has been hijacked by strong lobby groups with financial clout. Baron Rothschild in the nineteenth century said "he cared not who was elected to power in the UK. Whoever controls the money controls the British Empire and I (Rothschild) control the money". So, for centuries faceless moneymen have been running the show once politicians get elected with their money. In reality, the money men pull the strings and world leaders just obeying their masters.

US gave the world following narrative for the devastation of Gaza; namely "Hamas is a radicalised Islamic terrorist organization". For US, any person or organisation resisting injustice is worthy of this label. The late Nelson Mandela and the ANC in their resistance to racial apartheid were labeled by the West including late Baroness Thatcher, as terrorist. After Mandela, now revered by the West, became President and earned the Nobel award, US still had him on their terrorist list.

Another US narrative "Israel has the right to defend itself". The US is referring to the obsolete rockets with the effectiveness of a £2.99 Chinese Guy Fawkes fire crackers sent by understandably angry cave dwellers. It beggars belief as to how US sees the devastation of entire Palestinian communities and infrastructure as "Israel defending itself". Israel armed with these narratives and regular supplies of the most lethal arsenal from the US has embarked on one of the worst genocidal mission against the defenceless Palestinians in Gaza.

Gaza is boxed with no help from neighbouring countries. Britain helped to form Israel with similar destruction of mosques and civilians decades ago, and millions of tax payer's money handed over to Israel in foreign aid sponsoring their unrelenting push to take the entire region.Britain and US are guilty of arming Israel to the teeth with state-of-the-art military hardware to commit genocide and screaming "Israel has the right to defend themselves" whilst being fed by the tabloid media and Fox news.

International Role of Britain to end Illegal Sale of Arms by Warmongers

The clock on our colonial legacy cannot be turned back but it is vital efforts are ramped up with practical initiatives. With unfolding of Humanitarian disasters, we cannot afford to turn a blind eye to the root causes, namely sale of lethal weapons to countries supporting dissidents including Israel claiming to defend its borders.

With Britain's unique position in the UN, EU, NATO, Commonwealth, G7, G20, IMF, and more importantly the "Special Relationship" enjoyed with US, not only when it suits Americans, the UK can play a constructive role as an honest broker and galvanise countries involved in the manufacture and sale of lethal arsenal.

The real test for politicians and Parliamentary Select Committees is to set the hearts and minds to explore enforcement of a watertight International protocol or treaty. It should involve ALL major and secondary arms manufacturing countries in order to regulate strict sale of arms, purpose, monitoring actual end users and abolish illegal arms trade and deal violations with serious consequences. It has been possible to charge Nazis for heinous war crimes after 60 years, so it would be possible for it to work with a water tight treaty and willingness of International players. It will expose the ulterior motives of unwilling countries and dealt accordingly with sanctions.

Also, a coherent foreign policy, and not mantra or double standards should be declared and adhered by the West with specific reference to the Israel/Palestine situation. The West stopping sale of arms used by Israel to massacre innocent civilians and children would be a good starting point to restore faith in democracy and fairness. Similar restrictions imposed on other players in the region will be easy to enforce, unlike Israel most have no capability to manufacture and rely on imports. Any stockpile of weapons used by unscrupulous parties whilst various mechanisms and initiatives are taking shape should be dealt by International force, including making sure Israel does not capitalise from its superior arsenal.

A peaceful settlement was achieved in Northern Ireland when the mainland was bombed by the IRA through disarmament. It beggars belief as to why similar initiatives with right intentions, protocols and convictions cannot be achieved?

Let us give Peace a Real Chance – Stop Arm Sales and Quagmire of Crises

For a start, let us consider ending all illegal sales of arms and restrict export of legal sale of lethal weapons by the US, Britain, Russia, China...... including under the radar supply routes from other secondary countries namely Israel, Iran, India, Pakistan......relying directly or indirectly on technology from the major manufactures.

It is understandable the extreme reluctance of major arms producing countries not to engage as the export of arms and technology components constitutes a significant part of exports, employment and profits for shareholders. However, other successful economies have shown it is possible to export other commodities without too much dependence on the export sale of arms.

Let us ask ourselves whether it is "civilised", moral and humanitarian to export arms on one hand to inflict hardship and genocide on ordinary civilian lives, and provide foreign aid in millions as a humanitarian cause to keep a clear conscience. In addition, leaders and dictators of developing countries are encouraged to spend millions on arms with deals brokered by warmongers and "civilised" politicians, money which can be spent usefully to end starvation, ill health, disease, illiteracy and provide other opportunities for ordinary citizens to lead a dignified life.

The solution if we are to survive as "civilised" mankind is not to seize and squander resources of which we are not owners but custodians. Our curse has been, as Dwight Eisenhower had warned in his valedictorian presidential speech to American people in 1960, our submission to the military – industrial (financial and political) complex which profits prodigiously from confrontations, whether at the level of wars or that of unrest in the streets. The collusion of governments with the said complex distracts us from what exactly ails humanity.

Millions of people worldwide face the ultimate direct or indirect economic, education, social, health, immigration, cultural, terrorist and genocidal consequences of policies and actions of politicians, religious and rich elite ruling classes in their quest for power and greed to gain supremacy as legitimate means to propagate ideologies.
If only US and Britain would be forthright in applying sanctions to Israel and unelected rulers as they are to Russia's action in the Ukraine – affecting ordinary people, but not rich Russians willing to pay for a tennis match with David Cameron and Boris Johnson - only then we will have peace in the Middle East and elsewhere.

It may seem farfetched or naive, but we need to stop sending arms, as it has far reaching economic and other benefits instead of short-term gains. It's the only way to force them to talk in earnest for a peaceful settlement. As Philosopher Plato said "good actions give strength to inspire ourselves and inspire good actions in others.

I hope the above will be of use in your deliberations with cross party parliamentary colleagues and look forward to hearing your views."

With Kindest Regards.

Yours most sincerely',

(47) Reply on behalf of Sir Ming Campbell.

2 September 2014

'Dear Dr Akberali,

Sir Menzies has asked me to thank you for your e-mail which he has read with interest and which he will keep in mind when the issues are discussed in Parliament."

Donald Lothian
Constituency Assistant'

(48) Second follow-up letter to Priti Patel.

4 September 2014

'Dear Ms Patel

Re: A lack of courtesy to acknowledge receipt of letter dated 24 April 2014

"As I have not heard further from your goodself, David Leaf or Chris Albinson, I sense you agree I am vindicated by the contents of my letter of 16 July 2014.

A lack of response justifies that you or your office did not have a common courtesy to reply despite a curt attempt by David Leaf in his e-mail of 16 July 2014 to wriggle out by referring to the wrong correspondence dated 10 April 2014 as reply from you to my letter of 24 April 2014.

I felt pumped for a while as I thought you were a conviction politician. I gave you the benefit of doubt, and took the trouble to write to you in my own time and expense.
But it is a shame, I was wrong in thinking the political class are actually concerned with Plebe's views and well-being. It confirms public's perception of Westminster politicians as self-serving, meaningless and interchangeable class, as highlighted in the report to the Prime Minister by Lord Bew, Chairman of Standards in Public Life.

I suppose following your ministerial appointment, now it is most unlikely you will be forthright in your weekly announcements, as you will be more occupied addressing interests of lobby groups with financial clout so as not to rock the boat, and the newspaper wholesale monopoly will continue to reign at newsagent's expense.

I hope I am not being unreasonable. I trust you will understand why I feel aggrieved and insulted for the lack of common courtesy to acknowledge my letter of 24 April 2014 when I took the trouble to write in good faith at your own request.

Yours sincerely',

(49) Letter to Jonathan Lord.

20 January 2015

'Dear Mr Lord

Re: Voice of Reason and Concerns of Ordinary Muslims

I write to your goodself as a proud British citizen in the wake of Mr Eric Pickles' letter to Islamic leaders that they "had more work to do to root our extremists".

Mr Cameron says "everybody needs to help tackle the problem of radicalisation". But sadly, Mr Cameron or his office has no appetite or time to listen to the voice of ordinary people or as matter of common courtesy even acknowledge letters.

I once again attach letter addressed to Mr Cameron dated 30 July 2010 and 25 June 2013 highlighting underlying issues relating to the radicalisation and ethnic people.

Like minded ordinary British Muslim families do not subscribe to the despicable acts carried out in the name of Islam. But we are extremely worried and scared of going about our normal lives in schools, neighbourhood or place of work by being singled out as radicalised Muslims. In reality, such tactics are not defying the terrorists or addressing radicalisation but playing into the bloodstained hands of terrorists and the right-wing bigots by dividing and demonising as US and THEM.
Also, it is double standards when it comes to "free" speech and press including immigration rules when it suits politicians?

For example, Mr Cameron and Miliband have appointed foreign nationals Mr Crosby and Axelrod as election "gurus" affecting net migration. Presumably, appointments were conducted after exhaustive search for suitable British candidates as stipulated under the Immigration Rules which applies to ordinary people? Is it also in the spirit of the cherished values of "free" press when Mr Cameron dictates who should participate in the TV debates when the independent regulator has applied the rules?

I look forward to hearing from you of the concerns ignored years ago. Instead of vilifying certain sectors of society when things go wrong, Mr Cameron should occasionally listen to the concerns of ordinary people and not just chosen rich elite. Moreover, on a lighter note, Muslims do not spend all their time praying as depicted in the 'free' press.

With kindest regards.
Yours sincerely'

(50) Letter to Theresa May and a copy to Jonathan Lord.

14 July 2016

'Dear Prime Minister,

I write to convey heartfelt congratulations on your well-deserved appointment as the Prime Minister of our beloved country and accepting Her Majesty The Queen's invitation to form a new Government.

Your speech was moving, full of political convictions and vision eloquently based on the true meaning of the "Conservative and Unionist Party", and your belief "in a union not just between the nations of the UK but between all of our citizens - every one of us - whoever we are and wherever we're from".

I am a proud British Citizen of ethnic origin and your vision gives hope and fairness for the good of all the people irrespective of creed, class and race. I regard myself fortunate to call the great country UK my home because British people have good virtues. However, we cannot afford to take past and recent events for granted to threaten harmony in our multicultural society and British way of life.

I believe over the past years, multi-million-pound grants available to ethnic communities have unfortunately been wasted and not achieved desired objectives. Instead, it has rightly fueled anger and resentment amongst the indigenous people, causing alienation further exacerbated with grown-up stereotype prejudices in the neighbourhoods and workplaces amidst the minority which then gets imprinted on the innocent minds of children and future generations.

Moreover, despite well-meant initiatives from successive governments, sectors of ethnic people feel treated as second class citizens. However, it is equally important for ethnic communities to realise that it works both ways and by becoming an integral part of the UK, they will not get easily swayed or fall victims to the tiny minority with an unscrupulous agenda who promote and preach racial, political or religious hatred.

I think it is because in the past, too much emphasis has been placed on the politics of spin, sofa style leadership, appeasement and reliance on individuals claiming to be bastions of ethnic communities and not taking on board experiences of ordinary people leading everyday life.

Finally, I wish you well in all your endeavours and pray to God to give you strength and vision for the good of all the people to lead a prosperous life in peace for the good of humanity in the UK, the Commonwealth and worldwide.

I hope as a proud British citizen, I am given an opportunity to make practical contributions based on real life experience.

Yours most respectfully
cc. Jonathan Lord MP'

(51) Reply from the Direct Communications Unit with a rubber stamp signature.

19 August 2016

'Dear Dr Akberali

I am writing on behalf of the Prime Minister to thank you for your letter of 14 July.

Mrs May very much appreciates the time you have taken to write to her.

As the department for Communities and local government has responsibility for the matters you raise, I am forwarding your letter to them so that they are aware of your views.

Thank you once again, for writing.

Yours sincerely
Correspondence Officer'

(52) Letter to Prime Minister Theresa May and a copy to Jonathan Lord.

28 August 2016

'Dear Mrs May

Re: Launch of Race Audit of Public Services on 27 August 2016

Thank you kindly for the reply received on your behalf from The Direct Communications Unit dated 14 July 2016.

Further to my recent letter, I again sincerely apologise for taking the liberty to encroach on your valuable time by writing with reference to the above aptly timed launch.

I hope on this occasion valuable contributions from ordinary people from all backgrounds leading everyday life will be heard and allowed to engage unlike your three predecessors except during the Premiership of Sir John Major when The Direct Communications Unit did not even have the courtesy to acknowledge correspondence.

In the recent past, it has become the norm and fashionable to address concerns with complex expensive approach and close sofa-style leadership to absolve responsibilities instead of open simple less expensive accountable pragmatic approach. Over the years, multi-million-pound grants made available to enhance social mobility and integration have been squandered and failed to achieve the desired objectives. Instead, it has fuelled anger and resentment amongst hard working people, and alienated communities even further.

We need a pragmatic approach which will not only tackle radicalisation, Islamophobia, discrimination...but engage communities at grassroots level so as not to get swayed or dictated easily by individuals or organisations with their own agenda acting as gatekeepers.

I believe personal efforts over the years highlighting concerns are directly or indirectly interrelated within the context of the Race Audit in the following areas: -

- It will tackle forced marriages, women's rights and misuse/abuse of Sharia teachings.
- It confronts tax evasion/investment/money laundering and abuse of charitable status.
- It will encourage ethnic people to be proud British citizens and galvanise those from the Commonwealth countries as obvious partners of choice to trade following Brexit.
- It will alleviate unscrupulous immigration and misuse of public services.
- It will prevent radicalisation not only of young British born Muslims but also from other faiths including right wing extremism; and overcome subtle prejudice, second class status, stereotyping and discrimination in public sector, schools, streets, workplace...
- It places focus on policies based on practical non-patronising initiatives with less bureaucracy and red tape to encourage direct involvement into mainstream life and civic duty with less reliance on unscrupulous people. Initiatives for ethnic people would be better served if incorporated when formulating main policies and not in isolation or politics of appeasement as an afterthought.
- It emphasises significant past and present contributions made in various fields by ethnic people and what brings us together with less emphasis on what divides us.

Obviously, the above is a salient summary of points which needs to be developed with substance to realise desired objectives by asking honest questions so we can get to the reasons which undermines social cohesion and social mobility, and find solutions not only within the context of ethnic Muslims but all communities irrespective of race, creed or class.

Recent events are threatening the true harmony of our multicultural society and British way of life and we cannot afford to be complacent or take things for granted. The vast majority of the ethnic people are decent law-abiding and hardworking citizens with strong family and conservative values but like everything else, irrespective of one's background, we need to protect ourselves from bigots determined to create problems for us all. We feel encouraged by the launch of the

Race Audit by you and hope with a comprehensive plan it will come to fruition not like past inquiries when it was common to brush findings under the carpet to learn lessons and repeat the same old expensive mistakes with the same consequences.

I passionately believe you as our Prime Minister with strong political and leadership convictions will succeed further to achieve social equality, sexual violence, hate crime, social mobility, tackle gender discrimination, refugee crises, corporate corruption, exploitation of vulnerable workers, Islamophobia.... than your male predecessors.

On a lighter note, *Eid-ul-Adha* falls on 9 Sept, and hope like everything else it is not the fault of ordinary Muslims for the coincidence for Mr Donald Trump to come out and say: dem mozlems are celebrating 9/11.

I look forward to hearing from you.

Yours most respectfully
cc. Mr Jonathan Lord MP'

(53) Reply from the Direct Communications Unit with a rubber stamp signature.

20 September 2016

'Dear Dr Akberali

I am writing on behalf of the Prime Minister to thank you for your letter of 28 August.

Mrs May very much appreciates the time you have taken to write to her.

As the Cabinet Office has responsibility for the matter you raise, I am forwarding your letter to them so that they are aware of your views.

Thank you, once again, for your writing.

Yours sincerely
Correspondence Officer'

(54) Letter to Prime Minister Theresa May and a copy to Jonathan Lord.

14 October 2016

'Dear Mrs May

I have written to your goodself on three separate occasions with reference to your Prime Ministerial appointment, "Islamophobia, Radicalised Muslims and Islamist Terrorist – A Disingenuous Label" and "Launch of Race Audit of Public Services".

I am pleased to say despite standard "band aid" generic response, I am grateful to have at least received replies thanking on your behalf from the Communications Unit stating letters have been forwarded to the relevant Departments. I have received the expected standard "band aid" generic reply highlighting initiatives by the DCLG and further information can be obtained by visiting the Department's website.

We need to ask why despite years of well-meant government initiatives, projects, grants and audits, we are still faced with Islamophobia, discrimination, hate crimes, radicalisation, social mobility etc. I believe it is because initiatives are often "catch-up" measures instead of fixing root causes with pragmatic approach.

On this occasion, I am humbly requesting my constituent MP, Mr Jonathan Lord to bring my letter for the personal attention of your goodself. I hasten to add based on past experiences, I have drafted the letter on 3rd Sept 2016 soon after my letter of 28th Aug 2016 in full anticipation that I will either be ignored or shunned by the "establishment elite" with a patronising reply.

It has become the norm and fashionable for the "establishment elite" to reject views of ordinary folks as naïve and simplistic. But often simple ideas have led to major breakthroughs with far reaching benefits. A simple analogy would be delicacies termed as "street foods" eaten over years by common people taken for granted but since discovered by professional chefs hailed as the best thing since sliced bread and served with an expensive tag on a posh plate as healthy dietary option.

I believe not only professional politicians, advisors, lobbyists or eminent individuals but also ordinary people have a lot to offer to make a better society based on years of real-life experiences and observations if given a modicum of opportunity.

Like many ordinary British people, ethnic and non-ethnic whether Muslims or non-Muslims, I am equally concerned what is said, not said or done in the name of religion and democracy. We cannot afford to discard public's disenchantment with the "establishment elite" lightly as seen during the EU referendum, surge in UKIP, right wing political extremism and turmoil in the Labour party. Moreover, despite even more serious revelations or even intervention by the Republican grandee, I predict Donald Trump without any doubt will get elected as US President. I also said we cannot afford to discard public's disenchantment with the "establishment elite" lightly as seen during the EU referendum, surge in UKIP, right wing political extremism and turmoil in the Labour party.

With reference to my letter of 28 Aug 2016, I entreat you to give an opportunity to elaborate just one area requiring harmonising to achieve desirable objectives so you can assess viability, implementation and credibility e.g. "how to tackle forced marriages and women's rights" without compromising culture, UK and *Sharia* laws or any faith traditions before considering other areas. It will overnight help address women's matrimonial rights, protect vulnerable women and encourage involvement of women at grass root level with far reaching benefits. We have nothing to lose but a lot to gain at no extra cost.

I am optimistic with the esteemed support of Mr Lord; I will not be disappointed and based on past experiences even if nothing materialises when efforts have been ignored, I will feel satisfied to have tried to explore all possible avenues to get heard.

I sincerely wish you every success in all your endeavours to fulfil your vision of the true meaning of "conservative and unionist party", and your belief "in a union not just between nations of the UK but between all of our citizens - every one of us - whoever we are and wherever we're from."

Yours most respectfully,
cc. Jonathan Lord MP

(55) Letter to Jonathan Lord.

14 October 2016

'Dear Mr Lord

As my constituent MP, I write to entreat your goodself to make representation on my behalf. I would greatly appreciate if you would bring the attached self-explanatory letter for the personal attention of Mrs May or her advisor.

I have drafted the request well in advance in full anticipation based on previous experiences of receiving standard "band aid" generic reply (see enclosed replies).

I apologise for taking the liberty to encroach on your busy schedule. I passionately believe in social harmony and sincerely hope on this occasion I will not get shunned but given a well-deserved long overdue opportunity to get heard.

I am pleased one of the issues highlighted in my letter following the 2011 census to your goodself has now become a policy e.g. abuse of NHS by overseas mothers. We need to similarly address issues pertaining to the root causes of Islamophobia, hate crimes, radicalisation, discrimination...

Thanking you for your esteemed support. I look forward to hearing from you.

With best wishes.
Yours most gratefully,
encl.'

(56) Reply from Jonathan Lord

17 October 2016

'Dear Dr Akberali

Thank you very much for your letter and its attachments which I have now passed on to the Prime Minister's office in Downing Street.

You'll appreciate that the Prime minister has an extremely busy schedule and heavy workload which is why she has a tram of people who help her with her correspondence. I'm afraid that it's unlikely that she will be able to look at your letter personally but I'm sure that a member of her staff will consider your comments very carefully and make sure that they are passed on to the most appropriate person.

With best wishes.
Kind regards'

(57) Letter to Jonathan Lord and a copy to the Prime Minster Mrs May.

13 November 2016

'Dear Mr Lord

Re: Real Democracy, Fairness, Hope, Justice... or Divide & Rule, Money talks, Disdain, Apathy, Fear... - A Need for Democracy and Capitalism to Evolve to Reflect 21st Century

I write once again to your goodself as I am waiting in disappointing anticipation to hear following your letter to the Prime Minister's office on 17 October 2016.
It is hard to believe I am still ignored or shunned with "band aid" replies despite well-meant genuine selfless initiatives encompassing social harmony brought to your attention since 2010 and others ever since 2001 following 9/11. You may recall I had forwarded letter dated 30 July 2010 addressed to Mr Cameron – "Re: Community Cohesion, Big Society and Ethnic Communities" – which has not even been acknowledged to-date.

I appreciate the Prime Minister has an extremely busy schedule. But I was optimistic on this occasion that with your esteemed intervention, I stood a far better chance to get heard by her team of experts. Unless for inexplicable reasons, I would have thought the Westminster establishment elite would be interested to listen to pragmatic and less costly ideas to enhance social harmony and mobility. I hope I will get heard not before it is too late and not ignored as an irritant individual wasting time with nothing to offer.

By now, as your constituent, I would have hoped to be given a modicum of opportunity. It takes a lot of time and effort for an ordinary person to express thoughts on paper with no support. It reflects genuine convictions and not an obsession to write for the sake of it. It is painful when it gets ignored or given patronising "band aid" replies. Like many ordinary folks without media, lobbying or financial clout, it is disheartening genuine efforts to engage in the legitimate democratic process gets discarded lightly by the establishment.

Social disharmony allows radicalised individuals like Mr Trump, Mr Farage, Ms Le Pen or groups such as ISIS and right wing extremists to capitalise and triumph democratically or otherwise with undertones of religious and racial hatred e.g. "make America great again", "Hindus for Trump", "Trump for India and Israel", *"Caliphate Rule"*, *"Wahhabism"* by glossing over real motives and causes of conflicts or crises. Politicians like Mr Trump are here today gone tomorrow without affecting own comfortable lives but their divisive populist slogans lead to an aftermath of sufferings and killings faced for years by ordinary people worldwide.

Mr Trump ran a campaign full of rhetorical assertions to get elected fuelling flames of fear, exclusion, hatred and isolation appealing to selective America; one that is largely white, radicalised, weaponised, straight and Christian with promises to drain Washington DC swamp. The democratic outcome based on low electoral turnout has left vulnerable even more so with the brunt of effects faced by Immigrants, Muslims and humanity whether Mr Trump delivers on his pledges or not. How can democracy be so cruel? It will be a great pity if campaigns based on Xenophobia instead of real issues succeeds as accepted version of civilised radicalisation.

Just like the EU referendum result on 23 June 2016, it is widely reported "experts" of all persuasions from political scientists, commentators and pollsters are confounded by the US Presidential result. I am least surprised as you will recall I had mentioned in my letter of 14 Oct 2016. The trend will continue in 2017 elections in Italy, France and Germany whereby the extreme right-wing parties will capitalise on public disenchantment. I was least surprised by the outcome of the EU referendum, and voted Brexit for reasons other than the divide and rule campaign slogans adopted by Mr Farage *et al.*

Ordinary people's perception of democracy has been compromised and hijacked more now than before by individuals or lobby groups with financial clout, as highlighted in 19th century by Baron Rothschild - "I care not what puppet is placed on the throne of England to rule the Empire. The man that controls Britain's money supply controls the British Empire. And I control the money supply".

It has now become the norm for faceless moneymen to dictate politicians with their money. In reality, the money men pull the strings and leaders just obey their masters without leadership or political convictions. The eighties mantra of free market and "can't buck the market" has opened more doors for powerful individuals, bankers and multinationals to go for broke and do nothing wrong to manipulate tax evasion, currency markets, capitalism, justice, honours list and elections determined by those with most money to mobilise votes.

Neglect and lack of empathy are often the root causes that drive people to fall victims to the curse of various forms of radicalisation, Islamophobia, discrimination, racial hatred, social mobility, right wing extremism.... Ordinary people feel let down when politicians make empty promises on fairness, hope, "big society", equal opportunities for "working people" for short term gains to get elected.

I hope I am given an opportunity to make a positive contribution to enhance social harmony and mobility. I appreciate your advice in the letter dated 30 Nov 2010 "to stand for election or get involved in appropriate charities or pressure groups if I strongly feel about issues". However, I would rather to do so through existing legitimate democratic process because like the vast silent majority of Muslims, I fear the consequences including the risks of being labelled as radicalised Muslim, Jihadist or otherwise. Moreover, I have neither the financial backing for election expenses nor am I a career politician.

I passionately believe in the importance of thinking in terms of "US" and not "we" or "they"; whereby communities are at ease living in harmony and respect for mutual benefits instead of alienation, mistrust and getting swayed by the tiny minority with an unscrupulous agenda preaching religious, racial and political hatred based on Xenophobia.

I look forward to hearing from you.

Kind regards.
Best Wishes
Yours most respectfully
cc. The Rt.Hon. Theresa May MP'

(58) Reply for my continuing efforts from Jonathan Lord when I requested the copy of the reply from the Minster which I had not received.

23 November 2016

'Dear Dr Akberali,

I have read and carefully noted all you say in it.

However, I will not waste my staff's time digging out old letters from me; I assure you my forwarding note will have been sympathetic and straightforward. I saw the Minister's reply to you recently - the PM's office asked the Minister to reply on her behalf - and I thought it was very thoughtful and well written.

I also have to say that I do not agree with one point in particular in your email of the 23rd, namely that Governments don't want mobility and social harmony. Perhaps, just perhaps, one or two particularly cynical Opposition politicians maybe don't want this from time to time (near an election???), but

Governments tend to get re-elected if the country is thriving and people are happy. I prefer to think of politicians of all parties of having the best of motives and wishing the best of outcomes for the country, and I do actually have a very high regard for most of my colleagues, of all Parties, in this House. Some other countries, I agree with your point here, are not so fortunate.

Finally, please note that I and my very small team have to deal with huge amounts of casework every day and every week. Given that, after 6 years of very regular correspondence with you, I am now extremely well briefed on your views, I would be very grateful if you would only contact me very, very occasionally from now on, and preferably only if a NEW issue arises that you feel compelled to raise. This will then enable me to serve all my other 73,000 constituents and their families properly; I'm sure you understand '.

With best wishes.
Kind regards,

P.S. to my previous email. If you do have practical policy solutions to prevent radicalisation and promote social harmony, of course I would be very happy to receive this information. I would read such a letter or email very carefully indeed and send it to the most relevant Minister for their proper consideration and response'.

(59) Reply from the Direct communications Unit with rubberstamp signature.

5 December 2016

'Dear Dr Akberali

'I am writing on behalf of the Prime Minister to thank you for the copy of your letter of 13 November, addressed to Mr Jonathan Lord MP.

Mrs May appreciates the time you have taken to share your views.

Yours sincerely
Correspondence Officer'

(60) Letter to Jonathan Lord.

24 November 2016

'Dear Mr Lord,

Thank you for your e-mail of 23 Nov 2016. I have noted the tone of the contents.

Please be assured as my constituent MP, I will not even contact you "very very occasionally from now on" so you can serve the other 73,000 constituents and their families properly because of your chosen political career. I apologise for wasting your time never mind my own time and selfless efforts at no cost to the tax payer.

However, I would just like to make the following points for the record.

I have not received the letter mentioned by you from the Minister asked by the PM's office to reply. It is not question of wasting your "staff's time digging out old letters" as I would appreciate if I can have a copy of the recently sent letter for my file.

With reference to the e-mail point, I was mainly stating the fact that if Governments of all political parties were serious about social harmony and mobility then it beggars belief as to why during PM's speech outside 10 Downing Street from Late Baroness Thatcher to Mrs May on 14 July 2014 (incl.) after election victory reference is made in one way or other to address same old issues related to social harmony, mobility, racial hatred....If progress had already been made why would they all make it a top priority? Ironically, campaigns for Governments to get re-elected are mainly focused to better the lives of this class or that group. If this is not divisive politics with the issues relating to immigrants always lurking in the background in some way to win votes whether Brexit or otherwise than what else could it be?

Moreover, it is not my view but as advised to follow media reports, I have seen politicians of all parties whether in Government, opposition or cynical, not only during election time but in House of Commons there is cacophony, accusations.... One would expect agreement if divisions between various classes did not exist. Despite being a priority, Mrs May continues to mentions the "working poor" (JAMs).

I hasten to add I have not said politicians do not have "best of motives and wishing best of outcomes" but more to do with the difficulty ordinary people have to get heard within corridors of power in the Westminster village.

Finally, with reference to your P.S. note request after so long, I don't think I will bother you anymore by taking up your valuable time to address other 73,000 constituents and their families. In addition, I will not be taken seriously by the establishment. I will spend my time wisely as it takes a lot of time to put thoughts on paper like the present reply at 3 am in the morning only to receive "band aid" replies or being ignored. In the meantime, I will continue to watch events relating to social harmony, mobility, Islamophobia, racial hatred...... unfold in the media.

Kind regards and best wishes.
Yours respectfully,'

(61) Letter to Chris Hinde.

12 May 2017

'Dear Chris,

I am an Independent candidate contesting in Woking County Constituency.

It was only 3 weeks ago on 20 April that I decided to stand for election. As a lay person without any past election experience or party support, the first call I made was to the Electoral Commission.

Zoe answered and since that day, I have spoken to Zoe to learn the rules and regulations.

To-date, Zoe has acted in a very professional and polite manner with lots of patience when I have raised various queries. I thought to write to you to let know how impressed I am in my dealings with your staff Zoe.

I asked Zoe for your contact details as it is always good to give credit where it is due.

Kind regards.
Yours most gratefully'

(62) Reply from Chris Hinde

15 May 2017

'Dear Dr Akberali,

Thank you very much for your e-mail.
It is always pleasing to receive positive comments about staff at the Commission and I am grateful to you for having taken the time to write to me about the help that Zoe has given you. Thanks again for your comments which are much appreciated.

Regards
Chris Hinde
Regional Manager (Midlands)'

(63) Letter to Mr Khan, Mayor of London.

4 June 2017

'Dear Mr Khan,

We are horrified by the horrendous events in London last night, so soon after the similar senseless attack in Manchester. Today the whole country will grieve for the innocent people who have lost their lives.

We have once again seen the worst of cowardly acts and the best of humanity in last night's London terrorist attack. Few people are intent on harming and ending life, while countless hundreds, like our emergency services, tirelessly did their utmost to maintain and protect the lives of those they may not even have known. Our gratitude to you all for the brave instinctive behaviour and immense courage of resilience.

This and similar cowardly acts are meant to dishearten and defeat us; they are meant to take away our resolve, and aim to lead us into a spiral of revenge. However hard they try; it will not destroy our precious way of life and democracy. Despite evocative attempts to corrupt our hearts to hatred, we on the contrary have seen acts of unwavering sacrifices, selflessness and compassion.

Our thoughts and prayers are foremost with those who have lost loved ones, those who are injured and those who will carry the trauma of what they have experienced in their darkest hour.

London is a vibrant beautiful city with lovely people. We will not allow the sacrifices of London to be forgotten. The twisted evil minds of bigots are jealous of our civil rights and democracy denied to them, and they will not succeed in destroying our freedom'.

(64) Reply from Mayor's Office.

12 June 2017

'Dear Dr Akberali

'Thank you for your correspondence to the Mayor and for your kind words of support and sympathy from the Society of Independent Reformists following the attack at London Bridge and Borough Market on Saturday 3 June.

The Mayor appreciates you taking the time to write.

Kind regards',
Zoe Newcombe
Mayor's Office'

(65) Letter to Jonathan Lord. Letter after blunt message and 8 June 2017 election.

22 November 2017

'Dear Mr Lord

Re: 'The Truth About Muslim Marriage' – Channel 4 programme 21/11/2017

I write for the record in the wake of the above, bearing in mind Woking constituents will be affected, despite your blunt reply a year ago on 23 Nov 2016 not to waste time as you have important matters to attend on behalf of other 73,000 constituents.

I attach as reminder letters dated 14 Oct 2016 to you and Mrs May offering solutions on "women's rights and forced marriages", and as you are aware similar efforts as far back July 2010 (and before) have fallen on deaf ears with not even a courtesy to acknowledge. To say that irony is dead is an understatement as similar concerns have been raised well before the Channel 4 programme.

If the lawmakers are serious, it is still not late to tackle "woman's rights and forced marriages" by asking right questions as to why not all but some sectors of society remain affected!

We need real life pro-active measures with simple less costly solutions to address complex issues by listening to ordinary people, not complex solutions to simple issues at a cost. Extreme discrimination based on race, creed or sex has subtle social class origins built on a lack of opportunity, and if addressed with political conviction will yield sound results in terms of social harmony and mobility.

Occasionally, listening to ordinary people's concerns would alleviate not add further stereotyping of Muslims especially at a time when Islamophobia is rife, a scourge of every day misery and insults for Muslims on streets by right wing extremists as well as President Trump's tweets capitalising on any bad publicity.

The sufferings highlighted by Channel 4 has nothing to do with Islam but more to do with the egos of self-appointed custodians with own agendas, and our politicians have no qualms selling arms because of oil money. Let us not allow these hypocrites including their cohorts with egos tarnish Islam and get away at least in the UK!

A clear majority of like-minded ordinary Muslims and non-Muslims feel ignored by lawmakers until a disaster or press exposure followed by inquiries e.g. Grenfell, child abuse, Hillsborough. Whereas, "high powered individuals" set bad example as role models or bastions of society for us mere mortals e.g. sexual harassment, Panama tax scandal, with the cheek to remain in denial or ignorance when caught.

We can announce as many expensive "race audits", public inquiries and initiatives to learn lessons after damage has been done squandering valuable financial resources feathering lawyer's pockets without serving main objectives with laws drafted by lawyers with loop holes to exploit!

Kind regards'

(66) Reply from Jonathan Lord.

5 February 2018

'Dear Dr Akberali

Please find enclosed a copy of a letter from the Home Office regarding tolerance, anti-Muslim hatred, Sharia Law and the issue on forced marriage.

I hope you find the response informative.

With best wishes.
Kind regards
Jonathan Lord'

(67) Letter to Jonathan Lord.

7 February 2018

'Dear Mr Lord,

Re: Women's Rights and Forced Marriages

Thank you kindly for your letter dated 5 Feb 2018 with the enclosed reply from the Home Office Minister the Rt. Hon. Victoria Atkins MP.

With respect, I am disappointed by the patronising reply. I had taken the trouble to offer solutions to address the issue from a different perspective. Regrettably, the Minister has totally ignored and highlighted a list of expensive long-winded initiatives.

How long do women have to suffer? What I am proposing is not new legislation but simple solutions with checks and balances to make effective use of existing laws and less costly initiatives to empower women.

I agree Britain is a well-integrated society and we cannot afford to be complacent. It would serve us well if we have proactive measures to stop malpractices not reactive victim support initiatives relying on women to come forward. Moreover, most victims do not even know initiatives exist, lack confidence to approach or find out when it is too late. What we should do is empower women without having to rely on charitable acts, handouts or others. As mentioned previously, forced marriages has nothing to do with Islam and can be tackled easily with the right approach.

Let us not repeat past mistakes of ignoring public concerns only to be followed by expensive tax payer funded public inquiries to learn lessons after sufferings and loss of lives e.g. Grenfell, Hillsborough, child abuse, sexual grooming and harassment…. Valuable resources are squandered which can used to address real issues without adding to the national debt currently standing at about £1.73 trillion!

We are celebrating 100 years when women were given right to vote, a recognition of common humanity. Let us hope, we do not have to wait another 100 years to tackle other pertinent issues affecting women's everyday life.

As mentioned in my letter of 14 October 2016 to the Prime Minister, I have simple solutions worth listening and If implemented will go a long way. I look forward to your support for the worthy cause and hope I am not wasting your time.

Kind regards'.

(68) Letter to Jonathan Lord.

26 April 2018

'Dear Mr Lord

Re: Windrush and Hostile Immigrant Environment

I write for the record in the wake of the above despite your blunt reply of not to waste your time as you have important matters to attend on behalf of other 73,000 constituents of whom a number are immigrants and I am one of them.

The Prime Minister and the Home Secretary remain adamant that the Windrush debacle has nothing to do with legal immigrants but all to do with illegal immigrants. Sadly, the consequences are faced by all immigrants because it is the word "immigrant" not "illegal immigrants" which sticks in the public's mind. We British immigrants and our UK born children face hostility unlike white immigrants from Australia, New Zealand, Canada. We have also to be conscious that anything out of the ordinary whether in schools, workplace or neighbourhoods will be blamed on immigrants.

Any amount of compensation will not bring back lost ones or replace sufferings and missed opportunities. Moreover, it is tax payer's money not government's and it will come at cost to cuts in other public services without any effect on politicians.

I have also been a victim of hostile Home Office immigration policy when my late mother was refused a UK visitor visa after the bereavement of my father. It was granted on appeal I fought personally to save legal fees. I hope you will appreciate what we as immigrants have to endure layers of bureaucracy and expenses.

Recent family experience in the NHS despite being born in the UK makes you also wonder what we immigrants have to face in our daily lives with concerns falling on deaf ears and bureaucracy until a disaster happens e.g. Grenfell, Windrush. We have been reluctant to bring to your attention but mention in passing today.

Sadly, over the last 60 years and more so recently, politicians are out of touch of reality and use immigrants when it suits as cheap fodder to win votes e.g. elections, referendum, curtail rise in UKIP or when to apportion blame during crises in housing, school places, NHS.......

As you will be aware over the years, I have raised concern about hostility towards bonafide British immigrants who feel alienated at work place, schools, neighbourhoods and treated as second class citizens. You will remember the response to-date has not even been acknowledged with a thank you reply.

We can announce as many expensive "race audits", public inquiries and initiatives to learn lessons to combat institutional racism after damage squandering valuable financial resources feathering lawyer's pockets without serving main objectives but please do not make life more difficult for British immigrants to win votes.
I am not expecting a reply but please do not ignore public concerns as well as the important issue I have raised relating to forced marriages and women's rights.

Kind regards.
Yours sincerely'

(69) Reply from Jonathan Lord.

27 April 2018

'Dear Dr Akberali,

Thank you very much for your email.

With regard to the 'Windrush Generation', I'm very sorry indeed for the anxiety and confusion that recent events have caused. I'm hugely sympathetic to their situation and I think that officials have handled this matter, particularly in relation to its treatment of these entirely blameless and hardworking citizens, in an utterly shameful manner. The Government has taken a number of steps, including the establishment of a dedicated team within the Home Office to support anyone affected by this, the waiver of citizenship fees and language tests, and a promise of compensation for those affected. I'm very pleased that both the Home Secretary and the Prime Minister have expressed their profound regret and unreserved apologies for recent developments on a number of occasions now.

As far as your wider comments are concerned, I completely agree with you and the Prime Minister that there is no place whatsoever for discrimination of any kind, whether on the basis of colour, creed, gender or sexuality, against citizens with a bona fide right to be and remain in this country.

With best wishes '.
Kind regards',

(70) Letter to Jonathan Lord.

27 April 2018

'Dear Mr Lord

Re: Windrush and Hostile Immigrant Environment

Thank you for your reply.

'With great respect, your reply offers no assurances to a constituent with a 'legal' immigrant background.

Perhaps you feel "sorry" because you voted in favour of the draconian immigration passed in 2014/2016 when the Prime Minister was the Home Secretary without realising the harm it will cause 'legal' British this or that ethnic and black immigrant citizen. What a long definition for a British citizen of "legal" immigrant background! No wonder we are always in the lime light for no reason when it comes to attract votes or apportion blame.

It is symptomatic of a lack of understanding and empathy of what 'legal' immigrants actually have to endure in real life because of the hostile environment created by the government. It is not officials but the government who decide policies and blaming them is not the answer but an excuse to wriggle out of responsibility.

I had given specific examples which are not unique to me or uncommon and I was not referring to "illegal" but 'legal' immigrants like me and our children born in the UK with all the right paper work. I had also raised our recent NHS experience with a formal complaint which has been ignored and fallen on deaf ears with a bureaucratic response.

The Windrush debacle like every other major crisis does not happen overnight but from small beginnings and if pleas of help are ignored leads to disastrous consequences.

There is no reason for you to feel sorry about the Windrush saga. But it would have been reassuring if you had offered to look into the issues raised so they do not take root, a dilemma faced by the Windrush people of not being listened instead of politely fobbing me off as wider comments agreeing with the Prime Minister.

Also, what is not helpful is a constant reminder as British this or that ethnic or black immigrant citizen which just like the term 'illegal' sticks in people's mind as a different entity to the rest becoming easy target for blame or win votes.

I hope you will appreciate that all along I am actually trying to reach out so real-life issues get addressed not turn into a political football. I look forward to hearing from you hopefully not a bureaucratic reply.

With best wishes'.

(71) Reply from Jonathan Lord.

2 May 2018

'Dear Dr Akberali

Thank you very much for your further comments in your email of 27 April, which I'll certainly keep in mind over the coming weeks and months.

There's obviously work to be done around immigration at the Home Office, but I am delighted by the promotion of Sajid Javid to Home Secretary. You'll aware Sajid Has been very critical of the Home Office over the Windrush issue and brings to his new role his own experiences of emigration the UK from Pakistan as a child in the 1960s and 1970s. I believe that his promotion is assign that the Government is aware of the need to tackle this problem urgently and sensitively. I'm also confident that he's the right man for this job and I look forward to supporting him in his efforts to make sure that the Home Office works as fairly and effectively as possible for both the Windrush Generation and for everyone else.

With regard to the lives of everyone who is in the UK legally, either as a full UK citizens or as highly-valued people with leave to remain in the country, I would point out that we have very strong anti-discrimination laws here which say that everyone should be treated with the same level of respect in line with the fact that we are all equal before the law. The rise of Sajid Javid from the son of a bus driver to one of the great offices of state is a wonderful metaphor, I think, for the social mobility that we should all wish to see.

Thank you very much once again for taking the time to bring your thoughts to my attention.

I presume we may see each other at the count on Friday!

With best wishes,

Kind regards'

(72) Letter to Jonathan Lord.

5 May 2018

'Dear Mr Lord,

Re: Windrush and Hostile Immigrant Environment

Thank you very kindly for your reply of 2nd May.

As presumed by you, I was indeed on time at Friday's count and missed each other as I may have left because of prior engagements before your timely appearance.

I hope by now after all these years, you may have realised my intentions to reach out to you, your predecessors and cross-party politicians including Prime Ministers from Sir John Major to Mrs Teressa May (incl.) is based on genuine convictions to make a small but positive contribution to this great country of ours as a British citizen of "legal" this and that ethnic or black immigrant commonwealth background.

So much so, it has led me to heed your advice and contest two elections using own resources because like the majority of ordinary people irrespective of class, creed, age or race, I feel the political elite are out of touch of real life concerns as reflected in my election communication, hustings and articles which the electorate including Tory supporters alike have mentioned strongly reflect my sincerity and passion.

With respect, I will focus on the points in your reply indicative of a typical response with ample clues of fudging deployed by public institutions whilst ignoring salient real-life difficulties and issues faced by ordinary people e.g. racism, radicalisation, social mobility, social harmony, forced marriages, women's rights etc: -

1. We need to move away of treating important issues as a political football apportioning blame on predecessors and everyone else except ourselves.

2. For over nearly 20 years, I have raised not only to you but with many others that the Home Office and FCO visa section is not only fit for purpose but very incompetent and hostile when it comes to treating "legal" British citizens from ethnic background. I can prove it if you like from personal experiences which are not unique or uncommon.

3. I personally believe the term "illegal" is misleading to cover up the failures of the Home Office. I admit "illegal" immigrants do exist need to distinguish those from the thousands of pending historical cases or

records lost, and even if the Home Office tried would find it hard to extradite because of human rights. It is because the UK has been their home for years, and they not stepped outside and lost family connections in their country of origin. We need to explore ways to address their fate quickly so that those who are recent illegal immigrants can be deported before it is too late.

4. It is not the fault of civil servants because they serve and politicians decide not my words but said by the late Baroness Thatcher revered by the Tories.

5. Without the political will and an understanding of real-life experiences, Sajid Javid or Mrs May will not be able to tackle any problem, even if Sajid Javid being a son of a bus driver and changing words from hostile to compliant, is just meaningless.

6. The term "illegal" immigrant is a red herring to divert attention from failures in government policies. Immigrants are used as cheap fodder to win votes by pandering to the right-wing press and pollical groups e.g. vans with placards.

7. If you recall, I had often written to offer pro-active solutions to address "illegal" immigration on a number of occasions culminating in the usual bureaucratic reply from Mr Damian Green MP, the ex-front bencher and close adviser to Mrs May. It eventually wore me out as there is a limit how much an individual can endure in their own time at a personal cost (also see 8 below).

8. I am fully aware we have very strong anti-discrimination laws or complaints procedures but sadly they are ineffective namely: -

    a) Institutional racism or other forms in everyday life and social media, has become subtle instead of blatant making it difficult to prove.

    b) Complaints procedures are drawn out bureaucratic process designed to wear out or deter individuals in the first place to lodge a complaint even if they have the literacy skills or confidence to lodge a complaint.

    c) Individuals are often not aware of rights or let alone have the literacy skills to lodge a complaint in their own time and attend daily chores. A fact well known to those who break the law. Those who do pursue to seek justice have to rely on lawyers and they don't come cheap.

d)   With great respect, your reply is typical "establishment" response. It does not actually give a direct answer but patronising response of all the wonderful work with concerns falling on deaf ears until it is too late e.g. Grenfell, Windrush, Hillsborough, child abuse.

e)   In respect, of (d), I have raised personal experience relating to the NHS and despite following all complaint procedures including parliamentary ombudsman it is nearly a year and heard no further. Suppose wait until lives are lost, it will be followed by expensive public inquiry at a cost to the tax payer to learn lessons.

f)   We can put in place as many anti-discrimination laws or complaint procedures but the bureaucratic process is designed to wear out individuals without achieving the desired objectives.

9.   I would also refer to your keenness in the Get Surrey interview and fellow Woking Tories towards voter ID. I believe the present format will lead to voter apathy and undermine real democracy as not everyone is fortunate to have papers e.g. Windrush debacle. I am aware people without ID were able to register and agree the need to minimise vote rigging but not a sledge hammer approach without addressing the actual problem associated with postal voting.

10. In your Get Surrey interview you stated that no complaints have been made. I hope you will register my reservations and complaints I heard on the doorstep and hustings where a colleague of yours was present before the government rushes to roll out voter ID nationally without proper public consultation, if suits the Tory party.

I welcome and celebrate all forms of social mobility but let us not get carried away with a few cases here and there whilst ignoring numerous examples not only ethnic but indigenous people from disadvantaged backgrounds are affected. There is a lot a government can do with pro-active measures instead of just empty rhetoric on the doorstep of Downing Street announcing expensive public Race Audit enquiries.

It is also worth noting that a person with an ethnic background has to be a few-fold better qualified or work harder to attain social mobility in all aspects of life to compete against an indigenous counterpart and equally more prone to attract blame when things go wrong.

As already mentioned my intentions are well meant and constructive to reach out to you and the Prime Minister Mrs May based on genuine convictions to make a small but positive contribution to this great country of ours because for 45 years, despite difficulties faced as a "legal" immigrant, the UK has enriched my life and I would like to put something back into the society either directly or indirectly.

I look forward to hearing from you.

With best wishes,
Yours sincerely',

(73) Letter to Jonathan Lord.

31 May 2018

'Dear Mr Lord,

Re: Islamophobia in the Tory Party

'I write in the wake of the call by the Muslim Council of Britain for an independent inquiry into the claims of Islamophobia within the Tory party bearing in mind Woking constituents will be affected, despite your blunt reply not to waste your time as you have important matters to attend on behalf of other 73,000 constituents but not me.

I hope you will recall I have raised similar other concerns faced by British citizens of ethnic origin in their everyday life and therefore the specific allegations against the Tory party is not new but long overdue not forgetting the dog whistle politics adopted by the ex- Prime Minster David Cameron at the PMQs in his support of Tory Mayoral candidate Mr Zac Goldsmith by attacking Mr Sadiq Khan.

The Tory party have responded citing the recent promotion of Mr Salim Javid as the first Muslim Home Secretary claiming Islamophobia is not rife in the party just like you did when I had raised the Windrush debacle with you. Let us not get carried away by Mr Javid's promotion as an end to all our problems whilst ignoring many other injustices. It is worth bearing in mind Mr Javid on many occasions has maintained he is not a practicing Muslim but in name only and also did not speak often about his Pakistani background until recently. Maybe before he thought it might hinder his political and other careers but now seems fine to capitalised by publicising at every opportunity to make the most of his background.

As mentioned, I hope politicians will refrain from using British citizens of immigrant background as cheap fodder to attract votes as it has detrimental consequences in their everyday life. The country cannot progress by alienating sections of population and Islamophobia, a form discrimination just like antisemitism in the Labour party should be rooted out and the Tory party should not remain in denial.

As mentioned in my recent correspondence on interrelated issues e.g. Windrush debacle, forced marriages and women's rights real life solutions exist if we really want to address discrimination, Islamophobia, social harmony and mobility right across the country.

I look forward to hearing from you. I am also copying to my local Councillor including Baroness Warsi as members of the Conservative party to express views of Muslim constituents '.

Kind regards.
Yours sincerely'

(74) Reply from Jonathan Lord.

1 June 2018

'Dear Dr Akberali

Thank you for your thoughts in this and your previous email of 5th May, both of which I have read carefully and I carefully noted what you said in the emails too.

I do not accept all of what you say in this latest email and I think that the jaundiced and unacceptable way you speak about Sajid Javid (and his assumed motivations) perhaps betrays a wider animus you might have against the Conservative Party.

I am sure that my Party will look very carefully indeed at any accusations of Islamophobia, but a few idiots saying unacceptable things does not make a Party institutionally racist or Islamophobic. I believe that any proven transgressions have been dealt with both swiftly and very firmly by my Party - unlike the appalling lassitude shown by Labour towards anti-Semitism by its MPs, councillors, candidates and members.

Locally, I am delighted that a quarter of Conservative borough Councillors in Woking are of Muslim or BME backgrounds, and this is also true of more than a quarter of our Conservative Woking County Councillors. This is, I believe, a much larger figure than the actual percentage of Muslim and BME voters locally. The Conservatives also have more Muslim and BME Councillors locally than all the other local Parties put together, and the first ever Muslim Mayor of Woking, in

2010, my first year as MP, was also a Conservative. I gave this wonderful 'first' a 'high billing' in my maiden speech.

With regard to the Voter ID pilots, please feel free to share your views with Woking Borough Council, and/or the Electoral Commission which I think will be analysing the results. WBC has already published its key findings on the Woking pilot. Fewer than 55 people went to vote without proper ID and then failed to come back with valid ID, and the turnout in Woking was 37.7 per cent, which is very much in line with the historic turnout figures for recent local elections here (in non-Parliamentary election and non-European election years). I think that is a very encouraging result for such a strict pilot as took place here in Woking.

As you know there has been proven electoral fraud in Woking in the recent past. The Returning Officer for Woking fears and suspects that this has been a real problem in one ward in particular over several years, as I understand it. Given that Voter ID is believed to have virtually eliminated a widely accepted problem of impersonation fraud in Northern Ireland since its introduction many years ago, and has done so with no democratic ill effects that I am aware of, I do think that its introduction in the rest of the UK should be seriously considered.'

With best wishes.

PS. I am sorry that I missed you at the Count. We must have just missed each other, I think. I had an earlier engagement and I think that the first set of ward counts finished earlier than normal too!'

(75) Letter to the Rt. Hon. Jeremy Hunt.

2 January 2019

'Dear Mr Hunt,

Re: Sky News - Foreign Office makes forced marriage victims pay for their rescue according to an investigation by the Times

I write to your goodself in your capacity as a Foreign Secretary not a constituent MP following the above coverage by Sky news adding further misery to young women rescued by the Foreign Office after being sent abroad for forced marriages.

I apologise for taking the liberty of writing directly to you because I strongly feel the above misery could have been avoided with suffering alleviated for some of the victims if I had not been ignored and overlooked as an irritant.
I will send two self-explanatory correspondence later on confirmation from your office to give you a deeper insight addressed to my constituent MP, Mr Jonathan

Lord entitled "the Truth About Muslim Marriages" – Channel 4 programme 21/11/2017 and "Women's Rights and Forced Marriages".

It is with deep regret Mr Lord is of the opinion I am "wasting his time" and "if I feel strongly about local and national issues, I am always at liberty to stand for elections or join protest groups" when I have written to him on important real-life concerns affecting ordinary people e.g. illegal immigration, hostile Home Office environment, radicalisation, Islamophobia, discrimination …….

I look forward to hearing from you. I strongly believe solutions based on real life experiences do exist and other scourge affecting our society '.

Yours sincerely'

(76) Letter to Jeremy Hunt (reminder).

4 February 2019

'Dear Mr Hunt

Re: Still waiting for reply to my e-mail (letter) of 2 January 2019 following Sky News report on the rescue of forced marriage victims by the FCO (see encl.)

'I apologise for taking liberty to write in your capacity as Foreign Secretary and not as constituent MP despite website advice not to write to your constituency. It is because I have not heard further since I wrote to your FCO address over a month ago.
 I also appreciate you will not have time to reply because of your busy schedule. But unlike ordinary public have resources and staff at your disposal paid by the tax payer to serve civic duty. I hope you will reflect it is uncourteous and contemptuous not to reply when the public take the trouble of writing to lawmakers on important issues.

In the current climate, the political class need to reflect more of their actions in a democracy – whether we are from the same walk of life or not - and we either both receive the same treatment or we don't.

The politicians, celebrities, professionals and elders could serve well as effective role models by setting good example for the young and others to uphold social as well as moral values in society. In the past, the public held politicians in good faith but trust in MPs has slipped away due to recent events, leaving MPs ranked below bankers and estate agents in people's estimations.
The MPs should be mindful not to take the electorate for granted or we ignore the will of the people at our peril. We have seen an increase in social unrest because the ordinary public encouraged by the behaviour of superiors and MPs feel it is morally

acceptable to be greedy, irresponsible, deceitful and pay or accept bung for party-political and self-serving interests instead of national loyalty and hard work.

The father of the house Rt. Hon. Kenneth Clarke eloquently said during the Brexit debate on 29 Jan 2019 " the political class need to be aware the public are looking at the politicians with contempt, and if we are trying to restore confidence in our political system and if current shambles continues, I hate to think where populism and extremism will take us next in British democracy."

We have young adults looking to become the next MP or prime minister and if they see our current MPs getting away with such raucous behaviour in the chamber then they will follow suit in taking advantage of situations placed upon them. We need to be honest what politics and democracy is about in national interest?

In light of the above, I agree partly with your comment made in Singapore "stopping Brexit or a second referendum would be a catastrophic and unforgivable breach of mistrust in our democracy" but it is not the main reason for public apathy.

Brexit alone has not opened the door to extremist populist forces in the UK but the contempt with which the political class "servants of the people" treat ordinary people whilst readily listening to individuals with media, legal, financial and lobbying clout.

The abrogating of duties by the political class and ignoring real-life issues of ordinary people e.g. Windrush, Grenfell, food banks, homelessness, austerity are the main reasons for public apathy and social unrest not Brexit or referendum as claimed by Mrs May at PMQs who has also alluded Tories as 'the nasty party'.

Sadly, some real-life hardships can easily be avoided at no extra cost instead of waiting to worsen followed by disaster and expensive public inquiries costing the tax-payer's only to be penalised with austerity later to pay for lawmaker's mistakes e.g. Grenfell, Windrush. In reality, opinions are cheap but expensive in long-term with fatal consequences. Whereas, facts based on real- life experience provide lasting workable solutions with wider social and welfare benefits with much less suffering at a fraction of the cost to the nation.

For example, contrary to the lies peddled by the media and right-wing extremists to create a hostile atmosphere for Muslims, forced marriage has no place in Islam but it is more to do with the universal violation of women's rights witnessed in employment, communities, parliament and high office by individuals despite legislation e.g. sexual harassment, rape, up-skirting, domestic violence, pay gap, job prospects.

I am not chasing unicorns but firmly believe forced marriages and real- life concerns of ordinary people can be tackled with a realistic grown up approach with right safety checks and balances in legislature to alleviate the scourge of forced marriages and other atrocities. The victims should be left under no circumstances to face the future at the mercy of events and chance.

I hope on this occasion my efforts will be brought to your personal attention instead of a patronising reply blaming an oversight because of thousands of letters received by the FCO or austerity, and if possible, suggest ways other than to move home to get heard when ignored by a safe seat constituent MP abdicating responsibility.

I look forward to hearing from you on the best possible pragmatic way to proceed without much bureaucracy as I have limited available resources at my disposable '.

Yours sincerely
encl.'

(77) Final reminder to Jeremy Hunt (final reminder).

4 April 2019

'Dear Mr Hunt,

Re: An open letter – Discourteous behaviour by the establishment "elite"

'It is over 3 months, when I first wrote by e-mail to your goodself on 2nd Jan 2019 to your FCO address.

As I heard nothing further, I wrote to your constituency address on 3rd Feb on an important subject offering possible solutions on how to alleviate suffering of forced marriage victims.

I write again as I am still waiting to hear from you or your office. I hope you will agree it is discourteous not to acknowledge when public takes trouble to write, not once but twice, at a personal cost to a senior cabinet secretary on an important issue affecting women's rights. It does not set a good role model example for the public to follow when a politician reneges despite pledging "the main reason for entering politics is to make life better for others."

Is it any wonder with such an attitude as well as the political chicanery and in-fighting over the Brexit negotiations debacle, the public are left with no choice but feel disenchanted by the political class and the establishment elite?
It is also least surprising the country is on its knees, a great nation with fifth largest economy, UN permanent member, NATO - as well as a leader in the field of science, justice, courtesy, democracy and much more – has now become a subject of mockery!

Why should Iran and other countries take us seriously when we are now reduced to laughing stock in the EU and worldwide? But sadly, the price is paid by innocent hostages, victims of forced marriages and families whilst, the political class remain unaccountable and enjoy perks at tax payers' expense by treating electorate with discourtesy.

I entreat your goodself as a respected senior member of the government to listen to real-life concerns and "burning injustices" of ordinary people not get entangled in the shenanigans of Tory leadership ambitions to satisfy populist and extremists wing of the party.

I look forward to hearing from you on this occasion '.

Yours sincerely'

(78) Letter to the Rt.Hon. Jacinda Arden, The New Zealand Prime Minister.

31st March 2019

'Dear Prime Minister

An open letter of condolence and leadership courage – A hope for humanity

I write as an ordinary folk to express my heartfelt condolences and prayers following the darkest hour in the history of New Zealand on Friday, 15th March 2019.

I would also take the opportunity that like many, I feel humbled and grateful to the Almighty that ever since the fateful day, when the whole humanity irrespective of race and creed was dealt a severe blow, you have showed nothing but exemplary formidable leadership, vision and courage.

You also showed during the Remembrance Day service on 29th March 2019, when you spoke eloquently about "the ugliest viruses such as extremism, violence and racism an assault on the freedom of humanity." You went on further "we cannot confront these issues alone, none of us can ... The answer lies in our humanity. But for now, we will remember the tears of our nation and the new resolve we have formed."

You have become an epitome of leadership during challenging times with heartwarming words of wisdom and steel like determination lifting not only the image and people of New Zealand to new heights but also giving hope to the whole of humanity. But sadly, there is a distinct lack of leadership in the world today. The last leader we had was the late President Nelson Mandela with courage, conviction and foresight to tackle big issues.

You went further which no other leaders in the western world have ever done or ever dare. You greeted not only your nation but the world from the heart of democracy in your nation's parliament with the Islamic greeting *"Assalamu Alaykum"* (may peace be upon you). Your desire to include humanity into the depth of your heart was visible and came naturally. It flooded the hearts of many and I still feel the emotion at this very moment of writing to you.

Sadly, unlike your goodself, we have "leaders" with self-serving egos mollycoddling each other or countries with the sole purpose to protect export income from the sale of arms on their minds. At the same provide lip-service instead of challenging Islamophobia or burning injustices with heads buried in the sand. Meanwhile, the so-called custodians and world policeman are busy inciting hatred and waging wars in the Middle East pitting one nation against another whilst at the same time ignoring human rights abuse, racism and hatred at home, all in the name of Islam and democracy respectively.

What the world has witnessed since 15th March 2019 is a remarkable human being and a blessed leader in our midst, a beacon of hope and light. I entreat your goodself to pursue your vision "the world has been stuck in a vicious cycle of extremism breeding extremism and it must end" and as murdered Jo Cox MP said "we are far more united and have far more in common with each other than things that divide us."

Last but not least with your wisdom, compassion and courage, you have made strangers like me and many more your best admirers, and I sincerely hope it is not long before the Nobel peace prize is bestowed upon you not that unlike other so-called leaders you are touting for one but actions speak louder than words. Your name has already been enshrined in the annals of humanity as the best role model of our time.

I pray to God, Allah and Almighty of all faiths to give you continued strength and a long healthy life to accomplish your mission. New Zealand may be a small nation but it has a great world leader and citizens with an enormous heart and vision '.

Yours most respectfully
cc. HE Lieutenant General Sir Jerry Mateparae,
New Zealand High Commissioner'

(79) Reply received on behalf of Jacinda Arden.

11 April 2019

'Thank you for your kind words.

The Prime Minister has been deeply moved by the support and compassion shown in the wake of the attack in Christchurch, and by the thousands of people who have taken the time to share their condolences.

She has asked me to pass on the following statement:

My thoughts are with the families who have lost loved ones and who are now experiencing unimaginable pain and grief. While I can't take away this pain, I send the Muslim community my love, as so many New Zealanders have, and the reassurance that I will do all I can to support them. My focus is ensuring those who have been affected have the care and support they need - not just now, but in the coming months and year.

This is a tragic time, and all of New Zealand is feeling the impact. While we as a nation grapple with a form of grief and anger we have not experienced before, the compassion and kindness that has been expressed at community events, on social media, and by people right across the country show us who we are as a nation.

Going forward, I know those are the values we'll all work hard to protect.

Thanks again for getting in touch.
Kind regards
Office of the Prime Minister'

(80) Letter to Boris Johnson.

9 August 2019

An Open Letter to Mr Boris Johnson

'Dear Mr. Boris Johnson,

I hope with great respect what I have to say, you will take in good spirit because as a proud law-abiding British citizen of Muslim origin, like many Muslims and non-Muslims, my loyalty is foremost to the UK to live as a law-abiding citizen as well as contribute to social harmony, growth, development and prosperity for the benefit of us all.

Now that as expected, you have been elected by about 92,000 from a total of 160,000 Tory members, about 0.14% of UK citizens, and become the Prime Minister, we ask how you will address the following mendacious fiction of yours and continue to remain in denial.

We wonder, how would look into the eyes of over 2,000,000, 3% law-abiding British Muslims without prejudice or how the British Muslims could ever trust you as their true PM when you say "Islam inherently inhibits the path to progress and freedom" or refer to Muslim women with bigotry remarks as "letter boxes".

Mr Johnson, you are very good at making bombastic claims because of your oratory and writing skills - for which you are handsomely paid about £5,000 - under the pretext of free press and speech. But who are you kidding!

Mr Johnson, you know too well that the innocent people you like to attack cannot reply back because the very "free press" will not give them time of the day or an opportunity to pen an answer to your vile and puerile claims despite living in the same liberal democracy. As a journalist, one would expect you should not run scared but first check your facts by engaging in debates with other scholars to allay your fears instead of spouting drivel by hiding behind press articles or speech lecterns.

For example, Mr Johnson, in an essay titled "And Then Came the Muslims", added to the 2007 edition of your book, you wrote: "There must be something about Islam that indeed helps to explain why there was no rise of the bourgeoisie, no liberal capitalism and therefore no spread of democracy in the Muslim world."

With respect, as someone who claims to be a literate of Eton and Oxford University, can I ask if you have you ever read the Quran. Did you know the first word of revelation was "Read" and the first five verses of revelation was all about knowledge and learning - reading, reflecting, researching, writing, reasoning and sharing information!

When you say "Islam inherently inhibits the path to progress and freedom" you demonstrate your ignorance of the faith, the scripture, the traditions of the Prophet (saw) and the 1400 years of scholarship. I am afraid a man of your talent and position should check first before spouting such ignorance! After all, didn't you attend not only Eton but also Oxford University, surely you must have been taught how to check facts.

Mr Johnson, I entreat you not to pass judgement on Islam based on few rotten apples like Middle East Sheikhs claiming to be custodians of Islam with whom the West maintains a cosy relationship to earn blood money by selling arms to these regimes.

Your idea of bourgeoisie leading to rise in liberal capitalism is far from liberal. It is nothing less than elitist, nepotistic and conservative capitalism, where the aristocracy remains and retains control of the economy and power and the working class that you so patronisingly call bourgeoisie, and you pretend to champion, only are accepted when they operate as slaves to your system. They work on zero hour contracts, rent your "buy to let" properties or mansions that you have inherited from your landowning ancestors, they help you to pay your multiple mortgages, they work as nurses at your private hospitals earning peanuts or at the scarcely funded NHS hospitals earning even less, they are poorly paid teachers, firefighters, cleaners, police officers and so on, some of whom relying on foodbanks and charity. In your capitalist world, there is no room for the poor nor space for heart with compassion but Islam's economic philosophy is primarily based on compassion, sharing of wealth and care for each other. In your world of bourgeoisie capitalism, you reward wanton greed even if it destroys families, moral values and the environment. Islam invites its faithful to be caretakers and custodians of this earth and the environment.

Mr Johnson, perhaps a quick read of history would have put you in the right direction. Let me help you by quoting the future King, Prince Charles, in a historic speech: "Islam nurtured and preserved the quest for learning. In the words of the tradition, 'the ink of the scholar is more sacred than the blood of the martyr'. Cordoba in the 10th century was by far the most civilised city of Europe. We know of lending libraries in Spain, at the time King Alfred, was making terrible blunders with the culinary arts in this country. It is said that the 400,000 volumes in its ruler's library amounted to more books than all the libraries of the rest of Europe put together. That was made possible because the Muslim world acquired from China the skill of making paper more than 400 years before the rest of non-Muslim Europe. Many of the traits on which modern Europe prides itself came to it from Muslim Spain. Free trade, diplomacy, open borders, the techniques of academic research, anthropology, fashion etiquette, various types of medicine, hospitals, all came from this great city of cities."

Prince Charles went on to say "Medieval Islam was a religion of remarkable tolerance for its time, allowing Jews and Christians the right to practise their inherited beliefs, and setting an example which was not, unfortunately, copied for many centuries in the West. The surprise, ladies and gentlemen, is the extent to which Islam has been a part of Europe for so long, first in Spain, then in the Balkans, and the extent to which it has contributed so much towards the civilisation which we all too often think of, wrongly, as entirely Western. Islam is part of our past and our present, in all fields of human endeavour. It has helped to create modern Europe. It is part of our own inheritance, not a thing apart."
Surely, Mr Johnson you do not think the future King of the country you are currently the PM is wrong and you are right. Mr. Johnson, your ignorance has no bounds when it comes to Islam. Is it based on a deep-seated hatred of Islam or is it really based on an objective reading of the religion?

I get the distinct feeling that like Donald Trump, the President of USA, you really harbour extreme disdain for Islam. Where does this come from? Either you have had very bad experiences with Muslims or you have read Islamic text that clearly and irrefutably provide you with evidence that supports your view! You should sit down with someone who is more knowledgeable to explore your fear of Islam especially now you are the PM of Her Majesty's government and should represent all her subjects equally without prejudice or hatred. Maybe through enlightened discussions and explorations it will help you overcome the psychological barrier that is making your approach to Islam so erratic and biased!

You have gone further by saying "A fatal religious conservatism" and the further the Muslim world had "fallen behind, the more bitterness and confusion there has been, to the point where virtually every global flashpoint you can think of – from Bosnia to Palestine to Iraq to Kashmir – involves some sense of Muslim grievance."

But sadly, you have obviously forgotten your immediate history and the historic role played by the West in the systemic destruction of the Islamic world through colonisation, looting of the people's wealth and repeated barbaric massacres on those indigenous people. From Afghanistan to Egypt and from Syria to Sudan the colonial footprint of invasion, enslavement and genocide have left deeper and debilitating scars deeper than the deepest craters of pain you can ever imagine. And you mention Iraq, who is responsible for installing, sustaining and supporting a brutal dictator called Saddam Hussain in Iraq, and then toppling him by waging an illegal war and leaving the country totally destroyed?

Who was responsible for supporting Syria's Assad regime and when the people rebelled for democracy leaving them unaided at the front line to be slaughtered? Who was responsible for handing over Palestine to the Zionist lobby whilst making the indigenous Palestine people dispossessed and the entire region alight? Who was responsible for carving out the Middle East arbitrarily and handing them over to warlords and creating and thus far sustaining these illegitimate regimes? I am afraid the answer is the UK! So, before you point your fingers at Muslims you should examine the role of the West in breaking the backbones of the global Muslim community.

Mr. Johnson, in response to your misguided and totally disingenuous selective exposition of history let me remind you that when the Muslims were really free from economic and political imperialism and strangulation of the West, and they were able to build their lives on the Quranic paradigm of knowledge, enquiry, justice, fairness, excellence, charity, care and compassion they were able to transform the world.

Here is a summary of a speech given by a Professor of Politics at a University that puts into perspective a breath taking, striking and thoroughly riveting response to your ignorant rant and the ranting of all your ignorant friends like Messrs Trump, Farage and others like them.

"Apart from the windmills, water-mills, irrigation techniques, trade partnerships, bills of exchange and cheques, credit institutions, insurance and banking... Trigonometry, geometry and algebra, medicine and anaesthetics, public health and hygiene, philosophy and theology, literature and poetry, an optical revolution, astrology, astronomy and geography, all of which helped shape the European renaissance...Not to mention science and the experimental method that helped shape the European scientific revolution...As well as cartography, navigational techniques including the astrolabe, lunar and solar calendars, longitude and latitude tables, the lateen sail, all of which helped make possible the European voyages of discovery, in the absence of which the Europeans would have been confined to sailing within the Islamic Mediterranean...And... last but not least... the creation of an afro-Eurasian economy...After 650 CE that linked Europe into the mainstream of Afro-Asian trade and later the Eastern creation of the first global economy after 1492 that delivered not only a vibrant stream of Eastern trade but more importantly the many Asian inventions, institutions, ideas, technologies, production techniques, as well a list of agricultural, manufacturing and food products far too numerous to list here...".

Apart from all of this, what have the Muslims ever done for us?"

Mr. Johnson, perhaps next time when you write for the 'free press' for which you are well paid you should debate what have the Muslims not done for the world would be a more honest and genuine question. And the answer you will find is much shorter - for over a thousand years, Muslims build the foundation for many of the modern-day science and technology, art and architecture, philosophy and literature, geometry and astronomy, paving the way for many wholesome civilisations across the globe.

Mr. Johnson, there is another obvious question that needs answering - what have the Muslims done for the world in the last 400 years?
Apart from living the nightmare of being colonized, dehumanized, murdered, brutalized, enslaved, tortured, occupied, looted, their homes and lands carved-up then ruled by puppet regimes imposed on them... Apart from experiencing daily drone attacks, bombs, wars, death and destruction, Muslims have been living a normal life...

Wake up and smell the coffee Mr Boris Johnson - in fact the coffee beans were first brought to the West by the Ottomans that you so despise, smelling the coffee may be a cause for anti-Islamic allergic reaction - I would never want that for you.

Muslims are a compassionate bunch, so in the spirit of compassion we would like to extend our hand of friendship to you only if you promise to enlighten yourself with facts and how we have embraced UK as our home with loyalty and enterprise. The Muslims have done more not only in the UK but worldwide than any other people have ever done. Mr Johnson, do not forget Islam is the religion of freedom and equality, fairness and justice and progress and prosperity. You should try Islam; you may like it!

Finally, I hope you will not join the likes of Mr Trump and his cohorts who when confronted or lose an intellectual discussion tend to opt out with chants like "send them home" and more but I sincerely hope you will reflect on the above facts instead of dividing and alienating Muslims further for self-serving egos and political chicanery.

Mr Johnson, unlike your goodself, who gets paid for unsubstantiated facts by writing articles as well as making claims relating to £350m per week for the NHS, Brexit and much more, I am not getting paid for my efforts to highlight the above facts. I have done so in my own time because it hurts when we are subjected to hatred on daily basis in neighbourhoods, schools and work places based on unfounded facts made by politicians to woo voters or in the media blaming immigrants for housing shortage, NHS waiting times, school places, crime…

Lastly, I hope you have not forgotten the pledge you and other candidates made during the live ITV leadership debate to hold an independent investigation into Islamophobia within the Tory party or now that you have been elected, you will renege or come up with some excuse not to honour the pledge. If so, let me respectfully remind you, it is one of the main reasons as well as MP's expenses and other scandals that the public do not trust politicians!

I look forward to hearing from you because I sincerely believe we have all got a lot to offer, Muslims and non-Muslims alike, especially during the challenging times ahead of us after Brexit. I hope it is not just a routine acknowledgement from Downing Street Correspondence Unit thanking me on your behalf for taking the trouble of writing to you, a standard practice reserved for ordinary members of the public without legal, financial, media or lobbying clout.

Similarly, I also hope it is not a patronising reply highlighting ethnic appointments made by you, as it does not reflect reality faced by us mere mortals on daily basis, bearing in mind one only speaks of his faith when it suits him whereas another supports right wing politics at home and abroad, and had to resign because of misconduct in high office!

Yours sincerely'

(81) Letter to Boris Johnson.

12 August 2019

'Dear Prime Minister,

Re: A follow up to an Open Letter to Mr Boris Johnson dated 9 August 2019

'Thank you kindly for the *Eid ul Adha* message broadcasted by your goodself from Downing Street which has been circulating on social media network.

Your message is welcoming but would have gone a long way to build bridges, if broadcasted on national TV and also appeared in the same national press where Muslims are subjected to significant negative profiling in one form or another just like your previous attacks in your £5,000 a shot Daily Telegraph Monday columns which works out at about 4.08p a word.

As mentioned in my letter of 9 August 2019, such reports by you and others have not helped Muslims but each time exposes us to even more to racial hatred and ridicule from the bigots looking for scapegoats to vent anger encouraged after reading such articles.

Sadly, it also does not help, when asked during Tory party TV leadership debate, when such comments are casually discarded as "use of colourful language reflecting the views of British people" by a future PM. Similarly, your essay "And Then Came the Muslims", added to the 2007 edition of your book, which I have addressed at great lengths has also not helped, and it would go a long way to build bridges by putting the record straight.

Mr Johnson, you may have found the tone in my letter of 9 August 2019 aggressive. But, I hope you will believe me when I say, like many Muslims, it has been borne out of a direct result of years of every day frustrations as well as racial hatred directed by bigots to our old folks, women and children encouraged by media articles and speeches during referendum, general elections or otherwise when we are used as "cheap fodder" to woo voters.

It has also not been helped by your idol Donald Trump across the pond and our own Mr Nigel Farage fanning the flames of hatred, however hard they try later to make amends just like you in your *Eid ul Adha* message. As a nation, we should definitely value our "special relationship" status with the USA not by compromising but by standing up for our British values in terms of justice and fairness, especially in the Middle East, where Mr Trump is adamant to escalate crisis by listening not only to the oil rich Sheikh Kingdoms claiming to be the so-called custodians of Islam but also to the enemies of Islam.

As mentioned in my letter of 9 August 2019 just preceded by a day or two by your social media *Eid ul Adha*, I sincerely hope like a vast majority of likeminded law-abiding Muslims, you mean what you say in your *Eid ul Adha* message, and these are not just empty words as we have heard in the past from your other Downing Street predecessors.

Finally, as mentioned in my letter of 9 August 2019, I sincerely hope my letters are brought to your personal attention by one of your many Downing Street advisors and not discarded with routine acknowledgement or a condescending reply mentioning about the ethnic make-up of your current cabinet or how much you value Muslim contributions.

In the spirit of your *Eid ul Adha* message, I entreat you that as well your policy advisors, please listen to the ordinary people, Muslims and non-Muslims alike, the real victims of government policies, if we really want to tackle racial discrimination, radicalisation, social mobility, social harmony and other present day scourges and build bridges across the social divide instead of just listening to the same old so called "experts" with self-serving interests.

With kindest regards and best all good wishes.
Yours sincerely'

(82) Letter from Direct Correspondence Unit with a rubber stamp signature.

September 2019

'Dear Dr Akberali

'I am writing on behalf of the Prime Minister to acknowledge your rent correspondence '.

Yours sincerely
Correspondence Officer'

(83) Letter to Boris Johnson.

19th September 2019

'Dear Prime Minister,

I write in light of the two contradictory situations, your incident with the father of the child's patient during NHS hospital visit and my open letter to you dated 9th Aug 2019. It is very encouraging to read your twitter post after the NHS hospital visit "I've been PM for 57 days; part of my job is to talk to people on the ground and listen to what they tell me about the big problems. It doesn't matter if they agree with me. I'm glad this gentleman told me his problems. This isn't an embarrassment this is part of my job."

It is equally promising to note the following comment "The PM's spokesman said Mr Johnson was visiting the hospital to see for himself the reality of challenges that face the NHS and not going to hide away from those circumstances when he goes on theses, and so obviously is keen to talk to people and empathise and see what he can do to help."

But sadly, such comments mean nothing, just mere empty words. It does not reflect real-life experiences of ordinary people which leads to mistrust in our elected politicians and officials.

For example, just to cite my recent experience to interact with your goodself when I took the trouble in my own time and expenses at no cost to the tax-payer to write a 5-page open letter of 9th Aug 2019. It was critical but written in a constructive manner to build bridges to allay your fears about alienation and lack of contribution. It addressed unfounded allegations made by you directed towards certain disadvantaged sections of our multicultural society.

But regrettably, all I received for my efforts was a short note dated 11th Sept 2019 from your Direct Communications Unit with an illegible signed name, I quote "I am writing on behalf of the Prime Minister to acknowledge your recent correspondence." It reiterates the point that comments and speeches mean nothing. A dilemma also faced by ordinary public when we try to respond to well-paid newspaper columns by politicians which do not get published by the "free press" or speeches given protected by lecterns.

I hope my letter of 9th August will now be brought to your attention. I will send a copy if it has got misplaced. I look forward to hearing from you as stated on your twitter post.

Yours sincerely'

(84) Letter to Bill Gates and Melinda Gates.

27 December 2019

'Dear Mr and Mrs Gates,

Re: Book Manuscript – Contents page and Prologue

'I sincerely apologise for taking the liberty to write directly to your goodself and take up your valuable time.

I am hoping you will find a moment to read my letter despite heavy constraints on your valuable time.

The reason for writing is based on your experience with the Newsvendor at New York airport which after reading triggered a chain process that has led me to complete a book entitled "Hope and Fairness: A lay person's perception of reality". The manuscript is 225 pages and 114, 000 words. I attach the self-explanatory Prologue and the contents page.

It seems I have done the easy bit of writing. I now need professional guidance to get it published which is proving to be very difficult as I am an unknown entity.

I have tried in vain to attract a publisher. I am told that the public will not buy my book as I am not famous and therefore, I am not worth investing. I have the option to meet the costs myself by self-publishing and pay for professional editorial and marketing costs, something which I cannot afford.

In a way, the stumbling block I have reached reiterates your Newsvendor experience. In fact, I have addressed the same dilemma in a number of places faced by the ordinary people in real life in my book.

In light of the above, I was wondering if there is an opportunity in your foundation for people like me to get their work published, of course after close scrutiny. I am sure the book will inspire many people from disadvantaged background not to give up hope to fulfil their aspirations. It will also make the politicians aware of the handicaps faced by the public because of their intransigent party politics.

I pray to God to give you and other like-minded philanthropists continued vision and strength to serve humanity for the well-being of all the people in the world.

With kind regards. I wish you and your family a Happy Prosperous and a Peaceful New Year.'

Yours most respectfully'

Index

About The Author

D r Hassan Badrudin Akberali was born in Tanga, Tanzania, where he attended school. He came to study for PhD in marine biology in 1973 at Manchester University, after completing BSc (Hons) at Dar es Salaam. He left the world of scientific research in 1985 and went into business in Woking, making Knaphill his home ever since, and became interested in politics. He is retired and continues to focus his energy to serve public duty.

Printed in Great Britain
by Amazon

44077605R00215